MACMILLAN
English Study Dictionary

Brian Heaton

For Joe and Harry

The author would like to express his gratitude to Maggy Hendry for her editorial input as well as Dinah Jackson for the phonetics, Thelma Cooper for the illustrations, and Kathryn Harper.

© Copyright text Brian Heaton 1994
© Copyright illustrations The Macmillan Press Ltd 1994

All rights reserved. No reproduction, copy or transmission of this publication may be made without written permission.

No paragraph of this publication may be reproduced, copied or transmitted save with written permission or in accordance with the provisions of the Copyright, Designs and Patents Act 1988, or under the terms of any licence permitting limited copying issued by the Copyright Licensing Agency, 90 Tottenham Court Road, London W1P 9HE.

Any person who does any unauthorised act in relation to this publication may be liable to criminal prosecution and civil claims for damages.

First published 1994

Published by THE MACMILLAN PRESS LTD
London and Basingstoke
Associated companies and representatives in Accra, Auckland, Delhi, Dublin, Gaborone, Hamburg, Harare, Hong Kong, Kuala Lumpur, Lagos, Manzini, Melbourne, Mexico City, Nairobi, New York, Singapore, Tokyo.

ISBN 0-333-58269-1

Designed by Charles Design Associates
Printed in Hong Kong

A catalogue record for this book is available from the British Library

Contents

A Guide to the Dictionary	iv
A Guide to Pronunciation	vi
Grammar Notes	vii
Irregular Verb List	x

The Dictionary A-Z
Study Panels
Animals	10
Birds	22
The Body	25
Countries, People and Languages	51
Days, Months and Seasons	57
Fruit	89
Insects	114
Measures	137
Numbers	151
School and College Subjects	192
Vegetables	238

Exercises	254

A Guide to the Dictionary

This dictionary has been written for students in the early and lower intermediate stages of learning English as a Foreign Language. It defines 2,500 English words and provides examples of how they are used. Two special features of this dictionary are its language notes and collocations. These are explained in the guide which follows:

headwords are the words to be defined

pronunciation is given within slashes which follow the headwords – a complete list of symbols used can be found on page vi

parts of speech follow and are explained in the Grammar section on pages vii-viii

(where a word has more than one part of speech these are numbered after each headword)

alternatives and irregulars
alternative American words and spellings are given under the headwords in brackets

difficult forms of verbs and adjectives and irregular plurals of nouns are also shown under the headwords

definitions explain each word clearly and simply, using words contained in the dictionary (if a word has more than one meaning, these are numbered)

examples show the way a word can be used in a sentence

---

about /ə'baʊt/ adverb

building /'bɪldɪŋ/ noun (countable)

change [1] /tʃeɪndʒ/ noun (uncountable)
change [2] verb

waistcoat /'weɪskəʊt/ noun (countable)
(American English: vest)

swim /swɪm/ verb
swimming, swam, has swum

all /ɔːl/ determiner, pronoun
1 the whole of, every part of
   It rained **all** day yesterday.
2 every one or every thing
   All dogs eat meat.

discuss /dɪ'skʌs/ verb
talk about
I'd like to **discuss** my future with you.

collocations are a special feature of this dictionary. They show common ways in which the headword is used and will help you to avoid mistakes. They are sometimes followed by an explanation

language notes give useful information about how and how not to use them

answer

ask for/expect/seek an answer, give/offer an answer; a bad/good/excellent answer.

born

LANGUAGE NOTE

1 ALWAYS   I was born
  NEVER   ~~I have been born OR I am born~~
2 Don't *use* **by** after ***born***

A Guide to Pronunciation

The pronunciation of each word is given between slashes after the headword:

dog /dɒg/

The symbols used to show the pronunciation are from the International Phonetic Alphabet

• PRONUNCIATION TABLE •

Consonants		Vowels	
Symbol	**Key Word**	**Symbol**	**Key Word**
p	pot	iː	been
b	bit	ɑː	father
t	top	ɔː	north
d	dog	uː	soon
k	king	ɜː	bird
g	get		
w	wet	ɪ	bit
		e	pen
f	fat	æ	cat
v	very	ʌ	but
θ	thing	ɒ	not
ð	that	ʊ	put
s	sit	ə	another
z	zoo		
ʃ	shop	eɪ	may
ʒ	measure	aɪ	lie
		ɔɪ	boy
tʃ	chop	əʊ	go
dʒ	jump	aʊ	now
m	meet		
n	neat	ɪə	near
ŋ	sing	eə	fair
		ʊə	poor
h	hat		
l	leg	eɪə	player
r	red	əʊə	lower
j	young	aɪə	fire
		aʊə	flower
		ɔɪə	lawyer

Other symbols:
/ˈ/ comes before the syllable with main stress
/ˌ/ comes before the syllable with secondary stress
/*/ at the end of a word means that /r/ is usually pronounced if the next word starts with a vowel sound

*The pronunciations are based on the English Pronouncing Dictionary (14th Edition, edited by A.C. Gimson, Dent, London, 1977).

Grammar Notes

This dictionary contains only a few grammar words. The grammar words which appear are used after the headword and pronunciation, and sometimes in the language notes. Not all the grammar words in the following list are used in the dictionary.

active The verb is active when the subject does the action: eg Susan **has taken** my book. (Compare: My book **has been taken** by Susan.)

adjective An adjective is a word which tells you something about a noun: eg what kind it is (a **plastic** chair), what colour it is (a **red** car), how big it is (a **tall** building), how much it is (a **cheap** camera), or how good it is (an **excellent** answer).

You can put most adjectives either BEFORE or AFTER a noun (eg This is an **easy** exercise; This exercise is **easy**.) You must put some adjectives, however, AFTER a noun (eg The man was **asleep**.) Most adjectives are gradable and take comparative and superlative forms (easy, easier, easiest.)

adverb An adverb is a word which tells you something more about a verb (eg walk **quickly**), an adjective (eg **very** ill), another adverb (eg **quite** slowly), or a sentence (eg It didn't stop raining all week. **However**, there still wasn't enough water in the rivers.)

article The words **a**, **an** and **the** are articles. (These words are called **determiners** in this dictionary.)

auxiliary verb You can use an auxiliary verb with a main verb (eg **see**, **go**, **write**) to form a question, a tense, etc. **be**, **have**, or **do** are used as auxiliary verbs.
> Where **are** you **going**?
> Mr and Mrs Rodriguez **have** already **seen** the film.
> **Did** you **go** with them?

conjunction A conjunction is a word which joins words, groups of words and parts of sentences together: eg **and**, **but**, **although**, **when**.
> I've brought some pens **and** pencils.

continuous You can make the continuous (or progressive) form of a verb by using the verb **be** and the **-ing** form of the main verb.
> Bob and Tina **are playing** tennis.
> (Present Continuous)
> We'**ve been learning** English for two years.
> (Present Perfect Continuous)
> It **was raining** when I met them.
> (Past Continuous)
> What **have** you **been doing**?
> (Past Perfect Continuous)
> I **shall be waiting** for you.
> (Future Continuous)

countable A countable noun is a noun which has both a singular (eg **a car**) and a plural form (eg **cars**). You should use a determiner before the singular form of a countable noun.

determiner A determiner is a word like **a, an, the, some, any, all, every, each, another, this, that, these, those, my, your**, etc. Determiners tell you more about the meaning of a noun in a sentence: eg There's **a** strange man at the door. He has called at **all the other** houses in the street.

direct object The direct object of the verb **kicked** in the following sentence is **the ball**.
> Kick **the ball** to me.

direct speech When you write speech in the actual words which the speaker used, you use direct speech. (It isn't necessary for you to change the tenses and pronouns used by the speaker in any way at all.)
> "Come here tomorrow," Mr Uchida told Akiko.

future You can use the following forms to talk about things which will happen in the future.
> The winners **will play** against our own team next week.
> Tom and Dave **are playing** football tomorrow morning.
> Ali **is going to watch** the match.

indirect object The indirect object of the verb **gave** in the following sentence is **me**.
    My father gave **me** a new bike.

infinitive The infinitive is the form of a verb which you see in this dictionary: eg **come, go,** etc. Sometimes use the infinitive with **'to'**: eg **to come, to go** etc.

irregular You cannot form the plural of an **irregular noun** in the ordinary way (by adding **s** or **es**): eg **child, children; foot, feet.** You cannot form the past tense and past participle of an irregular verb in the ordinary way (by adding **ed**): eg **grow, grew, grown**. You cannot form the comparatives of an irregular adjective in the ordinary way (by adding **er** or **more** and **est** or **most**): eg **good, better, best; much, more, most; little, less, least**). In this dictionary all irregular forms of nouns, verbs and adjectives are given.

modal verb Modal verbs are used with other (main) verbs to show ideas such as wishes, intentions, ability, possibility, certainty, etc. These are modal verbs: **will, shall, should, would, can, could, may, might, must, ought to.**

negative You make a verb negative when you use words like **not**.
    I'm **not** going out tonight.

noun A noun is a word which you use to talk about people, animals, things, places and ideas: eg **a student, an elephant, houses, rivers, knowledge.** See also **countable, uncountable.**

object An object is a word or a group of words which you use to make the meaning of a verb or a preposition complete.
    Have you seen **the principal**?
    I've written to **him**.
See also **direct object, indirect object.**

participle There are two kinds of participles: the **present participle** (eg **kicking, seeing, throwing, walking**) and the **past participle** (eg **kicked, seen, thrown, walked**). This dictionary gives you the past participle of irregular verbs.

passive The verb is passive when the subject does not do the action: eg My book **has been taken** by someone. (Compare: Someone **has taken** my book.) The passive is often used when you are more interested in showing what is done than who or what is doing the action. The passive is also often used when you do not know who or what is doing the action: My book **has been stolen.**

past tense You can use the past tense to talk about things which happened at any time before now or which someone did before now.
    Tom and Dave **played** football yesterday.

perfect You can make the perfect form of a verb by using the verb **have** and the **-ed** form of the main verb.
    Bob and Tina **have just played** tennis.
    (Present Perfect)
    We**'ve been learning** English for two years.
    (Present Perfect Continuous)
    It **had rained** during the night. (Past Perfect)
    What **have** you **been doing?**
    (Past Perfect Continuous)
    We **shall have lived** here for five years
    by Christmas. (Future Perfect)

phrasal verb A verb which is used with an adverb or a preposition is called a phrasal verb: eg **break out, make up.** The meaning of the phrasal verb is often different from the meaning of the verb by itself: eg **blow up** (= destroy something by making it burst into small pieces). Sometimes, however, the adverb or preposition may add only slightly to the meaning of the verb, sometimes making it stronger: eg **cheer up, dry up, knock down.**

plural You use the plural form of a noun, a verb, etc to talk about more than one person or thing: eg three **boys**, a lot of **trees**. Some nouns are always plural and so you should use them only with plural verbs: eg **shorts, scissors, police,** etc.
    The police **are** coming.

predeterminer A predeterminer is a word which you can use BEFORE **a, an,** or **the:** eg **all, both, quite, half, twice, what:** eg all the students, **both** the men.

preposition A preposition is a word or group of words which you can use before a noun, a group of nouns or a pronoun: eg **after, at, by, from, off, out of, over, with:** eg the man standing **behind** me, **down** the hole.

present You use the present tense to talk about things which happen or are true now.
    Tom and Dave **are playing** football now.
    Ali **likes** to watch football.

pronoun You can use a pronoun in place of a noun or a group of nouns: eg **I, me, mine, you, yours, we, us, ours, he, him, his, she, her, hers, they, them, theirs.**
    Mr Lee is out. **He** won't be back until nine.
Words such as **who, whom, whose, which** and **that** are known as relative pronouns. However, they are shown simply as **pronouns** in this dictionary.

regular You can form the plural of a **regular noun** in the ordinary way (by adding **s** or **es**): eg **bicycle, bicycles.** You can form the past tense and past participle of a **regular verb** in the ordinary way (by adding **ed**): eg **believe, believed, believed.** You can form the comparatives of a regular adjective in the ordinary way (by adding **er** or **more, est** or **most**): eg **high, higher, highest; difficult, more difficult, most difficult.** In this dictionary regular forms of nouns, verbs and adjectives are usually not given.

reported speech When you write reported speech (also called **indirect speech**), you change the actual words which the speaker used (you must usually change the tenses and pronouns which the speaker uses).
    "Come here again tomorrow," Mrs Long told Alice. (direct speech)
    Mrs Long told Alice to go there again the next day. (reported speech)

singular You use the singular form of a noun, a verb, etc to talk about only one person or thing.

subject A subject is a word or a group of words about which you say something. You often put the subject of a verb at the beginning of a sentence (unless it is a question) and before the verb.
    The principal would like to see you.
    He wrote a long letter to me.

uncountable An uncountable noun is a noun which usually has no plural form (eg **advice, information**). You cannot normally put **a** or **an** in front of an uncountable noun: instead, you can put **some** or **any** (eg **some food, any music**).

verb A verb is a word which you use to show something **happening**, someone **doing** something or something/someone **being** in a certain way.
    The sun **shone** all morning but now it's **raining**.
    Look! That car **is going** very quickly.
    I **feel** tired but I **am** very happy.

verb phrase In this dictionary a verb which is not a phrasal verb but which consists of more than one word is called a verb phrase: eg **able to, used to, make sure, would rather.**
See also **phrasal verb**.

Irregular Verb List

Infinitive	Past simple	Past Participle	Infinitive	Past simple	Past Participle
beat	beat	beaten	meet	met	met
become	became	become	pay	paid	paid
begin	began	begun	put	put	put
bend	bent	bent	read	read	read
bite	bit	bitten	ride	rode	ridden
bleed	bled	bled	ring	rang	rung
blow	blew	blown	rise	rose	risen
break	broke	broken	run	ran	run
bring	brought	brought	saw	sawed	sawn
build	built	built			*(Am Eng: sawed)*
burn	burnt/burned	burnt/burned	say	said	said
burst	burst	burst	see	saw	seen
buy	bought	bought	sell	sold	sold
catch	caught	caught	send	sent	sent
choose	chose	chosen	set	set	set
come	came	come	sew	sewed	sewn
cost	cost	cost			*(Am Eng: also sewed)*
creep	crept	crept	shake	shook	shaken
cut	cut	cut	shine	shone	shone
dig	dug	dug	shoot	shot	shot
do	did	done	show	showed	shown/showed
draw	drew	drawn			(rarely)
drink	drank	drunk	shut	shut	shut
drive	drove	driven	sing	sang	sung
eat	ate	eaten	sink	sank/sunk	sunk
fall	fell	fallen	sit	sat	sat
feed	fed	fed	sleep	slept	slept
feel	felt	felt	slide	slid	slid
fight	fought	fought	sow	sowed	sown/sowed
find	found	found	speak	spoke	spoken
fly	flew	flown	spend	spent	spent
forget	forgot	forgotten	spit	spat	spat
forgive	forgave	forgiven		*(Am Eng: also spit)*	*(Am Eng: also spit)*
freeze	froze	frozen	spread	spread	spread
get	got	got *(Am Eng: gotten)*	spring	sprang	sprung
give	gave	given		*(Am Eng: also sprung)*	
go	went	gone			
grow	grew	grown	stand	stood	stood
hang	hung	hung	steal	stole	stolen
have	had	had	stick	stuck	stuck
hear	heard	heard	sweep	swept	swept
hide	hid	hidden	swim	swam	swum
hit	hit	hit	swing	swung	swung
hold	held	held	take	took	taken
hurt	hurt	hurt	teach	taught	taught
keep	kept	kept	tear	tore	torn
know	knew	known	tell	told	told
lay	laid	laid	think	thought	thought
lead	led	led	throw	threw	thrown
leave	left	left	understand	understood	understood
lend	lent	lent	undo	undid	undone
let	let	let	wake	woke	woken
lie (down)	lay (down)	lain (down)		*(Am Eng: waked)*	*(Am Eng: waked)*
light	lit/lighted	lit/lighted	wear	wore	worn
lose	lost	lost	win	won	won
make	made	made	wind	wound	wound
mean	meant	meant	write	wrote	written

The Dictionary A – Z

Aa

a /eɪ/(unstressed/ə/), **an** indefinite article, determiner
1 one (but not a special one)
   • *Is that **a** bowl or **a** saucer over there?*
   • *Is that **an** orange in the bowl over there?*
2 every
   • *"Surely **a** horse is bigger than **a** donkey." "Yes but **an** elephant is even bigger."*
3 one (not two, etc)
   • *There were **a** hundred people there.*
   • *We've been waiting for over **an** hour.*
4 for each, in each
   • *Oranges today are $4.20 **an** ounce, but I'm not sure how much they are **a** kilo.*

LANGUAGE NOTE

You can talk about *a cup*, *a saucer*, etc because you can count them: eg one cup, two cups, three cups. You cannot use *a* or *an* in front of words like *water*, *tea*, or *milk* because you cannot count these things. Instead you should use *some* or *any* in front of these words (or no word at all). Sometimes you can say *a glass of water, a cup of tea, a bottle of milk*, etc.

After you have used *a* in front of a word, you use *the* when you say or write the word again.

There's *a* strange woman at the door.
The woman says she knows you.

⚠ See also **an**; see also **the**.

able to /'eɪbl tuː/ verb phrase
be able to = can
   • *Are you **able to** use this dictionary? (= Can you use this dictionary?)*

about ¹ /əˈbaʊt/ adverb
1 here and there
   • *Two boys were kicking a ball **about**.*
   ❧ run/walk/hurry/rush/get/move/play about/kick/throw (something) about

2 a little more or less than
   • ***About** eighty people were at the concert.*
3 a little before or after
   • *Can you call me at **about** six o'clock?*

about ² preposition
of, concerning
   • *Is this book **about** Japan?*
   ❧ argue/cry/laugh/read/speak/talk about, tell (someone) about BUT NOT discuss about; a book/a film/a story about

about to /əˈbaʊt tuː/ verb phrase
If you are about to do something, you are going to do it immediately.
   • *Let's get on the bus now. It's **about to** leave; the engine's running.*

above /əˈbʌv/ preposition
higher than

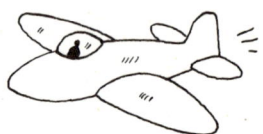

   • *The plane flew **above** the clouds.*

abroad /əˈbrɔːd/ adverb
in or to another country
   • *I've lived **abroad** for a year, but now I've come back home. I think my own country is best.*
   ❧ be/live/work/go/travel abroad

absent /'æbsənt/ adjective
not here, away
   • *"Is Alice here?" "No, she's **absent** today."*
   ❧ absent from (school/work, etc)

accident /'æksɪdənt/ noun (countable)
something which happens by chance (usually something bad)
   • *Ali had an **accident** because he was careless. He hit the car in front of him.*
   ❧ cause/have/meet with an accident; a bad/horrible/serious/terrible/unfortunate accident, a fatal accident (= an accident in which someone is killed)

θ	ð	ʃ	dʒ	tʃ	ŋ	ʒ	iː	ɜː	ɪ	æ	ʌ	ɒ
thing	that	shop	jump	chop	sing	measure	been	bird	bit	cat	but	not

ache¹ /eɪk/ noun (countable, uncountable)

a kind of pain or an unpleasant feeling which lasts for some time

- *We can't come to the party. Susie's got tooth**ache**, Helen's got back**ache**, Linda's got a head**ache** and I've got stomach**ache***

⚠ See **backache, earache, headache, stomachache, toothache.**

SPELLING NOTE

Sometimes *stomach ache* is written as two words.

✺ have an ache; have backache/toothache, etc; a bad headache, etc; a dull ache, a slight ache, a slight headache, etc

ache² verb

aching, ached, has ached
hurt, cause pain
- *I've been cycling too much. My legs **ache**.*

across /əˈkrɒs/ adverb, preposition

1 from one side (of something) to the other
   - *Carlos ran **across** the street when he saw us.*
✺ come/go/walk/run/hurry/rush across
2 on the other side of
   - *There's a post office **across** the road.*
✺ across the road/street/river/stream/lake/sea

act¹ /ækt/ noun (countable)

part of a play
- *The first **act** is rather dull, but the second and third **acts** are very exciting.*

act² verb

1 do something
   - *He **acted** very quickly to save her life.*
2 take the part of a person in a play or a film
   - *Susie is **acting** as the queen in the play.*

activity /ækˈtɪvətɪ/ noun

1 (countable) something you do (plural: activities)
   - *Their main **activities** at the weekend are swimming and playing tennis.*
✺ go in for /take part in an activity; indoor/outdoor activities
2 (uncountable) If there is a lot of activity, people are usually busy doing things.
   - *The school was full of **activity**. It was parents' evening.*

actor /ˈæktə*/ noun (countable)

a man who acts in a play or film
- *Bruce Lee was a famous **actor**.*

actress /ˈæktrɪs/ noun (countable)

plural: actresses
a woman who acts in a play or film
- *The **actress** was so good that everyone thought she was really crying.*

actual /ˈæktʃʊəl/ adjective

real
- *Noora looks thirty but her **actual** age is forty.*

actually /ˈæktʃʊəlɪ/ adverb

really
- *Henry pretends to be mean but he's **actually** very kind.*

LANGUAGE NOTE

Use *actually* in conversation when you want to show you disagree with someone. It is a polite way of saying someone is wrong or even of complaining.

"Hamed never arrives on time."
"Actually, this is the first time he's been late."

θ	ð	ʃ	dʒ	tʃ	ŋ	ʒ	iː	ɜː	ɪ	æ	ʌ	ɒ
thing	that	shop	jump	chop	sing	measure	been	bird	bit	cat	but	not

add /æd/ verb
1 put numbers together
- When you **add** five and seven, you get twelve.
- Five **added** to seven makes twelve.
2 put together with something else
- "Will you **add** my name to the list, please?" I asked.
3 say something else
- Rohanna **added** that we'd be welcome to stay for tea.

address¹ /əˈdres/ noun (countable)
plural: addresses

> **SPELLING NOTE**
>
> ALWAYS double **d** : a**dd**ress

the name or number of the house or flat, the street, town and country where someone lives or works
- My **address** is Flat 15, 62 Plum Tree Avenue, Singapore 1076.

address² verb
write a name and address on a letter or parcel
- The letter was **addressed** to someone called Mawani.

adult /ˈædʌlt/ noun (countable)
a man, a woman; not a child
- The film was for **adults** only.

adventure /ədˈventʃə*/ noun (countable)
something exciting (and often dangerous)
- Ann wanted to travel and have exciting **adventures**.

advertisement /ədˈvɜːtɪsmənt/ noun (countable)
words, pictures or signs which tell people about things or which try to sell them something
- As soon as I saw the **advertisement** for the camera, I decided to buy one.

> **LANGUAGE NOTE**
>
> You can sometimes use **ad** and **advert** as short forms when you speak (but not usually when you write letters to businesses, schools, etc).

advice /ədˈvaɪs/ noun (uncountable)
something which is said to people to help them to do things better
- Here's some good **advice**: always work hard.

> **LANGUAGE NOTE**
>
> ALWAYS   **some** advice or **a piece of** advice
> NEVER   an advice
> Note also the following phrases:
>   a bit of advice, a word of advice

advice on/about something;
ask for/seek / get/receive/give/offer/accept/follow/take/refuse advice,
go against advice (= not do what you are advised);
good/excellent/wise/friendly/bad advice,
sound advice (= good advice), valuable advice (= very useful advice), welcome advice (= advice which you are happy to accept)

advise /ədˈvaɪz/ verb
advising, advised, has advised

> **SPELLING NOTE**
>
> advi**ce** = noun   advi**se** = verb

tell someone how to do things better
- Mrs Lee **advised** going early to the concert.

> **LANGUAGE NOTE**
>
> advise **doing** something
> advise someone **to do** something

aeroplane /ˈeərəpleɪn/ noun (countable)
(American English: airplane)
a vehicle which has wings and an engine and which can fly
- Look at that large **aeroplane** over there.

board/get on an aeroplane, take an/go by aeroplane, fly/pilot an aeroplane

See also **aircraft**; see also **plane**.

θ	ð	ʃ	dʒ	tʃ	ŋ	ʒ	iː	ɜː	ɪ	æ	ʌ	ɒ
thing	that	shop	jump	chop	sing	measure	been	bird	bit	cat	but	not

afford /əˈfɔːd/ verb

have enough money to pay for something
- *Can you **afford** to buy this television set? It costs $600.*

> **LANGUAGE NOTE**
>
> You can often use **can** and **be able to** with **afford**.
> can afford, cannot afford, can't afford, could afford, couldn't afford, be able to afford, be unable to afford

afraid /əˈfreɪd/ adjective

1 frightened
- *Leila is **afraid** of dogs because a big dog bit her last year.*

> **LANGUAGE NOTE**
>
> 1 Don't use **afraid** in front of a noun.
>   NEVER   an afraid boy
>   ALWAYS a boy who is afraid
> 2 afraid **of** something
>   afraid **of** doing something
>   afraid **to do** something
>   afraid **that** something may/will happen

2 **I'm afraid** = used to show that you are worried or sorry about something
- ***I'm afraid** that your son is very sick. He'll have to stay in bed.*

after /ˈɑːftə*/

1 (preposition, conjunction) next, later (in time)
- *Let's set off on the picnic **after** breakfast.*
- *We watched TV **after** we had eaten.*
2 (preposition) behind, following
- *Look at the cat running **after** that mouse.*

ↄ come/go/hurry/run/rush after

> **LANGUAGE NOTE**
>
> Use **after** with words which show people or things moving.
> NEVER   the man sitting after me
> ALWAYS the man sitting **behind** me

afternoon /ˌɑːftəˈnuːn/ noun (countable)

the time of day between 12 noon and 6 pm
- *When we see someone at two o'clock in the **afternoon**, we say, "Good **afternoon**."*

> **LANGUAGE NOTE**
>
> **in** the afternoon   BUT   **on** Friday afternoon

afterwards /ˈɑːftəwədz/ adverb

later, after that time
- *I ate too much cake and **afterwards** I felt sick.*

again /əˈgen/ adverb

1 once more
- *Linda went to the cinema on Monday and then she went **again** on Wednesday.*
2 any more
- *Never do that **again**: it's very rude.*

against /əˈgenst/ preposition

1 touching
- *Did you put the ladder **against** the wall?*
2 be on the opposite side in a fight or a game
- *Which countries fought **against** Iraq in the war?*

age /eɪdʒ/ noun (countable, uncountable)

1 the number of years someone has lived, how old a person is
- *What are the **ages** of your two brothers?*
- *Children under sixteen years of **age** need only pay half fare.*
2 old age
- *If you are 70, you are in your **old age**.*

ↄ an early age (BUT RARELY a young age), a very young age, middle age, old age

aged /eɪdʒd/ adjective

1 at the age of, having lived a certain number of years
- *Boys **aged** sixteen must pay full fare.*
2 **middle-aged**
- *When you are about 40, you become **middle-aged**.*

ago /əˈgəʊ/ verb

before now
- *My uncle visited Japan ten years **ago**.*

θ	ð	ʃ	dʒ	tʃ	ŋ	ʒ	iː	ɜː	ɪ	æ	ʌ	ɒ
thing	that	shop	jump	chop	sing	measure	been	bird	bit	cat	but	not

agree

> **LANGUAGE NOTE**
>
> Don't use **ago** before **since.**
> NEVER   It is over a year ago since I last saw her.
> ALWAYS I last saw her over a year ago.
> OR   It is over a year since I last saw her.

agree /əˈgriː/ verb
agreeing, agree, has agreed
1. When you agree with people, you think the same about something as they do.
   - I **agree** with Vincento: he said the food at the hotel was very bad.
2. You say 'yes' to a person or a plan if you agree to do something.
   - Maria's just **agreed** to marry Ricardo, and the wedding will be next month.

> **LANGUAGE NOTE**
>
> agree **with** someone
> agree **on/about** something
> agree **to do** something
> agree **that** something should be done

ahead /əˈhed/ adverb
1. in front
   - Go straight **ahead**: don't turn left.
2. If a team or someone is ahead in a game, they are winning.
   - Brazil are now 3 goals **ahead** of Spain: the score is 4 - 1.
3. forward
   - We are going **ahead** with our plan.

air /eə*/ noun (uncountable)
1. what you breathe
   - What's that burning smell in the **air**?
   - fresh / open air (be in the open air = be outdoors)
2. **by air** = (travelling) in an aeroplane
   - If you send this parcel from London to Tokyo **by air**, it will arrive in three days.

air-conditioned /ˈeə kənˌdɪʃnd/ adjective
made cool or warm by a machine
- Is that hotel **air-conditioned**?

aircraft /ˈeəkrɑːft/ noun (countable)
plural: aircraft
(American English: airplane)
a vehicle which has wings and an engine and which can fly
- Six enemy **aircraft** were shot down.
- See also **aeroplane**; see also **plane**.

> **LANGUAGE NOTE**
>
> NEVER   go by aircraft
> ALWAYS go **by air** or go **by (aero)plane**

air hostess /ˈeə ˌhəʊstɪs/ noun (countable)
plural: hostesses
a woman who looks after the passengers on an aeroplane and brings them things to eat and drink
- The **air hostess** will bring you a drink.

airline /ˈeəlaɪn/ noun (countable)
the aeroplanes used by a country or company
- Hong Kong's **airline** is called Cathay Pacific.

airmail /ˈeəmeɪl/ noun (uncountable)
letters and parcels which we send in an aeroplane
- I sent the letter (by) **airmail**.

airplane /ˈeəpleɪn/ noun (countable)
(American English)
- See **aeroplane**; see **aircraft**; see **plane**.

airport /ˈeəpɔːt/ noun (countable)
the place where aeroplanes arrive or leave so that people can get on or off them
- Let's take a taxi to the **airport** so that we can be there before Rosie's plane lands.

aisle /aɪl/ noun (countable)
the space between rows of seats in a church or cinema
- Let's go further down the **aisle**. I can see two empty seats in the third row from the front.

θ	ð	ʃ	dʒ	tʃ	ŋ	ʒ	iː	ɜː	ɪ	æ	ʌ	ɒ
thing	that	shop	jump	chop	sing	measure	been	bird	bit	cat	but	not

alike[1] /əˈlaɪk/ adjective

almost the same, very similar

- *Anissa and Noora are so **alike**: it's hard to tell the difference between them.*

alike[2] adverb

in a similar way, almost the same
- *You should try to treat all the pupils **alike**: don't be kind to one and unkind to another.*

alive /əˈlaɪv/ adjective

living, not dead
- *"Is your grandfather **alive**?" "No, he's dead."*

LANGUAGE NOTE

Don't use **alive** in front of a noun.
NEVER   an alive fish
ALWAYS a *live* fish

---

all /ɔːl/ determiner, predeterminer, pronoun
1. the whole of, every part of
   - *It rained **all** day yesterday.*
   - *Ann ate **all** the cake herself.*
2. every one or every thing
   - ***All** dogs eat meat.*
3. **none at all** = not any
   - *Sam ate the cake and I had **none at all**.*

LANGUAGE NOTES

1 **all** or **all of**?
   All the students were present.
   All of the students were present.
   All of us were present.
   (NEVER All us were present.)

2 Word order
   We **all** finished five minutes ago.
   We have **all** finished.
   (Never We all have finished.)

Allah /ˈælə/ noun (proper)

the maker of the world, a name for God
- *Ahmad thanked **Allah** for everything.*

See also **God**.

all right /ˌɔːl ˈraɪt/ adjective phrase, adverb phrase
1. well (not ill)
   - *"How do you feel today?" "I'm **all right** now, thank you."*
2. Yes
   - *"Could you please lend me some money?" "**All right**. Here's a dollar."*

See also **okay / OK**; see also **right**.

allow /əˈlaʊ/ verb

say someone can do something
- *We're not **allowed** to smoke in this cinema.*

almost /ˈɔːlməʊst/ adverb

not quite, nearly
- *You **almost** passed the test. The pass mark was 50%, and you scored 49%.*

alone /əˈləʊn/ adverb

by oneself, with no one else present
- *No one went with Ken. He was (all) **alone**.*

LANGUAGE NOTE

Don't use **alone** instead of **lonely**.
NEVER   Do you ever feel alone living by yourself?
ALWAYS Do you ever feel **lonely** living by yourself?

---

along[1] /əˈlɒŋ/ adverb
1. (go) forward
   - *Please walk **along** quietly.*
   come/go/drive/get/hurry/run/walk along, bring/send/take/pull/push along
2. with you
   - *Come to my party tomorrow evening and bring a couple of friends **along**.*

along[2] preposition
1. from one end to the other
   - *I walked **along** the street several times but I couldn't find your house.*
2. by the side of a road, river, etc
   - *There are a lot of restaurants **along** this street.*

θ	ð	ʃ	dʒ	tʃ	ŋ	ʒ	iː	ɜː	ɪ	æ	ʌ	ɒ
thing	that	shop	jump	chop	sing	measure	been	bird	bit	cat	but	not

aloud /əˈlaʊd/ adverb
(say or read something) so that people can hear
- *Can you read that **aloud** to the class?*
↻ cry/read/shout/sing/think aloud

alphabet /ˈælfəbet/ noun (countable)
the letters which are used when writing a language
- *"Do you know the English **alphabet**?"*
  "Yes, of course. I'll say it for you: a, b, c, d, e, f, g, h, i, j, k, l, m, n, o, p, q, r, s, t, u, v, w, x, y, z."

alphabetical order /ˌælfəbetɪkl ˈɔːdə*/ adjective + noun
in the order of the alphabet
- *"Can you put these words in **alphabetical order**: tea, hand, animal, radio, park, lift?"*
  "Of course: animal, hand, lift, park, radio, tea."

already /ɔːlˈredɪ/ adverb
before now, before then
- *Have you finished your homework **already**?*

LANGUAGE NOTE

| NEVER | They already have come. |
| ALWAYS | They have **already** come. |

---

also /ˈɔːlsəʊ/ adverb
as well, too
- *Maria is wearing a red blouse, and Leila is **also** wearing a red blouse.*

although /ɔːlˈðəʊ/ conjunction
in spite of the fact that
- ***Although** I've just eaten, I still feel hungry.*

LANGUAGE NOTE

Don't use **but** after **although**.
NEVER	Although he worked hard, but he failed.
ALWAYS	**Although** he worked hard, he failed.
OR	He worked hard, **but** he failed.

⚠ See also **though**.

altogether /ˌɔːltəˈgeðə*/ adverb
with everyone, with everything
- *There are six hundred pupils in the school **altogether**.*

always /ˈɔːlweɪz/ adverb
1 for ever
   - *Dave said he'd **always** love Anna.*
2 all the time
   - *You're **always** complaining about something.*

LANGUAGE NOTE

I **always** leave home at five to eight and so far I have **always** arrived at school on time.
(NEVER I always have arrived)

---

am /æm/ (unstressed /əm/, /m/) verb
part of **be**
- *"Are you happy?"*
  *"Yes, I **am**. I'm very happy."*

amazing /əˈmeɪzɪŋ/ adjective
causing surprise
- *I don't know how Hassan managed to score that goal. It was **amazing**!*

ambulance /ˈæmbjʊləns/ noun (countable)
a van or car used to take people who are sick or hurt to hospital
- *When Dave broke his arm, an **ambulance** came within ten minutes and took him to the City Hospital.*
↻ go by ambulance, be taken by ambulance/in an ambulance

among /əˈmʌŋ/ preposition
1 in the middle of, part of (a group, etc)
   - *Your book is **among** these.*
2 between, to each of
   - *She divided the rice **among** the four boys.*

θ	ð	ʃ	dʒ	tʃ	ŋ	ʒ	iː	ɜː	ɪ	æ	ʌ	ɒ
thing	that	shop	jump	chop	sing	measure	been	bird	bit	cat	but	not

animal

> **LANGUAGE NOTE**
>
> Use **between** (with meanings 1 and 2) when there are two people or things.
> Use **among** when there are more than two.

3 to one another
  • *The students spoke quietly **among** themselves before they answered.*

amount /əˈmaʊnt/ noun (countable)
When you talk about the amount of something, you say how much there is.
  • *The government has spent a large **amount** of money on the new hospital.*

> **LANGUAGE NOTE**
>
> Use **amount** for things which you cannot count:
>   a large **amount** of meat   large **amounts** of meat
> BUT use **quantity** for things which you can count:
>   a large **quantity** of vegetables
>   large **quantities** of vegetables

amusing /əˈmjuːzɪŋ/ adjective
someone or something that makes you laugh
  • *That was a very **amusing** film: I couldn't stop laughing.*
  ᛋ very/most/highly amusing

an /æn/ (unstressed /ən/) indefinite article, determiner
  ⚠ See **a**.

> **LANGUAGE NOTE**
>
> Use **an** before a word which begins with a vowel sound: eg **an** apple, **an** egg, **an** insect, **an** orange, **an** umbrella, etc BUT **a** university (because this word does not begin with an ordinary u sound) .
> Also use **an** before words beginning with **h** when the **h** is not pronounced: eg **an** hour BUT **a** hospital.
> Use **a** for all other words.

and /ænd/ (unstressed /ənd/, /ən/) conjunction
1 Use **and** to join two words or phrases.
  • *I'm afraid I've forgotten my pen **and** ruler.*
  • *I went to a small restaurant near the beach **and** had breakfast there.*

2 Also use **and** when you say and write numbers after 100.
  • *There are two hundred **and** fifty pieces in the box.*

> **LANGUAGE NOTE**
>
> Do not use **and** when two adjectives come before a noun: *a beautiful, clever woman*.
> Use **and** only when (1) both adjectives are colours: *a red **and** yellow flag* and (2) both adjectives tell what something is made of: *a wool **and** nylon skirt*.

anger /ˈæŋgə*/ noun (uncountable)
When you feel anger, you are not pleased and you may want to hurt someone.
  • *Tim said he didn't feel any **anger** when his best friend took his money. He just felt sad.*

angle /ˈæŋgl/ noun (countable)
the space where two lines meet
  • *A triangle has three **angles** and a square four **angles**.*

angrily /ˈæŋgrɪlɪ/ adverb
in an angry way, with a strong feeling against someone or something
  • *The old man shook his fist and shouted **angrily** at the naughty boys.*

angry /ˈæŋgrɪ/ adjective
angrier, angriest
want to hurt someone for doing something wrong, not pleased with someone or something
  • *I was **angry** with Ann for laughing when I fell.*

> **LANGUAGE NOTE**
>
> angry **with** someone for doing something
> angry **about** something
> angry **at** something

animal /ˈænɪml/ noun (countable)
something living but not a plant (and not usually a person)
  • *There are a lot of different **animals** in the zoo: lions, tigers, elephants and many more.*
  ⚠ See box on page 10.

θ	ð	ʃ	dʒ	tʃ	ŋ	ʒ	iː	ɜː	ɪ	æ	ʌ	ɒ
thing	that	shop	jump	chop	sing	measure	been	bird	bit	cat	but	not

Animals

bat, deer, mouse, rabbit, horse, bear, dog, hippo, rat, buffalo, donkey, leopard, sheep, frog, elephant, snake, lion, camel, monkey, cow, crab, fox, ox, wolf, tiger, crocodile, cat, zebra, goat, giraffe

The following are the names of the young of some of the more common animals above:

cub (bear, fox, leopard, lion, tiger, wolf)	foal (horse)	lamb (sheep)
calf, calves (cow, cows)	kitten (cat)	puppy (dog)

announce /əˈnaʊns/ verb
announcing, announced, has announced
tell people something important
- *The headmistress **announced** that Mrs Law was leaving school at the end of the term.*

announcement /əˈnaʊnsmənt/ noun (countable)
something important to tell people
- *Did you see the **announcement** in the newspaper about the change in the dates of the examination?*
↻ hear/listen/read/see/make an announcement

annoy /əˈnɔɪ/ verb
make someone angry

- *Stop laughing. You're **annoying** me.*

θ	ð	ʃ	dʒ	tʃ	ŋ	ʒ	iː	ɜː	ɪ	æ	ʌ	ɒ
thing	that	shop	jump	chop	sing	measure	been	bird	bit	cat	but	not

annoyed /əˈnɔɪd/   adjective

not pleased, angry
- Mrs Ericsson was **annoyed** because we were late for dinner.

> **LANGUAGE NOTE**
>
> annoyed **at / with** someone for doing something
> annoyed **about** something
> annoyed **that/because** someone has done something or that something has happened

another /əˈnʌðə*/   determiner, pronoun

1 one more
- Have **another** biscuit: there are lots here.
- There are lots of apples here: have **another**.

> **LANGUAGE NOTE**
>
> Use **another** with a singular noun: eg **another student** BUT use **other** with a plural noun: eg **other students**.

2 **one another** (used to show each person in a group)
- Peter, Ken, Dave and Francis don't like **one another** and always quarrel.

△ See also **each other**.

answer¹ /ˈɑːnsə*/   noun (countable)

what is said or written when a question is asked
- I don't know the **answer** to this question. It's far too difficult.

✤ ask for/expect/seek/get/have/receive/give/offer an answer;
a bad/good/excellent answer, a blunt answer (= a very honest answer, often not polite)/an honest/a plain/a simple/ a straight/a quick/a polite/a clever/a foolish/ a silly/a firm/a clear/a full/a long answer; the correct/right/wrong answer

answer²   verb

1 what you say when someone asks you a question
- I can't **answer** this question: it's too hard.
2 what you write when someone writes to you
- Have you **answered** Alice's letter yet?

ant /ænt/   noun (countable)

△ See box on page 114.

any /ˈenɪ/

1 (determiner, pronoun) some, a little
- When Susie has **any** money, she spends it on clothes.
- I'll lend you some money if you haven't **any**.

> **LANGUAGE NOTE**
>
> Don't use **any** as a pronoun for a singular noun which we can count.
> Mr Long has a car but I don't think Mr Manson has **one**. (NOT **any**).
> Use **any** as a pronoun only for a singular noun which you cannot count or a plural noun which you can count.
> Tom has some paper but I haven't **any**.
> Ann has some scissors but Ken hasn't **any**.

△ See also **some**.

2 (determiner, pronoun)
Use **any** in sentences with **not** and in questions.
- "Did you have **any** cake?"
  "No, I wasn't given **any**."

> **LANGUAGE NOTE**
>
> Were **any girls** there?
> Were **any of the girls** we met there?

△ See also **some**.

3 (determiner) one (but not a special one)
- Come here again **any** day you like.
4 (adverb) even a little
- Can you drive **any** faster?

anybody /ˈenɪˌbɒdɪ/ **(anyone)** /ˈenɪwʌn/   pronoun

1 a person (but no special person: ie any person)
- Pedro has asked all his friends to come, but I haven't asked **anybody** yet.
2 (used in sentences with **not** and in questions)
- Have you ever seen **anyone** watching you?

anything /ˈenɪθɪŋ/   pronoun

a thing (but no special thing, something)
- "Is there **anything** I can pass you?"
  "I'd like some salt, please."

θ	ð	ʃ	dʒ	tʃ	ŋ	ʒ	iː	ɜː	ɪ	æ	ʌ	ɒ
thing	that	shop	jump	chop	sing	measure	been	bird	bit	cat	but	not

anyway /ˈenɪweɪ/ adverb
in spite of, in any case
- I locked the door but the thief got in **anyway**.

anywhere /ˈenɪweə*/ adverb
(in, at, or to) any place
Use **anywhere** mostly in sentences with **not** and in questions.
- I didn't go **anywhere** last night.

appear /əˈpɪə*/ verb
1 (begin) to be seen

- At last a ship **appeared** in the distance.
2 seem
- Vincent **appeared** to understand, but I'm not too sure he actually did.
3 arrive
- The party started at seven but Mr and Mrs Jottini didn't **appear** until nine!

apple /ˈæpl/ noun (countable)
⚠ See box on page 89.

apricot /ˈeɪprɪkɒt/ noun (countable)
⚠ See box on page 89.

are /ɑː*/ (unstressed /ə*/) verb
part of **be** (used after **we**, **they** and plural nouns)
- "**Are** you playing football this afternoon?"
 "No, we'**re** going swimming today."

LANGUAGE NOTE
you're = you are   we're = we are   they're = they are

area /ˈeərɪə/ noun (countable)
1 how much a space measures
- The **area** of the square is 40 square centimetres.
2 part of a place, a country, or a city
- This part of the town is a pleasant **area**.

aren't /ɑːnt/ verb
are not
- We **aren't** running: we're walking quickly.
⚠ See also **be**.

argue /ˈɑːɡjuː/ verb
arguing, argued, has argued
not agree with someone, quarrel
- "Hong Kong is bigger than Singapore."
 "It isn't!"
 "Stop **arguing**. Here is an atlas. I'll show you."

LANGUAGE NOTE
argue **with** someone
argue **about / over** something
argue **against** (doing) something
argue **that** something is good or bad, etc

argument /ˈɑːɡjʊmənt/ noun (countable)

SPELLING NOTE
argue (with an *e*) BUT **argument** (without an *e*)

When you have an **argument** with someone, you talk about something without agreeing.
- "What's the **argument** about?"
 "It's about which is bigger: Hong Kong or Singapore."
➪ get into / have / lose / win an argument

arm /ɑːm/ noun (countable)
part of your body between your hand and shoulder
- I fell and hurt my **arm** yesterday.
➪ bend / cross / fold / lower / raise / wave your arm(s)
⚠ See box on page 25.

armchair /ˌɑːmˈtʃeə*/ noun (countable)
a chair with sides for you to rest your arms
- This **armchair** is much more comfortable than the other chairs in your dining room.

LANGUAGE NOTE
sit **on** a chair BUT sit **in** an armchair

θ	ð	ʃ	dʒ	tʃ	ŋ	ʒ	iː	ɜː	ɪ	æ	ʌ	ɒ
thing	that	shop	jump	chop	sing	measure	been	bird	bit	cat	but	not

army /ˈɑːmɪ/ noun (countable)
plural: armies
a group of people who fight on land during a war
- Ken used to be a soldier and was in the **army** for five years.
- go into/join the army

around¹ /əˈraʊnd/ adverb
about
- I looked **around** to see if someone was there.
get/move/rush/run/walk around, sit/stand/wait around
See also **about¹**.

around² preposition
1 in a circle
   - Everyone stood **around** the fire.
2 about
   - I heard strange voices all **around** me.

arrange /əˈreɪndʒ/ verb
arranging, arranged, has arranged
1 put things in their place (usually in a tidy way)
   - Leila **arranged** the chairs round the table.
2 plan
   - I've **arranged** to see Dr Jones tomorrow.

arrest¹ /əˈrest/ noun (countable)
when someone who has done something wrong is caught
- The policeman made four **arrests** last week.
- be under arrest, make an arrest

arrest² verb
catch and keep someone who is believed to have done something wrong
- The policeman **arrested** the two men when he saw them steal the lady's bag.

LANGUAGE NOTE
arrest someone **for** doing something

arrival /əˈraɪvl/ noun (countable)
when someone comes to a place
- I want to be at the airport in time for Mr and Mrs Short's **arrival**.
- early/late/sudden arrival

arrive /əˈraɪv/ verb
arriving, arrived, has arrived
come to a place (usually at the end of a journey)
- I leave home at half past seven every morning and I **arrive** at school at eight o'clock.

LANGUAGE NOTE
arrive **at** a building, an address, a station, etc
BUT arrive **in** a city, a country
(NEVER arrive to)

article /ˈɑːtɪkl/ noun (countable)
1 a report in a newspaper
   - There was an interesting **article** about a blind girl in yesterday's newspaper.
2 a thing, an object
   - A pen, a ruler, a watch and several other **articles** had been stolen from my bag.

artist /ˈɑːtɪst/ noun (countable)
someone who draws and paints pictures
- Which **artist** painted that picture?

as¹ /æz/ (unstressed /əz/) preposition
to be (used) like
You can use this piece of wood **as** a spade.
See also **same²** (Language Notes).

as² conjunction
1 at the same time, when
   - **As** I opened the door, the phone rang.
2 for, because
   - I whispered **as** my father was sleeping.

as ... as /əz...əz/ adverb
Use these two words when you compare things in a certain way.
- He's **as** strong **as** a horse.

as soon as /əz ˈsuːn əz/ conjunction
at the moment when
- I'll come **as soon as** I finish the letter.

LANGUAGE NOTE
Use the Present Simple tense or the Present Perfect tense to show the future after **as soon as**.
I'll come as soon as I **finish**.
I'll come as soon as **I've finished**.
(NEVER I'll come as soon as I'll finish.)

θ	ð	ʃ	dʒ	tʃ	ŋ	ʒ	iː	ɜː	ɪ	æ	ʌ	ɒ
thing	that	shop	jump	chop	sing	measure	been	bird	bit	cat	but	not

as well as /əz 'wel əz/ preposition
added to
- *"Lee has a new watch **as well as** a new camera."*

ask /ɑːsk/ verb
1. want to know the answer to a question
   - *"Do you know what time it is?" Tamara **asked** me.*
2. ask someone to do something = want someone to do something
   - *"Can you get me a ruler, please?" "Pardon." "I **asked** you to get me a ruler."*
3. ask (someone) for something = want something
   - *I've **asked** Mrs de Sousa for an apple.*
4. **ask for someone** = want to see someone
   - *Someone was **asking for you**, but I told them you were out.*
5. invite
   - *Is Helen going to **ask** us to her party?*

LANGUAGE NOTE
ask a question **about** something
ask someone **to** do something
ask **for** something or someone
ask someone **to** a party, **to** our house, etc
ask **if** someone can do something
ask **where, how**, etc something is

asleep /əˈsliːp/ adjective
sleeping, not awake
- *Sue fell **asleep** in front of the television.*
- See also **fall asleep**.

LANGUAGE NOTE
Don't use **asleep** in front of a noun.
NEVER ~~an asleep boy~~
ALWAYS a boy *who is asleep*
OR a *sleeping* boy

assembly /əˈsembli/ noun (countable)
plural: assemblies
when the whole school or a group of people meet together
- *The first lesson will begin after **assembly**.*

astronaut /ˈæstrənɔːt/ noun (countable)
someone who travels in space
- *Did the two **astronauts** walk on the moon?*

at /æt/ (unstressed /ət/) preposition
1. You can use **at** to show places.
   - *I stayed **at** home yesterday.*
2. You can use **at** to show the time.
   - *Can you meet me **at** half-past six?*
   See also **on** 5 (and Language Note).
3. You can use **at** after certain verbs.
   - *Look **at** him! He's got blue hair! Mary pointed **at** the strange man.*
4. You can use **at** after certain adjectives.
   - *Sarka is very good **at** English.*

LANGUAGE NOTE
1. Use **at** in front of the name of a certain place (an address, a building).
   BUT use **in** in front of a large town, a city or a country.
   Note that you can often use either **at** or **in** in front of the name of a village or small town.
2. Use **at** in front of a point of time: eg **at** two o'clock.
3. Use **at** in front of such words as **Christmas, New Year, Easter**. eg **at Christmas**
   BUT use **on** if you mean an actual day: eg **on New Year's Day, on Easter Sunday**

ate /et/ verb
past tense of eat
- *Mrs Ming **ate** three large bowls of rice.*

athletics /æθˈletɪks/ noun (uncountable)
sports and exercises; running, jumping, etc
- *Tom Lane is very good at **athletics**: he won the 100-metres race yesterday.*

attend /əˈtend/ verb
be present at
- *Can you **attend** the meeting tomorrow?*

attention /əˈtenʃn/ noun (uncountable)
When you watch, listen or think carefully about something, you pay **attention**.
- *Pay **attention** to what I'm going to say.*
- ***Attention**, everyone! This is important!* (Note that this is a common way of getting people's attention.)

θ	ð	ʃ	dʒ	tʃ	ŋ	ʒ	iː	ɜː	ɪ	æ	ʌ	ɒ
thing	that	shop	jump	chop	sing	measure	been	bird	bit	cat	but	not

☋ catch/get/keep/hold/lose someone's attention, draw someone's attention to something

aunt /ɑːnt/ **auntie** /'ɑːntɪ/ noun (countable)
the sister of your mother or father, or your uncle's wife
- Mabel has three **aunts** but she likes **Auntie** Mary best.

author /'ɔːθə*/ noun (countable)
someone who writes a book
- Charlotte Brontë is my favourite **author**.

autumn /'ɔːtəm/ noun (countable, uncountable)
⚠ See box on page 57.

average /'ævərɪdʒ/ noun (countable)
- There are 20 pupils in Class A, 22 pupils in Class B and 27 pupils in Class C. The **average** number of pupils in the three classes is 23: 20+22+27 = 69 ÷ 3 = 23.
☋ above/below average, on average

awake /ə'weɪk/ adjective
not asleep
- Is Helena **awake** or is she still asleep?

away /ə'weɪ/ adverb
1 not here
  - I'm afraid you cannot see Dr Low. She is **away** on holiday this week.
2 in another place, usually where something belongs (used after **put**)
  - "Put your books **away**," the teacher said.
3 (used after certain verbs with the general meaning of disappear, go)
  - Don't throw your old clothes **away**. Give them **away** to some poor families.
☋ come/go/get/move/drive/fly/ride/sail/ march/walk/run/hurry away; give/take/ throw/pour/wash/wear away

awful /'ɔːfl/ adjective
very bad, terrible
- I didn't like the film at all. It was **awful**!

axe /æks/ noun (countable)
(American English: ax)
a tool which you use to chop wood
- Here's an **axe** for you to chop the tree down.

B b

baby /'beɪbɪ/ noun (countable)
plural: babies
a very young child
- Joe is still a baby. He's only ten months old.
☋ have a baby, a new-born baby

back [1] /bæk/ noun (countable)
1 opposite to front (usually singular)
  - Marcel always sits at the **back** of the classroom.
2 part of your body from your neck to the top of your legs
⚠ See box on page 25.

back [2] verb
move or make go backwards
- Can you **back** the car into the garage?

back [3] adjective
opposite to front
- Jenny sat on the **back** seat of the bus.

back [4] adverb
1 not forward
  - Ken decided to turn **back** and go home.
  bring/take/send/pull/push/hold/ keep/come/go/lie/sit/stand/get/ turn back
2 in return
  - Didn't you get my reply to your last letter? I wrote **back** immediately.
☋ answer back (= reply rudely to someone), get/give/phone/write back

θ	ð	ʃ	dʒ	tʃ	ŋ	ʒ	iː	ɜː	ɪ	æ	ʌ	ɒ
thing	that	shop	jump	chop	sing	measure	been	bird	bit	cat	but	not

backache /ˈbækeɪk/ noun (countable, uncountable)
usually uncountable in British English but usually countable in American English
a pain in your back
- *I've got (a) bad **backache**: it hurts a lot.*
⚠ See also **ache** 1; see also **back** [1] 2.

backwards /ˈbækwədz/ adverb
not forwards, with your back first or in front
- *The children were walking **backwards**.*

bad /bæd/ adjective
worse, worst
1 not good (at something)
   - *Tim is **bad** at French and scored only 10%.*
2 wicked
   - *The **bad** dog ate my sandwich.*

LANGUAGE NOTE

bad *at* (doing) something
bad *for* someone: eg *bad for your health*
bad *to* do something: eg *bad to lie*

---

badge /bædʒ/ noun (countable)
something which you wear to show you are a member of a group, club, team, etc
- *He was wearing a cap with the school **badge** on it.*
↻ an army badge, a club badge, a school/college/university badge

badly /ˈbædlɪ/ adverb
in a poor way, not well
- *You did very **badly** to get 8 out of 60 in the test.*

badminton /ˈbædmɪntən/ noun (uncountable)
a game like tennis. You play it by hitting a small object with feathers on it over a net.
- *Shall we play **badminton** this afternoon?*

bag /bæg/ noun (countable)
You use a bag to carry or keep things in. A bag can be made of paper, cloth, leather, plastic, etc.
- *Mrs Robson always puts her keys in her **bag**.*
↻ a handbag, a shopping-bag, a sleeping bag (= a large bag in which you can sleep when you go camping), a tea bag (= a small paper bag with tea in it), a toilet bag (= a very small bag in which you put a toothbrush, toothpaste, a bar of soap, etc)

baggage /ˈbægɪdʒ/ noun (uncountable)
bags, cases

LANGUAGE NOTE

NEVER a baggage
ALWAYS baggage or a piece of baggage

- *Collect your **baggage** before you leave.*

bake /beɪk/ verb
baking, baked, has baked
cook in an oven
- *Mrs Tan has **baked** a big cake for the party.*

baker /ˈbeɪkə*/ noun (countable)
someone whose job is to make bread and cakes in an oven
- *Paul's father is a **baker**.*

balcony /ˈbælkənɪ/ noun (countable)
plural: balconies
1 a place outside a room above the ground
   - *Mabel went onto the **balcony** for some fresh air.*
2 the top floor in a cinema or a theatre
   - *Two seats in the **balcony**, please.*

bald /bɔːld/ adjective
with little or no hair on your head
- *Mr Small is the **bald** man over there.*

ball /bɔːl/ noun (countable)
something round which you can throw or kick (usually in a game)
- *I kicked the **ball** and Erica caught it.*
↻ catch/drop a ball, play with a ball, throw/hit/kick a ball

balloon /bəˈluːn/ noun (countable)
a large bag filled with gas or hot air to make it float in the air
- *Look at the **balloon** high up in the sky.*

θ	ð	ʃ	dʒ	tʃ	ŋ	ʒ	iː	ɜː	ɪ	æ	ʌ	ɒ
thing	that	shop	jump	chop	sing	measure	been	bird	bit	cat	but	not

ballpoint (pen) /ˌbɔːlpɔɪnt ˈpen/ noun (countable)
a pen with a small ball at the end
- *Do you prefer a **ballpoint** to a pencil?*

⚠ See also **biro**; see also **felt-tip (pen)**.

banana /bəˈnɑːnə/ noun (countable)
⚠ See box on page 89.

band /bænd/ noun (countable)
1 a number of people who come together to do the same thing
   - *A small **band** of soldiers marched up the street.*
2 a group of people who play music together
   - *My father's favourite **band** is the Beatles.*
3 something round used to hold things together
   - *Estella had a rubber **band** round her hair.*

bang /bæŋ/ noun (countable)
a sudden loud noise
- *There was a loud **bang** when he fired the gun.*

bank /bæŋk/ noun (countable)
1 a place where you can keep money safely
   - *I'll go to the **bank** to get some money for you.*
2 the side of a river or lake

LANGUAGE NOTE

a river **bank**	BUT NEVER a lake bank
COMPARE	a river bank
	the sea shore

- *There are trees on both **banks** of the river.*

bar /bɑː*/ noun (countable)
1 a long piece of metal or wood

- *The prisoner bent one of the **bars** of the window and escaped.*
2 a piece of chocolate
   - *Would you like a **bar** of chocolate?*

bare /beə*/ adjective
without clothes, etc; without anything over it
- *Don't walk on the road in your **bare** feet.*

bark /bɑːk/ verb
make the sound a dog makes
- *The dogs **barked** loudly when I came in.*

base /beɪs/ noun (countable)
the lowest part of something
- *The **base** of the triangle is ten metres long.*

baseball /ˈbeɪsbɔːl/ noun (uncountable)
a team game played with a bat and ball on a large field with four bases
- ***Baseball** is popular in America and Japan.*

basin /ˈbeɪsn/ noun (countable)
1 a bowl which is used for putting food, water, etc in or for mixing food
   - *Put this flour in the **basin** and add water.*
2 something in a bathroom or kitchen which can hold water for washing things. There are usually taps from which water can run into the basin (sometimes called a washbasin in a bathroom).
   - *There's a **basin** in the bathroom where you can wash your hands.*

basket /ˈbɑːskɪt/ noun (countable)
You can use a basket to hold or carry things in. A basket is usually made of narrow pieces of wood or plastic.
- *Mrs Low's **basket** was full of fruit.*

basketball /ˈbɑːskɪtbɔːl/ noun (countable)
a game played between two teams. The players on each team try to throw a large ball into a high basket.
- *I like playing **basketball**.*

bat /bæt/ noun (countable)
1 something which you use in table tennis, baseball and cricket to hit a ball with
   - *Do you know how to hold a baseball **bat**?*
2 a small mouse-like animal with wings
⚠ See box on page 10.

θ	ð	ʃ	dʒ	tʃ	ŋ	ʒ	iː	ɜː	ɪ	æ	ʌ	ɒ
thing	that	shop	jump	chop	sing	measure	been	bird	bit	cat	but	not

18 bath

bath /bɑːθ/ noun (countable)
plural: **baths** /bɑːðz/
1 A bath is something which holds water and in which you can sit to wash yourself.
- Who filled the **bath** with hot water?
2 **have a bath** = wash your body.
- I ought to **have a bath**: I feel very dirty.
☞ have/take a bath

LANGUAGE NOTE

When you mean **swim**, say **bathe**
(NEVER bath NOR take a bath)
 Let's **bathe** in the lake.
take/have a bath = wash yourself in a bath
bathe = swim

---

bathrobe /ˈbɑːθrəʊb/ noun (countable)
(American English)
⚠ See **dressing gown**.

bathroom /ˈbɑːθrʊm/ noun (countable)
a room in a flat or house, usually containing a bath or shower, a basin and a toilet
- Could I use your **bathroom**, please?

battery /ˈbætərɪ/ noun (countable)
plural: batteries
something which makes electricity (in a radio, a torch, a travel clock, etc)
- I need two new **batteries** for my radio.

be /biː/ (unstressed/bɪ/) verb
is /ɪz/, are /ɑː*/(unstressed/ə*/), being,
was /wɒz/(unstressed/wəz/),
were /wɜː*/(unstressed /wə*/),
has been/biːn,bɪn/
1 Use **be** as a verb on its own.
- I **am** from London.
- She **is** sixteen years old.
- He **is** a doctor.
- It **is** a very narrow road.
- We **are** very happy to see you.
- **Are** you Helena's brother?
- The new students **are** over there.
- I **was** at home all evening.
- We **were** surprised when we heard the news.
- Fortunately, we **have** never **been** very poor.

2 Use **be** to make the continuous tense.
- "What **are** you doing tonight?"
 "I **am** going to the cinema."
 "**Is** Raisha going to the cinema with you?"
3 Use **be** to make the passive voice.
- "When **was** this room painted?"
 "I don't think it's ever **been** painted."

LANGUAGE NOTE

Don't use **being** to talk about how you are or how you feel.
NEVER   I'm being very happy today.
ALWAYS   I'm very happy today.

---

beach /biːtʃ/ noun (countable)
plural: beaches
the ground near the sea, usually flat and covered with sand

- Let's lie on the **beach** and have a rest.

beak /biːk/ noun (countable)
the (hard) mouth of a bird
- The big bird was holding a fish in its **beak**.

bean /biːn/ noun (countable)
⚠ See box on page 238.

bear /beə*/ noun (countable)
⚠ See box on page 10.

beard /bɪəd/ noun (countable)
the hair which grows on a man's face
- The old man had a long white **beard**.
☞ grow/ have a beard

beast /biːst/ noun (countable)
an animal
- Tie the **beast** up before it bites someone.
☞ a wild beast

θ	ð	ʃ	dʒ	tʃ	ŋ	ʒ	iː	ɜː	ɪ	æ	ʌ	ɒ
thing	that	shop	jump	chop	sing	measure	been	bird	bit	cat	but	not

beat /biːt/ verb

beating, beat, has beaten /ˈbiːtn/

1. hit something (hard) again and again
   - *Mrs Lee was **beating** the dust out of the carpet.*
2. win (beat someone = win against someone)
   - *Maria **beat** everyone in the school sports.*

↻ beat someone easily, just beat someone

LANGUAGE NOTE

You **win** a game, a prize, etc
BUT you **beat** the person you are playing or fighting against.
   I **won** a game of chess yesterday.
   I **beat** Cathy. I also **beat** her at cards.

⚠ See also **win**.

beautiful /ˈbjuːtɪfl/ adjective

lovely
- *Linda has a **beautiful** pair of shoes.*

because /bɪˈkɒz/ conjunction

for the reason that
- *We missed the film **because** we were late.*

because of /bɪˈkɒz əv/ preposition

for the reason of
- *We were late **because of** the accident.*

LANGUAGE NOTE

COMPARE   I didn't go out **because** it rained heavily.
          I didn't go out **because of** the heavy rain.

---

become /bɪˈkʌm/ verb

becoming, became /bɪˈkeɪm/, has become

1. come to be
   - *After university, Hassan **became** a teacher.*
2. grow or change into
   - *This little bird will become a **beautiful** swan.*

↻ become angry/famous/poor/rich/blind/deaf/lame/old/white/grey

---

LANGUAGE NOTES

1. Usually your hair **becomes, goes, turns** white or grey.
2. Never use **become** instead of **go** or **come** in: go mad, go bad, go wrong;   come right, come true

---

bed /bed/ noun

1. (countable) a piece of furniture for lying on when you go to sleep
   - *The **bed** was very hard so it kept me awake.*
2. (uncountable)
   - *Go to **bed** if you feel tired.*

↻ go to/lie in/stay in/get out of bed; put (a child) to bed, make the bed

bedroom /ˈbedrʊm/ noun (countable)

a room where you sleep
- *There are two beds in my **bedroom**.*

bedtime /ˈbedtaɪm/ noun (uncountable)

the time when you usually go to bed to sleep
- *Mr Eden reads his children a story at **bedtime**.*

bee /biː/ noun (countable)
⚠ See box on page 114.

beef /biːf/ noun (uncountable)

meat from a cow

LANGUAGE NOTE

NEVER   a beef
ALWAYS   beef OR a piece of **beef**

- *My favourite kind of meat is **beef**: I like it much better than chicken.*

been /biːn, bɪn/ verb

1. past participle of **be**
   - *I've **been** absent from school because I've **been** ill.*
2. (a past participle of a certain meaning of **go**) travelled to and returned from
   - *"Where have you **been**?" "I've **been** shopping."*

LANGUAGE NOTE

Sheila's **been** to Australia. (And she's come back.)
Sheila's **gone** to Australia. (And she's still there.)

⚠ See also **gone**.

θ	ð	ʃ	dʒ	tʃ	ŋ	ʒ	iː	ɜː	ɪ	æ	ʌ	ɒ
thing	that	shop	jump	chop	sing	measure	been	bird	bit	cat	but	not

beetroot /ˈbiːtruːt/ noun (countable, uncountable)
⚠ See box on page 238.

before¹ /bɪˈfɔː*/ adverb
earlier, up until now
• I've never eaten duck **before**.

before² preposition
1 earlier than
• We usually have breakfast **before** seven.
2 in front of
• The letter D comes **before** E.

> **LANGUAGE NOTE**
>
> Use **before** when you want to show the order of things in a list, but do not use **before** to show a place. Instead of **before**, use **in front of**.
>
> Who put the chair **in front of** the window? (NEVER before)

before³ conjunction
earlier than the time when
• Put your coat on **before** you go outside.

beggar /ˈbegə*/ noun (countable)
a poor person who asks people for money
• Did you give a dollar to the **beggar** we saw?

begin /bɪˈgɪn/ verb
beginning, began /bɪˈgæn/, has begun /bɪˈgʌn/
start
• The film **begins** at seven. Don't be late.

> **LANGUAGE NOTES**
>
> 1 You can often use either **begin** or **start**.
>   When did Ann **begin** / **start** to learn English?
>   BUT always use **start** (NOT begin) to talk about:
>   (1) starting a journey: We **started** (out) at eight.
>   (2) making machines work: "Can you **start** the car?" "No, it won't **start**."
>
> 2 Note the following patterns.
>   When did you start to **learn** English?
>   When did you begin/start **learning** English.
>   BUT I'm beginning/starting **to learn** the piano.
>   (NOT I'm beginning/starting learning the piano.)

⚠ See also **start**.

beginning /bɪˈgɪnɪŋ/ noun (countable)
start
• The hero was a very poor man at the **beginning** of the story, but at the end he was very rich.

> **SPELLING NOTE**
>
> double **n** : begi**nn**ing

behave /bɪˈheɪv/ verb
behaving, behaved, has behaved
do things in a good or a bad way
• My children **behave** well at school.

behaviour /bɪˈheɪvjə*/ noun (uncountable)
the way we do things
• Be on your best **behaviour** when you see the principal.
↻ on your best behaviour

behind¹ /bɪˈhaɪnd/ adverb
in the place where something or someone was
• Oh dear! I've left my glasses **behind**. Can you lend me yours?
↻ get/go/stay/leave (something) behind

behind² preposition
at the back of
• There is a tall tree **behind** that house. Can you see the top of it?

believe /bɪˈliːv/ verb
believing, believed, has believed
1 think that something is real or true
• Do you **believe** in God?
2 think that someone is telling the truth
• I don't **believe** Tom found the money.
3 think
• I **believe** he is Jane's brother.

> **LANGUAGE NOTE**
>
> NEVER   I am believing, they were believing, etc
> ALWAYS   I believe, they believed, etc

bell /bel/ noun (countable)
an object which makes a noise to let people know you're there
• Don't knock on the door. Ring the **bell**!

θ	ð	ʃ	dʒ	tʃ	ŋ	ʒ	iː	ɜː	ɪ	æ	ʌ	ɒ
thing	that	shop	jump	chop	sing	measure	been	bird	bit	cat	but	not

belong to /bɪˈlɒŋ tuː/ verb phrase
be owned by someone
- *This isn't your book. It **belongs to** me.*

LANGUAGE NOTE	
NEVER	~~The hat is belonging to Mr Smith.~~
ALWAYS	The hat **belongs** to Mr Smith.
OR	The hat **belonging** to Mr Smith has disappeared.

below /bɪˈləʊ/ preposition
lower than, underneath
- *We could hear shouting in the street **below**.*

belt /belt/ noun (countable)
a band which you wear round your waist to hold up your trousers or skirt
- *A **belt** will stop your trousers falling down!*

bend[1] /bend/ noun (countable)
a curved part of a road or river
- *Our house is by a **bend** in the river.*
⚭ a sharp bend, a slight bend

bend[2] verb
bending, bent /bent/, has bent
make something curve
- *Ahmed was so strong he could **bend** an iron bar.*

beneath /bɪˈniːθ/ preposition
lower than, under
- *The ship sank **beneath** the waves and disappeared.*

beside /bɪˈsaɪd/ preposition
next to, at the side of
- *Our new house is **beside** a small lake.*

besides[1] /bɪˈsaɪdz/ adverb
(and) also
- *He'll do very well in the job - **besides**, he can start work tomorrow.*

besides[2] preposition
as well as
- *Mr Jottini can speak French, English and Arabic **besides** Russian and Italian.*

best[1] /best/ adjective
good, better, best
- *Anna's composition is the **best** in the class.*
⚜ See also **good**.

best[2] adverb
well, better, best
- *"Which do you like **best**: reading, watching TV or playing games?" "I like playing games **best** of all."*
⚜ See also **well**[3].

better[1] /ˈbetə*/ adjective
good, better, best
- *Tony's picture is **better** than mine.*
⚜ See also **good**.

better[2] adverb
well, better, best
- *Susan likes History **better** than Geography.*
⚜ See also **well**[3].

better[3] adjective, adverb
well, better
- *I was quite ill last week, but I'm (getting) **better** now.*
be better, get better
⚜ See also **well**[2].

between /bɪˈtwiːn/ preposition
1 in the middle of

- *Maria stood **between** her two brothers.*

2 from one to the other
- *The ship sails **between** England and France.*

beyond /bɪˈjɒnd/ preposition
on the further side of
- *Our new school is **beyond** that wood.*

θ	ð	ʃ	dʒ	tʃ	ŋ	ʒ	iː	ɜː	ɪ	æ	ʌ	ɒ
thing	that	shop	jump	chop	sing	measure	been	bird	bit	cat	but	not

bicycle /ˈbaɪsɪkl/ noun (countable)
A bicycle has two wheels and you ride on it.
- *Do you go to school on your **bicycle**?*

go on a bicycle, go by bicycle
get on/pedal/ride a bicycle
(NEVER drive a bicycle)

LANGUAGE NOTE
You can sometimes say *bike* for *bicycle*.

big /bɪg/ adjective
bigger, biggest
large, not small
- *An elephant is a very **big** animal.*

LANGUAGE NOTES
1 You should usually use *large* with *amount* and *number* and NOT *big*:
a *large* amount of
a *large* number of
2 NEVER a big headache, etc
ALWAYS a bad headache, a terrible headache

bike /baɪk/ noun (countable)
See **bicycle**.

bill /bɪl/ noun (countable)
1 A bill is a piece of paper which shows how much you must pay when you have bought something.
(American English: check)
- *As soon as we had finished eating, I asked the waiter for the **bill**.*

ask for/pay/send the bill,
get/receive a bill

2 (American English) a piece of paper money
See **note** 3.

bird /bɜːd/ noun (countable)
a small animal which has wings and feathers and which can fly
- *There were several small **birds** on the branch.*
See box above.

Birds
duck, goose, hen, parrot, penguin, eagle

biro /ˈbaɪərəʊ/ noun (countable)
plural: biros
a ballpoint
- *This letter has been written with a **biro**.*
written with a biro/in biro
See also **ballpoint (pen)**; see also **felt-tip (pen)**.

birth /bɜːθ/ noun (countable)
being born
- *"What's your date of **birth**?"*
"I was born on 21 May 1983."

give birth (to a baby)

birthday /ˈbɜːθdeɪ/ noun (countable)
the same date every year as your date of birth (ie the date when you were born)
- *Are you going to Harry's **birthday** party?*

biscuit /ˈbɪskɪt/ noun (countable)
(American English: cookie)
a small thin cake (usually hard and quite sweet)
- *Do you enjoy chocolate **biscuits**?*

bit [1] /bɪt/ noun (countable)
a small part of something
- *Would you like a **bit** of cake?*

bit [2] verb
past tense of **bite**
- *The small dog ran after Tim and **bit** him.*

θ	ð	ʃ	dʒ	tʃ	ŋ	ʒ	iː	ɜː	ɪ	æ	ʌ	ɒ
thing	that	shop	jump	chop	sing	measure	been	bird	bit	cat	but	not

bit³ adverb

(used in speaking)
a little, rather
- *"How do you feel now?"*
  *"I'm a **bit** better, thank you."*

bite¹ /baɪt/ noun (countable)

when you cut something with your teeth
- *Would you like a **bite** of my apple?*
- have/take a bite of something

SPELLING NOTE

double *t*: bi**tt**en BUT bi**t**ing

---

bite² verb

biting, bit /bɪt/, has bitten /ˈbɪtn/

You **bite** something when you cut it with your teeth.
- *Be careful or the dog will **bite** you.*

bitter /ˈbɪtə*/ adjective

not sweet
- *The coffee is very **bitter** without sugar.*

black /blæk/ noun (uncountable), adjective

the colour of night when there is no light at all
- *Put some **black** in your painting to show that there are shadows.*
- *He was wearing **black** shoes.*
- *Piano keys are **black** and white.*

blackboard /ˈblækbɔːd/ noun (countable)

a flat piece of wood which is black and which teachers use in a classroom for writing on
- *The teacher wrote her name on the **blackboard**.*
- clean/wash /draw on/write on the blackboard

blank¹ /blæŋk/ noun (countable)

an empty space
- *Fill in the **blank** in this sentence:*
  "I felt very tired when I returned ____ ."

blank² adjective

without anything on it, with no writing on it
- *Noora wrote her name on a **blank** piece of paper.*

blanket /ˈblæŋkɪt/ noun (countable)

a thick piece of cloth to put over you to keep you warm (especially in bed)
- *In winter I have two **blankets** on my bed because it's very cold at night.*

bleed /bliːd/ verb

bleeding, bled /bled/, has bled
lose blood
- *I've just cut my hand and it's **bleeding** a lot.*

blew /bluː/ verb

past tense of **blow**
- *A strong wind **blew** my hat off.*

blind /blaɪnd/ adjective

unable to see
- *The **blind** man walks with a white stick.*

block¹ /blɒk/ noun (countable)

1 a number of buildings joined together
   - *Turn left at the end of the **block**.*
2 a large building divided into smaller parts
   - *I live on the 1st floor in a new **block** of flats.*
3 a large piece of stone, wood, etc
   - *This seat was made from a **block** of wood.*

block² verb

stop things from moving on or past
- *The large tree fell and **blocked** the road.*

blonde /blɒnd/ adjective

(of hair) yellow
- *Stephanie has **blonde** hair.*

blood /blʌd/ noun (uncountable)

If you cut yourself blood will flow from your body.
- *The knife was covered with **blood**.*

blouse /blaʊz/ noun (countable)

A piece of clothing which a girl or woman can wear on the top of her body.
- *Women wear **blouses** but men wear shirts.*

θ	ð	ʃ	dʒ	tʃ	ŋ	ʒ	iː	ɜː	ɪ	æ	ʌ	ɒ
thing	that	shop	jump	chop	sing	measure	been	bird	bit	cat	but	not

blow /bləʊ/ verb

blowing, blew /bluː/, has blown /bləʊn/
1 send out air
 • *Spiros began to **blow** over the tea to cool it.*
2 move with air
 • *Don't let the wind **blow** your hat off.*
3 send air into something to make a sound
 • *He **blew** the trumpet very loudly.*

blow up /ˌbləʊ ˈʌp/ phrasal verb

blow something up
1 destroy something by making it burst into small pieces
 • *The soldiers **blew** the bridge **up**.*
2 fill with air

 • *Your front tyre is flat: why don't you **blow** it **up**?*

blue /bluː/ noun (uncountable, countable), adjective

the colour of the sky when there are no clouds or the colour of the sea on a bright day
 • *His eyes are dark **blue**.*
 • *Moby Dick was a **blue** whale.*

blunt /blʌnt/ adjective

not sharp
 • *Use my penknife to sharpen your **blunt** pencils.*

board /bɔːd/ noun (countable)

1 a flat piece of wood, cardboard, plastic, etc
 • *There were one or two new pieces of paper on the notice**board**.*
 • *Let's play chess. Here's the chess**board**.*
2 a long, thin piece of wood
 • *The workmen are putting down some new **boards** on the floor.*
3 We often use the word **board** to mean **blackboard**.
 • *Mr Law wrote the sum on the **board**.*

4 **on board** = on a plane or ship
 • *The plane will leave as soon as everyone is **on board**.*

LANGUAGE NOTE

Don't use *of* after **on board**.
NEVER   on board of the plane
ALWAYS   on board the plane

boat /bəʊt/ noun (countable)

A boat is used to carry things or people on water.
 • *We sat in the small fishing **boat** all day and watched the big ships sail out to sea.*
 ↻ row/ sail a boat

body /ˈbɒdɪ/ noun (countable)

plural: bodies
1 every part of a person
 • *My whole **body** ached after cycling so far.*
2 all of a person or animal except for the head, arm and legs
 • *My **body** feels very hot but my head is cold.*
3 a dead person
 • *Two **bodies** were taken from the crash.*
 ⚠ See box opposite.

boil /bɔɪl/ verb

1 make water, etc very hot so that steam comes from it
 • ***Boil** the water before you pour it over the tea.*
2 cook something in very hot water
 • *Mrs Lee **boiled** some rice for lunch.*

bomb¹ /bɒm/ noun (countable)

something which blows up things or people
 • *Six people were killed when someone threw a **bomb** into the room.*

bomb² verb

drop bombs on
 • *Several aeroplanes **bombed** the bridge.*

bone /bəʊn/ noun (countable)

a hard part inside the body of a person or an animal
 • *The dog is eating a **bone**.*

θ	ð	ʃ	dʒ	tʃ	ŋ	ʒ	iː	ɜː	ɪ	æ	ʌ	ɒ
thing	that	shop	jump	chop	sing	measure	been	bird	bit	cat	but	not

The Body

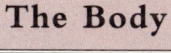

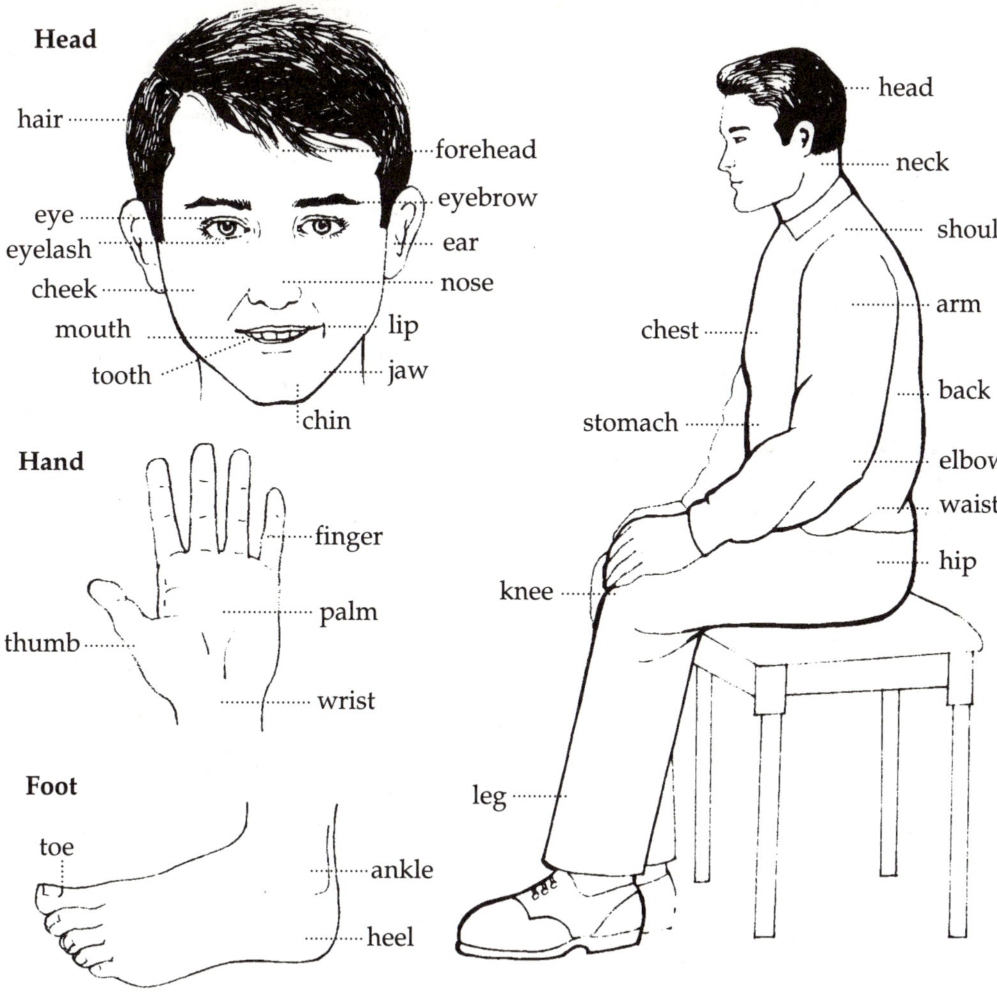

Head: hair, forehead, eye, eyebrow, eyelash, ear, cheek, nose, mouth, lip, tooth, jaw, chin

Hand: finger, palm, thumb, wrist

Foot: toe, ankle, heel

head, neck, shoulder, arm, chest, back, stomach, elbow, waist, hip, knee, leg

NOTE For more information, see also the following words in the dictionary:
arm, ear, eye, finger, hand, hair, head, leg, tooth

---

book[1] /bʊk/ noun (countable)
pieces of printed paper which are fastened together
- *Why don't you read a good **book** instead of watching television all day?*
- a history/geography/science book, etc, a picture/story/school book, a textbook (= a book which is used to study subjects at school)

book[2] verb
keep, save
- *I've **booked** two seats at the theatre tomorrow.*

bookcase /'bʊk-keɪs/ noun (countable)
a piece of furniture with shelves for books
- *The book is on the top shelf of your **bookcase**.*

bookshop /'bʊkʃɒp/ noun (countable)
a shop where books are sold
- *The book you want is in the **bookshop**.*

boot /buːt/ noun (countable)
a kind of shoe that covers the ankle
- *I've just bought a new pair of **boots** for walking in the countryside.*

θ	ð	ʃ	dʒ	tʃ	ŋ	ʒ	iː	ɜː	ɪ	æ	ʌ	ɒ
thing	that	shop	jump	chop	sing	measure	been	bird	bit	cat	but	not

bored /bɔːd/ adjective
not interested, unhappy because you have nothing to do
- *Why don't you read a book? Then you won't be so **bored**.*

LANGUAGE NOTE
bored **with** (doing) something

boring /ˈbɔːrɪŋ/ adjective
not interesting, dull
- *The film was so **boring**, I fell asleep.*

LANGUAGE NOTE
She is **bored** = Someone or something bores her
She is **boring** = She bores people

born /bɔːn/ verb (passive only)
When you are **born**, you come out of your mother's body and start your life.
- *"When were you **born**?"*
  *"I was **born** on 3rd October, 1987."*

LANGUAGE NOTES
1 ALWAYS   I **was** born
NEVER   ~~I have been born~~ OR ~~I am born.~~
2 Don't use **by** after **born**.

boss /bɒs/ noun (countable)
(used only in speaking)
plural: bosses
the person who tells people what to do when they are working, the manager
- *My **boss** told me to work much harder.*

bossy /ˈbɒsɪ/ adjective
always telling people what to do
- *My **bossy** sister is always shouting at me.*

both /bəʊθ/ determiner, pronoun
two (things or people)
- *I failed **both** the English and Maths exams.*

LANGUAGE NOTES
1 Don't use **both** after **the, these,** etc
NEVER   ~~The both students are working hard.~~
ALWAYS   **Both the** students are working hard.
2 Use only **both of** before **the, these, my,** etc
Do not use **both of** if there is only a noun by itself.
Hold it in both of your hands.
NEVER   ~~Hold it in both of hands.~~
ALWAYS   Hold it in **both** hands.
3 Note the position of **both** in these sentences.
We **both** enjoy parties.
We have **both** enjoyed the party.
(NOT USUALLY We both have enjoyed the party.)

bottle /ˈbɒtl/ noun (countable)
something made of glass or plastic in which water, milk, wine, etc are put. A bottle usually has a narrow top and no handle.
- *There is some milk in this **bottle**.*

bottom¹ /ˈbɒtəm/ noun (countable)
1 the lower end of something
   - *Our new house is at the **bottom** of the hill.*
2 the part of your body which you sit on

bottom² adjective
lowest
- *Please kneel down and put the books on the **bottom** shelf.*

bought /bɔːt/ verb
past tense and past participle of **buy**
- *Who **bought** you that book?*
- *We've just **bought** a new television set.*

bounce /baʊns/ verb
bouncing, bounced, has bounced
hit the ground and rise again
- *The ball **bounced** over the gate onto the road.*

bowl /bəʊl/ noun (countable)
a deep dish
- *Can I put some more rice in your **bowl**?*

θ	ð	ʃ	dʒ	tʃ	ŋ	ʒ	iː	ɜː	ɪ	æ	ʌ	ɒ
thing	that	shop	jump	chop	sing	measure	been	bird	bit	cat	but	not

box¹ /bɒks/ noun (countable)
plural: boxes
1 something which is square or like a rectangle in shape and which is made of wood, metal, plastic, paper, etc. You can put things in a box.
 • *I opened the **box** and found a pen inside.*
 a matchbox (= a box which is used for putting matches in)
2 **the box** = television (used only in speaking)
 • *"Is there anything interesting on **the box** tonight?"*
 ෴ a call box (= a box containing a telephone), a (tele)phone /letter box

box² verb
fight someone with your hands closed
 • *Pete is **boxing** Harry Hardy tonight.*

boy /bɔɪ/ noun (countable)
a child but not a girl
 • *The **boys** were enjoying the fight when the teacher came out and stopped it.*

brain /breɪn/ noun (countable)
something in your head which you use for thinking and feeling about things
 • *She's got a very good **brain**, and I'm sure she will succeed in everything she does.*
 ෴ an excellent/a good/first-class/quick brain

branch /brɑːntʃ/ noun (countable)
plural: branches
the arm of a tree

 • *The monkey sat on the bottom **branch** of the tree.*

brave /breɪv/ adjective
not feeling afraid, without fear
 • *The **brave** policeman took the gun from the thief.*

bravely /'breɪvlɪ/ adverb
in a brave way, without fear
 • *The two dead soldiers had fought very **bravely**.*

bread /bred/ noun (uncountable)
food which is made from flour and baked

LANGUAGE NOTE	
ALWAYS	bread, **some** bread, **a piece of** bread, **a slice of** bread and **a loaf of** bread
NEVER	a bread

 • *Could I have some **bread** please?*

break¹ /breɪk/ noun (countable)
a short rest (sometimes between lessons at school)
 • *I'm going to have a **break** and watch TV.*
 ෴ have/take a break
 a short/weekend break, a coffee/tea break

break² verb
breaking, broke /brəʊk/,
has broken /'brəʊkən/
1 divide into pieces (often by accident)
 • *The cup fell to the floor and **broke**.*
2 drop or hit something so that it divides into pieces
 • *Tina has **broken** one of the cups.*

break down /ˌbreɪk 'daʊn/ phrasal verb
breaking down, broke down, has broken down
stop working
 • *Oh dear! The car has **broken down** again.*

break out /ˌbreɪk 'aʊt/ phrasal verb
breaking out, broke out, has broken out
1 start (suddenly)
 • *A fire has **broken out** in the shop.*
2 escape, run away from prison
 • *Six prisoners **broke out** yesterday and haven't been caught yet.*

θ	ð	ʃ	dʒ	tʃ	ŋ	ʒ	iː	ɜː	ɪ	æ	ʌ	ɒ
thing	that	shop	jump	chop	sing	measure	been	bird	bit	cat	but	not

break up /ˌbreɪk ˈʌp/ phrasal verb
breaking up, broke up, has broken up
1. break into small pieces
   - Mrs Rodriguez **broke up** the chocolate.
2. stop, finish
   - When do we **break up** for the holidays?

breakfast /ˈbrekfəst/ noun (uncountable, countable)
the first meal of the day (in the morning)
- We all had a big **breakfast** before we left.

🔄 eat/have breakfast, make breakfast

LANGUAGE NOTE
NEVER make a breakfast
ALWAYS make breakfast or make the breakfast

breath /breθ/ noun (countable)
air which you take in and send out through your nose and mouth
- How long can you hold your **breath** underwater?

🔄 catch/get/lose your breath, take a (deep) breath;
a big/deep breath

breathe /briːð/ verb
breathing, breathed, has breathed
take air in and out through your nose and mouth
- Dr Stein told me to **breathe** deeply.

brick /brɪk/ noun (countable)
something in the shape of a small rectangle used for building walls and houses
- I'm using these **bricks** to build a wall.

bride /braɪd/ noun (countable)
a woman who is just getting married
- Was the **bride** late for her wedding?

bridegroom /ˈbraɪdɡrʊm/ noun (countable)
a man who is just getting married
- The **bridegroom** was wearing a white suit.

bridge /brɪdʒ/ noun (countable)
a way across a river or a road
- Is there a **bridge** over the river?

brief /briːf/ adjective
short (in time)
- Ali's going on a **brief** one-day visit to Singapore.

bright /braɪt/ adjective
1. giving a lot of light
   - The moon and stars are very **bright** tonight.
2. not dark, clear in colour
   - Nadia was wearing a **bright** red blouse.
3. clever
   - Ann is a very **bright** girl. She is always top of her class.
4. cheerful, happy
   - Stephen is always very **bright** and cheerful.

brightly /ˈbraɪtlɪ/ adverb
in a bright way, giving a lot of light
- The sun was shining **brightly** when we set off.

bring /brɪŋ/ verb
bringing, brought /brɔːt/, has brought
When you bring someone or something with you, you have them with you or they come with you.
- Did you **bring** a friend with you?

LANGUAGE NOTE
bring = carry someone or something **here** (to the speaker)
take = carry someone or something **there** (away from the speaker)

⚠ See also **take** [1].

broad /brɔːd/ adjective
wide, large from one side to the other
- Amran saw us and he gave us a **broad** smile.

LANGUAGE NOTE
The word **wide** is used much more often than **broad**: eg a **wide** street, a **wide** river.

broke /brəʊk/ verb
past tense of **break**
- Who **broke** the window?

broken /ˈbrəʊkən/ verb

past participle of **break**
not working
- *My watch is **broken**. What's the time, please?*

brother /ˈbrʌðə*/ noun (countable)

a boy or man with the same parents as someone else
- *I've got two **brothers**: Henry and Peter.*
- a big/little/elder/older/younger brother

brought /brɔːt/ verb

past tense and past participle of **bring**
- *Anna **brought** her new baby with her.*

brown /braʊn/ noun (uncountable, countable), adjective

the colour of chocolate
- *She was dressed all in **brown**.*
- *The **brown** cow was in the field.*

brush¹ /brʌʃ/ noun (countable)

plural: brushes
something we use to sweep or clean things
- *Use this **brush** to sweep up the dirt.*
- a clothesbrush, a hairbrush, a paintbrush, a toothbrush

brush² verb

sweep, use a brush
- *Please **brush** your hair. It's very untidy.*

Brussels sprout /ˌbrʌsəl ˈspraʊt/ noun (countable)

See box on page 238.

bucket /ˈbʌkɪt/ noun (countable)

You can put water in a bucket. It is round and is usually made of metal, plastic or wood.
- *Can you carry this heavy **bucket** of water?*

buffalo /ˈbʌfələʊ/ noun (countable)

See box on page 10.

bug /bʌg/ noun (countable)

1 (American English)
 See **insect**.
2 something that causes a disease (used only in speaking and in letters to friends)
- *I think I've got a **bug**. I feel sick.*

build /bɪld/ verb

building, built /bɪlt/, has built
make something (usually by putting stones, bricks, etc together)

- *Look at those men **building** a wall.*

builder /ˈbɪldə*/ noun (countable)

a person who builds things
- *My brother works as a **builder** in Dahran.*

building /ˈbɪldɪŋ/ noun (countable)

something which has been built
- *The post office is the **building** next to this.*

LANGUAGE NOTE

A building may be a block of flats, offices, etc, a house, a shop, a cinema, a church, a mosque, etc BUT NOT a bridge, a tunnel, a road, etc

built /bɪlt/ verb

past tense and past participle of **build**
- *Ken **built** the model bridge with matches.*

bulb /bʌlb/ noun (countable)

the glass part of a lamp which gives out light
- *We need to put a new **bulb** in this light.*
- a light bulb

θ	ð	ʃ	dʒ	tʃ	ŋ	ʒ	iː	ɜː	ɪ	æ	ʌ	ɒ
thing	that	shop	jump	chop	sing	measure	been	bird	bit	cat	but	not

bullet /ˈbʊlɪt/ noun (countable)
something small and sharp which is fired from a gun
- Several **bullets** hit my leg as I tried to run away.

bunch /bʌntʃ/ noun (countable)
plural: bunches
a lot of flowers etc put together
- The pupils gave the headmistress a lovely **bunch** of flowers for her birthday.

☞ a bunch of flowers/grapes/keys

burglar /ˈbɜːglə*/ noun (countable)
a thief who enters a building to steal things
- **Burglars** broke into our house and stole a TV.

⚠ See also **robber**; see also **thief**.

burn /bɜːn/ verb
burning, burnt /bɜːnt/ or burned, has burnt or has burned
1. be on fire
   - This wood is very dry and will **burn** quickly.
2. set fire to something
   - Mrs Torres is **burning** wood and not coal.

burnt /bɜːnt/ adjective
having been set on fire, destroyed or damaged by fire
- All that was left were a few **burnt** pieces of wood.

burst /bɜːst/ verb
bursting, burst, burst
open suddenly
- Don't **burst** the balloon with that pin.

☞ burst into flames, burst into tears

bury /ˈberɪ/ verb
burying, buried, has buried
put a dead body in the ground, put something in the ground
- Mr Newman's first wife is **buried** here.

bus /bʌs/ noun (countable)
plural: buses
a vehicle which carries several people from one place to another
- Mr Yamani always travels to work by **bus**.

☞ go/travel by bus; go/travel/ride on a bus; catch/take a bus; get on/get off a bus

bus station /ˈbʌs ˌsteɪʃn/ noun (countable)
a place where buses start and finish their journeys
- I have to go to the **bus station** to meet my aunt.

bus stop /ˈbʌs stɒp/ noun (countable)
a place where you can get on or off a bus

- There are a lot of people waiting at the **bus stop**.

bush /bʊʃ/ noun (countable)
plural: bushes
a small tree
- Mrs Law planted several **bushes** in her garden.

business /ˈbɪznɪs/ noun
plural: businesses
1. (countable) a factory, a shop
   - Mr Wong has a **business** in Singapore.
   ☞ build up/carry on/have/open up/start a business
2. (uncountable) buying and selling things
   - **Business** is very good at present, and a lot of people are quickly becoming very rich.
   ☞ be in/do business, get down to business (= start working seriously), go into/out of business
3. something that interests a person (uncountable)
   - That's my **business**. It's no **business** of yours. (= It has nothing to do with you.)

businessman /ˈbɪznɪsmən/ noun (countable)
plural: businessmen
someone who buys and sells things
- *"Are you a **businessman**?" "No, I'm a teacher."*

busy /ˈbɪzi/ adjective
busier, busiest
1 have a lot of things to do
   - *The headmaster is too **busy** to see you now.*
2 with a lot of things happening
   - *The town centre was very **busy** this morning.*

LANGUAGE NOTE

busy at/with something
busy doing something

---

but /bʌt/ (unstressed / bət/) conjunction
used between two phrases to show different ideas or things
- *I'm very thin **but** my elder sister is very fat.*

LANGUAGE NOTE

When you use *although* in part of a sentence, don't begin the other part of the sentence with *but*.
EITHER   **Although** it was raining heavily, a lot of people came to see the football match.
OR   It was raining heavily **but** a lot of people came to see the football match.
(NEVER   Although it was raining heavily, but a lot of people came to the football match.)

---

butcher /ˈbʊtʃə*/ noun (countable)
someone who sells meat
- *I've got to go to the **butcher's** to get some meat.*

butter /ˈbʌtə*/ noun (uncountable)
something which is made from milk and is yellow. You spread butter on bread or use it when you cook.
- *David put a lot of **butter** on his bread.*

butterfly /ˈbʌtəflaɪ/ noun (countable)
⚠ See box on page 114.

button¹ /ˈbʌtn/ noun (countable)
1 something small and round for fastening clothes
   - *One of the **button**s has come off my shirt.*
2 something small which we push to start and stop a machine
   - *Push this **button** to turn the radio on.*

button² verb
fasten clothes by pushing buttons through small holes
- ***Button** (up) your coat: it's very cold today.*

buy /baɪ/ verb
buying, bought /bɔːt/, has bought
pay money for something
- *I've just **bought** a new camera from that shop.*

LANGUAGE NOTE

buy something *for* someone *from* someone else

---

by¹ /baɪ/ adverb
past
- *A small piece of wood floated **by**.*
↪ come/go/drive/ride/hurry/run/walk/pass by

by² preposition
1 beside, near
   - *The new college is **by** a small mosque.*
2 during
   - *The soldiers marched **by** night.*
3 on or before
   - *I'll be back **by** seven o'clock.*
4 (used with the passive voice to show who did something)
   - *This book was written **by** Charles Dickens. (= Charles Dickens wrote this book.)*
5 (used with *myself, yourself, himself,* etc)
   - *Did you paint the picture **by** yourself? Yes, I painted it all **by** myself. No one helped me.*

θ	ð	ʃ	dʒ	tʃ	ŋ	ʒ	iː	ɜː	ɪ	æ	ʌ	ɒ
thing	that	shop	jump	chop	sing	measure	been	bird	bit	cat	but	not

☙ go by bus/train/boat/road/rail/sea/air
BUT go on foot (= walk); by accident/
chance/ hand/machine/day/night/
day/night/law, etc

bye (bye) /ˌbaɪ 'baɪ/ interjection
Goodbye
- *Bye bye*. I'll see you tomorrow.

Cc

cabbage /'kæbɪdʒ/ noun (countable, uncountable)
See box on page 238.

cafe /'kæfeɪ/ noun (countable)
a place where you can get food and drinks (tea and coffee)
- Let's go to a *cafe* and have some coffee.

cage /keɪdʒ/ noun (countable)
a box with bars, wires or pieces of wood round it
- I don't like to see tigers in *cages* in zoos.

cake /keɪk/ noun (countable)
a sweet kind of food, almost like a soft biscuit

- Mrs Lowe made a big *cake* for Joan's birthday. She put twelve candles on it.
☙ bake/make a cake; a birthday/wedding cake, chocolate cake; a piece of cake

calculator /'kælkjʊleɪtə*/ noun (countable)
a machine you can use to do sums
- "What's 45 + 389 x 34.6?" "Just a moment, please. I'll use my *calculator*."
☙ a pocket calculator

calendar /'kælɪndə*/ noun (countable)
a piece of paper which shows the days, weeks and months of the year
- Look at a *calendar* and find out what day we leave.

θ	ð	ʃ	dʒ	tʃ	ŋ	ʒ	iː	ɜː	ɪ	æ	ʌ	ɒ
thing	that	shop	jump	chop	sing	measure	been	bird	bit	cat	but	not

candy 33

LANGUAGE NOTE

In British English a **diary** is a book with a space or page for each day but in American English such a book is usually called a **calendar.**

In Britain a **calendar** is often printed on a large piece of paper which you can put up on a wall.

⚜ See also **diary**.

calf /kɑːf/ noun (countable)
plural: calves /kɑːvz/
a young cow
⚜ See box on page 10.

call [1] /kɔːl/ noun (countable)
1 make or give someone a (phone) call
 • Give Sue a **call** to find out how she is.
 ✦ give someone a call, make/take a call
2 a shout or a cry (for something)
 • We heard a **call** for help. A man was lying in the road!

call [2] verb
1 telephone
 • Helen and Dave **called** their aunt (up) to ask if they could visit her.
2 shout or cry for someone or something
 • The teacher **calls** (out) the pupils' names before the first lesson.
3 ask someone to come
 • **Call** (for) the police at once! Someone's stolen my ring!
4 give someone a name
 • I'm **called** Susan. What's your name?

call for /'kɔːl fɔː*/ phrasal verb
go and get someone or something, collect
 • I'll **call for** you on my way to town.

caller /'kɔːlə*/ noun (countable)
1 a person who makes a telephone call
 • What number do you want, **caller**?
2 a visitor
 • There were several **callers** while you were out.

calm /kɑːm/ adjective
still, peaceful, quiet
 • The sea is very **calm** today.

came /keɪm/ verb
past tense of **come**
 • How many people **came** to the meeting?

camel /'kæml/ noun (countable)
⚜ See box on page 10.

camera /'kæmərə/ noun (countable)
You use a camera to take photographs.
 • Have you taken any photographs with your new **camera** yet?

camp [1] /kæmp/ noun (countable)
a piece of land where people live in tents or huts (usually for a short time)
 • The three men made their **camp** half-way up the mountain.
✦ make/set up a camp

camp [2] verb
live for a short time in a tent or hut
 • We decided to **camp** in the valley.

can [1] /kæn/ noun (countable)
a tin for keeping food or drink inside
 • Each of us took a **can** of fruit on the picnic.
✦ a tin can

can [2] /kæn/ (unstressed /kən/) modal verb
1 be able to do something
 • Lisa **can** speak French and English .
2 let someone do something
 • Ann **can** go to the cinema, too, but she has to be back home before ten o'clock.
3 **Can I, can we, can you** = used to ask politely for something
 • "**Can I** go to the cinema tonight?"
⚜ See also **could**.

candle /'kændl/ noun (countable)
a long round stick which we burn to give light
 • When all the lights went out, we used **candles**.
✦ blow out/light a candle

candy /'kændɪ/ noun (countable)
plural: candies
(American English)
⚜ See **sweet** [1] 1.
✦ a box of/a piece of candy

θ	ð	ʃ	dʒ	tʃ	ŋ	ʒ	iː	ɜː	ɪ	æ	ʌ	ɒ
thing	that	shop	jump	chop	sing	measure	been	bird	bit	cat	but	not

cannot /'kænɒt/ or **can't** /kɑːnt/ modal verb
1 not be able to do something
   • Mei Ling **cannot** speak English very well.
2 not let someone do something
   • You **can't** go to the cinema tonight. You must do your homework.

> **LANGUAGE NOTE**
> You should USUALLY write **cannot** or **can't** and NOT can not.

cap /kæp/ noun (countable)
soft, flat hat
• That **cap** is too big for you.

capital /'kæpɪtl/ noun (countable)
the city or town which is the centre of the government of a country
• London is the **capital** of England.

capital letter /ˌkæpɪtl 'letə*/ noun (countable)
A, B, and C are capital letters but a, b, and c are small letters.
• Sentences begin with a **capital letter**.

captain /'kæptɪn/ noun (countable)
1 the leader of a team
   • Antonia was **captain** of the hockey team.
2 the chief person on a ship
   • The **captain** was the last to leave the ship.
3 an officer in the army or in the navy
   • **Captain** Lee told his men to fire at the enemy.

car /kɑː*/ noun (countable)
a vehicle in which a small number of people can travel along roads
• The Jones family has just got a new **car**.
↻ drive/park/start/stop a car, ride/travel in a car, travel/go by car

> **LANGUAGE NOTE**
> NEVER — go by a car, go by your car
> ALWAYS go **by car**, go **in a car**, go **in your car**

car park /'kɑː pɑːk/ noun (countable)
a place where we can leave a car
• We parked in the **car park** and walked to the shops.

card /kɑːd/ noun (countable)
1 a piece of thick paper
   • The new teacher gave the pupils small **cards** to write their names on.
2 We send or give people birthday cards, Christmas cards and New Year cards.
   • I must send Anne a birthday **card**.
↻ a greeting/birthday/wedding/Christmas/New Year/Easter card, a get-well card; send/receive a card
3 a piece of thick, strong paper used for playing certain games
   • There are 52 **cards** in a pack.
↻ playing card/play cards

cardboard /'kɑːdbɔːd/ noun (uncountable)
thick paper used for making boxes, etc
• He carried his clothes in a **cardboard** box.

care¹ /keə*/ noun (countable)
1 **take care** = be careful
   • **Take care** when you wash these glasses: don't break any.
2 **take care of someone** = look after someone
   • Mabel always **takes care of** her small brother when they go to school.
↻ take good/great care of

care² verb
caring, cared, has cared
feel interested in
• "I don't **care** (about) what happens to the two thieves."
↻ couldn't care less about someone/something (= have no interest in them)

care for /'keə fɔː*/ phrasal verb
caring for, cared for, has cared for
1 look after
   • Who **cared for** you while you were ill?
2 like
   • I don't **care for** cheese.

θ	ð	ʃ	dʒ	tʃ	ŋ	ʒ	iː	ɜː	ɪ	æ	ʌ	ɒ
thing	that	shop	jump	chop	sing	measure	been	bird	bit	cat	but	not

careful /ˈkeəfl/ adjective
If you are careful, you think a lot about what you are doing so you can do it well.
- I wish Sita would be more **careful** with her homework. She often makes mistakes.

> **LANGUAGE NOTE**
>
> careful *about* / *of* something
> careful *about doing* something
> careful *with* something (which may be dangerous)
> careful *(not)* *to do* something.
> careful *that* you (don't) do something
> careful *how* you do something

carefully /ˈkeəflɪ/ adverb
with a lot of care, thinking a lot
- Think **carefully** about what you want to do.

careless /ˈkeəlɪs/ adjective
not careful, not taking any care at all
- It was **careless** of you to lose your watch.

> **LANGUAGE NOTE**
>
> Don't use **careless** to mean **carefree**.
>
> NEVER I wish I were young and careless again.
> ALWAYS I wish I were young and carefree again.

carpenter /ˈkɑːpɪntə*/ noun (countable)
a person who makes furniture and other things out of wood
- I want to be a **carpenter** when I leave school.

carpet /ˈkɑːpɪt/ noun (countable)
a woven piece of wool which you use to cover floors
- There was a large red **carpet** on the floor of the living room in Shirley's new flat.

carriage /ˈkærɪdʒ/ noun (countable)
the part of a train which people travel in
- The train had six **carriages**, and Henry and his sister were in the last one.
- railway carriage

carrot /ˈkærət/ noun (countable, uncountable)
See box on page 238.

carry /ˈkærɪ/ verb
carrying, carried, has carried
pick something up and take it from one place to another
- Mr Timms always **carries** a shopping bag.

> **LANGUAGE NOTE**
>
> Don't use **carry** with cars, etc in sentences like the following.
>
> NEVER An ambulance carried her to hospital.
> ALWAYS An ambulance **took** her to hospital.

carry on /ˌkærɪ ˈɒn/ phrasal verb
carrying on, carried on, has carried on
continue
- The pupils **carried on** working even after their teacher had left the room.

cart /kɑːt/ noun (countable)
a vehicle used for carrying people or things which is pulled by an animal (usually a horse) or a person
- There was only a horse and **cart** in the street.
- pull/push a cart; horse and cart

cartoon /kɑːˈtuːn/ noun (countable)
1 a funny drawing (often of someone or something well-known)
   - Simon likes to look at the **cartoons** in the newspaper every morning.
2 a film which is made with drawings

- Let's watch this **cartoon**.

θ	ð	ʃ	dʒ	tʃ	ŋ	ʒ	iː	ɜː	ɪ	æ	ʌ	ɒ
thing	that	shop	jump	chop	sing	measure	been	bird	bit	cat	but	not

case /keɪs/ noun (countable)
1 a box or large bag for carrying things in when you travel
  • *Mr Mann took two large **cases** to Japan.*
  a briefcase (= a case for papers and books which opens at the top)
  a suitcase (= a large box for clothes, etc)
2 a box for holding things
  • *I won a **case** of wine.*
  ↻ a packing case (= the box in which something new is sold)

cassette /kə'set/ noun (countable)
  a small tape for recording and playing sounds
  • *I'd like to buy a **cassette** of those songs.*
  ↻ listen to/play a cassette

cassette player /kə'set ˌpleɪə*/ or

cassette recorder /kə'set rɪˌkɔːdə*/
  noun (countable)
  a machine for recording and playing music, speaking, etc
  • *Can we listen to your new **cassette recorder**?*

castle /'kɑːsl/ noun (countable)
  a strong building (built in the past) where soldiers and people could usually be safe
  • *There are a lot of old **castles** in Britain.*

cat /kæt/ noun (countable)
  ⚠ See box on page 10.

catch /kætʃ/ verb
  catching, caught /kɔːt/, has caught
1 hold something (without dropping it)
  • *Can you **catch** the ball if I throw it to you?*
2 run after someone and stop them
  • *The police have just **caught** the thief.*
3 **catch a bus, a train, a plane**
  • *If we hurry, we'll **catch** the nine o'clock train.*
4 **catch a cold** = have a cold
  • *You'll **catch a cold** if you don't change your wet clothes.*
5 **catch fire** = start to burn
  • *Don't stand too near the burning wood or your dress may **catch fire**.*

cauliflower /'kɒlɪflaʊə*/ noun (countable, uncountable)
  ⚠ See box on page 238.

cause¹ /kɔːz/ noun (countable)
  someone or something that makes something happen, a reason for something
  • *The oil was the **cause** of the accident.*

cause² verb
  causing, caused, has caused
  make something happen
  • *The drunk driver **caused** the accident.*

cave /keɪv/ noun (countable)
  a large hole in a hill or under the ground
  • *A long time ago people lived in **caves**.*
  ↻ a dark/deep cave

CD /ˌsiː 'diː/ noun (countable)
  the short form of **compact disc**
  a small circle of hard plastic on which sounds have been recorded
  • *Would you like to listen to my new **CDs**?*

ceiling /'siːlɪŋ/ noun (countable)
  the part of a room which is above your head
  • *This room has a very high **ceiling**.*
  ↻ a high/low ceiling

celery /'selərɪ/ noun (uncountable)
  ⚠ See box on page 238.

cement /sɪ'ment/ noun (uncountable)
  something mixed with water in order to join bricks together to build a house, etc
  • *Put some more **cement** between these bricks.*

cent /sent/ noun (countable)
1 ten cents = 10c
  • *There are a hundred **cents** in a dollar.*
  not have a cent (= not have any money at all)
2 **per cent** = one part in a hundred parts
  • *Four **per cent** (4%) of $100 is $4.*

θ	ð	ʃ	dʒ	tʃ	ŋ	ʒ	iː	ɜː	ɪ	æ	ʌ	ɒ
thing	that	shop	jump	chop	sing	measure	been	bird	bit	cat	but	not

centigrade/Centigrade /ˈsentɪgreɪd/ or **Celsius** /ˈselsɪəs/ adjective
a way of measuring temperature
- Water freezes at 0° **centigrade** and boils at 100° **centigrade**.

⚠ See also **Fahrenheit**.

centre /ˈsentə*/ noun (countable)
(American English: center)
middle
- There is a circle in the **centre** of the square.

☞ at the centre of, in the centre of

century /ˈsentʃərɪ/ noun (countable)
plural: centuries
a period of a hundred years
- He was born at the beginning of the nineteenth **century**, in 1803, I think.

certain /ˈsɜːtn/ adjective
1 sure about something
   - I am **certain** the meeting starts at eight.

> **LANGUAGE NOTE**
>
> **certain of doing** something = feel sure you will do it
> **certain to do** something = will really do it

2 some, not all
   - **Certain** pupils in the class like maths, but others like English.

certainly /ˈsɜːtnlɪ/ adverb
yes, of course
- "Will you carry this chair, please?" "**Certainly**."

> **LANGUAGE NOTE**
>
> Put **certainly** just after the first auxiliary verb (eg **will, am, has**) BUT NOT just after the main verb.
>   She will **certainly** come.
>   She **certainly** wants to come.
> When you use **be** on its own, you can put **certainly** either just before or just after it.
>   She **certainly** is clever.
>   She is **certainly** clever.

certificate /səˈtɪfɪkət/ noun (countable)
a piece of paper with important information
- My father keeps his birth **certificate** and his marriage **certificate** in a strong metal box.

☞ a birth/marriage/death certificate, a school (-leaving) certificate, a teaching certificate

chain [1] /tʃeɪn/ noun (countable)
pieces of metal which are joined together
- A **chain** is stronger than a rope because it doesn't break easily.

> **LANGUAGE NOTE**
>
> keep something **on** a chain

chain [2] verb
tie or fasten something with a chain
- I **chained** my bicycle to the gate.

> **LANGUAGE NOTE**
>
> chain something **to** something else

chair /tʃeə*/ noun (countable)
a piece of furniture on which we sit
- There were six small **chairs** round the table.

> **LANGUAGE NOTE**
>
> sit **on** a chair BUT sit **in** an armchair

chalk /tʃɔːk/ noun (uncountable)
We use **chalk** to write on the blackboard.
- The teacher gave me some **chalk** and told me to write the answer on the blackboard.

> **LANGUAGE NOTE**
>
> ALMOST ALWAYS **chalk** NOT chalks

☞ a box/piece/stick of chalk

θ	ð	ʃ	dʒ	tʃ	ŋ	ʒ	iː	ɜː	ɪ	æ	ʌ	ɒ
thing	that	shop	jump	chop	sing	measure	been	bird	bit	cat	but	not

chance /tʃɑːns/ noun (countable)
1 anything which happens without us planning to do it
• I met Linda by **chance** this morning.
2 hope
• Our team has a good **chance** of winning.
☞ have/stand/get a chance of; lose/miss your chance; an excellent/good/fair/last chance

change¹ /tʃeɪndʒ/ noun (uncountable)
1 When you go into a shop and give more money than something costs, you will get some money back. This is your change.
• This pen costs $8. If you give me a $10 note, I can give you $2 **change**.
2 coins
• I didn't have any **change** for the phone.
☞ count one's change, give change for, keep the change

change² verb
changing, changed, has changed
1 take or put one thing in place of another
• Tina **changed** the radio she had bought because it didn't work.
2 become different
• You've **changed** since I last saw you.
3 make different
• Rita's **changed** her holiday plans.

LANGUAGE NOTE

change **from** something **to/into** something else

---

change purse /'tʃeɪndʒ pɜːs/ noun (countable)
(American English)
⚠ See **purse**¹.

chapter /'tʃæptə*/ noun (countable)
part of a book
• Have you read the first **chapter** of the book yet?
☞ first/second/opening/closing chapter

charge¹ /tʃɑːdʒ/ noun (countable)
the price asked or paid for something, the cost
• The dentist's **charges** are very high.
☞ make a (small) charge/a charge (for something)

charge² verb
charging, charged, has charged
ask to be paid
• That hairdresser **charges** a lot for a haircut.

chart /tʃɑːt/ noun (countable)
a piece of paper or card with information on it (often with numbers or like a map)
• The weather **chart** tells us how cold or hot it will be and if it will rain.

cheap /tʃiːp/ adjective
not dear, costing only a little money
• Vegetables are **cheap** but meat is expensive.

LANGUAGE NOTE

NEVER cheap wages   ALWAYS **low** wages

---

cheat /tʃiːt/ verb
1 behave in a dishonest way
• Spiros always **cheats** when he plays games.
2 treat someone in a dishonest way
• The shopkeeper has **cheated** you out of £20.

check¹ /tʃek/ noun (countable)
(American English)
⚠ See **cheque**; see **bill**¹.

check² verb
make sure something is right
• Please **check** your answer again.

check-out /'tʃek aʊt/ noun (countable)
a desk in a large shop where you pay for everything you have bought

θ	ð	ʃ	dʒ	tʃ	ŋ	ʒ	iː	ɜː	ɪ	æ	ʌ	ɒ
thing	that	shop	jump	chop	sing	measure	been	bird	bit	cat	but	not

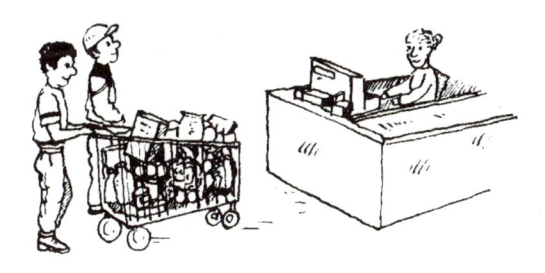

- *I think we've got everything. Let's go to the **check-out** and pay for it.*

cheer[1] /tʃɪə*/ noun (countable)

a shout (because something or someone is very good)
- *Charles has just won the class prize. Three **cheers** for Charles!*

↻ a loud cheer, three cheers

cheer[2] verb

shout out when you want someone to win
- *We **cheered** loudly when our team won.*

↻ cheer loudly

cheer up /ˌtʃɪər ˈʌp/ phrasal verb

stop being sad
- ***Cheer up**, Jane. Things will soon get better.*

cheerful /ˈtʃɪəfl/ adjective

happy
- *Mabel is a **cheerful** girl who always smiles.*

cheerfully /ˈtʃɪəfli/ adverb

in a happy way
- *She was singing **cheerfully** to herself.*

cheese /tʃiːz/ noun (uncountable, countable)

something hard or soft (but not a liquid) which is usually made from milk
- *Would you like some **cheese** and biscuits?*

↻ bread and cheese, cheese and biscuits

chemist /ˈkemɪst/ noun (countable)

(American English: drugstore)

a shop which sells medicine, etc
- *Dr Johansson told us to get the medicine at that **chemist's** over there.*

LANGUAGE NOTE

An apostrophe + s is often used to show a shop:-
chemist's = chemist's shop
butcher's = butcher's shop

⚠ See also **pharmacy**.

cheque /tʃek/ noun (countable)

(American English: check)

a printed piece of paper which you can use instead of money. You must write the name of the person and the amount you want to pay them.
- *I've forgotten to bring any money with me. Can I pay for this book by **cheque**?*

LANGUAGE NOTE

In American English **check** can mean
EITHER   **cheque** (British English)
OR   **bill** (British English)

"Shall I pay cash or by cheque?"
"Waiter, please bring me the check."

↻ make (out)/write (out) a cheque, pay a cheque (into a bank), pay someone by cheque; a cheque book

cherry /ˈtʃerɪ/ noun (countable)

plural: cherries

⚠ See box on page 89.

chess /tʃes/ noun (uncountable)

a game played on a board with black and white squares
- *Let's have a game of **chess**.*

↻ a game of chess, a chess match; play chess

chest /tʃest/ noun (countable)

1 a large, heavy box
- *Mrs White kept her clothes in a large **chest**.*

θ	ð	ʃ	dʒ	tʃ	ŋ	ʒ	iː	ɜː	ɪ	æ	ʌ	ɒ
thing	that	shop	jump	chop	sing	measure	been	bird	bit	cat	but	not

chew

2 a piece of furniture with drawers in it
- *Let's put the toys in the **chest**.*
3 the front part of the top of your body
⚠ See box on page 25.

chew /tʃuː/ verb
bite food so that you can swallow it
- ***Chew** the meat well before you swallow it.*

chicken /'tʃɪkɪn/ noun (countable, uncountable)
a young hen
⚠ See box on page 22.

LANGUAGE NOTE

When you are talking about **a chicken** as a bird on a farm, etc, use **a**.

Look! There's **a chicken** running across the road.

When you are talking about **chicken** as a food on a dish, you should not use **a** before it.
Would you like **chicken** or fish?

---

chief [1] /tʃiːf/ noun (countable)
the leader of a group of people
- *Can you take us to your **chief**, please?*
ಸ a fire/police chief

chief [2] adjective
main, most important
- *The murder of the President was one of the **chief** causes of the war.*

child /tʃaɪld/ noun (countable)
plural: children /'tʃɪldrən/
a young boy or girl (older than a baby)
- *Mr and Mrs Tomiko have two **children**.*
ಸ have a child, bring up/raise a child (= look after and teach until the child has grown up); a bright/clever/dull/slow child

chimney /'tʃɪmni/ noun (countable)
a hole or pipe through the roof of a building for smoke to pass through.
- *The factory over there has a very tall **chimney**.*

chocolate /'tʃɒklɪt/ noun
1 (uncountable) sweet food which is made from cocoa
- *Helena gave Susie a big bar of **chocolate**.*
ಸ a bar of/a piece of chocolate
2 (countable) piece of sweet food made from cocoa
- *Let's buy a box of **chocolates** for Tina.*

choir /'kwaɪə*/ noun (countable)
a group of people who sing together
- *My brother and I sang in the school **choir**.*

choose /tʃuːz/ verb
choosing, chose /tʃəʊz/, has chosen /'tʃəʊzn/
take something you like best
- *It was difficult to **choose** which camera to buy: they all seemed very good.*

LANGUAGE NOTE

choose **between** two things
choose **among** three or more things
choose **from** a lot of things
choose something (eg a present) **for** someone

---

chopsticks /'tʃɒpstɪks/
noun (countable and usually plural)
long thin pieces of wood, plastic or ivory used for eating
- *Some English people find it very hard to eat rice with **chopsticks**.*
ಸ eat with/use chopsticks

Christmas /'krɪsməs/ noun (uncountable, countable)
a holy day when Jesus Christ was born, December 25th
- *My aunt and uncle will stay with us at **Christmas**.*

LANGUAGE NOTE

at Christmas BUT **on** Christmas day

θ	ð	ʃ	dʒ	tʃ	ŋ	ʒ	iː	ɜː	ɪ	æ	ʌ	ɒ
thing	that	shop	jump	chop	sing	measure	been	bird	bit	cat	but	not

church /tʃɜːtʃ/ noun (countable)
plural: churches
a building where people meet and pray to God
- *Mabel and Anna go to **church** on Sundays.*

> **LANGUAGE NOTE**
>
> Usually you shouldn't use **a** before **church** after **go**.
> go to church, go to school, go to hospital, etc

cigarette /ˌsɪɡəˈret/ noun (countable)
Some people smoke cigarettes.
- *She took out a **cigarette** and lit it.*
↻ light (up) / put out / smoke a cigarette

cinema /ˈsɪnəmə/ noun (countable)
(American English: movies)
a building where you can go to see a film
- *There's a good film at that **cinema** tonight.*

circle [1] /ˈsɜːkl/ noun (countable)
a round shape
- *The number 10 has a line and a **circle**.*

circle [2] verb
circling, circled, has circled
move round
- *The police **circled** the building to stop the burglars escaping.*

circus /ˈsɜːkəs/ noun (countable)
plural: circuses
a place (usually a tent) where people watch other people and animals doing tricks
- *I like watching the lions at the **circus**.*

city /ˈsɪti/ noun (countable)
plural: cities
a very big town
- *Tokyo is one of the world's largest **cities**.*
↻ the city centre; a fine / great / large / old city

clap /klæp/ verb
clapping, clapped, has clapped
hit your hands together when you are pleased with what someone has done
- *When Don finished singing, everyone **clapped**.*

class /klɑːs/ noun (countable)
plural: classes
a group of people who study together (at school, etc)
- *Susie is the oldest pupil in our **class**.*

classmate /ˈklɑːsmeɪt/ noun (countable)
a friend in your class
- *Peter Yuen and Victor Sun are my **classmates**.*

classroom /ˈklɑːsrʊm/ noun (countable)
a room where pupils have lessons
- *Our **classroom** is next to the library.*

clean [1] /kliːn/ verb
wash, take away dirt
- *How often do you **clean** your teeth?*

clean [2] adjective
not dirty
- *Wash your hands if they aren't **clean**.*

clear /klɪə*/ adjective
1 You can see through something which is clear.
   - *The water in the lake is very **clear**.*
2 easy to understand
   - *Do you understand how it works? Is it **clear** now?*
3 with nothing in the way
   - *You can pass the car in front now. The road is **clear**.*
   ↻ clear of snow / traffic
4 A clear day is a day when there are no clouds in the sky.
   - *You can see France on a **clear** day.*

clearly /ˈklɪəli/ adverb
easily seen, easily understood
- *Did the teacher explain everything **clearly**?*

θ	ð	ʃ	dʒ	tʃ	ŋ	ʒ	iː	ɜː	ɪ	æ	ʌ	ɒ
thing	that	shop	jump	chop	sing	measure	been	bird	bit	cat	but	not

clerk /klɑːk/ noun (countable)
someone who works in an office and types, writes letters, puts papers away, etc
- *My sister was a **clerk** before she became a secretary.*

clever /ˈklevə*/ adjective
cleverer or more clever, cleverest or most clever
able to learn quickly
- *Ann was very **clever** at school.*

LANGUAGE NOTE

clever **at** (doing) something
clever **with** your hands
clever **of** someone **to do** something

---

climate /ˈklaɪmɪt/ noun (uncountable, countable)
the kind of weather in a certain country or place
- ***Climate** is very important for health.*
- a bad/good/excellent/dry/wet/cold/warm/hot/mild/healthy/unhealthy/pleasant/unpleasant climate

climb /klaɪm/ verb
1 go up

- *We have to **climb** a lot of steps to get to our flat. It's on the top floor.*
- climb down/up/in/out/on
2 rise, slope up
- *The road **climbs** (up) a steep hill before it drops into the valley.*

climber /ˈklaɪmə*/ noun (countable)
a person who likes to climb mountains and rocks
- *The **climber** was near the top when he fell.*

clinic /ˈklɪnɪk/ noun (countable)
a building or part of a hospital which people visit to see a doctor or nurse
- *Go to the **clinic** if you still have earache.*

clock /klɒk/ noun (countable)
something to show the time
- *We were late home because the school **clock** had stopped.*
- turn the clock back/forward
This clock is fast/slow/right.
This clock keeps (good) time.
This clock loses/gains (time). (= This clock is slow/fast.)
This clock has stopped.
- See also **o'clock**.

close¹ /kləʊz/ verb
closing, closed, has closed shut
- *We couldn't buy anything as the shop was **closed**.*

close² /kləʊs/ adverb, preposition (when followed by to)
near
- *Come **closer**. I can't hear you.*
- *The market is **close (by)**. We also live **close to** a bus station.*
- close by, close to

cloth /klɒθ/ noun
1 (uncountable) cotton, silk, wool, etc
- *Is this made of **cloth**? Yes, I think it's made of cotton.*
2 (uncountable) a piece of cotton, silk, wool, etc
- *Mrs Lokollo has just bought some blue **cloth** to make a new dress.*
3 (countable) a piece of cloth used for covering the table and washing dishes, floors, and our face
- *The waiter put a clean **cloth** on the table.*
- a dish-cloth, a face-cloth, a floor-cloth, a table-cloth

clothes /kləʊðz/ noun (plural)
dresses, skirts, shirts, trousers, etc
- *I need some new **clothes** because most of my old ones no longer fit me.*

θ	ð	ʃ	dʒ	tʃ	ŋ	ʒ	iː	ɜː	ɪ	æ	ʌ	ɒ
thing	that	shop	jump	chop	sing	measure	been	bird	bit	cat	but	not

LANGUAGE NOTE

1 Don't use a number before **clothes**.
   NEVER ~~I packed six clothes in the case.~~
   ALWAYS I packed **some/a lot of/a few** clothes in the case.
2 ALWAYS wash your **clothes**
   NOT ~~cloths~~ (unless you mean dish-cloths, etc)

↻ change/put on/take off your clothes, wear your best clothes

clothing /'kləʊðɪŋ/ noun (uncountable)

dresses, skirts, shirts and trousers, etc
- Bring some warm **clothing** with you.

LANGUAGE NOTE

NEVER ~~a clothing~~
ALWAYS some clothing, a piece of clothing

cloud /klaʊd/ noun (countable)

a collection of drops of water in the sky
- Look at the **clouds**. It's going to rain!

cloudy /'klaʊdɪ/ adjective

cloudier or more cloudy, cloudiest or most cloudy
full of clouds
- A **cloudy** sky means that it may rain.

club /klʌb/ noun (countable)

1 a group of people who have the same interest in something: eg sports, dancing
   - I joined the swimming **club** last week.
2 a large, heavy stick
   - The thief hit the man on the head with a **club** and stole his money.

clue /kluː/ noun (countable)

something which helps to give the answer to a problem or crime
- The fingerprints gave the policeman a **clue** to the murderer.

↻ find/discover a clue, look for a clue

coach /kəʊtʃ/ noun (countable)

plural: coaches
1 bus (usually for travelling a long way)
   - The tourists travelled by **coach**.
   ↻ go by/travel by coach; go on/travel on a coach
2 part of a train
   - The train was pulling six **coaches**.

coal /kəʊl/ noun (usually uncountable)

something hard and black, used for burning
- I'm cold. Put some more **coal** on the fire.

↻ burn/use coal

coast /kəʊst/ noun (countable)

piece of land next to the sea
- Amsterdam is on the **coast** of the Netherlands.

LANGUAGE NOTE

off the coast of Spain (= at sea near the coast of Spain)
on the Spanish coast (= on the land in Spain near the sea)

coat /kəʊt/ noun (countable)

something we wear on top of our clothes to keep warm or dry
- It's snowing outside. Put on a **coat**.

↻ wear/put on/take off your coat; an overcoat, a raincoat

coconut /'kəʊkənʌt/ noun (countable)

⚠ See box on page 89.

code /kəʊd/ noun (countable)

1 a set of rules
   - You must learn the Highway **Code** before you can pass your driving-test.
2 secret writing (which is difficult for anyone else to understand)
   - Can you work out the **code**?

↻ break/make up a code; Morse code

θ	ð	ʃ	dʒ	tʃ	ŋ	ʒ	iː	ɜː	ɪ	æ	ʌ	ɒ
thing	that	shop	jump	chop	sing	measure	been	bird	bit	cat	but	not

coffee /ˈkɒfɪ/ noun
1 (uncountable) something we drink (usually hot and brown)
 • "Would you like some tea or **coffee**?" "I'll have a cup of **coffee**, please."
 ↻ make (the) coffee
 fresh/strong/weak/black/white coffee (= coffee without/with milk)
2 (countable) a cup of coffee
 • Could you bring us two **coffees**, please?

coin /kɔɪn/ noun (countable)
money made out of metal (and not paper)
 • Have you got **coins** for the telephone?

cold[1] /kəʊld/ noun (countable)
When you cough and use a handkerchief a lot, you are ill and have a cold.
 • Bernadette is off school with a **cold**.

LANGUAGE NOTE
catch cold BUT NEVER ~~have cold~~
ALWAYS have **a** cold

 ↻ a bad/slight cold

cold[2] adjective
not warm
 • The milk was very **cold** when I took it out of the fridge.
 ↻ be/feel cold

collar /ˈkɒlə*/ noun (countable)
the part of a blouse, shirt or coat which you wear round your neck
 • The **collar** of this shirt is too tight.

collect /kəˈlekt/ verb
1 put together in one place
 • Susie **collected** the exercise books and gave them to the teacher.
2 save over a long time
 • My sister **collects** foreign stamps.
3 fetch or bring back
 • Mr Lee **collects** the children from school.
4 ask for money
 • We're **collecting** (money) for the blind today.

collection /kəˈlekʃn/ noun (countable)
things which have been put together
 • Henry showed me his large stamp **collection**.
 ↻ a coin/stamp collection

college /ˈkɒlɪdʒ/ noun (countable)
a place where people study after they leave school
 • Mei Ling went to **college** to learn how to type, and her brother went to university.
 ↻ go to/drop out of/finish college

colon /ˈkəʊlən/ noun (countable)
used in writing
This is a colon :
 • You use a **colon** before writing an example.

colour[1] /ˈkʌlə*/ noun (countable)
(American English: color)
red, blue, yellow, green, brown, etc
 • "What **colour** is the sea?" "It's blue and green, isn't it?"

LANGUAGE NOTE
1 Use **be** (NEVER have) when you talk about the colour of something.
2 NEVER ~~Her dress was red colour.~~ ALWAYS Her dress was **red**. OR Her dress was **a red colour**.
Note that the third sentence above is not usual unless you want to show something is almost red or red and another colour.

 ↻ a bright/dull/dark/deep/cold/warm/rich/soft colour

comic 45

colour²   verb
(American English: color)
give something colour, paint something
- We have to **colour** this picture.
- **Colour** the trees green.

coloured   /ˈkʌləd/   adjective
(American English: colored)
Anything which is not white or black is coloured.
- There are a lot of **coloured** pictures in my new book.

colourful   /ˈkʌləfl/   adjective
(American English: colorful)
bright, with many colours
- Flowers make a garden very **colourful**.

comb¹   /kəʊm/   noun (countable)
something small and flat which you can pull through your hair to make it tidy
- May I borrow your **comb**, please? My hair is very untidy.

comb²   verb
pull a comb through your hair to make it tidy
- Why don't you **comb** your hair? It's untidy.

come   /kʌm/   verb
coming, came, has come
1 move towards the speaker
- "**Come** here at once!" the teacher told Alice.

> **LANGUAGE NOTE**
>
> COMPARE **come** here (to the speaker)
>   **go** there (away from the speaker)

2 arrive
- Has Augustus **come** yet or is he late again?
3 is
- Monday **comes** after Sunday.

come back   /ˌkʌm ˈbæk/   phrasal verb
coming back, came back, has come back
return
- "**Come back** as soon as you've finished work," Mrs Lee said to her husband.

come down   /ˌkʌm ˈdaʊn/   phrasal verb
coming down, came down, has come down
move or become lower
- The price of these cameras has **come down** to $180. They used to cost $250.

come from   /ˌkʌm frɒm/   phrasal verb
coming from, came from, has come from
be born, live
- The tourist told me he **came from** Japan.

> **LANGUAGE NOTE**
>
> NEVER   They are coming from Malaysia.
> ALWAYS   They **come from** Malaysia.

come in   /ˌkʌm ˈɪn/   phrasal verb
coming in, came in, has come in
enter
- "**Come in**", shouted Samy as soon as he heard me knock on the door.

come on   /ˌkʌm ˈɒn/   phrasal verb
coming on, came on, has come on
try harder, do better
- **Come on**, hurry up! You can win if you run faster.

comfortable   /ˈkʌmfətəbl/   adjective
1 soft, easy to wear or sit on
- These chairs are soft and **comfortable**.
2 feeling very well, without any pain, etc
- Are you **comfortable** in that chair?

comic   /ˈkɒmɪk/   noun (countable)
a children's magazine
- "Do you like reading **comics**?" "Yes, I enjoy Superman **comics** most."

θ	ð	ʃ	dʒ	tʃ	ŋ	ʒ	iː	ɜː	ɪ	æ	ʌ	ɒ
thing	that	shop	jump	chop	sing	measure	been	bird	bit	cat	but	not

comma /ˈkɒmə/ noun (countable)
This is a comma ,
- There is a **comma** between the words "pens" and "pencils": We have pens, pencils and rulers.

common /ˈkɒmən/ adjective
happening often, found in many places
- Sheep are very **common** in Australia.

> **LANGUAGE NOTE**
> NEVER ~~common that someone does something~~
> ALWAYS common **for** someone **to do** something

compact disc (or compact disk) /ˌkɒmpækt ˈdɪsk/ noun (countable)
⚠ See CD.

company /ˈkʌmpənɪ/ noun (countable)
plural: companies
a business, a group of people who work in the same factory or office
- David's father works for a car **company**.

compare /kəmˈpeə*/ verb
comparing, compared, has compared
see how similar or different things are
- If you **compare** the two cars, you'll find the bigger one faster than the smaller one.

> **LANGUAGE NOTE**
> compare something **with** / **to** something else

compete /kəmˈpiːt/ verb
competing, competed, has competed
try to win
- Are you going to **compete** in any of the races?

> **LANGUAGE NOTE**
> compete **with** / **against** someone
> compete **in** a game, a race, etc
> compete **for** a prize

competition /ˌkɒmpɪˈtɪʃn/ noun (countable)
a game or a test which people try to win
- Our school is going to have a painting **competition**.
↻ go in for / enter / take part in / win / lose a competition; healthy / strong / fair / unfair competition

competitor /kəmˈpetɪtə*/ noun (countable)
a person who takes part in a game, a race or a competition
- There were over a hundred **competitors** in the singing competition.

complain /kəmˈpleɪn/ verb
say you do not like something because it is bad, unpleasant, painful, etc
- Ann **complained** of a pain in her leg.

> **LANGUAGE NOTE**
> complain **about** someone or something (NEVER complain on)
> complain **of** an illness, etc
> complain **to** someone
> complain **that** something is bad, etc

complete /kəmˈpliːt/ adjective
1 having everything which is necessary
- Is this tea set **complete**?
2 as much as possible (used before a noun to make its meaning much stronger)
- This is a **complete** surprise.

completely /kəmˈpliːtlɪ/ adverb
as much as possible, in every way, totally
- I **completely** forgot about the meeting.

composition /ˌkɒmpəˈzɪʃn/ noun (countable)
a piece of writing or music which someone has written
- Mary wrote a very good **composition** about her best friend.
↻ do / write a composition

θ	ð	ʃ	dʒ	tʃ	ŋ	ʒ	iː	ɜː	ɪ	æ	ʌ	ɒ
thing	that	shop	jump	chop	sing	measure	been	bird	bit	cat	but	not

computer /kəmˈpjuːtə*/ noun (countable)
a machine which can keep information so that you can use it
- *I can do the problem on my **computer** in a minute!*

concert /ˈkɒnsət/ noun (countable)
music played in a hall, etc for people to listen to
- *I enjoyed all the songs in the **concert**.*
- give/hold a concert

concrete /ˈkɒŋkriːt/ noun (uncountable)
something which is made by mixing sand, small stones, cement and water and which is often used for building
- *The walls of this building are made of **concrete**.*

conductor /kənˈdʌktə*/ noun (countable)
someone who sells tickets on a bus
- *The bus **conductor** will give you a ticket.*

congratulate /kənˈɡrætjʊleɪt/ verb
congratulating, congratulated, has congratulated
praise someone, give them your good wishes
- *Everyone **congratulated** Annie Law when they heard she had won the prize.*

LANGUAGE NOTE
congratulate someone **on** (doing) something

connect /kəˈnekt/ verb
to join two or more things together
- *The radio will work if we **connect** these two wires.*

consonant /ˈkɒnsənənt/ noun (countable)
a letter or sound which is not a,e,i,o or u
B, c, d, f, g, h, m, n and p are consonants.

contain /kənˈteɪn/ verb
hold or have something inside it
- *The small box **contained** a beautiful ring.*

continent /ˈkɒntɪnənt/ noun (countable)
The seven large areas of land on the Earth are called continents.

- *Africa, Asia and Europe are three **continents**.*

continue /kənˈtɪnjuː/ verb
continuing, continued, has continued
1 go on further, carry on
   - *This road **continues** for another mile before it reaches the beach.*
2 keep on doing something (sometimes after a break or rest)
   - *Let's **continue** our talk after lunch.*

LANGUAGE NOTE
EITHER continue **to do** something
OR continue **doing** something
continue **with** something

control /kənˈtrəʊl/ verb
controlling, controlled, has controlled
have power over, influence
- *The new teacher couldn't **control** the class, and the pupils began throwing things.*

convenient /kənˈviːnjənt/ adjective
1 easy, very suitable
   - *Will it be **convenient** if we meet here?*

θ	ð	ʃ	dʒ	tʃ	ŋ	ʒ	iː	ɜː	ɪ	æ	ʌ	ɒ
thing	that	shop	jump	chop	sing	measure	been	bird	bit	cat	but	not

LANGUAGE NOTE

Will Friday be convenient *for* you?
Is it convenient *to* talk now?
It is very convenient *that* you've come.
It will be convenient *if* you can come with us.

2 near, easy to reach
- Their new flat is very **convenient** for schools and shops.

LANGUAGE NOTE

This place is very convenient *for* the shops.
It is very convenient *for* shopping.

conversation /ˌkɒnvəˈseɪʃn/ noun (countable)
talking with other people
- Jonathan and I had a long **conversation** about leaving school.
- carry on/enter into/get into/have/hold a conversation

cook¹ /kʊk/ noun (countable)
a person who makes food for people to eat
- My aunt works as a **cook** in a small hotel.

cook² verb
make food for people to eat
- What are you going to **cook** for our next meal?
- cook a dish/a meal, cook food

cooker /ˈkʊkə*/ noun (countable)
a machine on which food is cooked
- Mrs Simpson is cooking the vegetables and fish tonight on her new **cooker**.

cookie /ˈkʊkɪ/ noun (countable)
(American English)
See **biscuit**.

cool /kuːl/ adjective
not warm but not cold
- It's quite **cool** and pleasant today.

copy¹ /ˈkɒpɪ/ noun (countable)
plural: copies
something which looks the same as something else
- This picture is a **copy** of a famous French painting.
- make/take a copy

copy² verb
copying, copied, has copied
make something look the same as something else
- Adam couldn't do his homework, and so he **copied** Dave's homework.

corn /kɔːn/ noun (uncountable)
a kind of plant or seeds which you can eat
- Hens and other birds like to eat **corn**.

corner /ˈkɔːnə*/ noun (countable)
the point where two sides meet
- Our television is in the **corner** of our living-room.

correct¹ /kəˈrekt/ adjective
without making mistakes
- David always gives the **correct** answer in class.
- the correct answer; get something correct

correct² verb
put something right which was wrong
- You must **correct** mistakes.

correction /kəˈrekʃn/ noun (countable)
putting the right word or answer in place of a wrong word or answer
- Do your **corrections** before you begin the new exercise. In future, try to be more careful.
- make a correction

cost[1] /kɒst/ noun (countable)

amount of money that we pay for something
- The **cost** of petrol has risen a lot recently.
  cut/reduce/increase costs; cost of living
- See also **price**.

LANGUAGE NOTE

Use **price** when you talk about paying for things.

NEVER   What is the cost of that watch?
ALWAYS What is the **price** of that watch?
OR   How much did that watch **cost** ?

When you talk about paying someone to do something for you, you should usually use **cost**.
What is the **cost** of having the room painted?

Note that **cost** is not often used with a.

---

cost[2] verb

costing, cost, has cost

put a price on something
- Cecilia's new dress **cost** over $200.

cotton /ˈkɒtn/ noun (uncountable)

a kind of cloth from which clothes are made
- Is your shirt made of **cotton** or nylon?
- Is that a **cotton** shirt or a nylon one?

cough[1] /kɒf/ noun (countable)

the noise you make when you send out air from your mouth and throat
- I can't speak too well: I've got a bad **cough**.
- have a cough; a bad cough

cough[2] verb

send air quickly out of your mouth and throat
- Lisa **coughed** so much she kept me awake.

could /kʊd/ (unstressed /kəd/) modal verb

1 can (past tense)
   - I **could** read when I was your age.

LANGUAGE NOTE

When you talk about actually doing something (often difficult) in the past, use **was able to** or **were able to** (NOT could).

NEVER   I could finish my homework early.
ALWAYS I **was able** to finish my homework early.
OR   I **managed** to finish my homework early.

When you talk about being able to do something like swimming, playing the piano, speaking Japanese, etc (ie an ability or power), use **could** or **was able to**.

I **could** speak Spanish when I was six.
I **was able to** speak Spanish when I was six.

---

2 **Could I, could we, could you** = used to ask politely for something
   - **Could I** have some more cake, please?
- See also **can**[2] 3.

LANGUAGE NOTE

Could is a little more polite than can.

---

3 be able to
   - I wish I **could** go with you.
4 be able to (used to show that something is possible)
   - If you spoke French, you **could** come.

couldn't /ˈkʊdnt/ modal verb

could not
- I **couldn't** meet you last night because I had to stay at home to do my homework.

count /kaʊnt/ verb

1 say one number after another
   - **Count** from one to a hundred in English.
2 add up numbers
   - Have you finished **counting** (up) your money yet?

counter /ˈkaʊntə*/ noun (countable)
a long table in a shop, a bank or a post office
- *The assistant put the pen on the **counter**.*

country /ˈkʌntrɪ/ noun
plural: countries
1 (countable) an area of land: eg Spain, England
- *"Which **country** is he from?"
"I think he comes from France."*
⚠ See box opposite.
2 (uncountable with the) land which is not in a town
- *I like living in **the country**: it's so peaceful.*

couple /ˈkʌpl/ noun (countable)
1 two people or things,
a few (American English)
- *There are a **couple** of handkerchiefs in the top drawer.*
2 a man and his wife, a boy and his girlfriend, etc
- *Two **couples** were sitting in the cafe.*

course /kɔːs/ noun (countable)
a set of lessons, books, etc
- *I'm going to take a French **course**.*
๛ attend/take/give/teach a course

course, of course adverb phrase
certainly
- *"Are you going to the meeting?"
"**Of course**. I'm going to give a talk."*

cousin /ˈkʌzn/ noun (countable)
the son or daughter of your uncle and aunt
- *How many **cousins** have you got?*

cover[1] /ˈkʌvə*/ noun (countable)
1 something which you put over something else to keep it clean or safe
- *Don't forget to put a **cover** over the cheese when you finish.*
2 the outside of a book
- *Oh dear! I've torn the **cover** of this book.*

cover[2] verb
put something over something else to keep it clean or safe
- ***Cover** the chairs with this cloth before you paint the room.*

cow /kaʊ/ noun (countable)
male: bull
⚠ See box on page 10.

LANGUAGE NOTE
The meat from a **cow** is called **beef**.

crab /kræb/ noun (countable, uncountable)
⚠ See box on page 10.

LANGUAGE NOTE

When you talk about **a crab** as a living sea animal, etc, use **a**.
   Be careful or you'll put your foot on **a crab**!
When you are talking about **crab** as food on a dish you should not use **a** before it.
   Would you like **crab** or duck?

crack[1] /kræk/ noun (countable)
a thin line which is caused when something is broken
- *There was a small **crack** in the wood.*

crack[2] verb
break something in such a way as to cause a thin line to appear (but not break something into separate parts)
- *What a pity! Sheila **cracked** this lovely plate when she dropped it.*

crash[1] /kræʃ/ noun (countable)
1 an accident in which cars, etc hit each other or other things
- *There was a bad **crash** when a lorry hit a car round this corner.*
๛ a bad/big/serious/terrible crash
2 a loud noise when something breaks or hits something else
- *Suddenly we heard a loud **crash**. Poor Linda had dropped all the plates!*

θ	ð	ʃ	dʒ	tʃ	ŋ	ʒ	iː	ɜː	ɪ	æ	ʌ	ɒ
thing	that	shop	jump	chop	sing	measure	been	bird	bit	cat	but	not

Countries, People and Languages

Country	People	Language	Adjective
Algeria	an Algerian	Arabic	Algerian
Argentina	an Argentinian	Spanish	Argentinian
Australia	an Australian	English	Australian
Austria	an Austrian	German	Austrian
Belgium	a Belgian	French, Flemish	Belgian
Brazil	a Brazilian	Portuguese	Brazilian
Bulgaria	a Bulgarian	Bulgarian	Bulgarian
Burma	a Burmese	Burmese	Burmese
Canada	a Canadian	English, French	Canadian
Chile	a Chilean	Spanish	Chilean
China	a Chinese	Chinese	Chinese
the CIS	a Russian, etc	Russian, etc	Russian, etc
Colombia	a Colombian	Spanish	Colombian
Cuba	a Cuban	Spanish	Cuban
Denmark	a Dane	Danish	Danish
Egypt	an Egyptian	Arabic	Egyptian
England	an Englishman	English	English
Finland	a Finn	Finnish, Swedish	Finnish
France	a Frenchman	French	French
Germany	a German	German	German
Great Britain	a Brit, a Briton	English	British
Greece	a Greek	Greek	Greek
Holland	a Dutchman	Dutch	Dutch
Hungary	a Hungarian	Hungarian, Magyar	Hungarian
India	an Indian	Hindi, Urdu, etc	Indian
Indonesia	an Indonesian	Bahasa Indonesia	Indonesian
Iran	an Iranian	Arabic	Iranian
Iraq	an Iraqi	Arabic	Iraqi
Ireland	an Irishman	Irish, English	Irish
Israel	an Israeli	Hebrew, Arabic	Israeli
Italy	an Italian	Italian	Italian
Japan	a Japanese	Japanese	Japanese
Korea	a Korean	Korean	Korean
Libya	a Libyan	Arabic	Libyan
Malaysia	a Malaysian	Bahasa Malaysia	Malaysian
Mexico	a Mexican	Spanish	Mexican
Morocco	a Moroccan	Arabic	Moroccan
New Zealand	a New Zealander	English	New Zealand
Norway	a Norwegian	Norwegian	Norwegian
Pakistan	a Pakistani	Urdu, etc	Pakistani
Peru	a Peruvian	Spanish	Peruvian
the Philippines	a Filipino	Tagalog, Filipino	Philippine, Filipino
Poland	a Pole	Polish	Polish
Portugal	a Portuguese	Portuguese	Portuguese
Romania	a Romanian	Romanian	Romanian
Scotland	a Scot, a Scotsman	English, Gaelic	Scottish
South Africa	a South African	English, Afrikaans	South African
Spain	a Spaniard	Spanish	Spanish
the Sudan	a Sudanese	Arabic	Sudanese
Sweden	a Swede	Swedish	Swedish
Switzerland	a Swiss	French, German, Italian, Romansch	Swiss
Thailand	a Thai	Thai	Thai
Turkey	a Turk	Turkish	Turkish
Uruguay	a Uruguayan	Spanish	Uruguayan
the USA	an American	English	American
Venezuela	a Venezuelan	Spanish	Venezuelan
Wales	a Welshman	English, Welsh	Welsh

crash [2]   verb
1   hit something hard
    - *The lorry **crashed** into a tree and the driver was badly hurt.*
2   fall and break with a loud noise
    - *A brick **crashed** through the window.*

cream [1]   /kriːm/   noun (uncountable)
1   the top part of the milk which is often quite thick
    - *Do you take **cream** in your coffee?*
2   something you rub into your skin to make it soft
    - *She puts **cream** on her face every morning.*
    face/hand cream

cream [2]   adjective
very pale yellow
    - *The classroom walls were **cream** but the ceiling was white.*

credit card   /ˈkredɪt ˌkɑːd/   noun (countable)
a plastic card which you can use instead of money to buy things
    - *Does this shop take **credit cards**?*
    pay by credit card, take credit cards

creep   /kriːp/   verb
creeping, crept /krept/, has crept
walk quietly (often to surprise someone)

- *Dave didn't want his parents to know he was going out and so he **crept** out of the house.*

cricket   /ˈkrɪkɪt/   noun (uncountable)
a game which you play in a field with a bat and a small ball
    - *Let's have a game of **cricket** today.*
    a game of cricket, a cricket match

cried   /kraɪd/   verb
past tense and past participle of **cry**
    - *Poor Mary **cried** for days when Susan left.*

crime   /kraɪm/   noun (countable)
something bad or wrong you do, something you do when you break the law
    - *There have been a lot of **crimes** recently, and it is dangerous to walk alone at night.*
    cut down on/reduce/fight / keep down/prevent crime

criminal   /ˈkrɪmɪnl/   noun (countable)
someone who does something very bad and breaks the law
    - *The **criminal** had stolen a lot of money.*
    a dangerous criminal

crocodile   /ˈkrɒkədaɪl/   noun (countable)
See box on page 10.

crop   /krɒp/   noun (countable)
corn, plants, vegetables and fruit which farmers grow
    - *The storm destroyed the rice **crop**, and so people had very little food to eat.*
    grow/plant a crop; a good/successful/a thin/poor crop

cross [1]   /krɒs/   noun (countable)
plural: crosses
This is a cross: X
    - *My teacher put a **cross** at the side of every spelling mistake I made.*

cross [2]   verb
go or pass over
    - *Be careful when you **cross** the road.*

LANGUAGE NOTE

cross **from** one side of a street, a river, etc **to** another

---

θ	ð	ʃ	dʒ	tʃ	ŋ	ʒ	iː	ɜː	ɪ	æ	ʌ	ɒ
thing	that	shop	jump	chop	sing	measure	been	bird	bit	cat	but	not

cross out /ˌkrɒs ˈaʊt/ phrasal verb
put a line through something because it is wrong or because you want to change it
- Mrs Lee **crossed out** what I had written.

crossing /ˈkrɒsɪŋ/ noun (countable)
a place where it is safe to go from one side of the road to the other
- It's always safer to use a zebra **crossing** when you can.
↻ zebra/pelican crossing/pedestrian/railway crossing

crossroads /ˈkrɒsrəʊdz/ noun (countable)
plural: crossroads
the place where two or more roads cross
- The bus stopped when it reached the **crossroads**.

crowd /kraʊd/ noun (countable)
a lot of people in one place
- There was a large **crowd** at the football match.

crowded /ˈkraʊdɪd/ adjective
We say that a place is crowded when there are too many people in it.
- The buses are **crowded** at this time in the morning because everyone is rushing to work.

cruel /krʊəl/ adjective
unkind, hard
- The **cruel** boy hit the dog with a stick.

cry¹ /kraɪ/ noun (countable)
plural: cries
the noise people make when they are sad or when they need help
- I heard a **cry** for help coming from the river.
↻ give a cry, have a good cry

cry² verb
crying, cried, has cried
1 make a sound because something hurts you or because you are very sad
   - The little girl was **crying** because she'd fallen and hurt her ankle.
2 shout out
   - "Help! Help!" he **cried** as he ran away.

cucumber /ˈkjuːkʌmbə*/ noun (countable)
△ See box on page 238.

cup /kʌp/ noun (countable)
1 a bowl with a handle on it
   - Andy is filling a **cup** with water.
2 something to drink which is in a cup
   - Would you like a **cup** of coffee or tea?

cupboard /ˈkʌbəd/ noun (countable)
a piece of furniture where you can keep things
- Aileen put the cups and plates in the **cupboard**.

cure /kjʊə*/ verb
curing, cured, has cured
make well again, stop someone from being ill
- Dr Lee gave Jenny some medicine which **cured** her cough.

curry /ˈkʌrɪ/ noun (uncountable, countable)
plural: curries
meat, vegetables, fish, etc cooked in a hot sauce and usually eaten with rice
- Do you like Indian **curry**?

curtain /ˈkɜːtn/ noun (countable)
a piece of cloth which is put across a window or the front of a stage
- Can you put the light on and close the **curtains**?
↻ close/open/draw the curtains

curve /kɜːv/ verb
curving, curved, has curved
bend, not be straight, go round
- The road **curves** to the right before it reaches the village.

cushion /ˈkʊʃn/ noun (countable)
a soft bag like a pillow which you put on a seat to make it more comfortable
- "Would you like another **cushion** for the sofa?" "No, thanks. I'm already very comfortable."

θ	ð	ʃ	dʒ	tʃ	ŋ	ʒ	iː	ɜː	ɪ	æ	ʌ	ɒ
thing	that	shop	jump	chop	sing	measure	been	bird	bit	cat	but	not

customer /ˈkʌstəmə*/ noun (countable)
a person who buys things in a shop
- *Several **customers** were waiting to pay.*

customs /ˈkʌstəmz/ noun (plural)
a place where customs officers look at the things which you bring into a country
- *Everyone arriving from abroad must take their luggage through (the) **customs**.*
- get/go/pass through (the) customs

customs officer /ˈkʌstəmz ˌɒfɪsə*/ noun (countable)
someone who works in the customs and looks at what people have brought into the country
- *The **customs officer** wanted to see everything I had in my case. He was looking for gold!*

cut[1] /kʌt/ noun (countable)
a hole made by a knife, some scissors or something sharp
- *Tony had a **cut** on his wrist after playing with his new knife.*
- a deep/small cut

cut[2] verb
cutting, cut, has cut
1. break something with a knife, scissors, etc
   - *Can you **cut** this string with your knife?*
2. make shorter
   - *Who **cut** your hair?*
3. divide or break into smaller pieces
   - *Miss Smart **cut** the cake into two pieces.*

cut down /ˌkʌt ˈdaʊn/ phrasal verb
cutting down, cut down, has cut down
cut something so that it falls down
- *The men in the picture are **cutting down** a tree.*

cut out /ˌkʌt ˈaʊt/ phrasal verb
cutting out, cut out, has cut out
take out part of something with a knife, scissors, etc
- *There's a picture of your college in today's newspaper. Why don't you **cut** it **out**?*

cut up /ˌkʌt ˈʌp/ phrasal verb
cutting up, cut up, has cut up
cut into small pieces
- *You have to **cut** the meat **up** into small pieces before you cook it.*

cycle[1] /ˈsaɪkl/ noun (countable)
See **bicycle**.

cycle[2] verb
cycling, cycled, has cycled
ride a bicycle
- *Henry **cycles** to work every day.*

cyclist /ˈsaɪklɪst/ noun (countable)
a person who rides a bicycle
- *When the car hit the bicycle, the **cyclist** fell off.*

Dd

dad /dæd/ noun (countable)
a name which people often call their father
- Peter's **dad** will take us to college this morning.

daddy /ˈdædɪ/ noun (countable)
a name which children often call their father
- **Daddy**, can I have another ice cream, please?

daily¹ /ˈdeɪlɪ/ noun (countable)
plural: dailies
a newspaper which comes out every day.
- The news of our rescue was in all the **dailies**.

daily² adverb
every day
- I'm getting very fat and unhealthy. I must start doing exercises **daily**.

damage¹ /ˈdæmɪdʒ/ noun (uncountable)
If something causes damage to something else, it spoils it or makes it less useful.
- The fire did a lot of **damage** to the house.

LANGUAGE NOTE
NEVER The fire caused a lot of damages.
ALWAYS The fire caused a lot of **damage**.

cause/do/prevent/repair damage; great/serious/slight/lasting damage

damage² /ˈdæmɪdʒ/ verb
damaging, damaged, has damaged
spoil, make less useful
- Don't hit the door with the hammer. You'll **damage** it.

LANGUAGE NOTE
Things are **damaged** BUT people and animals are hurt.

dance¹ /ˈdɑːns/ noun (countable)
1 a way of moving in time with music
- Would you like to have a **dance** with me?
2 a time or a place at which people dance (ie move their bodies in time with music)
- Is there a **dance** at your college tonight?

dance² verb
dancing, danced, has danced
move in time with music
- Tom **danced** all night with Linda.

dancer /ˈdɑːnsə*/ noun (countable)
a person who is moving in time to music
- Tom and Linda are very good **dancers**.

θ	ð	ʃ	dʒ	tʃ	ŋ	ʒ	iː	ɜː	ɪ	æ	ʌ	ɒ
thing	that	shop	jump	chop	sing	measure	been	bird	bit	cat	but	not

danger /ˈdeɪndʒə*/ noun (uncountable)
something which can hurt you
- *Be careful if you see a red flag: it's usually a sign of **danger**.*
↻ face/look out for danger
in/out of danger

dangerous /ˈdeɪndʒərəs/ adjective
likely to cause harm
- *Don't play with matches: it's **dangerous**.*

dark¹ /dɑːk/ noun (uncountable)
the time when it is not light, night
- *Light a match, please. I can't see in the **dark**.*
↻ get/grow dark

dark² adjective
1 without light
   - *It's very **dark**. Can you put on the light?*
2 not light in colour
   - *Look for a man with **dark** hair in a **dark** blue suit.*

date¹ /deɪt/ noun (countable)
the name given to the number of the day, the month and the year
- *"What's the **date** today?"*
  "It's July 12th."
↻ a convenient/suitable date

date² noun (countable)
⚠ See box on page 89.

daughter /ˈdɔːtə*/ noun (countable)
someone's child who is a girl
- *Mr and Mrs Law have two **daughters** and a son.*

day /deɪ/ noun (countable)
1 a period of 24 hours
   - *Are there thirty or thirty-one **days** in January?*
   ↻ a clear/sunny/nice/cold/warm/hot day;
   a rainy/windy/cloudy/foggy day;
   a bad/busy/full day;
   a good/happy/pleasant/an important/special day; a working day;
   someone's birthday;
   the other day (= recently);
   have/take a day off (= have a holiday)
   ⚠ See box opposite
2 the time when it is usually light and not night
   - *It was so hot that the travellers walked at night and rested by **day**.*

LANGUAGE NOTE
1 Note the following phrases.
We rested **by day** and travelled **by night**.
Where have you been **all day**?
Did he leave **the next day**?
Maria phoned **the following day**.
Was it you I saw **the other day**?
There are a lot of crimes **these days**.
2 Use **on** before the name of a day or a date and NOT **at** or **in**.
Will you come again **on** Thursday?

↻ day breaks (=day begins)

θ	ð	ʃ	dʒ	tʃ	ŋ	ʒ	iː	ɜː	ɪ	æ	ʌ	ɒ
thing	that	shop	jump	chop	sing	measure	been	bird	bit	cat	but	not

Days, Months and Seasons

Days
Monday	
Tuesday	
Wednesday	**weekdays**
Thursday	
Friday	
Saturday	**the weekend**
Sunday	

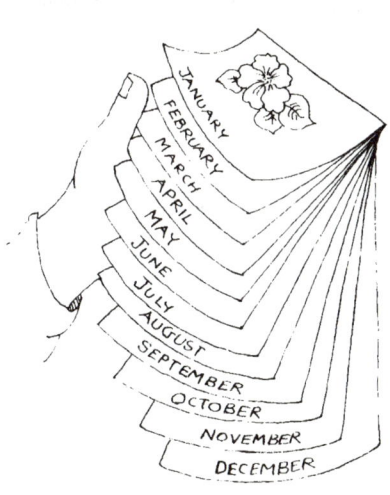

Months
January
February
March
April
May
June
July
August
September
October
November
December

Seasons

spring
The weather in Britain becomes warmer.

summer
The weather in Britain is warm.

winter
The weather in Britain is cold.

autumn
The weather in Britain becomes cooler.

---

daylight /ˈdeɪlaɪt/ noun (uncountable)

the part of the day which is not dark
- *Let's continue working while it's still **daylight**. We may be able to finish before it gets dark.*
  in broad daylight (= during the day)

dead /ded/ adjective
1 not alive
- *Ahmed's grandparents are **dead**, but his mother and father are still alive.*

LANGUAGE NOTE

Note the difference between **dead** and **died**.
   This plant is **dead**.
   This plant has **died**.

---

2 You can use **dead** about a telephone to mean that it doesn't work or it is broken.
- *"What did he say?"*
  *"I don't know. The phone went **dead** before he finished."*

⚠ See also **die**.

θ	ð	ʃ	dʒ	tʃ	ŋ	ʒ	iː	ɜː	ɪ	æ	ʌ	ɒ
thing	that	shop	jump	chop	sing	measure	been	bird	bit	cat	but	not

deaf /def/ adjective
unable to hear properly
- *Speak very clearly. Leila is rather **deaf**.*

dear /dɪə*/ adjective
1 costing a lot of money
   - *We shouldn't waste meat: it's very **dear**.*
   ⚠ See also **expensive**.
2 loved a lot
   - *She's a very **dear** friend of ours.*
3 You use **Dear** to begin a letter
   - ***Dear** Sir, **Dear** Uncle Ben*

decide /dɪˈsaɪd/ verb
deciding, decided, has decided
choose between two or more things
- *"Do you want to take the bus or train to Rome?"*
*"I don't know. I'll **decide** tomorrow."*

LANGUAGE NOTE

decide **against** doing something
decide **(up)on / about** (doing) something
decide (**not**) **to do** something
decide **whether** to do something **or** not
decide **what** to do
decide **that** you ought to do something

---

deep /diːp/ adjective
1 going a long way down, not shallow
   - *We can't cross the river there: the water's too **deep**.*
2 dark, strong (when you use it to describe a colour)
   - *Is the sky in this picture black or **deep** blue?*
3 low (when you use it to describe a voice or a sound)
   - *John's voice is very **deep**.*

deer /dɪə*/ noun (countable)
plural: deer
⚠ See box on page 10.

degree /dɪˈɡriː/ noun (countable)
1 a unit which you use to measure the temperature
   - *Today's temperature is thirty-one **degrees** centigrade.*
2 You get a **degree** after you have passed certain university examinations.
   - *Has Mr Johansson a BSc **degree** from an English university?*
☞ get/have/study for/take a degree

dentist /ˈdentɪst/ noun (countable)
someone who takes care of your teeth
- *I'm going to the **dentist**. I've got toothache.*

LANGUAGE NOTE

the dentist's = the place where the dentist works
I'll have to go to the **dentist's** tomorrow.

---

department store /dɪˈpɑːtmənt ˌstɔː*/
noun (countable)
plural: department stores
a big shop which sells lots of different things
- *Why don't you buy all your Christmas presents at this **department store**?*

depth /depθ/ noun (uncountable, countable)
how deep it is from the top to the bottom
- *What's the **depth** of the swimming pool?*

describe /dɪˈskraɪb/ verb
describing, described, has described
1 say what someone or something is like
   - *Can you **describe** the two men you saw last night?*
2 say what has happened
   - *Mr Oldfield **described** the attack to the police.*

LANGUAGE NOTE

describe something **to** someone
ALWAYS I'll describe **to** you where he lives.
NEVER ~~I'll describe you where he lives.~~

θ	ð	ʃ	dʒ	tʃ	ŋ	ʒ	iː	ɜː	ɪ	æ	ʌ	ɒ
thing	that	shop	jump	chop	sing	measure	been	bird	bit	cat	but	not

description /dɪˈskrɪpʃn/ noun (countable)
act of saying what someone or something is like
- *I gave the police a **description** of the man.*
- answer a description (= look like someone, etc who has been described); a close/good/true/full/poor/vague/wrong description

desert /ˈdezət/ noun (countable)
a large piece of land covered with sand
- *The travellers had to walk a long way across the **desert** before they found water.*

desk /desk/ noun (countable)
a kind of table where you read and write
- *Leave your books on your **desk** before you go out.*

destroy /dɪˈstrɔɪ/ verb
1 spoil something so that it cannot be repaired
   - *The building was **destroyed** by the bomb.*
2 kill a very sick animal
   - *Our dog was in pain and so we had it **destroyed**.*

detective /dɪˈtektɪv/ noun (countable)
a policeman or policewoman whose job is to find out who has stolen something, killed someone, etc
- *The **detective** found a small gun in Dave's case.*

develop /dɪˈveləp/ verb
grow or change (to something better or more complete)
- *This part of the country has been **developed**, and there are now good roads and new buildings.*

development /dɪˈveləpmənt/ noun (countable)
the act of growing or changing to something better or more complete
- *There have been several **developments** which have made our country much richer.*

diagram /ˈdaɪəgræm/ noun (countable)
a drawing to explain something, a plan to show how something works
- *The **diagram** below shows how a camera works.*
- draw/make a diagram; a clear/rough diagram

dial¹ /daɪəl/ noun (countable)
a flat circle with numbers or letters round the outside
- *The **dial** on this watch shines in the dark.*

dial² verb
dialling, dialled, has dialled
You can dial a number on some telephones when you phone someone (ie you put your finger in the hole above a number and move it round).
- *Are you sure you **dialled** the right number when you phoned Ken?*

SPELLING NOTE
double l: dialling, dialled BUT dials

diamond /ˈdaɪəmənd/ noun (countable)
1 a hard jewel which is very expensive
   - *The **diamond** Rosa bought cost $250,000!*
2 a shape almost like a square
   - *The piece of wood was the same shape as a huge **diamond**.*

diary /ˈdaɪərɪ/ noun (countable)
plural: diaries
a book with pages or spaces for the days, weeks and months. You write what you do each day in a diary.
- *I can come on Wednesday. I haven't got anything in my **diary** that day.*
- See also **calendar**.

θ	ð	ʃ	dʒ	tʃ	ŋ	ʒ	iː	ɜː	ɪ	æ	ʌ	ɒ
thing	that	shop	jump	chop	sing	measure	been	bird	bit	cat	but	not

dictate /dɪk'teɪt/ verb
dictating, dictated, has dictated
speak slowly so that someone can write down what you say
- *Mrs Soegondo is **dictating** a letter to Elsa.*

dictation /dɪk'teɪʃn/ noun (countable)
something which is spoken slowly and written down
- *Mr Lee has just given his class a **dictation**.*
- give/take (down) dictation

dictionary /'dɪkʃənrɪ/ noun (countable)
plural: dictionaries
a book which gives the spellings and meanings of words. The words are written in alphabetical order: A, B, C, D, etc.
- *The book you are now looking at is a **dictionary**.*
- look up (something in)/use a dictionary; a good/useful/large/small/pocket dictionary

did /dɪd/ verb
past tense of **do**
- *"**Did** you see Anna yesterday?"*
  *"No, I stayed at home and **did** my homework."*

didn't /'dɪdnt/ verb
did not
- *We **didn't** go out last night: we stayed at home.*
- See also **do**.

die /daɪ/ verb
dying, died, has died
stop living
- *The old man was 92 when he **died**.*
- See also **dead 1**; see also **kill**.

LANGUAGE NOTE

1 die **of** a disease

2 COMPARE   The flowers **died** because no one watered them.
The cold weather **killed** the flowers.

---

differ /'dɪfə*/ verb
be different, not be the same as
- *The two pieces of wood **differ** in size but not in shape.*

difference /'dɪfrəns/ noun (countable)
the way in which things are not the same
- *What's the **difference** between a letter and a parcel?*
- make/notice/see/point out a difference
a big/clear/sharp/wide/great/important/real/serious/small/slight difference, much difference, the chief/main difference

---
LANGUAGE NOTE

It doesn't make any (or much) difference = It doesn't matter.

---

different /'dɪfrənt/ adjective
not the same
- *These two books are **different**: one is about birds and the other is about fish.*

LANGUAGE NOTE

1 NEVER   different than something
  ALWAYS   different *from/to* something

2 NEVER   more different from
  ALWAYS   different *from*

---

difficult /'dɪfɪkəlt/ adjective
not easy, hard
- *"Efficient" is a **difficult** word to say and spell.*

difficulty /'dɪfɪkəltɪ/ noun (countable, uncountable)
plural: difficulties
If you have difficulty in doing something, you cannot do it easily.
- *I had great **difficulty** with this homework.*
- cause/make/come across/meet/face a difficulty, get over a difficulty, have difficulty (with), run into difficulties (= meet a difficulty); great/serious difficulty

---

θ	ð	ʃ	dʒ	tʃ	ŋ	ʒ	iː	ɜː	ɪ	æ	ʌ	ɒ
thing	that	shop	jump	chop	sing	measure	been	bird	bit	cat	but	not

LANGUAGE NOTE

have difficulty **with** something or someone
have difficulty **(in)** doing something

dig /dɪɡ/ verb
digging, dug /dʌɡ/, has dug
make a hole in the ground
- We **dug** a deep hole and hid the money in it.

dining room /'daɪnɪŋ rʊm/ noun (countable)
the room in a house or flat where people eat their meals
- The table was too big for our **dining room**.

dinner /'dɪnə*/ noun (uncountable, countable)
the main meal of the day (Some people eat dinner in the middle of the day but other people eat dinner in the evening.)
- What are we having for **dinner**?
- dinner-time;
  eat/have/have something for dinner;
  make/prepare dinner
- See also **lunch**.

direct¹ /dɪ'rekt/ verb
show or tell someone the way to a place
- Can you **direct** me to the nearest chemist's?

direct² adjective, adverb
the shortest or quickest way from one place to another
- Is this a **direct** train to Madrid?
- Does this bus go **direct** to Madrid?

direction /dɪ'rekʃn/ noun (countable)
1 the way you should go to reach a place
   - Our flat is in that **direction** over there.
2 how to do something (used in the plural)
   - Read the **directions** carefully before you take the medicine.
- follow/get/give directions,
  clear/vague directions

dirt /dɜːt/ noun (uncountable)
anything that is not clean: dust, mud, etc
- The workmen left some **dirt** on the clean floor.

dirty /'dɜːtɪ/ adjective
dirtier, dirtiest
not clean, covered with mud

- Ramon fell in the mud and got his shirt very **dirty**.

disappear /ˌdɪsə'pɪə*/ verb
When someone or something **disappears**, you can no longer see them.
- The ship sank and **disappeared** beneath the waves.

disappointed /ˌdɪsə'pɔɪntɪd/ adjective
When you are **disappointed**, you are sad because you did not get something which you wanted.
- We were all **disappointed** when it began to rain and we couldn't go on the picnic.

discover /dɪ'skʌvə*/ verb
find for the first time
- "Who **discovered** America?" "Columbus."
- When I got home, I **discovered** a big hole in my sock.

discovery /dɪ'skʌvərɪ/ noun (countable)
plural: discoveries
something which you find (and which no one else has found before)
- I made an interesting **discovery** when I got home: I found an old letter from my father.
- make a discovery; a big/great/exciting/
  pleasant/unpleasant discovery;
  a scientific discovery

θ	ð	ʃ	dʒ	tʃ	ŋ	ʒ	iː	ɜː	ɪ	æ	ʌ	ɒ
thing	that	shop	jump	chop	sing	measure	been	bird	bit	cat	but	not

discuss /dɪˈskʌs/ verb
talk about
- *I'd like to **discuss** my future with you.*

> **LANGUAGE NOTE**
>
> Don't use **about** after **discuss**.
> NEVER We discussed about the new road.
> ALWAYS *We **discussed** the new road.*
> OR *We had a discussion **about** the new road.*

discussion /dɪˈskʌʃn/ noun (countable)
You have a **discussion** about something when you talk seriously about it with other people.
- *We were having a **discussion** about the new college when Anna called.*
- ℞ have/hold/lead/start/take part in a discussion; a brief/short/long/friendly/serious/useful discussion

disease /dɪˈziːz/ noun (countable, uncountable)
an illness
- *I think Mr Peacock died of a rare **disease**.*
- ℞ come down with/fall ill with/have/cure/die of/pass on a disease, prevent disease; a dangerous/painful/serious/cruel/deadly/fatal/infectious/rare disease

> **LANGUAGE NOTE**
>
> You can often use the words **disease** and **illness** with the same meaning. However, remember that a certain disease (usually named) causes an illness (= a general period of being unwell). Also a disease can be passed on from one person to another.
>
> *Vincento is absent from college because of **illness**: three years ago he got malaria - or a similar **disease**.*

⚠ See also **illness**.

dish /dɪʃ/ noun (countable)
plural: dishes
1 a small bowl or plate for food
   - *Can you put the meat on this **dish** and the fish on that **dish** over there?*
2 **the dishes** = all the plates, saucers, etc
   - *I'll wash **the dishes** and you dry them.*
3 a type of food or meal
   - *Tamara's favourite **dish** was fried fish.*
℞ someone's favourite dish, the main dish

distance /ˈdɪstəns/ noun (countable)
1 the amount of space between two objects, places, etc
   - *What is the **distance** between Taipei and Tokyo?*
2 **in the distance** = far away
   - *I could just see a man **in the distance**.*
℞ the far distance; a good/great/long/short/safe distance (= far enough away from someone/something to be safe)

> **LANGUAGE NOTE**
>
> a distance **of** 250 kilometres, etc

dive /daɪv/ verb
diving, dived, has dived
jump downwards (into water) with your head and hands first
- *We all **dived** into the swimming pool together.*

divide /dɪˈvaɪd/ verb
dividing, divided, has divided
1 cut into different parts
   - *Mrs Gikas **divided** the cake into six pieces and gave us each a piece.*
2 move or go into different parts
   - *Mr Robinson **divided** the class into three teams.*
3 find out how many times one number is contained in another number
   - *Thirty **divided** by six is five: 30 ÷ 6 = 5.*

θ	ð	ʃ	dʒ	tʃ	ŋ	ʒ	iː	ɜː	ɪ	æ	ʌ	ɒ
thing	that	shop	jump	chop	sing	measure	been	bird	bit	cat	but	not

do /duː/ verb

do, does /dʌz/ , doing, did /dɪd/ , has done /dʌn/

1 Use **do** to make questions and to give short answers.
   - "***Do*** *you like your new college?*" "*Yes, I* ***do.***" (OR "*No, I* ***don't.***")

2 Use **do** to make negative forms of verbs.
   - *Peter **doesn't** want to leave school yet.*
   - ***Don't*** *play with matches. They're dangerous.*

3 You can use **do** to make the meaning of a main verb more important.
   - *I **do** enjoy drawing and painting.*

4 Use **do** in the following type of sentence instead of using the same verb twice.
   - "*I like swimming very much.*" "*So **do** I.*" (OR "*I **do**, too.*")

5 carry out an action
   - *Laura **did** her homework before she went out.*

6 If you want to know what someone's job is, you can ask them what they **do**.
   - "*What does Mr Ho **do**?*" "*He's a teacher.*"

7 If you want to ask someone if they are well, busy, etc, you ask "*How are you **doing**?*"
   - *Constantine, how are you **doing** at your new school?*

8 When you meet someone for the first time, you can say "*How do you do?*"
   - *I'm Sam Lee. **How do you do?***

LANGUAGE NOTE

Note the reply: "How do you do?"
"How do you do?"
(NEVER "Very well, thank you.")

See also **did**; see also **didn't**; see also **doesn't**; see also **don't**.

doctor /ˈdɒktə*/ noun (countable)

a person who treats sick people or who has a special degree from a university
- *You should see a **doctor** if you feel ill.*
- a family doctor

doesn't /ˈdʌznt/ verb

does not
- *Why **doesn't** the teacher say anything to Ann?*

See also **do**.

dog /dɒg/ noun (countable)

See box on page 10.

doll /dɒl/ noun (countable)

a children's toy which looks like a baby or a person
- *Linda is always playing with her new **doll**.*

dollar /ˈdɒlə*/ noun (countable)

one dollar = $1

money used in the United States of America, Canada, Australia, New Zealand, Singapore, Hong Kong, Zimbabwe, and several other countries
- *This camera cost over six hundred **dollars**.*

done /dʌn/ verb

past participle of **do**
- "*What have you **done**?*" "*I'm afraid I've broken this bowl.*"

See also **do**.

donkey /ˈdɒŋkɪ/ noun (countable)

See box on page 10.

don't /dəʊnt/ verb

do not
- ***Don't*** *run across this busy road.*

See also **do**.

door /dɔː*/ noun (countable)

You usually open or close a door to get into a building, a room, or a cupboard.
- *When I opened the **door**, I saw two strange men in the room.*
- close/shut/open/lock a door, knock on a door

θ	ð	ʃ	dʒ	tʃ	ŋ	ʒ	iː	ɜː	ɪ	æ	ʌ	ɒ
thing	that	shop	jump	chop	sing	measure	been	bird	bit	cat	but	not

down ¹ /daʊn/ adverb
1 (from a higher place) to a lower place
 • *Let's take the lift **down** to the sixth floor.*
2 to a lower level in price, loudness, etc
 • *Prices of cameras have come **down** recently.*
3 at, in or near a lower place
 • *We're on the sixth floor and Ted's **down** on the ground floor.*
4 Sometimes you can use **down** with certain verbs to add to their meanings.
 • *I'm going to lie **down** and have a rest.*
 ⟳ bend/break/burn/die/fall/kneel/lie/sit down

down ² preposition
1 (from a higher place) to a lower place
 • *Is that Fatima Alvarez coming **down** the stairs?*
2 along, to the far end of
 • *When he saw the policeman, Oswald turned and ran **down** the street.*

downstairs /daʊnˈsteəz/ adverb
down the stairs
 • *"Close your bedroom door and come **downstairs** at once," Mrs Law told Tony.*

dozen /ˈdʌzn/ determiner, noun (countable)
twelve
 • *I'd like a **dozen** eggs, please.*

LANGUAGE NOTE

1 COMPARE *a **dozen** eggs*
 *five **dozen** eggs*
 ***dozens** of eggs*

2 ALWAYS *five **dozen***
 NEVER ~~*five dozens*~~

---

drank /dræŋk/ verb
past tense of **drink**
 • *Nicola **drank** a whole bottle of milk.*

draw ¹ /drɔː/ noun (countable)
the score when both sides have the same number of points
 • *"Who won the match?" "It was a **draw**."*

draw ² verb
drawing, drew /druː/, has drawn /drɔːn/
1 make pictures with a pen, pencil or crayon
 • *I'd like to **draw** that beautiful scene.*
2 pull
 • *The cart was **drawn** by two horses.*
3 draw (out) = take out
 • *Mrs Kempf has gone to the bank to **draw** (out) $500 for a new dress.*
4 score the same number of points in a game
 • *Wanchai Wanderers **drew** with Redston Rovers: the score was 2-2.*

drawer /drɔː*/ noun (countable)
the part of a table or a cupboard which you can pull out and push in
 • *"Where's my red shirt?"*
 *"It's in the top **drawer** of the chest."*

drawing /ˈdrɔːɪŋ/ noun (countable)
the picture which someone makes with a pen, a pencil, etc
 • *Mrs de Sousa likes my **drawing** of the tiger.*
 ⟳ do/make a drawing

drawn /drɔːn/ verb
past participle of **draw**
 • *Ben's just **drawn** a picture of his house.*

dream ¹ /driːm/ noun (countable)
things which you see in your mind when you are asleep
 • *I had a strange **dream** last night. I was playing football for Brazil!*
 ⟳ have a dream; a bad/horrible/terrible/strange dream; sweet dreams (= good night: may you have pleasant dreams)

θ	ð	ʃ	dʒ	tʃ	ŋ	ʒ	iː	ɜː	ɪ	æ	ʌ	ɒ
thing	that	shop	jump	chop	sing	measure	been	bird	bit	cat	but	not

dream [2]   verb

dreaming, dreamed or dreamt /dremt/, has dreamed or has dreamt

see things in your mind when you are asleep
- *"What did you **dream** about last night?"*
  *"I **dreamt** I was in a small boat on the sea."*

LANGUAGE NOTE

NEVER   I dreamed to go home.
ALWAYS I dreamed **of going** home.

---

dress [1]   /dres/   noun

plural: dresses

1 (countable) a piece of clothing for a girl or a woman
   - *Do you like Jenny's new **dress**?*
   ↻ a long/short/loose/tight dress
2 (countable, uncountable) clothing for men or women
   - *Jane's bought a lovely evening **dress** for the big party. Everyone will be in evening **dress**.*

LANGUAGE NOTE

1 COMPARE   *an evening dress* (= a long dress worn by a woman)
  WITH   *evening dress* (= clothes worn for dances, etc in the evening by both women and men)

2 COMPARE   *an evening dress* (= a long dress worn by a woman in the evening for dances, etc)
  WITH   *a nightdress* (= a loose dress worn by a woman in bed)

---

dress [2]   verb

1 When you **dress** yourself or get dressed, you put your clothes on.
   - *Please get **dressed** before you have your breakfast.*
2 When you are **dressed**, you are wearing clothes.
   - *Just a moment, please. I'm not **dressed**, but it won't take me a minute to put a shirt and some trousers on.*

↻ be/get dressed;
  fully dressed, dressed in black

dressing gown   /'dresɪŋ gaʊn/   noun (countable)

(American English: bathrobe)

a type of long coat which you can wear over your pyjamas, etc
- *Put on your **dressing gown** and come downstairs to have supper with us.*

drink [1]   /drɪŋk/   noun (countable)

water, tea, coffee, beer, cola, etc
- *I'm very thirsty. Can I have a **drink**, please?*
↻ have/take/make/pour a drink;
  a cold/hot/strong/weak drink;
  soft drink, a drink of water, etc

drink [2]   verb

drinking, drank /dræŋk/, has drunk /drʌŋk/,

take water, tea, coffee, beer, cola, etc
- *You've made too much coffee for me. I'm afraid I can't **drink** it all.*

drive   /draɪv/   verb

driving, drove /drəʊv/, has driven /'drɪvn/,

make a car go where you want to go

- *My mother **drives** to work every day but my father goes by bus.*

driver   /'draɪvə*/   noun (countable)

a person who drives a car, a bus, a lorry, a train, etc
- *"Is your uncle a bus **driver**?"*
  *"No, he's a lorry **driver**."*
↻ a bus/lorry/taxi/tram/train/
  (an)engine driver, a learner-driver

θ	ð	ʃ	dʒ	tʃ	ŋ	ʒ	iː	ɜː	ɪ	æ	ʌ	ɒ
thing	that	shop	jump	chop	sing	measure	been	bird	bit	cat	but	not

drop¹ /drɒp/ noun (countable)
1 a very small amount of water, tea, cola, etc (like a tiny ball)
 • *I felt a few **drops** of rain on my face.*
2 a fall (in temperature, amount, price, etc)
 • *"Yesterday it was very hot, but today it's cool."*
 *"Yes, there's been a big **drop** in temperature."*
↻ a big/sharp/slight/small/sudden drop

drop² verb
dropping, dropped, has dropped

SPELLING NOTE
double **p**: dropping, dropped BUT drops

1 fall
 • *The apple **dropped** to the ground.*
2 let something fall
 • *Tony **dropped** the cup, and it broke.*
3 become weaker or lower (used about the wind)
 • *I wanted to fly my kite but the wind had **dropped**.*
4 let someone get out of a car
 • *Mr Patel gave us a lift in his car and **dropped** us at the post office.*

drove /drəʊv/ verb
past tense of **drive**
 • *Ken **drove** from Leeds to London yesterday.*

drown /draʊn/ verb
go under the water and die
 • *Two sailors **drowned** when the ferry sank.*

drug store /'drʌg stɔː*/ noun (countable)
(American English)
⚠ See **pharmacy**.

drum /drʌm/ noun (countable)
a round instrument which you hit with a stick to make a noise
 • *Simon plays the **drums** in the new band.*

drunk¹ /drʌŋk/ verb
past participle of **drink**
 • *Have you **drunk** all the milk?*

drunk² adjective
If someone is **drunk**, they have had too much beer or wine.
 • *I was so **drunk** I could hardly stand up.*

dry¹ /draɪ/ verb
drying, dried, has dried
make dry
 • *You can **dry** your hands on this towel.*

dry² adjective
drier, driest
without any water in it or on it, not wet
 • *This towel is **dry**: it's been in the sun all day.*
↻ go/run dry

dry up /ˌdraɪ 'ʌp/ phrasal verb
drying up, dried up, has dried up
become dry
 • *"Look at the stream: it's **dried up**."*
 "Where has all the water gone?"

duck /dʌk/ noun (countable, uncountable)
⚠ See box on page 22.

duckling /'dʌklɪŋ/ noun (countable)
a young duck
⚠ See box on page 22.

LANGUAGE NOTE
When you are talking about **duck** as food on a dish, you should not use **a** before it. Would you like crab or **duck**? When you are talking about **a duck** as a living bird, use **a**. There was **a large duck** swimming on the lake.

dug /dʌg/ verb
past tense of **dig**
 • *Who **dug** your garden and put in those plants?*

θ	ð	ʃ	dʒ	tʃ	ŋ	ʒ	iː	ɜː	ɪ	æ	ʌ	ɒ
thing	that	shop	jump	chop	sing	measure	been	bird	bit	cat	but	not

dumb /dʌm/ adjective
not able to talk
- Poor Mr Green is both deaf and **dumb**.

durian /ˈdjʊərɪən/ noun (countable)
⚠ See box on page 89.

during /ˈdjʊərɪŋ/ preposition
at some moment in a period of time
- Several boats sank **during** the storm last week.

LANGUAGE NOTE

1. Use a noun (phrase) after **during**.
   - NEVER: I saw him during I visited the hospital.
   - ALWAYS: I saw him **during my visit** to the hospital.
   - OR: I saw him **when I visited** the hospital.

2. **during** = how long something took
   for = when something took place
   - NEVER: Anna was absent from school during two months.
   - ALWAYS: Anna was absent from school **for two months**.
   - OR: Anna was absent from school **during March and April**.

3. COMPARE: The school will be closed **during** (the whole of) January. (= from the beginning to the end of January)
   WITH: The school will be closed **in** January. (= for some days or weeks in January - but not usually for the whole of January)

---

dust¹ /dʌst/ noun (uncountable)
tiny dry pieces of dirt
- 🐍 Everything in the flat was covered in **dust**.
  collect/gather/pick up dust;
  a cloud of dust, a piece of dust

dust² verb
wipe or brush tiny pieces of dirt off something
- Sarah **dusted** the chair before she sat on it.

duster /ˈdʌstə*/ noun (countable)
the cloth which you use to wipe dust off something
- May I borrow your **duster** to dust the chairs.

dusty /ˈdʌstɪ/ adjective
dustier, dustiest
covered with tiny pieces of dirt
- The whole house is **dusty**; I must clean it.

dying /ˈdaɪ-ɪŋ/ verb
present participle of **die**
- "The soldier won't live much longer. I'm sure he's **dying**."

θ	ð	ʃ	dʒ	tʃ	ŋ	ʒ	iː	ɜː	ɪ	æ	ʌ	ɒ
thing	that	shop	jump	chop	sing	measure	been	bird	bit	cat	but	not

E e

each /iːtʃ/ determiner; pronoun
1 everyone or everything in a group
- *The teacher gave **each** child a pencil.*

> **LANGUAGE NOTE**
>
> 1 You should usually use a singular countable noun and a singular verb after **each**.
> > We went to bed early each **night**.
> > There were several books on the shelf but each **was** damaged.
>
> 2 Use **of** after **each** when there are other determiners: eg **the**, **these**, **your**, etc. However, remember that you must use a singular verb.
> > Each **of the pupils** is going to bring something to eat. (BUT NOT Each of pupils .....)
>
> 3 COMPARE **Each of us** has brought a ball.
> > We have **each** brought a ball.
> > We **each have** a ball.

2 for one
- *"How much are these mangoes?" "Two dollars **each**."*

3 each other
- *We looked at **each other** and smiled.*

⚠ See **another** ².

> **LANGUAGE NOTE**
>
> You should usually use **each other** for two people and **one another** for more than two people.
> > Why are the two men shouting at each other?
> > Why were all the men shouting at one another?

eagle /ˈiːgl/ noun (countable)
⚠ See box on page 22.

ear /ɪə*/ noun (countable)
You hear with your **ears**.
- *The sudden noise hurt my **ears**.*
⚠ See box on page 25.

earache /ˈɪəreɪk/ noun (countable, uncountable)
usually uncountable in British English but usually countable in American English
a pain in (one of) your ears
- *I've got bad **earache**. (British English)*
- *I've got a bad **earache**. (American English)*
⚠ See also **ache** ¹.

early /ˈɜːlɪ/ adjective
earlier, earliest
1 at or near the beginning of a period of time, not late
- *We all got up **early** this morning.*
2 before the time for something to take place
- *I missed the bus because it came five minutes **early**.*

earn /ɜːn/ verb
receive money after you have done some work
- *How much does Pedro **earn** a week?*

earth /ɜːθ/ noun (uncountable)
1 (often Earth or the Earth) the world, the planet on which we live
- *The **earth** is a long way from the sun.*
2 the ground or soil
- *The **earth** here is very good for growing vegetables.*

east ¹ /iːst/ noun (singular with the)
where the sun rises
- *Everyone knows the sun rises in **the east** and goes down in the west.*

> **LANGUAGE NOTE**
>
> You can use the **East** (with a capital E) to mean India, China, Japan, etc.
> the Far East (= countries of east Asia), the Middle East (= countries of the east Mediterranean)

east ² adjective
the part of a country, a building, a place, etc facing where the sun rises, in the east
- *The **east** side of the house is cooler than the south.*
- *Is Malawi in **East** Africa?*

θ	ð	ʃ	dʒ	tʃ	ŋ	ʒ	iː	ɜː	ɪ	æ	ʌ	ɒ
thing	that	shop	jump	chop	sing	measure	been	bird	bit	cat	but	not

eastern, Eastern /'iːstən/ adjective
in or from the east part of a country
- *He's just bought a house in **Eastern** England.*

easily /'iːzɪlɪ/ adverb
without any difficulty
- *Victor was the fastest runner and **easily** won the race.*

easy /'iːzɪ/ adjective
easier, easiest
1 not difficult to do
   - *I think maths is **easy** but English is very hard.*
2 comfortable, without any problems
   - *Elsa had an **easy** life after her marriage.*

eat /iːt/ verb
eating, ate /et/, eaten /'iːtn/
put something into your mouth and swallow it
- *I couldn't **eat** all the rice: there was far too much.*

edge /edʒ/ noun (countable)
outside end of something

- *The cup fell off the **edge** of the table and broke.*

education /ˌedjʊ'keɪʃn/ noun (uncountable)
teaching and learning (often in a school)
- *Mrs Lim finished her **education** in London.*
- begin/finish/receive (your) education; a broad/general/an excellent/good/narrow/poor education; primary/secondary/further/higher/university/adult/private/health/physical education

egg /eg/ noun (countable)
Eggs are almost round and can be eaten; they have a thin shell and are laid by birds.
- *Would you like an **egg** for breakfast?*
- break/boil/fry an egg; a boiled/fried egg

either /'aɪðə*/ pronoun, determiner
1 one of two things
   - *I haven't seen **either** of the two men you asked about.*
2 You can also use **either** at the end of sentences with not as in the following:-
   - *"I haven't got any money." "I haven't **either**."*

See also **neither**[1]; see also **too**[1].

LANGUAGE NOTE

1 Use a singular countable noun after **either** in such sentences as:-
   Either **book** will be suitable.
2 Use **of** after **either** when there are other determiners: eg **the**, **these**, **your**, etc. However, remember that you must use a singular verb.
   Either **of those pupils** will be able to do it.
   (NEVER Either of pupils .....)

---

either ... or /ˌaɪðə* ....ɔː*/ conjunction
(do) one of two things
- *You can **either** stay **or** leave now.*

LANGUAGE NOTE

Take care to use **either** .... **or** in the correct position.
   Either a pen **or** a pencil is necessary for this exam.
   You'll need **either** a pen **or** a pencil for this exam.
   You'll need a pen **either** for the exam **or** for your homework. I'm not sure which.
   You can **either** use your pen **or** borrow my pencil for the exam.

---

electric /ɪ'lektrɪk/ adjective
An electric machine is a machine which is worked by electricity.
- *Paul has just bought a new **electric** kettle.*

electrician /ɪˌlek'trɪʃn/ noun (countable)
someone who repairs electric machines, lights, etc or puts them in a building
- *I've called the **electrician** to fix the lights.*

θ	ð	ʃ	dʒ	tʃ	ŋ	ʒ	iː	ɜː	ɪ	æ	ʌ	ɒ
thing	that	shop	jump	chop	sing	measure	been	bird	bit	cat	but	not

electricity /ɪˌlekˈtrɪsɪtɪ/ noun (uncountable)
You use electricity when you turn on an electric machine, a light, the television, etc.
• *Someone turned off the **electricity**.*

elephant /ˈelɪfənt/ noun (countable)
⚠ See box on page 10.

elevator /ˈeləveɪtə*/ noun (countable)
(American English)
↻ take the elevator
⚠ See lift ¹1.

else /els/ adverb
1 You can use **else** after **anyone** and **anything**
  • *"Could I have a drink, please?"*
    *"Certainly. Would **anyone else** like a drink?"*
2 You can use **else** after **no one** and **nothing**
  • *I wanted to watch the film on TV but **no one else** did.*
3 You can use **else** after **somewhere**.
  • *I went to see my friends in Tampines but they'd gone **somewhere else**.*
4 You can use **else** after **who**, **what**, **where**, etc.
  • *Linda went on the picnic. Who **else** went?*
  • *What **else** do you want?*
5 **or else** = if not
  • *Hurry up **or else** we'll be late for college.*

empty ¹ /ˈemptɪ/ verb
emptying, emptied, has emptied
take everything out
• *Rose **emptied** her bag on to her desk.*

empty ² adjective
emptier, emptiest
with nothing inside it
• *I was hungry but the fridge was **empty**.*

end ¹ /end/ noun (countable)
1 where something stops or finishes
  • *We watched to the **end** of the film.*
2 the last part of a period of time
  • *I'll see you again at the **end** of August.*
  ↻ bring to an end, put an end to

end ² verb
stop or finish (something)
• *We turned the television off when the film **ended**.*

enemy /ˈenəmɪ/ noun (countable)
plural enemies
1 someone who wants to hurt you in some way
  • *Nicola and I are friends: we're not **enemies**.*
2 someone or something (often a country) which you fight against
  • *China and Japan were **enemies** during the Second World War.*
  ↻ a bitter/powerful/secret enemy, one's worst enemy

engine /ˈendʒɪn/ noun (countable)
1 a machine which gives power or makes things move
  • *Hassan's new fast car has a very big **engine**.*
  ↻ start/warm up/run/turn on/turn off/repair an engine
  a diesel/an electric/a steam engine
2 a machine which pulls a train
  • *The first trains had steam **engines** but most **engines** are now electric.*

engineer /ˌendʒɪˈnɪə*/ noun (countable)
someone who plans or makes machines, roads, bridges, etc
• *I want to be an **engineer** when I leave college.*
↻ a chemical/a civil/an electrical/a mechanical engineer

enjoy /ɪnˈdʒɔɪ/ verb
1 like something a lot
  • *Children **enjoy** going to the seaside for holidays.*

θ	ð	ʃ	dʒ	tʃ	ŋ	ʒ	iː	ɜː	ɪ	æ	ʌ	ɒ
thing	that	shop	jump	chop	sing	measure	been	bird	bit	cat	but	not

equal 71

> **LANGUAGE NOTE**
>
> enjoy + ing
> NEVER ~~I enjoy to sing and dance.~~
> ALWAYS I enjoy *singing* and *dancing*.

2 **enjoy yourself** = do what you like doing
- We really *enjoyed ourselves* at the party.

enjoyable /ɪnˈdʒɔɪəbl/ adjective

very nice and pleasant
- We spent an *enjoyable* day with Helen and Joe swimming and playing on the beach.
- ៛ very/most/highly enjoyable

enough /ɪˈnʌf/ pronoun, determiner

1 as much as you need or want, as many as you need or want
- Have you had *enough* biscuits?

> **LANGUAGE NOTE**
>
> 1 Use *of* after *enough* when there are other determiners: eg *the*, *these*, *your*, etc.
> COMPARE Have you had *enough* rice?
> Have you had *enough of* the rice?
> (NEVER ~~Have you had enough of rice?~~)
> 2 NEVER ~~The rice isn't enough.~~
> ALWAYS There isn't enough rice.

2 as much as is necessary
- You aren't trying hard *enough* to win.

> **LANGUAGE NOTE**
>
> NEVER ~~enough hard~~
> ALWAYS hard *enough*

enter /ˈentə*/ verb

1 go into, come into
- An old man *entered* the room.
2 become a member of
- Mary was only thirteen when she *entered* King's College.

> **LANGUAGE NOTE**
>
> NEVER ~~enter into a room~~
> ALWAYS *enter* a room

entrance /ˈentrəns/ noun (countable)

1 way into a place (usually a gate or a door)
- The *entrance* to the school is in Elm Road.
- ៛ a back/rear/front/side entrance, the main entrance
2 the right to go in or join
- The *entrance* examination for Oxbridge College is very difficult.

entry /ˈentrɪ/ noun (countable)

plural: entries
1 way into a place
- Wait for us at the *entry* to the building.
2 someone or something taking part in a competition or race
- There were over fifty *entries* for the competition.
- ៛ a winning entry

envelope /ˈenvələʊp/ noun (countable)

a paper cover in which you can send a letter
- Remember to stamp the *envelope* before you post it.
- ៛ address/seal an envelope; a self-addressed/ a stamped addressed envelope

equal¹ /ˈiːkwəl/ verb

equalling, equalled, has equalled

> **SPELLING NOTE**
>
> double l: equalling, equalled
> BUT equals

be exactly the same amount as something else (often used in maths)
- Four plus four *equals* eight. (4 + 4 = 8)

θ	ð	ʃ	dʒ	tʃ	ŋ	ʒ	iː	ɜː	ɪ	æ	ʌ	ɒ
thing	that	shop	jump	chop	sing	measure	been	bird	bit	cat	but	not

equal² adjective

the same as something else, as big as, as much as, as good as, etc
- A kilo of feathers is **equal** in weight to a kilo of rice, but much bigger in amount.

equally /ˈiːkwəlɪ/ adverb

1 by exactly the same amount
- Divide the cake **equally** among the six pupils.
2 just like, just as much as
- I know Anna is good at tennis, but Tina is **equally** good.

escalator /ˈeskəleɪtə*/ noun (countable)

moving stairs

- Shall we take the lift up or the **escalator**?

escape /ɪˈskeɪp/ verb

escaping, escaped, has escaped
get away from someone or something, become free
- While the police were taking them to the police station, the two thieves **escaped** from the car.

especially /ɪˈspeʃəlɪ/ adverb

chiefly, above all
- Laura likes playing games, **especially** tennis and badminton.

even¹ /ˈiːvn/ adjective

1 flat, smooth, level
- "The new road isn't very **even**."
  "That's right. It's quite rough, isn't it?"
2 the same in height, length or weight
- "Do you think those curtains are **even**?"
  "No, one of them is longer than the other."

3 When the scores in a game are the same, they are even.
- "What's the score?" "2-2, so it's **even**."
4 **an even number** = a number which will divide by two
- 2,4,6,8,10 and 12 are all **even numbers**.

even² adverb

You can use **even** to show your surprise.
- **Even** Susie had forgotten to do her homework.

LANGUAGE NOTE

You should put **even** in front of the word to which it refers.

COMPARE Sam is very strong but **even** he can't lift the heavy box.
Sam can't move the heavy box - he can't **even** lift it.
Sam is so weak he can't lift anything: he can't lift **even** the small box.

---

evening /ˈiːvnɪŋ/ noun (countable)

the part of the day just after the afternoon, early at night
- Mr Alvarez usually arrives home at half past six but this **evening** he'll be late.

evening dress /ˌiːvnɪŋ ˈdres/

noun (countable, uncountable)
⚠ See **dress**¹ 2 (Language Notes).

event /ɪˈvent/ noun (countable)

1 something that happens (usually interesting or important)
- Hiroshi's visit to Canada was the most important **event** in his young life.
∽ an event happens/takes place/occurs; a coming/an exciting/a happy/important/ special event; world events
2 a race or sport in a competition
- The next **event** will be the high jump.
∽ enter for /take part in/watch an event

θ	ð	ʃ	dʒ	tʃ	ŋ	ʒ	iː	ɜː	ɪ	æ	ʌ	ɒ
thing	that	shop	jump	chop	sing	measure	been	bird	bit	cat	but	not

ever /ˈevə*/ adverb
at any time
- Have you **ever** been to Singapore?

> **LANGUAGE NOTE**
>
> 1 NEVER ~~Ann said she would ever love Ken.~~
>   BUT   Ann said she would **always** love Ken.
>   OR   Ann said she would love Ken **for ever**.
>
> 2 NEVER ~~Has Ben already driven a car before?~~
>   BUT   Has Ben **ever** driven a car?
>
> **Ever** is used in questions to mean **at any time up to now**.

every /ˈevrɪ/ determiner
all or each
- Mabel cries **every** time she sees a sad film.

> **LANGUAGE NOTE**
>
> COMPARE Every pen **was** broken.
>   All the pens **were** broken.

everybody /ˈevrɪˌbɒdɪ/
(everyone) /ˈevrɪwʌn/ pronoun
each person or all the people
- **Everybody** was very kind to me after I had the accident.
- Susie said she knew **everyone** at the party, but I knew no one at all.

> **LANGUAGE NOTE**
>
> 1 **Everybody** and **everyone** take a singular verb.
>   NEVER   ~~Everybody are going.~~
>   ALWAYS Everybody is going.
>
> 2 **Everybody** and **everyone** can take a singular or plural pronoun.
>   EITHER Everyone's taking their lunch with them.
>   OR   Everyone's taking his/her lunch with him/her.
>
> 3 Note the difference between **everyone** and **every one**.
>   **Everyone** is very tired.
>   **Every one** of these children is tired.
>   **Every one** of the pens I bought was broken.

everything /ˈevrɪθɪŋ/ pronoun
each thing or all the things
- Alice liked **everything** she got for her birthday.

everywhere /ˈevrɪweə*/ pronoun
each place or all the places
- **Everywhere** Mr Low went in Hong Kong, he always met someone he knew.

exactly /ɪgˈzæktlɪ/ adverb
1 correctly, accurately
- Tell me **exactly** what happened.

> **LANGUAGE NOTE**
>
> 1 Use **exactly** with numbers
>   It's **exactly** 300 days since he left.
> 2 Use **exactly** with **what**, **which**, **when**, **where**, **who**, **how**, etc.
>   **Exactly** when did you leave?

2 just, quite, no more and no less
- $380 is **exactly** what I need for a new dress.

exam /ɪgˈzæm/
examination /ɪgˌzæmɪˈneɪʃn/ noun (countable)
1 an important test to find out how much you know about something
- The history **examination** was very easy, and everyone passed.
ஃ give/pass/fail/sit (for)/take an exam; a difficult/easy/entrance/final/oral/written exam
2 When a doctor gives you an **examination**, he looks at your body to see if you are healthy.
- Why don't you go to Dr Lee for an **examination** if your headaches continue?
ஃ a medical examination (= an examination by a doctor); a careful/a thorough examination

examine /ɪgˈzæmɪn/ verb
examining, examined, has examined
1 give someone an important test to find out how much they know about something

θ	ð	ʃ	dʒ	tʃ	ŋ	ʒ	iː	ɜː	ɪ	æ	ʌ	ɒ
thing	that	shop	jump	chop	sing	measure	been	bird	bit	cat	but	not

74 example

- Our new teacher is going to **examine** us on what we learnt in geography last term.
2 look closely or carefully at someone's body to see if they are healthy and well
- Dr Hill **examined** my chest when I told him about my cough.

example /ɪgˈzɑːmpl/ noun (countable)
1 something which shows a general idea, what something is like or how it works

- This picture is a good **example** of modern art.
2 **for example** = here is an example
- Sam is very lazy. **For example**, he stays in bed as long as he can every morning.

excited /ɪkˈsaɪtɪd/ adjective
happy and no longer calm (usually because something is going to happen)
- We were all very **excited** because Uncle Ben had promised to take us to Australia with him.

exciting /ɪkˈsaɪtɪŋ/ adjective
Something which is exciting makes you feel happy and no longer calm.
- The book was so **exciting** I couldn't put it down.

exclamation mark /ˌeksklə'meɪʃn ˌmɑːk/
noun (countable)
(American English: exclamation point)
This is an exclamation mark: !
- Class, be quiet at once!

excuse [1] /ɪkˈskjuːs/ noun (countable)
When you explain why you are wrong or late, you make an excuse.
- "What is your **excuse** this time for being late?" "I missed the bus."

give/find/look for/make (up)/think up an excuse;
a good/bad/poor/lame excuse

excuse [2] /ɪkˈskjuːz/ verb
excusing, excused, has excused
pardon or forgive
- Please **excuse** my terrible handwriting.
- **Excuse** me, but could you say that again?

LANGUAGE NOTE
You should say **Excuse me** BEFORE you do or say anything which you think may annoy or trouble someone.
You should say **Sorry** or **I beg your pardon** AFTER you do it.

exercise [1] /ˈeksəsaɪz/ noun (countable)
1 a piece of written work you do to help you learn something
- Have you finished the grammar **exercises**?
2 movements of your body to keep it strong and healthy
- Angela does **exercises** every morning.

exercise [2] verb
exercising, exercised, has exercised
move your body to keep it strong and healthy
- Angela **exercises** every morning before she gets dressed.

exit /ˈeksɪt/ noun (countable)
the way out of a public building
- The **exit** is that green door over there.

expect /ɪkˈspekt/ verb
believe something will happen
- Don't worry. I **expect** Rita will come soon.

expensive /ɪkˈspensɪv/ adjective
costing a lot of money
- Leila's ring was **expensive**. It cost $8,000!
- See also **dear** [1].

θ	ð	ʃ	dʒ	tʃ	ŋ	ʒ	iː	ɜː	ɪ	æ	ʌ	ɒ
thing	that	shop	jump	chop	sing	measure	been	bird	bit	cat	but	not

experiment /ɪkˈsperɪmənt/ noun (countable)
something you do to find out something or show that something is true
- *We did an interesting **experiment** to find out how much damage loud noises can cause.*

↻ do/carry out an experiment

explain /ɪkˈspleɪn/ verb
1 talk about something so that someone else can understand it
   - *Will you **explain** what this word means?*
2 talk about how something happens so that someone else can understand it
   - *Did Khaled **explain** how the accident happened?*

LANGUAGE NOTE	
NEVER	~~Please explain us how to do it.~~
ALWAYS	Please explain it ***to*** us.

explanation /ˌekspləˈneɪʃn/ noun (countable)
1 giving a reason for something
   - *Did he give an **explanation** for his behaviour?*
2 talking about how something happens so that someone else can understand it
   - *I didn't believe her **explanation** of how the accident happened.*

↻ ask for/look for/ give an explanation; a clear/good/satisfactory/simple/full/long explanation

extra¹ /ˈekstrə/ adjective
more than what is usual or necessary, etc
- *Don't forget to take an **extra** pair of socks.*

extra² adverb
more than usually
- *This is **extra** strong coffee.*

eye /aɪ/ noun (countable)
You see with your **eyes**.
- *As soon as May's baby brother went to bed, he closed his **eyes** and fell asleep.*

↻ close/shut/open/roll /rest your eyes; a black eye; good/sharp/poor eyes

⚠ See also box on page 25.

θ	ð	ʃ	dʒ	tʃ	ŋ	ʒ	iː	ɜː	ɪ	æ	ʌ	ɒ
thing	that	shop	jump	chop	sing	measure	been	bird	bit	cat	but	not

F f

face /feɪs/ verb
facing, faced, has faced
When you **face** something, you look towards it.
- *Our room in the hotel **faces** the sea.*

fact /fækt/ noun (countable)
something that is true
- *It is a **fact** that the world is round. You can't possibly argue about it.*

LANGUAGE NOTE

You can often use **the fact that** to begin a sentence.
The fact that he was so late made me angry.
If you feel you must tell someone something which is unpleasant but which is true, you can use **the fact is** to begin the sentence.
The fact is that your best friend has been lying to you for over a year.

☞ check your facts (= examine your facts), collect/gather facts, present the facts; the bare/basic/hard/plain/real facts

fact, in fact adverb phrase
truly, really (You can say **in fact** to remind someone that what you are saying is true.)
- *"Cindy, I thought you were in your bedroom." "No, I wasn't. **In fact**, I was in the bathroom."*

factory /ˈfæktərɪ/ noun (countable)
plural: factories
a building where people make things with machines

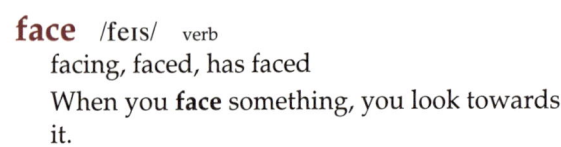

- *Jenny works in a clothes **factory**: she makes shirts and trousers.*
☞ open/close/shut down/manage/run a factory

Fahrenheit /ˈfærənhaɪt/ adjective, noun
a way of measuring temperature
- *Water freezes at 32° **Fahrenheit** and boils at 212° **Fahrenheit**.*
△ See also **Centigrade**

fail /feɪl/ verb
1 try to do something but be unable to do it
   - *I tried to run as fast as Ann but I **failed**.*
☞ fail badly/miserably
2 **fail (in) an exam** = not pass
   - *I **failed** maths but passed English.*

LANGUAGE NOTE

fail **to do** something = not do it at all
fail **in doing** something = do it but not well enough to be successful

fair /feə*/ adjective
1 light in colour, not dark
   - *Sheila's got **fair** hair: it isn't dark like mine.*
2 right and honest
   - *That's not **fair**! It's my turn!*
3 neither good nor bad
   - *Sheila's work was only **fair** because she didn't work hard enough.*

θ	ð	ʃ	dʒ	tʃ	ŋ	ʒ	iː	ɜː	ɪ	æ	ʌ	ɒ
thing	that	shop	jump	chop	sing	measure	been	bird	bit	cat	but	not

fairly /ˈfeəlɪ/ adverb
1 in a right and honest way
- *The new teacher marked all the students' compositions **fairly**.*
2 quite
- *Fatima's composition was **fairly** good, but yours was better.*

LANGUAGE NOTE

1 weak < -- >strong
   fairly good   quite good   rather good   very good
2 Do not use *fairly* when you compare people or things:
   NEVER   ~~fairly better than~~
   ALWAYS **rather** better than

---

fall¹ /fɔːl/ noun (countable)
1 a drop, a movement quickly downwards
- *Poor old Mrs Ene had a bad **fall** yesterday.*
- *There's been a sharp **fall** in the price of oil.*
- break/have/take a fall; a bad/nasty/big/sharp/serious/painful/sudden fall
2 (American English) autumn
- *Did you visit Japan in the **fall** of 1993?*

fall² verb
falling, fell /fel/, has fallen /ˈfɔːlən/
drop, move quickly downwards
- *I **fell** off my bike and hit my head.*

fall asleep /ˌfɔːl əˈsliːp/ noun (countable) verb phrase
falling asleep, fell asleep, has fallen asleep
go to sleep
- *Nadia **falls asleep** as soon as she goes to bed.*
⚠ See also **asleep**.

false /fɔːls/ adjective
1 not true
- *The thief gave the police a **false** name and address.*
2 not real
- *The lady sitting next to me laughed so much that her **false** teeth fell out!*

family /ˈfæməlɪ/ noun (countable)
plural: families
1 your parents, your brothers and sisters
- *The Lee **family** used to live next door.*
- a big/large/small/famous/happy family
2 You can also use **a family** to mean only children.
- *Mr and Mrs Gill want **a family** very much. They'd like a boy and a girl.*
3 your **family name** = your surname and the surname of your parents
- *Sue Hicks: Hicks is Sue's **family name**.*
⚠ See also **name**.

LANGUAGE NOTE

You can use a singular or plural verb after **family**. If you are thinking of the family as one group, use a singular verb.

Your family has come to see you.

If you are thinking of the family as different people in the group, use a plural verb.

My family are always quarrelling amongst themselves.

---

famous /ˈfeɪməs/ adjective
known by a lot of people
- *Elizabeth Taylor is a **famous** film star.*

fan /fæn/ noun (countable)
1 something we can use to move the air to keep cool

- *Turn the **fan** on if you're too hot.*

| θ | ð | ʃ | dʒ | tʃ | ŋ | ʒ | iː | ɜː | ɪ | æ | ʌ | ɒ |
| thing | that | shop | jump | chop | sing | measure | been | bird | bit | cat | but | not |

2 If you are a **fan** of someone, you like them very much.
- *My mother was a Beatles **fan** in her youth.*

☙ a great/keen fan

far /fɑː*/ adverb
farther, farthest; also further, furthest
1 a long way, not near
- *"Do you live **far** from Rome?"*
  "Yes, about two hundred kilometres."

LANGUAGE NOTE

Far is used mostly in questions and in sentences with ***not***. However, in ordinary sentences ***a long way*** is often used instead of ***far***.

   Have you travelled far?
   I'm not going far on my holidays.
BUT She lives **a long way** from school.
   (NOT far)

Note that you can use far after ***too***, ***so*** and ***as far as***.

   It's **too far** to walk.
   I agree with you **so far**.
   Tony gave Jill a lift **as far as** the bus stop.

2 **how far** = how many kilometres, etc away
- *"How **far** is it from here to the bus station?" "Not **far**, about fifty yards."*

fare /feə*/ noun (countable)
money which you pay to travel on a bus, a train or taxi
- *The **fare** from here to school is fifty cents.*

☙ pay your fare;
  full/half fare

farm /fɑːm/ noun (countable)
fields and buildings for keeping animals or growing plants, etc
- *Do you grow potatoes on your **farm**?*

LANGUAGE NOTE

live **in** a house BUT live/work **on** a farm

farmer /ˈfɑːmə*/ noun (countable)
a man who owns fields and buildings and keeps animals or grows plants there
- *Like all **farmers**, Mr Obasuyi works very hard.*

farther /ˈfɑːðə*/ adjective, adverb
far, farther, farthest
- *Our house is **farther** from town than yours.*

LANGUAGE NOTE

Don't use ***farther*** to mean ***extra*** or ***more***.
   Do you need any ***further*** information?
   (NEVER farther)

⚠ See also **far**; see also **further**.

farthest /ˈfɑːðɪst/ adjective, adverb
far, farther, farthest
- *Our house is the **farthest** of all the houses in the row.*
- *I live the **farthest** from school of all my friends.*

⚠ See also **far**; see also **furthest**.

fast¹ /fɑːst/ adjective
quick
- *"Have you already finished reading this book?" "Yes, I have. I'm a very **fast** reader."*

fast² adverb
faster, fastest
quickly
- *Run as **fast** as you can or you'll miss the bus.*

fasten /ˈfɑːsn/ verb
join together, close
- *Just a moment while I **fasten** my coat, please.*

fat /fæt/ adjective
fatter, fattest
round and heavy
- *You'll get very **fat** if you eat so much.*

⚠ See also **thick 1**; see also **thin 2**.

father /ˈfɑːðə*/ noun (countable)
a man who has a child or some children, the man who is one of someone's parents
- *Ken's **father** takes him to school every day.*

fault /fɔːlt/ noun (countable)
1 something wrong, a mistake
   - *There was a **fault** in the computer I bought, and so I took it back to the shop.*
2 **be someone's fault** = be something which they have done wrong
   - *I'm sorry. It's my **fault** we're late.*
↻ a bad/serious/slight fault

favourite /ˈfeɪvərɪt/ adjective
(American English: favorite)
the most liked
- *My **favourite** flower is the rose. I've always liked it more than any other flower.*

LANGUAGE NOTE

NEVER	Maths is my most favourite subject.
ALWAYS	Maths is *my favourite* subject.
OR	Maths is the subject **which I like best**.

---

fax¹ /fæks/ noun (countable)
a written message which is sent by phone
- *Did you get a **fax** from Mr Jones today?*

fax² verb
send a written message by phone
- *I'll **fax** Mr Musowake: it'll be cheaper than phoning or sending a letter.*

fear /fɪə*/ noun (uncountable)
being afraid of someone or something
- *A lot of people have a great **fear** of snakes but I like them.*

LANGUAGE NOTE

NEVER	I feel fear of them.
ALWAYS	I feel *afraid* of them.

↻ have a fear of, show your fear of; a deep/great/real/strong/hidden fear

feather /ˈfeðə*/ noun (countable)
the soft and light covering of a bird's body
- *Some birds have brightly coloured **feathers**.*

fed /fed/ verb
past tense and past participle of **feed**
- *I **fed** all the animals this morning.*

fee /fiː/ noun (countable)
1 money you pay to do something
   - *What is the **fee** to join the club?*
2 money which is paid for work, etc
   - *Dr Smith's **fees** are very high.*
↻ charge a fee; an entrance/membership fee

feed /fiːd/ verb
feeding, fed /fed/, has fed
give food to
- *Mr Gikas gets up early to **feed** the cows.*

feel /fiːl/ verb
feeling, felt /felt/, has felt
1 touch
   - ***Feel** the fruit to find out if it's fresh.*
2 find out what something is like when you touch it
   - *Your hands **feel** very cold.*

LANGUAGE NOTE

Don't use the continuous tense when you use *feel* with the second meaning above.

NEVER	The water was feeling very cold when I had a shower this morning.
ALWAYS	The water **felt** very cold when I had a shower this morning.

---

3 be
   - *We **felt** very happy when we won the prize.*

θ	ð	ʃ	dʒ	tʃ	ŋ	ʒ	iː	ɜː	ɪ	æ	ʌ	ɒ
thing	that	shop	jump	chop	sing	measure	been	bird	bit	cat	but	not

feet /fiːt/ noun (countable)
plural of **foot**
△ See **foot**.

fell /fel/ verb
past tense of **fall**
- I *fell* and hurt my foot because I didn't look where I was walking.

felt /felt/ verb
past tense and past participle of **feel**
- The blind boy *felt* my face before he spoke to me.

felt-tip (pen) /ˌfelt tɪp ˈpen/ noun (countable)
a pen with the end made of cloth (not metal)
- This picture was drawn with a *felt-tip (pen)*.
△ See also **ball-point (pen)**; see also **biro**.

female /ˈfiːmeɪl/ noun (countable), adjective
a girl, a woman, an animal that can have babies
- Was the thief a male or a *female*?
△ See also **male**.

fence /fens/ noun (countable)
wood or metal sticks in the ground around a garden or field

- The cows escaped from the field because the *fence* was broken.
↻ build/put up/mend a fence; a high/low fence

ferry /ˈferɪ/ noun (countable)
plural: ferries
a boat which carries people or things across water
- Several *ferries* cross the harbour daily.
↻ take a ferry, travel by ferry

fetch /fetʃ/ verb
go and bring back
- Could you please *fetch* me some chocolate?

fever /ˈfiːvə*/ noun (countable)
If you have a **fever**, you have a high temperature and you are ill.
- Last week I had a *fever*. I think it was flu.
↻ a high fever, a slight fever

few /fjuː/ adjective
1 **a few** = some, a small number of
   - There are *a few* oranges left. Can I have one?
2 **few** = not many
   - *Few* people came to the meeting: I counted only five!
△ See also **little 2**.

LANGUAGE NOTE

Use **few/a few** with things which you can count:
a few trees, a few people, few cars
Use **little/a little** with things which you cannot count:
a little water, a little noise, little traffic

COMPARE **few** children (= not many)
   little children (= small or young children)

---

field /fiːld/ noun (countable)
1 a piece of land on a farm where plants are grown or where animals are kept
   - There were cows in one *field* and vegetables in another *field*.
2 a piece of land where sports and games are played
   - I think the town needs a new football *field*.

fig /fɪg/ noun (countable)
△ See box on page 89.

fight¹ /faɪt/ noun (countable)
You have a fight when you use your hands or guns, etc against other people (usually to stop them doing something or as a sport).

θ	ð	ʃ	dʒ	tʃ	ŋ	ʒ	iː	ɜː	ɪ	æ	ʌ	ɒ
thing	that	shop	jump	chop	sing	measure	been	bird	bit	cat	but	not

- *Charlie Buster won the big **fight**.*
- end in/have/start/stop/win/lose a fight; a fight breaks out/starts; a big/brave/clean/fair/good/hard fight

fight ² verb
fighting, fought /fɔːt/, has fought

use your hands or guns, etc against other people (usually to stop them doing something)
- *The two countries **fought** against each other for five years before they made peace.*
- fight bravely, fight fairly/cleanly, fight hard

LANGUAGE NOTE

fight someone/something
fight **against / with** someone
fight **about / over** something
fight **for** something you like or believe in

NEVER   fight against a fire, etc
ALWAYS   fight a fire, fight a disease

---

figure /ˈfɪgə*/ noun (countable)
a number
- *1,2,3,4,5,6,7,8,9 and 10 are **figures** but A, B, C, D, E, F and G are letters.*

LANGUAGE NOTE

Figures are not usually used in compositions for small numbers.

six pupils, fifteen people, thirty days
BUT 87 pupils, 623 people, 5,184 days

---

fill /fɪl/ verb
1 put something in something else (eg a box, a pan, a bowl) so that there is no empty space
   - ***Fill** the bowl with water so I can wash.*
2 **fill in** = write
   - ***Fill in** your name and address on this form.*

film /fɪlm/ noun (countable)
1 the paper which you put into a camera to take photographs
   - *I must buy a new **film** for my camera.*
2 moving pictures which you can see on television or at the cinema (American English: movie)
   - *I'm going to the Odeon tonight to see "Superman 10." I hear it's a very good **film**.*
- make/see/watch/ show a film; a film star
- See also **star 3**.

find /faɪnd/ verb
finding, found /faʊnd/, has found
1 see or learn something either by looking for it or by chance, discover
   - *I **found** my pen in your room!*
2 **find out** = learn
   - *Can you **find out** how many people came?*

fine ¹ /faɪn/ noun (countable)
an amount of money which you have to pay because you have done something wrong
- *Mr Mawani had to pay a **fine** of $500 because he parked his car outside the post office.*
- pay a fine; a big/small fine, a heavy fine (= a very big fine)

fine ² adjective
1 very good
   - *You have a **fine** view of the sea from here.*
2 dry, not raining
   - *Do you think it'll be **fine** tomorrow?*

fine ³ adverb
very well
   - *"How do you feel?" "I feel **fine**, thanks."*

θ	ð	ʃ	dʒ	tʃ	ŋ	ʒ	iː	ɜː	ɪ	æ	ʌ	ɒ
thing	that	shop	jump	chop	sing	measure	been	bird	bit	cat	but	not

> **LANGUAGE NOTE**
>
> When it is used with this meaning, **fine** is usually used on its own and NOT with an adverb (apart from the adverb **absolutely**).
>
> NEVER ~~I'm very fine.~~
> ALWAYS I'm **fine**.

finger /ˈfɪŋə*/ noun (countable)
You have fingers on your hand.
- Sarka had a ring on her wedding **finger**.

> **LANGUAGE NOTE**
>
> You can talk about your five fingers to mean your four fingers and your thumb.
> BUT you should never use the word **finger** in the singular to mean a **thumb**.

↻ your little finger, your middle finger

⚠ See also box on page 25.

finish /ˈfɪnɪʃ/ verb
finishes, finishing, finished, has finished
1 end, not continue any longer
- School **finishes** at half-past three every day.
2 bring to an end
- I can **finish** my homework in an hour.

fire /faɪə*/ noun (countable)
1 flames and heat when something is burning
- I'm going to light a **fire** to keep warm.
↻ build/make/light/start/put out a fire; a fire breaks out/burns/dies down/spreads; a big/small/dangerous/roaring fire
2 **on fire** = burning
- The pan's **on fire**! Put a wet towel over it!

fire alarm /ˈfaɪər əˌlɑːm/ noun (countable)
a bell which rings if there is a fire
- We got out when we heard the **fire alarm**.
↻ a fire alarm goes off/rings/sounds

fire brigade /ˈfaɪə brɪˌɡeɪd/ noun (countable)
(American English: fire department)
a group of people who put out fires
- The **fire brigade** arrived at the burning building in three minutes.

fire engine /ˈfaɪər ˌendʒɪn/ noun (countable)
a kind of lorry which is used to take firemen and their things to a fire
- Two **fire engines** arrived at the burning building.

fireman /ˈfaɪəmən/ noun (countable)
plural: firemen
someone who puts out fires
- Two **firemen** rescued the old woman from the fire.

fish[1] /fɪʃ/ noun (countable, uncountable)
plural: fish or fishes
an animal which lives and swims in water and which you can eat

- I caught six large **fish**.
- I prefer **fish** to meat, don't you?
↻ catch a fish; fish swim

> **LANGUAGE NOTE**
>
> 1 catch a **fish** (= an animal living in the water)
>   BUT
>   eat **fish** (= food which is the body of the animal)
> 2 The plural **fishes** is not often used now. Use it only to talk about **the different kinds of fish**.

θ	ð	ʃ	dʒ	tʃ	ŋ	ʒ	iː	ɜː	ɪ	æ	ʌ	ɒ
thing	that	shop	jump	chop	sing	measure	been	bird	bit	cat	but	not

fish [2] verb
try to catch a fish
- *Adam wants to **fish** under the bridge today.*

fisherman /ˈfɪʃəmən/ noun (countable)
plural: fishermen
someone who tries to catch fish (as a job or for sport)
- *Peter's uncle is a **fisherman** and often spends several days at sea.*

fit [1] /fɪt/ verb
fitting, fitted, has fitted
1. be the right size
   - *These shoes don't **fit**: they are too big.*
2. find room for
   - *Maria can't **fit** any more clothes in her case.*

fit [2] adjective
fitter, fittest
1. well or healthy
   - *I hear you've been ill. Do you feel **fit** now?*
   ↻ feel fit, keep fit
2. good enough
   - *The flat was so dirty it wasn't **fit** to live in.*

fix /fɪks/ verb
1. put or fasten something so that it will not move
   - *Geeta asked Ramesh to **fix** the fence.*
2. make something work again, repair
   - *Could you **fix** my radio? It keeps going off.*

flag /flæg/ noun (countable)
a piece of cloth with the colours of a certain country
- ***Flags** were flying from many buildings when the President arrived.*
↻ fly/hang out/raise/wave a flag

flame /fleɪm/ noun (countable)
part of a fire
- *A candle burns with a single **flame**.*
↻ a flame burns, burst into flame

flat [1] /flæt/ noun (countable)
American English: apartment
a group of rooms in a large building
- *Our **flat** is on the top floor of this building.*
↻ block of flats (American English: apartment house)

flat [2] adjective
flatter, flattest
smooth, level
- *Is there anything **flat** to write this letter on?*

flew /fluː/ verb
past tense of **fly**
- *An aeroplane **flew** above us as we were talking.*

flies [1] /flaɪz/ noun (countable)
plural of **fly**
- ***Flies** are a problem in hot weather.*

flies [2] /flaɪz/ verb
present tense (with he, she, it) of **fly**
- *Mr Lee **flies** to New York every month.*

flight /flaɪt/ noun (countable)
a journey in the air, usually in an aeroplane
- *Farid is taking the early **flight** to Paris.*
↻ be on/book/take a flight;
a direct /nonstop/rough/smooth flight;
a space flight, a test flight

float /fləʊt/ verb
stay on top of water
- *My hat **floated** down the river.*

flood [1] /flʌd/ noun (countable)
a large amount of water covering a piece of land which is usually dry
- *Mr and Mrs Ito lost everything in the **flood**.*

flood [2] verb
cover with a large amount of water
- *The river has risen and **flooded** the fields.*

θ	ð	ʃ	dʒ	tʃ	ŋ	ʒ	iː	ɜː	ɪ	æ	ʌ	ɒ
thing	that	shop	jump	chop	sing	measure	been	bird	bit	cat	but	not

floor /flɔː*/ noun (countable)
1 part of a room you can walk on
  • *There were no chairs so Ann sat on the **floor**.*
2 all the rooms or flats on the same level in a building
  • *I live on the tenth **floor** of a block of flats.*

LANGUAGE NOTE

1	floor	=	*inside* a building
	ground	=	*outside* a building

2 NEVER   We live in the fourth floor.
  ALWAYS We live **on** the fourth floor.

flour /flaʊə*/ noun (uncountable)
fine white or brown powder which is used to make bread and cakes
  • *Helen is buying some **flour** for her mother.*

flow /fləʊ/ verb
move along without stopping (especially used with air and water)
  • *Where does this river **flow** into the sea?*
  • *The crowd **flowed** out of the football ground as soon as the game had finished.*

flower /ˈflaʊə*/ noun (countable)
the coloured or white parts which usually grow at the top of a plant

  • *Elisa's favourite **flower** is a rose.*
  ↻ grow / plant / pick flowers

flown /fləʊn/ verb
past participle of **fly**
  • *Two of the birds have **flown** out of the cage.*

LANGUAGE NOTE

flowed = past tense of **flow**
    *The river **flowed** very quickly.*
flew = past tense of **fly**
    *The bird **flew** away.*
flown = past participle of **fly**
    *I've never **flown** from here to Madrid before.*

flu /fluː/ noun (uncountable)
short for influenza
fever, sickness
  • *Poor Dave has **flu** and is staying in bed today.*

fly¹ /flaɪ/ verb
flying, flew /fluː/, has flown /fləʊn/
move in the air (not on the ground)
  • *Jonathan's learning to **fly** a small plane.*

fly² noun (countable)
plural: flies
⚠ See box on page 114.

flyover /ˈflaɪəʊvə*/ noun (countable)
a road which runs above other roads and buildings
  • *Turn left down this road and take the **flyover** to Newtown.*

fold /fəʊld/ verb
bend something so that one part is on top of the other
  • *Tina **folded** the towels neatly before she put them in the drawer.*

follow /ˈfɒləʊ/ verb
1 go after someone or something
  • *Oswald **followed** me home yesterday.*
2 do what someone says
  • *I'll **follow** your instructions very carefully.*
  ↻ follow blindly (= following without thinking), follow closely
3 understand what someone says
  • *"Do you **follow** me?" "Yes, I understand."*

θ	ð	ʃ	dʒ	tʃ	ŋ	ʒ	iː	ɜː	ɪ	æ	ʌ	ɒ
thing	that	shop	jump	chop	sing	measure	been	bird	bit	cat	but	not

food /fuːd/ noun (uncountable)
everything people and animals eat
- *Do you like Chinese food?*
- cook/prepare food; frozen/fresh/tasty food, health food (= special food which is good for your health), healthy food (= ordinary food which is good for your health - not special food), fast food (= food which is quickly prepared to eat at once or take home)

foolish /ˈfuːlɪʃ/ adjective
silly, stupid
- *The foolish man spent all his money.*

foolishly /ˈfuːlɪʃlɪ/ adverb
in a silly way, without thinking carefully
- *He foolishly crossed the road without looking.*

foot /fʊt/ noun (countable)
plural: feet
1 part of your body on which you walk and stand (at the end of your leg)
- *Mabel hurt her foot and couldn't walk.*
See also box on page 26.

LANGUAGE NOTE
go by car, go by bus, go by train, etc
BUT go **on** foot

2 You can use the words **foot** and **feet** when you measure something:
1 foot = .305 metres.

LANGUAGE NOTE
When you are using the words *foot* and *feet* to measure something, you can say:

EITHER She's almost six foot tall.
OR She's almost six feet tall.

But you should use only *foot* in the following phrases:
She climbed a **six-foot** wall.
That's a **ten-foot** stick.

3 the lowest point of something (singular only)
- *We rested at the foot of the mountains.*

football /ˈfʊtbɔːl/ noun
1 (uncountable) a game which you play by kicking a ball
- *Do you like playing football?*
2 (countable) a large ball filled with air and used for playing football
- *Have you brought a football with you?*

LANGUAGE NOTE
1 a football match BUT *a game* of football
American English only: *a football game*
2 American football = a special type of football game/match

- play football

footpath /ˈfʊtpɑːθ/ noun (countable)
a narrow way for people to walk on
- *There was a small footpath through the wood.*

for /fɔː*/ (unstressed /fə*/) preposition
1 You can use **for** to show the person you are giving something to.
- *Susie bought a pen for her sister.*
2 You can use **for** to show what something is used to do.
- *We use a knife for cutting things.*

LANGUAGE NOTE
NEVER	~~We're going to a restaurant for having a Chinese meal.~~
ALWAYS	We're going to the restaurant for a Chinese meal.
OR	We're going to the restaurant to have a Chinese meal.

3 You can use **for** to show you are doing something as part of your school, your club, your town, your country, etc.
- *Are you playing hockey for the college?*
4 You can use **for** to show how long.
- *Adam talked for three hours without stopping.*

LANGUAGE NOTE

Use either the Present Perfect tense or the Present Continuous tense before **for** in sentences like the following.
I **have studied** English for five years.
I **have been studying** English for five years.
(NEVER ~~I am studying English for five years.~~)

5 You can use **for** to show how far.
   • *We walked **for** twelve kilometres yesterday.*
6 You can use **for** to show how much something is.
   • *"How much are these apples?" "Three **for** $10."*
7 You can use **for** to show why someone is going somewhere.
   • *Let's go out **for** a meal tonight.*
8 You can use **for** to mean **because of**.
   • *I got a prize **for** being top of my class.*
9 You can use **for** to show one thing in place of another.
   • *I'll give you a pen **for** this stamp.*
10 You can use **for** after several adjectives like **easy**, **difficult**, **good**, etc.
   • *This kind of food is good **for** you.*

forest /ˈfɒrɪst/ noun (countable)
a large piece of land where trees grow close together
• *It is important to stop cutting down **forests**.*
↻ a thick forest

forget /fəˈget/ verb
forgetting, forgot /fəˈgɒt/ ,
has forgotten /fəˈgɒtn/
not remember, not be able to think of something
• *What's she called? I've **forgotten** her name.*

LANGUAGE NOTE

I forgot to do it. = I didn't do it.
I forgot about doing it. = EITHER I didn't do it.
                          OR   I can't remember doing it.

forgive /fəˈgɪv/ verb
forgiving, forgave /fəˈgeɪv/ ,
has forgiven /fəˈgɪvn/
stop being angry with someone
• *He could never **forgive** the bus driver for causing the accident.*

fork /fɔːk/ noun (countable)
something you use to eat with

• *Put your **fork** down and use a spoon.*

form[1] /fɔːm/ noun (countable)
1 a printed piece of paper with spaces for you to fill in
   • *Fill this **form** in if you want to join the club.*
   ↻ fill a form in, fill a form out (especially in American English)
2 kind
   • *Cycling and swimming are **forms** of exercise.*
3 class at school or college
   • *Tom is in **Form** 4 at New College.*

form[2] verb
start to be, start to make
• *Clouds were **forming** in the sky.*
• *Let's **form** a music club.*

fortnight /ˈfɔːtnaɪt/ noun (countable)
two weeks
• *We're going on holiday for a **fortnight**.*

fortunate /ˈfɔːtʃənət/ adjective
lucky
• *We were very **fortunate** not to be killed in the accident.*

θ	ð	ʃ	dʒ	tʃ	ŋ	ʒ	iː	ɜː	ɪ	æ	ʌ	ɒ
thing	that	shop	jump	chop	sing	measure	been	bird	bit	cat	but	not

fortunately /ˈfɔːtʃənətlɪ/ adverb
luckily
- *Fortunately no one was killed in the accident.*

forward /ˈfɔːwəd/ , **forwards** /ˈfɔːwədz/
adjective, adverb
in front, towards the front
- *The crowd made a forward movement.*
- *Who moved forwards?*

fought /fɔːt/ verb
past tense and past participle of **fight**
- *The old man had fought in two wars.*

found /faʊnd/ verb
past tense and past participle of **find**
- *Who found the money?*

fountain /ˈfaʊntɪn/ noun (countable)
water which goes up into the air and falls down again
- *The garden was full of small fountains.*

fox /fɒks/ noun (countable)
plural: foxes
⚠ See box on page 10.

free /friː/ adjective
freer, freest
1 If you are **free**, you can do or go where you want.
   - *I'll be free to go with you when I finish.*
   ✥ set/turn someone free (= make someone free from prison etc)
2 not costing any money
   - *A lot of poor people were given a free meal after the concert.*
   ✥ free of charge

freeze /friːz/ verb
freezing, froze /frəʊz/, has frozen /ˈfrəʊzn/
When it freezes, it is so cold that water turns into ice.
- *The cold weather will freeze the lake.*

fresh /freʃ/ adjective
1 not old, newly made
   - *Fresh bread is much better than old bread.*
2 clean
   - *Let's go to the countryside and get some fresh air.*

fridge /frɪdʒ/ noun (countable)
short for refrigerator
a cupboard or box for keeping food cold
- *Put the milk in the fridge, please.*

fried /fraɪd/ verb
past tense and past participle of **fry**
- *Who fried this rice?*

friend /frend/ noun (countable)
someone you know well and spend time with
- *I always go to the beach with my friends on Saturdays.*
✥ make/win friends; a good/old/new/close/false/true friend

friendly /ˈfrendlɪ/ adjective
friendlier or more friendly, friendliest or most friendly
If you are friendly to someone, you act in a kind and pleasant way to them.
- *Mr Lim was always very friendly to children and used to give them apples and sweets.*

LANGUAGE NOTE

friendly **to / towards** someone
= treat in a kind way, act as a friend to
friendly **with** someone
= be friends with, have as a friend

---

frighten /ˈfraɪtn/ verb
make (someone) feel afraid
- *Don't shout! You'll frighten the baby.*

frog /frɒg/ noun (countable)
⚠ See box on page 10.

from /frɒm/ (unstressed /frəm/) preposition
1 You can use **from** to show the place where someone or something starts.
   • Mrs Wilson travelled **from** Cairo to Dubai.
2 You can use **from** to show the time when someone or something starts.
   • Lunch is **from** twelve to half-past one.

LANGUAGE NOTE	
NEVER	We've lived here from 1992.
ALWAYS	We've lived here **since** 1992.

3 You can use **from** to show how far away someone or something is.
   • The main post office is two miles **from** here.
4 You can use **from** to show who gave or sent something.
   • Did you get a present **from** your sister?
5 You can use **from** after words like **away** and **absent**.
   • Why were you absent **from** school?
↻ different/far/free/safe from

front¹ /frʌnt/ noun (countable, usually singular)
something which faces forward
   • The **front** of the car has been damaged.

front² preposition
the first or main place, facing forward
   • Dave sat on the **front** row.
   in front of = further forwards than
   • Ken was sitting **in front of** Ahmed.

LANGUAGE NOTE	
NEVER	Our hotel room is in front of the sea.
ALWAYS	Our hotel room **is facing** / **faces** the sea.

froze /frəʊz/ verb
past tense of **freeze**
   • The lake **froze** and so we were able to walk across it.

frozen /ˈfrəʊzn/ verb
past participle of **freeze**
   • The milk has **frozen**: I can't pour it out of the bottle.
   • It's so cold that I'm **frozen**. (= I feel very cold.)

fruit /fruːt/ noun (countable, uncountable)
plural: fruit or fruits
part of a plant which you can eat
   • Oranges are my favourite **fruit**.
   • Is a tomato a vegetable or a **fruit**?

LANGUAGE NOTE
The plural **fruits** is not often used now. Use it only to talk about **the different kinds of fruit**; apples, oranges, mangoes, etc

↻ canned fruit (American English), tinned fruit (British English) (= fruit in tins), dried/fresh/frozen/ripe fruit (= fruit ready to eat)
⚠ See box opposite.

fry /fraɪ/ verb
frying, fried, has fried
cook in hot oil
   • Ted's **frying** some fish and chips for you.

full /fʊl/ adjective
not empty, no space left
   • We couldn't all get on the bus because it was **full**.

LANGUAGE NOTE
be full **of** something   NEVER be full with something
COMPARE   The car is full of petrol.
The car has been filled with petrol.

full stop /ˌfʊl ˈstɒp/ noun (countable)
(American English: period)
This is a full stop .
   • You should use a **full stop** at the end of a sentence.

θ	ð	ʃ	dʒ	tʃ	ŋ	ʒ	iː	ɜː	ɪ	æ	ʌ	ɒ
thing	that	shop	jump	chop	sing	measure	been	bird	bit	cat	but	not

Fruit

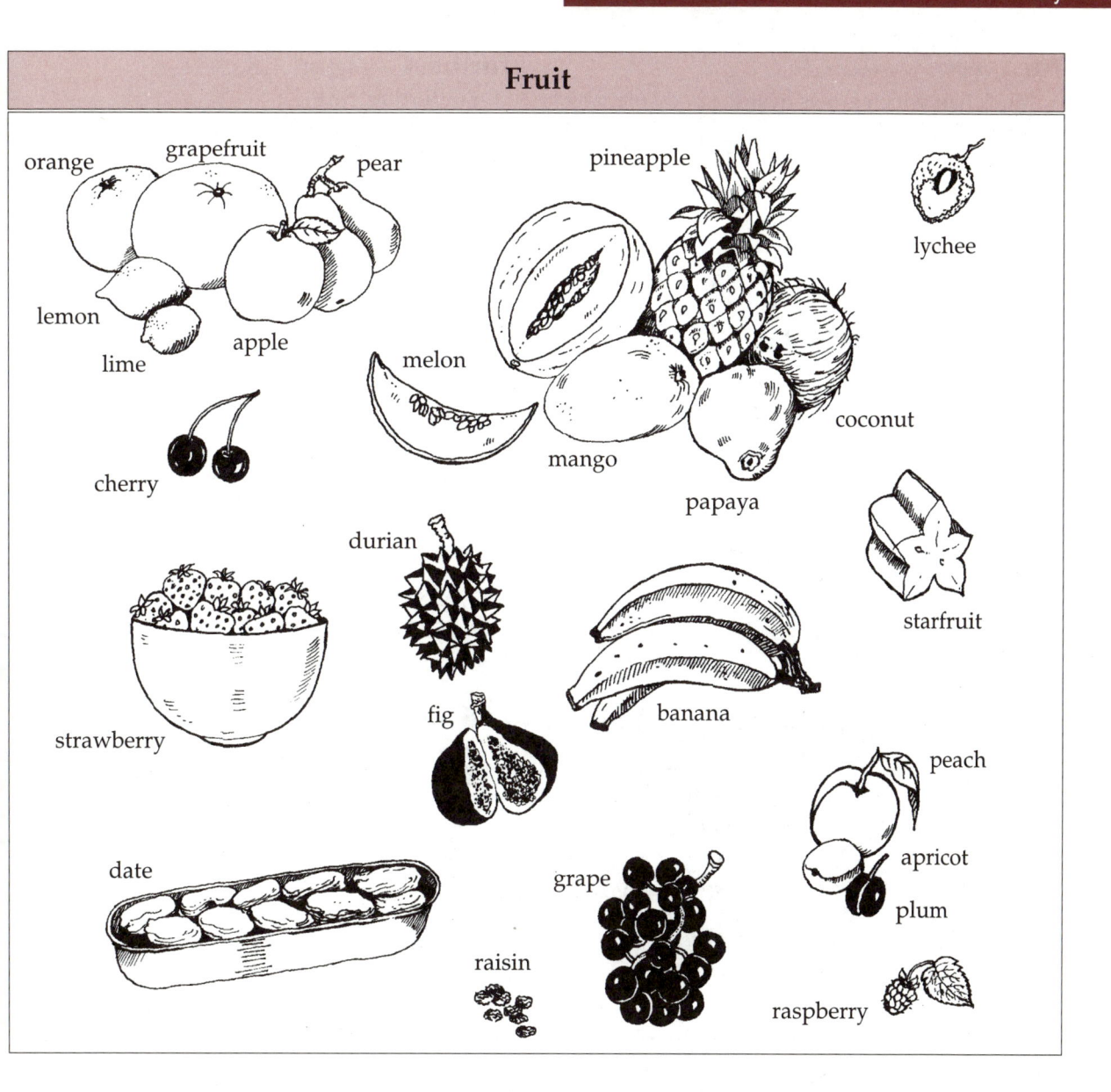

orange, grapefruit, pear, pineapple, lychee, lemon, apple, lime, melon, mango, papaya, coconut, cherry, durian, starfruit, strawberry, fig, banana, peach, apricot, plum, date, grape, raisin, raspberry

fun /fʌn/ noun (uncountable)
1 something which we enjoy or which makes us laugh
 • Going to watch a football match is **fun**, isn't it?
  have fun
2 **make fun of** = laugh about (someone)
 • Harry was sorry that he'd **made fun of** Betty.

LANGUAGE NOTE	
NEVER	Listening to pop music is a good fun.
ALWAYS	Listening to pop music is **good** fun.

funny /ˈfʌnɪ/ adjective
funnier, funniest
When you say or do something which is funny, it makes you laugh or smile.

fur /fɜː*/ noun (uncountable)
thick hair which grows over the body of many animals

- It's nice to touch the cat's soft **fur**.

furniture /ˈfɜːnɪtʃə*/ noun (uncountable)
chairs, tables, cupboards, beds, etc
- You've put too much **furniture** in this small room.
- garden/office/modern/old/secondhand furniture

LANGUAGE NOTE

1 NEVER ~~There were a lot of furnitures.~~
  ALWAYS There was a lot of **furniture**.

2 NEVER ~~I bought a nice furniture.~~
  ALWAYS I bought **a nice piece of furniture**.
  OR   I bought **a nice chair**, etc.

further /ˈfɜːðə*/ adjective, adverb
far, further, furthest
- Have you anything **further** to say?
- Leila walked **further** than anyone else.
- See also **far**; see also **farther**.

LANGUAGE NOTE

Do not use **farther** to mean **extra** or **more**.
NEVER ~~Do you need any farther information?~~
ALWAYS Do you need any **further** information?

furthest /ˈfɜːðɪst/ adjective, adverb
far, further, furthest
- Everyone walked a long way, but Tom and Rita walked the **furthest**.
- See also **far**; see also **farthest**.

future /ˈfjuːtʃə*/ noun (singular with *the*)
tomorrow, next week, etc or what will happen tomorrow, next week, etc
- It may be possible for people to live on the moon in the **future**.

LANGUAGE NOTE

In future (= **from now on**) is often used in warning people.
   Don't ever come late again. **In future**, make sure you arrive on time.

- face/look into/plan for the future; a bright/great/promising/rosy future; the immediate/near/distant future

Gg

game /geɪm/ noun (countable)

something we play. For example, some people play football, others play hockey and others tennis.
- *Dave Hill is good at **games**.*

LANGUAGE NOTE

Basketball is my favourite ***game***.
BUT ***Swimming*** is my favourite ***sport***.
Games = football, hockey, tennis, cricket, golf, table tennis, badminton
Sports = swimming, running, jumping, etc

☞ have/play/win/loose a game; a close/exciting/friendly/good/important/quick game (= a short game)
⚠ See also **match 2**; see also **sport**.

gaol /ˈdʒeɪl/ noun (countable)
⚠ See **jail**.

garage /ˈgæraːʒ/ noun (countable)
1 a building where cars are kept
   - *Leave your car in my **garage** when you go.*
2 a building where cars are repaired or sold
   - *My car won't start. I'll have to take it to the **garage**.*

garden /ˈgɑːdn/ noun (countable)
a piece of land (often around a house) often used for growing flowers and vegetables
- *Mr Low is cutting the grass in his **garden**.*

garlic /ˈgɑːlɪk/ noun (countable)
⚠ See box on page 238.

gas /gæs/ noun
plural: gases
1 (countable) something like air
   - *Oxygen and hydrogen are **gases**.*
2 (uncountable) something which is used for heating or cooking
   - *Mrs Mawani uses **gas** to cook with.*
☞ light the gas, turn the gas off/on
3 (American English)
⚠ See **petrol**.

gate /geɪt/ noun (countable)
1 like a door but used at the entrance to a garden or field
   - *Please close the **gate** behind you.*
2 an exit in an airport through which people pass on their way to go on board an aeroplane
   - *Passengers for Air India flight 206 should go to **gate** 5.*

gave /geɪv/ verb
past tense of **give**
- *Oswald **gave** Ann a new camera.*

general /ˈdʒenərəl/ adjective
1 as a whole
   - *Can you give the police a **general** idea of what the man looked like?*
2 of all, for most people
   - *There was a **general** feeling that the war would soon end.*

generous /ˈdʒenərəs/ adjective
kind, pleased to help
- *It was very **generous** of you to give me $100.*

gentle /ˈdʒentl/ adjective
gentler or more gentle, gentlest or most gentle
soft, not rough, kind
- *Maria is a very **gentle** person who likes to look after old people.*

gentleman /ˈdʒentlmən/ noun (countable)
plural: gentlemen
You can use **gentleman** as a polite word for man.
- *Ladies and **gentlemen**, I'm very pleased to talk to you tonight.*

θ	ð	ʃ	dʒ	tʃ	ŋ	ʒ	iː	ɜː	ɪ	æ	ʌ	ɒ
thing	that	shop	jump	chop	sing	measure	been	bird	bit	cat	but	not

get /get/ verb

getting, got /gɒt/, has got
(American English: has gotten /'gɒtn/)
1 become
- *Did you **get** wet when it rained?*
2 receive, be given
- *What did you **get** for your birthday?*
3 buy
- *Mr Simpson's **getting** a new car soon.*
4 fetch, bring
- *Could you **get** me a glass of water, please?*
5 arrive
- *We'll **get** there in half an hour.*
6 make, cause
- *Can't you **get** the door open?*
7 have
- *Poor Tom's **got** flu.*
8 catch
- *Are we in time to **get** the nine o'clock train?*

get along with /ˌget əˈlɒŋ wɪð/ phrasal verb

getting along with, got along with, has got along with
agree with, manage to live or work with
- *It is hard to **get along with** Tracy.*

get back /ˌget ˈbæk/ phrasal verb

getting back, got back, has got back
1 return
- *I **got back** from my holidays yesterday.*
2 obtain again
- *I hope you **get** your book **back** from Dave.*

get down /ˌget ˈdaʊn/ phrasal verb

getting down, got down, has got down
1 come down
- *Don't sit on that wall. **Get down** at once.*
2 write
- *Did you **get down** everything he said?*

get in /ˌget ˈɪn/ phrasal verb

getting in, got in, has got in
enter
- *The two men **got in** by a small window.*

get off /ˌget ˈɒf/ phrasal verb

getting off, got off, has got off
1 leave
- *We **get off** (the bus) at the next stop.*
2 take off
- *These shoes are so tight I can't **get** them **off**!*

get on /ˌget ˈɒn/ phrasal verb

getting on, got on, has got on
1 go on or inside (a bus, etc)
- *Is this bus full or can we all **get on** (it)?*
2 dress, put on
- ***Get** your coat **on** and come with me.*
3 be successful, enjoy life, manage to do things
- *How's Ali **getting on**? Is he doing well in his job?*

get on with /ˌget ˈɒn wɪð/ phrasal verb

getting on with, got on with, has got on with
1 continue
- ***Get on with** your work and stop talking.*
2 agree with, manage to live or work with
- *Do you think Dave **gets on with** Ken?*

get up /ˌget ˈʌp/ phrasal verb

getting up, got up, has got up
1 get out of bed
- *What time do you **get up** every morning?*
2 rise, stand
- *John **got up** when the visitors came in.*

ginger /ˈdʒɪndʒə*/ noun (countable)

See box on page 238.

giraffe /dʒɪˈrɑːf/ noun (countable)

See box on page 10.

girl /gɜːl/ noun (countable)

a child but not a boy (A girl later becomes a woman.)
- *Look at the picture of the two **girls**. They're standing near their mother and father.*

θ	ð	ʃ	dʒ	tʃ	ŋ	ʒ	iː	ɜː	ɪ	æ	ʌ	ɒ
thing	that	shop	jump	chop	sing	measure	been	bird	bit	cat	but	not

give /gɪv/   verb

giving, gave /geɪv/, has given/ 'gɪvn/
1 let someone have or hold
   - Please **give** me your attention.
2 bring or send something as a present
   - He **gave** me a new watch for my birthday.

LANGUAGE NOTE	
EITHER	give someone something
OR	give something to someone

3 allow someone to have
   - **Give** me a few minutes to solve the problem.
4 cause someone to have
   - You **gave** me a surprise.
5 We also use **give** in front of words like **smile**, **shout**, **cry**, etc
   - He **gave** Tina a smile as he passed her.
6 pay
   - Mrs Wilson **gave** $15,000 for the car.

give back /ˌgɪv 'bæk/   phrasal verb

giving back, gave back, has given back
return (something to its owner)
   - Have you **given** Sheila her book **back**?

give in /ˌgɪv 'ɪn/   phrasal verb

giving in, gave in, has given in
bring (to someone)
   - All the pupils have **given in** their homework.

give out /ˌgɪv 'aʊt/   phrasal verb

giving out, gave out, has given out
give (to each of several people)
   - He helped the teacher to **give out** the books.

glad /glæd/   adjective

happy
   - I'm **glad** so many of my friends have passed the test.

LANGUAGE NOTE
glad **about** something
glad **to do** something
glad **that** something will happen

glass /glɑːs/   noun

plural: glasses
1 (countable) something for drinking out of
   - Could I have a **glass** of water, please?
   ⚐ have/drink a glass of something
2 (uncountable) You can see through glass. Windows are made from glass.
   - It's hard to see out of these windows. The **glass** is very dirty.

glasses /'glɑːsɪz/   noun (plural)

You wear glasses to help you to see better.

- Old people often need **glasses**.

LANGUAGE NOTE	
NEVER	I've lost my new **glass**.
ALWAYS	I've lost my new **glasses**.
OR	I've lost my new **pair of glasses**.

⚐ dark/sun/reading glasses

glue /gluː/   noun (uncountable)

You can use glue to join things together.
   - Use some **glue** to stick the pieces of paper together.

go /gəʊ/   verb

goes, going, went /went/, has gone /gɒn/
1 move, travel
   - We're **going** to Japan tomorrow.

θ	ð	ʃ	dʒ	tʃ	ŋ	ʒ	iː	ɜː	ɪ	æ	ʌ	ɒ
thing	that	shop	jump	chop	sing	measure	been	bird	bit	cat	but	not

2　do (something)
- Are you **going** swimming today?

LANGUAGE NOTE	
NEVER	He's gone to swim today.
ALWAYS	He's gone **swimming** today.

↻ go climbing/cycling/dancing/fishing/sailing /shopping/skiing/swimming/walking

3　become
- Mr Robinson's hair is **going** grey.

LANGUAGE NOTE	
ALWAYS	go blind, go deaf, go grey, go mad
NEVER	go ill, go tired
ALWAYS	grow tired, become ill, become tired

4　work
- My watch has stopped. It won't **go**.
5　lead
- This road **goes** to London.
6　attend
- Do you **go** to school?

go off /ˌgəʊ ˈɒf/　phrasal verb
goes off, going off, went off, has gone off
stop working
- The lights suddenly **went off**.

go on /ˌgəʊ ˈɒn/　phrasal verb
goes on, going on, went on, has gone on
1　pass, continue
- The concert **went on** until midnight.
2　happen
- What's **going on**?
3　start working
- The lights suddenly **went on** again.

go out /ˌgəʊ ˈaʊt/　phrasal verb
goes out, going out, went out, has gone out
1　leave a house or other building
- We're **going out** for dinner. Can you look after the children?
2　spend time with someone of the opposite sex
- I've been **going out** with William for a year.
3　stop burning, stop shining
- Has the fire **gone out**?

go with /ˈgəʊ wɪð/　phrasal verb
goes with, going with, went with, has gone with
look good with
- Your red tie doesn't **go with** your yellow shirt.

goal /gəʊl/　noun (countable)
1　the space between two posts which football players must aim at
- The ball went into the **goal**.
2　a point in a football or hockey match
- Our team won by three **goals** to two.
↻ kick/score a goal

goat /gəʊt/　noun (countable)
⚠ See box on page 10.

LANGUAGE NOTE
When you are talking about **a goat** as a living animal, use a. 　Oh dear! There's a goat eating your hat. When you are talking about **goat** as a food on a dish, you should not use **a** before it. 　Do they eat goat?

God /gɒd/　noun (proper, also countable)
the maker of the world
- Alice thanked **God** for giving her a happy life.

LANGUAGE NOTE
Note the use of the capital letter. COMPARE　Christians worship **God**. 　　　　　Some Chinese and Indian people worship many **gods**.

θ	ð	ʃ	dʒ	tʃ	ŋ	ʒ	iː	ɜː	ɪ	æ	ʌ	ɒ
thing	that	shop	jump	chop	sing	measure	been	bird	bit	cat	but	not

☪ believe in God, praise God
△ See also **Allah**.

going to /ˈɡəʊɪŋ tuː/ verb phrase
be going to = will
- Are you **going to** meet Leila tonight?

gold[1] /ɡəʊld/ noun
a yellow metal which is worth a lot of money
- Did they find **gold** in this part of Australia?

gold[2] adjective
1 made of a valuable yellow metal
- Stefan gave Maria a **gold** ring.
2 yellow (and shining)
- Use some **gold** paint.

golf /ɡɒlf/ noun (uncountable)
Golf is a game in which you hit a small hard ball with a long stick (called a **club**). You have to hit the ball into a small hole in the ground.
- Would you like a game of **golf** this afternoon?

gone /ɡɒn/ verb
past participle of **go**
- Where's Ted **gone**? I can't seen him now.

LANGUAGE NOTE

COMPARE Sarah's **gone** to Hong Kong.
(= She went to Hong Kong and she is still there.)

Sarah's **been** to Hong Kong.
(= She went to Hong Kong and she has already come back.)

△ See also **been**[2].

good /ɡʊd/ adjective
better /ˈbetə*/, best
1 enjoyable, interesting
- We all had a **good** time at Anna's party.

2 nice, kind
- Ramon's a very **good** man and helps everyone he meets.
3 When you are good at (doing) something, you are clever at it and able to do it well.
- Are you **good** at maths?
4 If something is good for you, it helps you in some way.
- Exercise is **good** for you, isn't it?

LANGUAGE NOTE

good **at** (doing) something
good **for** something (= suitable for)
good **of** someone **to do** something
good **to someone** (= kind to)
good **with** children, etc (= able to control and get on with)

---

good afternoon /ɡʊd ˌɑːftəˈnuːn/ interjection
You say **Good afternoon** when you meet someone between noon and five or six o'clock.
- "**Good afternoon**, John." "**Good afternoon**, Mr Wright."

goodbye /ɡʊd ˈbaɪ/ interjection
You say **Goodbye** when you leave someone.
- **Goodbye**, Mabel, I'll see you tomorrow.

good evening /ɡʊd ˈiːvnɪŋ/ interjection
You say **Good evening** when you meet someone between afternoon and night.
- "**Good evening**, Ann." "**Good evening**, Bob."

good morning /ɡʊd ˈmɔːnɪŋ/ interjection
You say **Good morning** when you meet someone before noon.
- "**Good morning**, Rosa." "**Good morning**, Tom."

goodnight /ɡʊd ˈnaɪt/ interjection
You say **Goodnight** to someone when you go to bed or when you leave them in the evening.
- I think I'll go to bed now. **Goodnight**, Harry.

θ	ð	ʃ	dʒ	tʃ	ŋ	ʒ	iː	ɜː	ɪ	æ	ʌ	ɒ
thing	that	shop	jump	chop	sing	measure	been	bird	bit	cat	but	not

goose /guːs/ noun (countable)
plural: geese
⚠ See box on page 22.

got /gɒt/ verb
past tense and past participle of **get**
• I **got** a birthday card from Mr and Mrs Azuma.

gotten /ˈgɒtn/ verb
past participle of **get**
(American English)

government /ˈgʌvnmənt/ noun (countable)
the group of people who control a country and say what will happen
• Will the **government** build a lot of new hospitals in your country?
↻ bring down a government (= make a government end or fall), form/set up a government (= start a government); a good/strong/weak government

grandchild /ˈgræntʃaɪld/ noun (countable)
plural: grandchildren
the child of someone's son or daughter
• Mr and Mrs MacDonald have three **grandchildren**: Peter, Elsa and Shirley.

granddaughter /ˈgrændɔːtə*/ noun (countable)
the daughter of someone's son or daughter
• Elsa is Mrs Howard's **granddaughter**.

grandfather /ˈgrænfɑːðə*/
grandad /ˈgrændæd/
grandpa /ˈgrænpɑː/ noun (countable)
the father of someone's father or mother
• Mr MacDonald is Peter's **grandfather**.

grandmother /ˈgrænmʌðə*/
granny /ˈgrænɪ/ noun (countable)
grandma /ˈgrænmɑː/
the mother of someone's father or mother
• Mrs Howard is Elsa's **grandma**.

grandson /ˈgrænsʌn/ noun (countable)
the son of someone's son or daughter
• Peter and Vincent are Mr and Mrs Howard's **grandsons**.

grape /greɪp/ noun (countable)
⚠ See box on page 89.

grapefruit /ˈgreɪpfruːt/ noun (countable, uncountable)
⚠ See box on page 89.

grass /grɑːs/ noun (uncountable)
Grass is the very common plant which grows in fields.
• The cows have eaten almost all the **grass**.
↻ cut the grass; high/tall/short grass

great /greɪt/ adjective
1 large, a lot of
• There is a **great** difference between my age and my grandma's age.
2 important
• Dr Sun Yat Sen was a **great** man. He's called the father of modern China.

greedy /ˈgriːdɪ/ adjective
greedier or more greedy, greediest or most greedy
When you take more than you need or when you want too much, you are **greedy**.
• You're very **greedy** if you've eaten all six cakes.

green /griːn/ noun (uncountable, countable), adjective
the colour of grass or leaves, the colour between yellow and blue
• Paint the fields a light **green**.
• The children were playing on the **green** grass.

θ	ð	ʃ	dʒ	tʃ	ŋ	ʒ	iː	ɜː	ɪ	æ	ʌ	ɒ
thing	**that**	**shop**	**jump**	**chop**	**sing**	**measure**	**been**	**bird**	**bit**	**cat**	**but**	**not**

greengrocer /ˈgriːnˌgrəʊsə*/ noun (countable)
someone who sells fruit and vegetables
- *I'm going to the **greengrocer's** to buy some apples.*

⚠ See **grocer** (Language Note).

grew /gruː/ verb
past tense of **grow**
- *The grass **grew** quickly during the wet weather.*

grey /greɪ/ noun (uncountable, countable), adjective
colour between black and white, the colour of clouds before it rains
- *The old man had a **grey** beard.*
- *His hair was dark **grey** in colour.*
- *Elephants are **grey**.*

grocer /ˈgrəʊsə*/ noun (countable)
someone who sells coffee, tea, flour, eggs, tinned food, etc
- *You can get tins of soup at this **grocer's**.*

LANGUAGE NOTE

An apostrophe + s is often used to show a shop:
grocer's = grocer's shop
greengrocer's = greengrocer's shop

---

ground /graʊnd/ noun
1 (uncountable) the top of the earth

- *Victor jumped off the wall and landed with both feet on the **ground**.*

LANGUAGE NOTE

ground = outside a building
floor = inside a building

---

2 (countable) land which is used for playing games and doing sport
- *The football **ground** is next to the school.*
3 **the grounds** = the land round a building (and belonging to it)
- *There are lots of trees in the school **grounds**.*

group /gruːp/ noun (countable)
a number of people, animals or things together in the same place at the same time
- *Have you got a favourite pop **group**?*

LANGUAGE NOTE

COMPARE   The group was waiting for us.
(= the group as ONE body)
The group were arguing among themselves.
(= the group as different people)

🔗 belong to/form a group;   a big/large/small/important/special/pop group

grow /grəʊ/ verb
growing, grew /gruː/, has grown /grəʊn/
1 get bigger
  - *The baby began to **grow** very quickly and soon all its clothes were too small.*
2 make something get bigger or longer
  - *Linda is **growing** her hair long and her husband is **growing** a beard!*
3 put seeds in the ground and look after them
  - *Susie is **growing** some flowers in this box.*
4 become
  - *It suddenly **grew** dark.*

🔗 grow dark/light/big/fat/old/wise

⚠ See **go 3**.

grow up /ˌgrəʊ ˈʌp/ phrasal verb
growing up, grew up, has grown up
change from a child to a man or woman
- *David has **grown up** and is studying to be a teacher.*

grown-up /ˈgrəʊn ʌp/ noun (countable)
plural: grown-ups
a man or a woman
- *Only **grown-ups** can see this film. It isn't for children.*

θ	ð	ʃ	dʒ	tʃ	ŋ	ʒ	iː	ɜː	ɪ	æ	ʌ	ɒ
thing	that	shop	jump	chop	sing	measure	been	bird	bit	cat	but	not

guard[1] /gɑːd/ noun (countable)

someone who watches people, places and things to keep them safe
- *Mr Carvalho is a **guard** at this bank. He's got a gun and he stands outside.*

↻ keep/stand guard over

guard[2] verb

watch people, places and things to keep them safe or to stop them escaping
- *The large house is **guarded** by several dogs.*

guess[1] /ges/ noun (countable)

an answer which you give when you are not certain whether it is correct or not
- *He made a **guess** but he was quite wrong.*

↻ make a guess; a close/good/lucky/rough guess, a wild guess (= a guess made without any knowledge at all)

guess[2] verb

give an answer without knowing whether it is correct or not
- *I had to **guess** some of the answers to the exam questions. I hadn't done any work.*

↻ guess correctly/wrongly/wildly

LANGUAGE NOTE
In colloquial American English **guess** means *think*.
"We ought to leave soon."
"I **guess** so."

guide /gaɪd/ noun (countable)

1 someone who shows you places and tells you about them
   - *We had a very good **guide** who showed us round the old building.*
2 a book which tells you about places
   - *I'm reading an excellent **guide** to Bangkok.*

↻ a handy guide (= a convenient guide), a clear/simple/useful/helpful guide

guitar /gɪˈtɑː*/ noun (countable)

something which you play by pulling strings

- *Ibrahim is learning to play the **guitar**.*

LANGUAGE NOTE	
NEVER	Can you play guitar?
ALWAYS	Can you play **the** guitar?

gun /gʌn/ noun (countable)

something which you hold in your hand to shoot with
- *Don't point that **gun** at me! It's very dangerous to play with **guns**.*

H h

habit /ˈhæbɪt/ noun (countable)
something which you often do without thinking about it and which you cannot stop doing
- *Smoking is a bad **habit** and is very unhealthy.*
- break/fall/get into/get out of/grow out of/give up/lose/have the habit of; make a habit of, pick up/form (bad) habits
a bad/dangerous/horrible/unfortunate/unpleasant habit

had /hæd/ (unstressed /həd/) verb
past tense and past participle of **have**
- *We all **had** breakfast early this morning.*
- *Maria **had** already left when we arrived.*

hadn't /ˈhædnt/ verb
had not
- *Simon **hadn't** been there for more than five minutes when Anna and her friend came.*
- See also **have**.

hair /heə*/ noun
1 (countable) Hairs are long thin threads which grow on your head, on certain parts of your body or on the bodies of certain animals.
   - *The cat left a lot of **hairs** on the sofa.*
2 (uncountable) You can use the word **hair** to mean a group of these hairs (eg all the hairs on your head).
   - *Lily has beautiful, long black **hair**.*

LANGUAGE NOTE	
NEVER	He's the fair-hair boy.
ALWAYS	He's the *fair-haired* boy.
OR	He's the boy **with fair hair**.

- brush/comb/cut/wash/lose your hair (= go bald); your hair falls out/grows; long/short/straight/curly/wavy/fair/dark/black/blond/brown/grey/red/white hair
- See also box on page 25.

haircut /ˈheəkʌt/ noun (countable)
When you have a haircut, someone cuts your hair for you.
- *Her hair is too long. She needs a **haircut**.*
- get/have/need a haircut, give someone a haircut

LANGUAGE NOTE	
COMPARE	I'm having my hair cut. (*hair cut* = two words) I'm having a haircut. (*haircut* = one word)

hairdresser /ˈheəˌdresə*/ noun (countable)
the person who cuts and washes your hair
- *I'm going to the **hairdresser** this morning.*

half [1] /hɑːf/ noun (countable)
plural: halves /hɑːvz/
1 When you divide something into two equal parts, you cut it into **halves** (or in **half**).
   - *Sam and Tony both wanted the apple, and so Mrs Lee cut it in **half**.*
2 a ticket for a child on a bus or train, etc (often sold at half price)
   - *Two and three **halves** return to London.*

half [2] predeterminer
1 an equal part or number of a larger part or number
   - ***Half** a dozen eggs, please.*
   - *A **half** dozen eggs, please.*
   - ***Half** the furniture was broken.*
   - ***Half** the pupils were absent.*

θ	ð	ʃ	dʒ	tʃ	ŋ	ʒ	iː	ɜː	ɪ	æ	ʌ	ɒ
thing	that	shop	jump	chop	sing	measure	been	bird	bit	cat	but	not

LANGUAGE NOTE

1 You can say or write:
   EITHER half a dozen (= 6)
   OR   a half dozen (= 6)
   EITHER half an hour (= 30 minutes)
   OR   a half hour (= 30 minutes)

2 NEVER   It takes one and a half hour.
  ALWAYS It takes one and a half **hours**.

3 Note the use of the plural and singular:
   One and a half weeks **have** now passed.
   One week and a half **has** now passed.

4 You can say or write:
   EITHER   I gave him half the cake.
   OR   I gave him half of the cake.
   BUT ONLY I gave him half **of** it.(of+ pronoun)
   AND   I gave him my half **of** the cake.
   (NOT   I gave him my half the cake.)

5 Don't use **of** after **half** when you are talking about numbers or about measuring.
   NEVER   I'd like half of a metre of cloth.
   ALWAYS I'd like **half a metre** of cloth.

2 **half an hour** = thirty minutes
 • I'll see you in **half an hour**.
3 **half past** = thirty minutes after
 • Come back at **half past** four.

LANGUAGE NOTE

British English: half past four
American English: half **after** four

hall /hɔːl/ noun (countable)
1 part of a house near the door between the rooms
 • Nicola opened the door and asked us to wait in the **hall**.
 ↻ an entrance hall
2 a large room where people can meet, especially in a public building, a school, etc.
 • The party will take place in the village **hall** because there will be over a hundred guests.
 ↻ a concert/dance hall, city/town/village hall

halves /hɑːvz/ noun (countable)
plural of **half**
 • Cut the apples into **halves** and put them here.
 ⚠ See also **half** [1].

hamburger /ˈhæmbɜːgə*/ noun (countable)
some meat inside two pieces of round bread
 • I often buy a large **hamburger** for lunch.

hand /hænd/ noun (countable)
1 the part of your body at the end of your arm
 • My **hands** are very dirty. Can I wash them?

LANGUAGE NOTE

NEVER   You're holding it in the hand.
ALWAYS You're holding it in **your** hand.

 ↻ hold hands, shake someone's hand(s), take someone's hand, clap your hands; hand in hand (= holding hands)
 ⚠ See also box on page 25.
2 the thin part on the face of a clock which shows the time
 • The minute **hand** of the clock was broken.

handbag /ˈhændbæg/ noun (countable)
(American English: purse)
a bag which a woman uses to carry money and small things in
 • Helen took her pen out of her **handbag**.

handkerchief /ˈhæŋkətʃɪf/ noun (countable)
a small piece of cloth which you use to blow your nose on
 • Have you got a clean **handkerchief**?

handle [1] /ˈhændl/ noun (countable)
a part of something which you can hold
 • Oh dear! The **handle** of my case has broken and I can't carry it now.

θ	ð	ʃ	dʒ	tʃ	ŋ	ʒ	iː	ɜː	ɪ	æ	ʌ	ɒ
thing	that	shop	jump	chop	sing	measure	been	bird	bit	cat	but	not

handle [2] verb
handling, handled, has handled
touch or hold in your hands
- Don't **handle** the fruit unless you want it.

hang /hæŋ/ verb
hanging, hung /hʌŋ/, has hung
1 tie or hold something at the top
   - Mr Baker **hung** the wet clothes on the line to dry.
2 be tied or held at the top by something
   - There were clothes **hanging** on the line.

LANGUAGE NOTE

Note the forms of **hang** when it is used with the meaning of killing someone by putting a rope round their neck and hanging them up:
hanging, **hanged**, **has hanged**
The killer was **hanged** a hundred years ago.
(NEVER hung)

---

happen /ˈhæpən/ verb
1 take place without being planned
   - "What will **happen** if Dave doesn't do his homework?" "He'll be punished."
2 result
   - I put my foot on the brake but nothing **happened**!

LANGUAGE NOTE

happen to someone
What's happening **to** the children?

---

3 be or do something by chance
   - We **happened** to see Alice Zeera last night.

happily /ˈhæpɪlɪ/ adverb
gladly, not sadly
- Helen sang **happily** as she was painting.

happy /ˈhæpɪ/ adjective
happier, happiest
1 glad, not sad
   - I felt very **happy** when I heard I had won.

2 good, successful
   - "I'm ten today." "**Happy** Birthday, Nigel."

LANGUAGE NOTE

happy **about** something good
happy **with** someone else, your work, etc
happy **to do** something
happy **that** something has happened

☞ Happy Birthday/Christmas/New Year

harbour /ˈhɑːbə*/ noun (countable)
American English: harbor
a place where boats can land safely

- Three ships are coming into the **harbour**.

hard [1] /hɑːd/ adjective
1 difficult, not easy
   - The English exam was very **hard**. I could answer only six questions out of twenty.
2 not soft
   - Susie didn't like sleeping on the **hard** bed.

hard [2] adverb
harder, hardest
1 a lot
   - You must work **hard** if you want to pass.

LANGUAGE NOTE

NEVER — He worked hardly.
ALWAYS — He worked **hard**. (= a lot)
OR — He **hardly** worked. (= not very much)
Remember that **hard** and **hardly** mean almost the opposite in the sentences above.

θ	ð	ʃ	dʒ	tʃ	ŋ	ʒ	iː	ɜː	ɪ	æ	ʌ	ɒ
thing	that	shop	jump	chop	sing	measure	been	bird	bit	cat	but	not

2 strongly
- David hit the ball **hard** and then ran.

hardly /ˈhɑːdlɪ/ adverb
1 If you can hardly do something, you can only just do it or do it with great difficulty.
- The boy was so small that he could **hardly** reach the doorbell.

> **LANGUAGE NOTE**
>
> Always use **hardly** BEFORE the main verb.
> He could **hardly** see us.

⚠ See **hard** ²1 (Language Note).
2 **hardly ever** = almost never, almost not at all
- I **hardly ever** saw Susie even though we lived so near to each other.

harvest /ˈhɑːvɪst/ noun (countable)
the collection of fruit and vegetables on farms
- The **harvest** in Russia was very poor last year and many people will now be very hungry.

has /hæz/ (unstressed /həz/) verb
part of **have** (used after **he**, **she**, **it** and singular nouns)
- Ann **has** two sisters and one brother.

hasn't /ˈhæznt/ verb
has not
- Peter **hasn't** a watch like yours, has he?
- Ann **hasn't** eaten anything yet.
⚠ See also **have**.

has to /ˈhæz tuː/ verb phrase
part of **have to** (used after **he**, **she**, **it** and singular nouns)
- Spiros **has to** take his driving test again.

hat /hæt/ noun (countable)
something which you wear on your head
- Leila's wearing her new **hat**.

hate /heɪt/ verb
hating, hated, has hated
not like in any way
- I **hate** people who lie.
↻ be filled with hate (towards someone), be full of hate

> **LANGUAGE NOTE**
>
> Do not use **hate** in the continuous form.
> NEVER I am hating potatoes.
> ALWAYS I **hate** potatoes.

have /hæv/ (unstressed /həv/) verb
has /hæz/ (unstressed /həz/), having,
had /hæd/ (unstressed /həd/), has had
1 own
- Do you **have** a bike?
2 You should use **have** with the past participle of a verb to make the present perfect tense.
- **Have** you finished your homework yet?
3 **have a cold** = suffer from a cold
- I'm staying at home: I **have a** bad **cold**.
↻ have a cough/a (high) temperature/ a sore throat/a pain/a bad stomach, etc; have cholera/flu/malaria/measles/ typhoid, etc; have backache/earache/ stomachache/toothache, etc
4 **have a meal** = eat (and drink)
- What time do you usually **have** breakfast?
↻ have breakfast/dinner/lunch/tea; have a drink/ a (cup of) coffee, a glass of milk/water, etc
5 **have a rest** = rest (See below)
- You look tired: you should **have a** (short) **rest**.
↻ have a bath/shave/shower/wash/ sleep, have a holiday/good time/ nice day/swim/walk/talk, etc
6 **have something to eat** = eat something
- "I'm very hungry."
"Why don't you **have something to eat**?"

θ	ð	ʃ	dʒ	tʃ	ŋ	ʒ	iː	ɜː	ɪ	æ	ʌ	ɒ
thing	that	shop	jump	chop	sing	measure	been	bird	bit	cat	but	not

7 **have something done** = ask or get someone else to do something for you
- *Tina is **having** her hair cut today.*

LANGUAGE NOTE

1 In 1 - 3 above, **have** does not have a continuous form.
NEVER ~~Ken's father is having a lot of money.~~
ALWAYS Ken's father **has** a lot of money.
NEVER ~~I'm having flu.~~
ALWAYS I **have** flu.

2 **Have** and **has** can only be shortened to **'ve** and **'s** when they are used to form tenses (as in 2 above).
We **'ve** already finished our tea.
NEVER ~~We've tea at four o'clock every day.~~
ALWAYS We **have** tea at four o'clock every day.

3 When you use **have** with the meanings 3 - 7, you should use **do** and **did** to form questions and to make sentences with **not** when the present and past simple tenses are used.
NEVER ~~Had you a rest?~~
ALWAYS **Did** you **have** a rest?
NEVER ~~I haven't usually breakfast at nine o'clock.~~
ALWAYS I don't usually **have** breakfast at nine o'clock.

---

haven't /'hævnt/ verb
have not
- *Mr and Mrs Hill **haven't** returned from Cairo yet.*
⚠ See also **have**.

have to /'hæv tuː/ verb phrase
has to, having to, had to, has had to
must
- *When do we **have to** get up tomorrow?*

he /hiː/ pronoun
You can use **he** to talk about a man or a boy when you have already spoken or written about him before.
- *"Where's Mr White?" "**He** is in Madrid."*

LANGUAGE NOTE

Only use **he** to show a boy or a man. In the past, **he** was used a lot more than now because people usually thought they were talking or writing about boys or men. For example, many people still say, "Why don't you see your dentist? **He'll** know what to do." They never think that a dentist may be a woman!

Now it is better to say:
Why don't you see your dentist?
They'll know what to do.

And it is better to write:
Why don't you see your dentist? **He/she'll** or **He/she'll** know what to do.

Where it is possible, use the plural form of the noun and **they**.

Dentists are useful people to see.
They usually know what to do in such cases.

---

head /hed/ noun (countable)
1 the part of your body above your shoulders
- *Mrs Jones has a hat on her **head**.*
℧ bow/hang your head, hold your head up, lift/raise/nod/shake/scratch/turn your head
⚠ See box on page 25.
2 the headmaster or headmistress of a school
- *Mr Lim wrote a letter to the **head** to explain why his son was absent.*

headache /'hedeɪk/ noun (countable)
a pain in your head
- *The bright lights gave me a **headache**.*

LANGUAGE NOTE

have stomachache BUT have **a** headache

℧ get/have a headache;
a bad/splitting headache,
a sick headache (American English)
⚠ See also **ache**[1].

θ	ð	ʃ	dʒ	tʃ	ŋ	ʒ	iː	ɜː	ɪ	æ	ʌ	ɒ
thing	that	shop	jump	chop	sing	measure	been	bird	bit	cat	but	not

104　headmaster

headmaster /ˌhedˈmɑːstə*/ noun (countable)
the most important teacher in a school
- *The **headmaster** wanted to see the two boys.*

headmistress /ˌhedˈmɪstrɪs/ noun (countable)
plural: headmistresses
the most important teacher in a school
- *Our **headmistress** is having a meeting with all the teachers.*

health /helθ/ noun (uncountable)
how your body is, how well you feel
- *Doing exercises is good for your **health**.*
- ↻ damage/look after your health, enjoy good health; bad/poor/broken/ill/failing/good/excellent/perfect health; in good/poor health

healthy /ˈhelθɪ/ adjective
healthier, healthiest
well, in good health
- *Dave was always a strong and **healthy** boy. He was never ill even for a day.*

hear /hɪə*/ verb
hearing, heard /hɜːd/, has heard
1 You **hear** things when sounds reach your ears.
  - *Please speak louder. I can't **hear** you.*

LANGUAGE NOTE

1 Avoid using *hear* in the continuous form.
   NEVER ~~I'm hearing someone singing.~~
   ALWAYS I hear someone singing.

2 hear = receive sounds with your ears
        (whether you want to or not)
   listen to = pay attention to sounds (= want or try to hear)
   I listened to Mr Green's talk but I couldn't hear everything.

3 Note the pattern: I heard him come in.
   (NOT I heard him came in.)

⚠ See also **listen**.

2 be told something
  - *Have you **heard** the news about the crash?*
3 receive a letter, etc
  - *I haven't **heard** from Adam for a over a month.*

heart /hɑːt/ noun (countable)
1 the part of your body which sends blood round it
  - *I felt my **heart** beating very fast after the race.*
  - ↻ your heart beats/fails/stops; your heart aches for someone (= you feel very sorry for them), your heart leaps (= feel happy and excited), your heart sinks (= feel unhappy and disappointed) ; a healthy/strong/weak heart, a good/kind/soft/a cold heart (= cruel or unkind) , a warm heart (= kind and friendly)
2 the centre
  - *This is the old part of the city - its true **heart**!*
3 **learn by heart** = remember
  - *We all had to **learn** the poem **by heart**.*

heat¹ /hiːt/ noun (uncountable)
a high temperature, being hot
- *The **heat** from the burning building was too much for the firemen and they had to leave.*
- ↻ great heat

heat² verb
make hot or warm
- *This food is cold. Put it in a pan and **heat** it*

heavily /ˈhevɪlɪ/ adverb
a lot, a great amount
- *It rained very **heavily** this afternoon.*

heavy /ˈhevɪ/ adjective
heavier, heaviest
weighing a lot
- *The bed was difficult for us to move because it was so **heavy**.*
- ↻ with a heavy heart (= sadly) , heavy traffic (= a lot of cars)

θ	ð	ʃ	dʒ	tʃ	ŋ	ʒ	iː	ɜː	ɪ	æ	ʌ	ɒ
thing	that	shop	jump	chop	sing	measure	been	bird	bit	cat	but	not

he'd /hiːd/
1 he would
   • *He'd do it if you asked him.*
2 he had
   • *He said he'd lived there for ten years.*

hedge /hedʒ/ noun (countable)
a row of small trees along a garden, a field or a road
   • *Can you see the field behind this hedge?*

height /haɪt/ noun (uncountable, countable)
how tall someone or something is
   • *"What's the height of this hedge?"*
     "It has a height of almost two metres."

held /held/ verb
past tense and past participle of **hold**
   • *Have you ever held such a small baby before?*

helicopter /ˈhelɪˌkɒptə*/ noun (countable)
an aeroplane which can fly straight up in the sky

   • *My Sims waved at his family from the helicopter.*
   ⌗ fly/pilot a helicopter; fly in a helicopter, travel by helicopter

he'll /hiːl/
he will
   • *Andy is in bed but he'll get up soon.*

hello /həˈləʊ/ interjection
You say Hello when you meet someone or start a telephone conversation.
   • *Hello, are you all right?*
   • *Hello. This is Bill Jones speaking.*

help¹ /help/ noun (uncountable)
work which you do for someone to make it easier for them; or money or advice which you give them
   • *I saw that the old woman needed some help.*
   ⌗ ask/beg/call for help, need/want/get/bring/send/offer/give/receive/refuse help; (be of) big/great/little help (to someone), kind help; a cry for help

help² verb
1 do some work for someone, give them money or advice (to make it easier for them)
   • *My friend helped start my business by lending me some money.*

LANGUAGE NOTE

EITHER   help someone to do something
OR   help someone do something

---

2 **help yourself** = take
   • *Please help yourself to some more cake.*

helpful /ˈhelpfl/ adjective
Someone is helpful when they make it easier for you by doing some work or giving you money or advice.
   • *David is very helpful. He always washes up.*

hen /hen/ noun (countable)
male: cock
⚠ See box on page 22.

her¹ /hɜː* (unstressed /hə*/)/ determiner
belonging to a girl or woman
   • *Rita is looking for her pen. Have you seen it?*

her² pronoun
You can use her to show a girl or a woman when you have already spoken or written about the girl or woman before.
   • *That's Mabel over there. Can you see her?*

here /hɪə*/ adverb
1 at or in this place, near you
   • *Please write your name here.*

θ	ð	ʃ	dʒ	tʃ	ŋ	ʒ	iː	ɜː	ɪ	æ	ʌ	ɒ
thing	that	shop	jump	chop	sing	measure	been	bird	bit	cat	but	not

> **LANGUAGE NOTE**
>
> Use **here** for the place where you are and **there** for all other places.
> NEVER ~~I'm at home now and I'll stay there until you come.~~
> ALWAYS I'm at home now and I'll stay **here** until you come.

2 We can use **here** to draw attention to someone or something.
   - **Here** comes Anna.

> **LANGUAGE NOTE**
>
> Note the word order.
>   Here come **Ken and Rosa**.
>   Here **they** come.
> The verb comes before the subject unless it is a pronoun.

hers /hɜːz/ pronoun
something belonging to a girl or woman
- This pen is yours and that pen is **hers**.

herself /həˈself/ pronoun
1 You can use **herself** as the object of a verb or preposition.
   - Poor Mary cut **herself** on the broken glass.
   - She looked at **herself** in the mirror.
2 You can use **herself** to make the subject or object seem more important or to make the pronoun **she** stronger.
   - She painted the picture **herself**.
   - She **herself** told me the news.
3 without any help
   - Renata made the dress (all by) **herself**.
4 **by herself** = without anyone else
   - Raisha has gone on holiday (all) **by herself**.

he's /hiːz/
1 he is
   - **He's** going to Tokyo tomorrow.
2 he has
   - He says **he's** lived here all his life.

hide /haɪd/ verb
hiding, hid /hɪd/, has hidden /ˈhɪdn/
1 go where you cannot easily be seen or found
   - Let's **hide** behind this cupboard.
2 put something (or someone) where they cannot be seen
   - Let's **hide** Susan's present under your bed.

high ¹ /haɪ/ adjective
1 tall
   - "How h**igh** is this wall?"
     "It's over two metres **high**!"

> **LANGUAGE NOTE**
>
> Use **high** for mountains, hills, etc.
> Use **tall** for people, trees, etc.
> However, note that you can often use either **high** or **tall** for buildings (although many people still use **tall**).
>   That's a very **high building**.
>   That's a very **tall building**.

   See also **tall**.
2 a long way above the ground
   - The kite was **high** in the sky when I saw it.
3 much, great, a lot
   - The painting was sold for a **high** price.

high ² adverb
far up (in the sky)
- The plane flew **high** above the clouds.

hill /hɪl/ noun (countable)
a high piece of land (but not as high as a mountain)

- Let's push our bikes up this **hill**.

θ	ð	ʃ	dʒ	tʃ	ŋ	ʒ	iː	ɜː	ɪ	æ	ʌ	ɒ
thing	that	shop	jump	chop	sing	measure	been	bird	bit	cat	but	not

him /hɪm/ pronoun
You use **him** to show a boy or a man.
- *That's Peter over there. Can you see **him**?*

himself /hɪm'self/ pronoun
1 You can use **himself** as the object of a verb or preposition.
   - *Poor Tom hurt **himself** when he fell off his bicycle.*
   - *He looked at **himself** in the mirror and laughed.*
2 You can use **himself** to make the subject or object seem more important or to make the pronoun he stronger.
   - *Mark built the house **himself**.*
   - *Mr Khan **himself** phoned me.*
3 without any help
   - *Adam made this piece of furniture (all by) **himself**.*
4 **by himself** = without anyone else
   - *Ben has gone to the beach (all) **by himself**.*

hippo /'hɪpəʊ/ noun (countable)
plural: hippos
short for hippopotamus /ˌhɪpə'pɒtəməs/;
(plural: hippopotamuses or hippopotami /ˌhɪpə'pɒtəmaɪ/)
⚠ See box on page 10.

hire /'haɪə*/ determiner
hiring, hired, has hired
pay to borrow or use something
- *Let's **hire** a boat and go fishing.*

LANGUAGE NOTE

1 You **hire** something for a short time.
eg hire a bicycle, hire a boat, hire a dress, hire a car, hire a hall (for a party, etc)
You **rent** something for a longer time.
eg rent a flat, rent a house, rent a TV set
Note that in American English **hire** is used for all the cases above.

2 You can also use the verb **hire (out)** to mean **lend** (for money).
I've already **hired out** all my boats.

his /hɪz/ determiner
belonging to a boy or man
- *Look at Professor Bradley in **his** new car.*

hit /hɪt/ verb
hitting, hit, has hit
touch something very hard with your hand or a stick, etc
- *Linda **hit** the ball and scored a goal.*
℧ hit something hard

hobby /'hɒbɪ/ noun (countable)
plural: hobbies
something which you enjoy doing in your free time
- *My **hobbies** are stamp collecting and reading.*
℧ go in for/have a hobby

hockey /'hɒkɪ/ noun (uncountable)
a game you play by hitting a ball with a stick
- *I play **hockey** for my school.*
⚠ See also **ice hockey**.

hold /həʊld/ verb
holding, held /held/, has held
1 keep something in your fingers, hands or arms
   - *Tony **held** my hand while we crossed the road.*
2 have inside it
   - *This bucket **holds** five litres of water.*

LANGUAGE NOTE

Although you can use **hold** in the continuous form for the first meaning above, you cannot use the continuous form of **hold** for the second meaning.
They're holding hands.
BUT This box **holds** a lot of books.
(NEVER ~~This box is holding a lot of books.~~)

hole /həʊl/ noun (uncountable)
a space in something
- *I've lost all my money. There must be a **hole** in my pocket.*
℧ dig/make a hole (in something);
a big/deep hole

θ	ð	ʃ	dʒ	tʃ	ŋ	ʒ	iː	ɜː	ɪ	æ	ʌ	ɒ
thing	that	shop	jump	chop	sing	measure	been	bird	bit	cat	but	not

holiday /ˈhɒlɪdeɪ/ noun (countable)
1. the time when you are away from home having a rest (often plural)
   - We're going to Switzerland for our **holidays**.
   - have/take a holiday
2. the time when you are not at work/school
   - We have five weeks' **holiday** every summer.
3. **on holiday** = having a holiday
   - I'm going to Spain **on holiday** next week.

> **LANGUAGE NOTE**
>
> The word **holiday** is often used when you mean only a short time (eg two days' holiday) and **holidays** when you mean a longer time (eg the summer holidays, the school holidays). In many cases, however, you can use either **holiday** or **holidays**.
> Where are you going for your holiday(s)?

home /həʊm/ noun (uncountable, countable)
the place where you live with your family
- I work in Leeds but my **home** is in Weeton, a village a few miles away.
- go home, leave home, at home

> **LANGUAGE NOTE**
>
> NEVER go to home   ALWAYS go home

homework /ˈhəʊmwɜːk/ noun (uncountable)
exercises which a teacher gives pupils to do at home
- I've got too much **homework**.

> **LANGUAGE NOTE**
>
> 1. NEVER a homework   ALWAYS homework
> 2. COMPARE   I have to learn a poem and finish the rest of my **homework**.
>   I have to dust all the furniture and do all the **housework**!
>
> homework = exercises which are done to help pupils to study and learn
> housework = work which is done to look after a house (eg washing, cleaning)

- do/give in/hand in your homework

honest /ˈɒnɪst/ adjective
truthful, saying what is true, not stealing
- Hiroshi and Paulo are very **honest**: I'm sure they didn't take your watch.

honey /ˈhʌnɪ/ noun (uncountable)
something sweet which is made by bees and which you can eat
- People say that **honey** is good for sore throats.

hook /hʊk/ noun (countable)
a piece of bent metal for hanging things on
- Put your coat on the **hook** behind the door.

hop /hɒp/ verb
hopping, hopped, has hopped
1. jump on one foot
   - Why are you **hopping**? Have you hurt your left foot?
2. move by jumping (used for birds and small animals)
   - The small bird **hopped** across the grass.

hope¹ /həʊp/ noun (uncountable, countable)
a feeling that what you want to happen will actually happen
- **Hopes** of finding the two lost sailors are now increasing.

> **LANGUAGE NOTE**
>
> Note the prepositions after **hope**:
> no hope **for** someone
> no hope **of** success, **of** doing something

- bring hope to someone, give up/have/hold out hope; keep your hopes up; every hope/a faint/slight/real/great/strong hope, high hopes, your last hope, not much hope, your only hope

hope² verb
hoping, hoped, has hoped
want something (not) to happen
- I **hope** it doesn't rain on Saturday. We're all going on a picnic.

θ	ð	ʃ	dʒ	tʃ	ŋ	ʒ	iː	ɜː	ɪ	æ	ʌ	ɒ
thing	that	shop	jump	chop	sing	measure	been	bird	bit	cat	but	not

LANGUAGE NOTE

1 COMPARE I hope he **comes**. (future)
           I hope he **will come**. (future)
  WITH   I wish he **would come**. (future)
  COMPARE I hope I know the answer.
           (I think I do)
           I wish I knew the answer.
           (I know I don't)

2 Note the short answer after **hope**:
  "I hope he comes."
  "So do I."

See also **wish** [1] 1.

hopeful /ˈhəʊpfl/ adjective
1 feeling that something you want to happen will actually happen
  • I'm **hopeful** that our team will win.
2 causing you to feel that something you want to happen will actually happen
  • There are **hopeful** signs that the country will improve.

hopeless /ˈhəʊplɪs/ adjective
1 causing you to feel that something you want to happen will not happen
  • It's **hopeless**. We can't save the animals.
2 very bad (often at games, art, music, etc)
  • Tina's **hopeless** at hockey.

horrible /ˈhɒrɪbl/ adjective
used mostly in speaking to friends
very unpleasant
  • The meal was **horrible**! I couldn't eat a thing!

horse /hɔːs/ noun (countable)
See box on page 10.

hospital /ˈhɒspɪtl/ noun (countable)
a large building where doctors and nurses take care of sick people

• My friend's in **hospital** with a broken leg.
be taken/go to/stay in hospital

LANGUAGE NOTE

BRITISH ENGLISH	be in hospital
	go to hospital
AMERICAN ENGLISH	be in the hospital
	go to the hospital

hot /hɒt/ adjective
hotter, hottest
1 not cold, very warm
  • This classroom gets very **hot** in summer.
2 giving a strong, burning taste
  • This food is very **hot**. Pass the water, please.

hotel /həʊˈtel/ noun (countable)
a place where people can stay and have meals
  • Which **hotel** will you stay in when you visit Hong Kong?
check in at a hotel (= fill in forms and take a room), check out of a hotel (= pay your bill and leave), stay at/in a hotel

hour /ˈaʊə*/ noun (countable)
There are 60 minutes in one hour and 24 hours in one day.
  • It takes two **hours** to fly from Paris to Rome.

LANGUAGE NOTE

| NEVER | a fourteen hours flight |
| ALWAYS | a fourteen-hour flight |

house /haʊs/ noun (countable)
plural: houses /ˈhaʊzɪz/
a building where people live (but not a block of flats)
  • We're moving to a new **house** next month.
  an apartment house (American English only)
See **flat**.
a detached house (= a house on its own, not joined to another house); a semi-detached house (= a house joined to one other house); a terraced house (= a house joined to several other houses)

| θ | ð | ʃ | dʒ | tʃ | ŋ | ʒ | iː | ɜː | ɪ | æ | ʌ | ɒ |
| thing | that | shop | jump | chop | sing | measure | been | bird | bit | cat | but | not |

how /haʊ/ adverb

1. You can use **how** to ask questions about numbers, amounts, prices, etc.
   - *How many people were at the football match?*
   - *How much petrol is there left?*
   - *How much are these oranges?*

2. You can use **how** to ask questions about length, height, weight, etc.
   - *How long are these pieces of wood?*
   - *How high is this ceiling?*
   - *How heavy are you?*

3. You can use **how** to ask questions about the way something is done.
   - *How can I start this engine?*

4. You can use **how** to ask questions about the way something happened.
   - *How did the fire start?*

5. You can use **how** to ask questions about someone's health or how they feel.
   - *How are you? How do you feel now?*

> **LANGUAGE NOTE**
>
> *How* is used to ask about things which can change after a short time (eg how you are feeling).
> *How* are things with you?
> *How's* your work?
> *How* did Leila look when you saw her?
>
> *What's........ like* and *What are........ like* are used to ask about things and people which do not change after a short time.
> *What's* your sister like?
> *What* are the new pupils like?
> *What's .... like* is often used for the weather.
> *What* was the weather *like* in Italy?
>
> COMPARE "What's your sister like?"
>   "She's very nice."
> WITH   "How's your sister?"
>   "She's been ill but she's recovered."

6. You can use **how** when you meet someone for the first time.
   - *"How do you do. I'm Ted Green"*
   - *"How do you do. I'm Susie Lee."*

however /haʊˈevə*/ adverb
Use **however** when you want to say something surprising or the opposite of what you have just said.
- *It rained on Saturday, and spoiled the picnic. However, we enjoyed playing games in the village hall.*

hum /hʌm/ verb
humming, hummed, has hummed
sing quietly without opening your lips
- *She hummed as she painted.*

hung /hʌŋ/ verb
past tense and past participle of **hang**
- *Leila hung her coat on the hook behind the door.*

hungry /ˈhʌŋgrɪ/ adjective
hungrier, hungriest
the feeling which you have when you want food and you haven't eaten for a long time
- *We're very hungry. We haven't eaten all day.*

hunt /hʌnt/ verb
1. try to catch a wild animal
   - *It should be against the law to hunt tigers.*
2. look for, find
   - *I hunted everywhere for my maths book but I couldn't find it. Did you borrow it?*

hurry¹ /ˈhʌrɪ/ noun (singular)
in a hurry = without any time, quickly
- *Vincent is always in a hurry when I see him.*

hurry² verb
hurrying, hurried, has hurried
1. go quickly, do something quickly or immediately
   - *Jenny hurried out of the flat to catch the bus, but she just missed it.*
2. **hurry up** = do something sooner or more quickly
   - *Hurry up or you'll miss the bus.*

θ	ð	ʃ	dʒ	tʃ	ŋ	ʒ	iː	ɜː	ɪ	æ	ʌ	ɒ
thing	that	shop	jump	chop	sing	measure	been	bird	bit	cat	but	not

hurt /hɜːt/   verb

hurting, hurt, has hurt

1 give or cause pain
- I **hurt** my knee when I fell down the stairs.

2 feel pain
- I wrote so much that my hand began to **hurt**.

3 **hurt oneself** = cause oneself pain
- Did you **hurt yourself** when you fell?

ಆ hurt badly/slightly/a little;
be badly/seriously hurt, be slightly hurt

husband /ˈhʌzbənd/   noun (countable)

the man to whom a woman is married
- Mike is Helen's **husband**. They've been married for over five years.

hut /hʌt/   noun (countable)

a small building (usually made of wood)
- Old Mr Wong lives in a **hut** on the side of a hill.

I i

I /aɪ/   pronoun

You can use **I** to talk about yourself.
- "Where are you?" "**I'm** here."

LANGUAGE NOTE	
NEVER	I and my brother saw her.
ALWAYS	My brother and **I** saw her.
Always put **I** AFTER the other person	

ice /aɪs/   noun (uncountable)

water which is frozen, water which is so cold that it has been made hard
- Be careful when you drive in Britain in winter. There's often a lot of **ice** on the roads.

ಆ ice forms/melts

ice cream /ˌaɪs ˈkriːm/   noun (uncountable, countable)

something very cold and quite sweet which we eat (made from milk and eggs, etc)

LANGUAGE NOTE	
EITHER	Could I have an ice cream?
OR	Could I have some ice cream?

- Let's have an **ice cream**.

ice hockey /ˈaɪs ˌhɒkɪ/

a game like hockey but played on ice
- There is a good **ice hockey** match on TV.

⚠ See also **hockey**.

θ	ð	ʃ	dʒ	tʃ	ŋ	ʒ	iː	ɜː	ɪ	æ	ʌ	ɒ
thing	that	shop	jump	chop	sing	measure	been	bird	bit	cat	but	not

I'd /aɪd/
1 I would
- *I'd* do it if you asked me.
2 I had
- I said *I'd* lived there for ten years.

idea /aɪˈdɪə/ noun (countable)
1 a plan, a thought, a suggestion
- It's a good *idea* to keep a cat if there are mice in your house.
- get/have/hit upon an idea; a bright/brilliant/clever/good/fresh/new/clear/general/rough/silly/strange idea
2 a general description
- Give me an *idea* of what he was like.
- a broad/general idea, the main idea
3 **have (got) no idea** = not know (about something or how to do something)
- *I've got no idea* what to buy Linda.
- not have the faintest/slightest idea

if /ɪf/ conjunction
1 You can use **if** to talk about something which may happen.
- *If* it rains, I'll stay in and watch TV.
2 You can use **if** to mean **when**.
- I always feel tired *if* I go to bed late.
3 You can use **if** for questions after **know**, **ask**, etc.
- Do you know *if* Maria is at school today?

LANGUAGE NOTE
1 Note the use of the Present Simple tense in the following *if*-clauses to show the future.
 If we *leave* now, we'll arrive in time.
 Water will boil if you *heat* it to 100° C.
2 Note the tenses in the following kinds of *if*-clauses about "unreal" events.
 If we *left* now, we'd be in time.
 We would all get wet if it *rained* now.
3 Note the tenses in the following kinds of *if*-clauses about events which are both "unreal" and impossible.
 If we *had left* now, we'd have been in time.
 We would all have got wet if it *had rained*.
4 We can use **had** at the beginning of this last kind of clause instead of *if*.
 Had we left now, we'd have been in time.
 We would all have got wet *had* it rained.

ill /ɪl/ adjective
sick, not well
- Mabel ate so much ice cream that she was *ill*.

LANGUAGE NOTE
1 In British English you can say:
 EITHER My friend was *sick*.
 OR   My friend was *ill*.
 However, you should not use *ill* before a noun.
 NEVER I've been with my ill friend.
 ALWAYS I've been with my *sick* friend.
2 In American English *sick* is usually used (NOT ill).
 I feel quite *sick*: I'm hot and my legs ache.
 In British English, however, **to be sick** is often used when you have a bad stomach and want to bring back the food in it.
 Try to be sick. You'll feel better after you've been sick.

- fall/ be taken ill; very/seriously ill
- See also **sick**.

illness /ˈɪlnɪs/ noun (countable)
being unwell
- Dr Jones gave Adam some medicine to cure his *illness*.
- have/cure someone of/get over/recover from an illness/a fatal illness (= an illness which causes death)/serious/ sudden illness
- See also **disease**.

I'll /aɪl/
I shall, I will
- *I'll* see you soon.

I'm /aɪm/
I am
- *I'm* Don and this is Dave.
- *I'm* going swimming this afternoon.

imagine /ɪˈmædʒɪn/ verb
imagining, imagined, has imagined
1 have a picture in your mind
- *Imagine* living here fifty years ago!
2 think that something may happen
- I *imagine* Lesley will pass the test.

θ	ð	ʃ	dʒ	tʃ	ŋ	ʒ	iː	ɜː	ɪ	æ	ʌ	ɒ
thing	that	shop	jump	chop	sing	measure	been	bird	bit	cat	but	not

indeed   113

> **LANGUAGE NOTE**
>
> NEVER ~~imagine to do something~~
> ALWAYS imagine ***doing*** something

immediately /ɪˈmiːdɪətlɪ/   adverb
at once, this moment
- Please come ***immediately***. Don't wait.

important /ɪmˈpɔːtənt/   adjective
1. something which you should do
   - It is ***important*** to exercise daily.

> **LANGUAGE NOTE**
>
> important **for** someone **to do** something
> something can be important **to** someone

2. not common, special
   - The president is a very ***important*** person.

impossible /ɪmˈpɒsɪbl/   adjective
When something is impossible, it cannot happen or you cannot do it.
- It's ***impossible*** to live without water.

improve /ɪmˈpruːv/   verb
improving, improved, has improved
1. get better
   - It will stop raining soon and the weather will ***improve***.
2. make better
   - You must try to ***improve*** your English.

in /ɪn/   preposition
1. You can use **in** to show where someone or something is.
   - Rio de Janeiro is ***in*** Brazil.
2. You can use **in** to show the year or month when something happened.
   - Mr and Mrs Hill were married ***in*** 1992.
3. You can use **in** to mean **during**.
   - We'll have a long holiday ***in*** the summer.
4. You can use **in** to mean **after.**
   - I'll come ***in*** ten minutes.

5. You can use **in** to show how something is written or said.
   - This dictionary is written ***in*** English.
6. You can use **in** to show that you can read or see something in a book, a play or a film.
   - There are a lot of famous stars ***in*** the film.
7. You can use **in** to show what someone is wearing.
   - Catherine came ***in*** a red and blue dress.
8. You can use **in** to mean **at home**.
   - Hassan isn't ***in*** but he'll be back soon.
9. You can use **in** in phrases like **in pain, in good health**, etc.
   - Why do you always speak ***in*** such a loud voice?
   ↻ in anger/doubt/fear/surprise/danger/ safety/silence/secret/use/brief/short/ general/good health, in a hurry

increase¹ /ˈɪŋkriːs/   noun (countable)
a rise in price, numbers, etc
- There's a small ***increase*** in the price of oil.
↻ a big/large/sharp/slight/small/sudden increase, a steady increase

> **LANGUAGE NOTE**
>
> an increase **of** ten dollars, etc **in** the price

increase² /ɪŋˈkriːs/   verb
increasing, increased, has increased
make something bigger or add to it
- People became poorer as food prices ***increased***.

indeed /ɪnˈdiːd/   adverb
You can use **indeed** at the end of a group of words to make **very** stronger.
- Your composition is very good ***indeed***.

> **LANGUAGE NOTE**
>
> ***very*** tall ***indeed***
> a ***very*** tall boy ***indeed*** (BUT NOT a tall boy indeed)

θ	ð	ʃ	dʒ	tʃ	ŋ	ʒ	iː	ɜː	ɪ	æ	ʌ	ɒ
thing	that	shop	jump	chop	sing	measure	been	bird	bit	cat	but	not

indoors /ɪnˈdɔːz/ adverb
inside a building, not outside
- He told me to stay **indoors** until I got better.

influenza /ˌɪnfluˈenzə/ noun (uncountable)
⚠ See **flu**.

information /ˌɪnfəˈmeɪʃn/ noun (uncountable)
what you tell someone, what someone knows
- Have you any **information** about Japan?
- ask for/find/gather/get/have/give information; false/full/important/useful/inside information (= information from someone who knows)

LANGUAGE NOTE	
NEVER	~~an information~~
ALWAYS	some information
OR	a piece of information

ink /ɪŋk/ noun (uncountable)
something which we use in pens to write
- I can't write. There's no **ink** in this pen.

insect /ˈɪnsekt/ noun (countable)
a very small animal with six legs
- Look at the **insect** on the window. It's a bee.
⚠ See box below.

inside¹ /ˈɪnsaɪd/ noun (countable)
a part of something
- Have you painted the **inside** of your flat?

inside² /ɪnˈsaɪd/ adjective
in a building, room, etc
- The **inside** wall of the building is made of brick.

inside³ /ˈɪnsaɪd/ adverb
in a house, a place, etc.
- Let's go **inside** and have a meal.

inspector /ɪnˈspektə*/ noun (countable)
1 someone who sees that everything is all right or working properly
   - My father is a ticket **inspector** on the buses.
2 a policeman
   - The **inspector** told his men to wait outside.

instead /ɪnˈsted/ adverb
in place (of something)
- I don't feel hungry and I don't want any dinner. I'd like an apple **instead.**

instead of /ɪnˈsted ɒv/ preposition
in place of
- I don't feel hungry. I'd like an apple **instead of** my dinner.

LANGUAGE NOTE
Instead of someone/something
Instead of **doing** something
(NEVER ~~instead of to do something~~)

Insects

- bee
- ant
- butterfly
- moth
- fly
- spider

θ	ð	ʃ	dʒ	tʃ	ŋ	ʒ	iː	ɜː	ɪ	æ	ʌ	ɒ
thing	that	shop	jump	chop	sing	measure	been	bird	bit	cat	but	not

invent 115

instructions /ɪnˈstrʌkʃnz/
noun (countable and usually plural)
something which tells you how to do something
- Read the **instructions** carefully before you try to put the film in the camera.
- carry out/follow/give/leave instructions; wait for further instructions; clear instructions, written instructions

> **LANGUAGE NOTE**
>
> instructions **on** / **about** something
> instructions **on** / **about** how to do something

interest /ˈɪntrɪst/ noun (countable)
If you take an interest in something, you like it and want to get to know a lot about it
- I've got no **interest** in this subject.
- take/show/keep up an interest in, lose interest in, have no interest in; a close/great/deep/keen/strong/serious/lively interest in; of great/general interest

interested /ˈɪntrɪstɪd/ adjective
having a liking for something (and wanting to know a lot about it)
- I'm very **interested** in stamp collecting and I've got over 5,000 foreign stamps.
- deeply/greatly/highly/very (much) interested in

> **LANGUAGE NOTE**
>
> COMPARE The lesson was very **interesting**.
> The students were very **interested** in the lesson.

interesting /ˈɪntrɪstɪŋ/ adjective
causing you to like something (and want to know a lot about it)
- I'm reading a very **interesting** book: it's about the world in a hundred years' time!
- highly/very interesting

international /ˌɪntəˈnæʃnəl/ adjective
for, from or to different countries; used by different countries
- Heathrow is a large **international** airport.

interrupt /ˌɪntəˈrʌpt/ verb
When you interrupt someone speaking, you do something to make them stop.
- It's bad manners to **interrupt** the teacher.

interval /ˈɪntəvl/ noun (countable)
a short break between two parts of a film, a play or a concert
- Let's have a cup of coffee during the **interval**.
- a brief/short/long interval

interview /ˈɪntəvjuː/ noun (countable)
a meeting with a person to ask him or her questions
- I'm going for an **interview** for a good job.
- attend/give/have an interview; a job/radio/TV interview

into /ˈɪntuː/ (unstressed /ˈɪntə, ˈɪntʊ/) preposition
1 When you go **into** a place, you go inside (from the outside).
   - Ahmed rushed **into** the shop.
2 You can use **into** to show that things change.
   - Seeds grow **into** flowers.

introduce /ˌɪntrəˈdjuːs/ verb
introducing, introduced, has introduced
1 bring or help someone to meet someone else for the first time; tell someone a person's name or your own name
   - I **introduced** my parents to my teacher.
2 bring something to another place or thing for the first time
   - Who **introduced** rubber trees into Malaysia?

invent /ɪnˈvent/ verb
make something new
- Thomas Edison **invented** the electric light bulb.

θ	ð	ʃ	dʒ	tʃ	ŋ	ʒ	iː	ɜː	ɪ	æ	ʌ	ɒ
thing	that	shop	jump	chop	sing	measure	been	bird	bit	cat	but	not

invention

LANGUAGE NOTE	
COMPARE WITH	discover (= find for the first time)
	invent (= make something new)
discover	a new country, river, lake, etc
	a medicine, a cure
	a new fact
invent	a new machine
	a new way of doing something

invention /ɪnˈvenʃn/ noun (countable)
something completely new which has just been made
- *The electric light bulb was one of Thomas Edison's inventions.*

inventor /ɪnˈventə*/ noun (countable)
someone who makes something completely new for the first time
- *Thomas Edison was a great inventor.*

inverted commas /ɪnˌvɜːtɪd ˈkɒməz/
noun (countable and usually plural)
See **quotation marks**.

invitation /ˌɪnvɪˈteɪʃn/ noun (countable)
When you ask someone to go somewhere or do something with you, you give them an invitation.
- *I sent out twenty invitations to my party.*
- give/send (out)/receive/get/reply/accept/refuse an invitation; a kind invitation (eg *Thank you for your kind invitation....*)

invite /ɪnˈvaɪt/ verb
inviting, invited, has invited
ask someone to go somewhere or to do something with you
- *Why don't you invite Stefan to dinner?*

iron[1] /ˈaɪən/ noun
1 (uncountable) a heavy metal which cannot easily break
- *The old bridge is very strong; it's made of iron.*

2 (countable) something which you can use to make clothes smooth (after you have washed and dried them)
- *Can I borrow your iron, please?*

iron[2] verb
make clothes smooth (with an iron)
- *Could you iron my shirt for me?*

is /ɪz/ (unstressed /z, s/) verb
part of **be** (used after *he, she, it* and singular nouns)
- *"Is Harry at home?"*
"No, he's playing football at school."

LANGUAGE NOTE		
he's = he is	she's = she is	it's = it is

island /ˈaɪlənd/ noun (countable)
a piece of land with sea or water round it
- *Indonesia is a large island in the Pacific Ocean.*

LANGUAGE NOTE	
ALWAYS	the island **of** Bali
NEVER	~~the island Bali~~

isn't /ˈɪznt/
is not
- *It's very hot here, isn't it?*
See also **be**.

it /ɪt/ pronoun
1 You can use **it** to show an animal or object when you have already spoken or written about the animal or object before.
- *Miss Samson bought a new lamp, but when she got home it was broken.*

θ	ð	ʃ	dʒ	tʃ	ŋ	ʒ	iː	ɜː	ɪ	æ	ʌ	ɒ
thing	that	shop	jump	chop	sing	measure	been	bird	bit	cat	but	not

2 You can use **it** to answer questions with *who, what, when,* etc.
   - "*Who is in the bathroom?*" "***It****'s Peter.*"
3 You can use **it** to talk about the weather.
   - ***It****'s raining, isn't **it**?*
4 You can use **it** with the verb **be** followed by adjectives like **difficult, easy, necessary, possible, probable, likely**.
   - ***It****'s difficult to say how I feel.*
   - ***It** won't be necessary for you to come.*

it'll /ˈɪtl/
it will
- ***It'll** be good to see Adam again.*

it's /ɪts/
1 it is
   - ***It's** going to be fine tomorrow.*
2 it has
   - *He says **it's** rained for a month there.*

its /ɪts/ pronoun
belonging to it
- *The little dog has hurt **its** leg.*

LANGUAGE NOTE	
NEVER	Has the poor bird broken it's wing?
ALWAYS	Has the poor bird broken its wing?
it's = it is	its = of it

itself /ɪtˈself/ pronoun
1 You can use **itself** as the object of a verb or preposition.
   - *The cat cut **itself** on the broken glass.*
2 You can use **itself** to make the subject or object seem more important or to make the pronoun it stronger.
   - *The little donkey **itself** opened the gate.*
3 without any help
   - *The dog opened the gate (all by) **itself**.*
4 **by itself** = without anything else
   - *The cat was in a cage **by itself**.*

I've /aɪv/
I have
- ***I've** already finished my homework.*

LANGUAGE NOTE
Use the short form **I've** (= I have) only to make the Present Perfect tense.

	I've bought a new bike.
NEVER	I've a new bike.
ALWAYS	I have a new bike.
OR	I've got a new bike.

θ	ð	ʃ	dʒ	tʃ	ŋ	ʒ	iː	ɜː	ɪ	æ	ʌ	ɒ
thing	that	shop	jump	chop	sing	measure	been	bird	bit	cat	but	not

Jj

jacket /ˈdʒækɪt/ noun (countable)
a short coat
- *Ken's wearing a new **jacket**.*

jail /dʒeɪl/ noun (countable)
also gaol in British English
a prison, a place where criminals are kept
- *The thieves were sent to **jail** for bank robbery.*
  be sent to jail, go to jail
△ See also **prison**.

jar /dʒɑː*/ noun (countable)
something (usually made of glass) in which you can put food, etc
- *Mrs Lawson gave Tina a **jar** of sweets.*

jeans /dʒiːnz/ noun (plural)
trousers made from strong blue cloth
- *Nadia even wears **jeans** at school.*

LANGUAGE NOTE	
EITHER	These jeans **are** dirty.
OR	This pair of jeans **is** dirty.

jewel /ˈdʒuːəl/ noun (countable)
a very expensive stone: eg a diamond

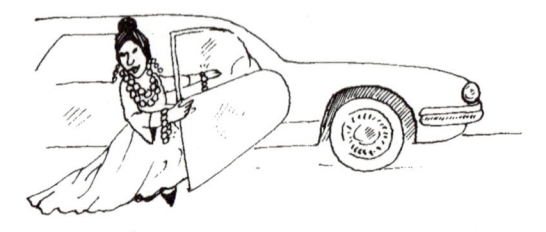

- *Soraya has a lot of **jewels**. She's very rich.*

job /dʒɒb/ noun (countable)
1 work which you do for money
   - *Ken's just got a new **job** in a large office.*
   ✥ do/look for/find/get/land/take (up)/give up/lose a job, offer someone a job, a badly paid/boring/difficult/hard/easy/good/satisfying/steady/well-paid/unpaid/full-time/part-time/desk job/office job
2 a piece of work
   - *"Whose **job** is it to wash up tonight?" "Yours! I did it yesterday."*

join /dʒɔɪn/ verb
1 come together
   - *Go down this road until it **joins** the main road.*
   - ***Join** these two pieces together with glue.*
3 meet
   - *I can't come now but I'll **join** you later.*
4 become a member of a group
   - *I'm going to **join** the school basketball club.*

joke¹ /dʒəʊk/ noun (countable)
a short funny story which makes people laugh
- *I couldn't stop laughing when I heard the **joke**.*
✥ play a joke on someone (= play a trick on someone), tell a joke; a good/poor/old joke

joke² verb
joking, joked, has joked
say something which makes people laugh
- *Mr Lee likes to laugh and **joke** with people.*

LANGUAGE NOTE
joke **with** someone **about** something

journey /ˈdʒɜːnɪ/ noun (countable)
a trip somewhere, going from one place to another
- *It's a two hour **journey** from here to London.*
✥ go on/make/set out on a journey; a dangerous/safe/long/short/tiring/pleasant journey

θ	ð	ʃ	dʒ	tʃ	ŋ	ʒ	iː	ɜː	ɪ	æ	ʌ	ɒ
thing	that	shop	jump	chop	sing	measure	been	bird	bit	cat	but	not

LANGUAGE NOTE

COMPARE a **journey** (by road)
a **flight** (= a "journey" by air)
a **voyage** (= a "journey" by sea)

judge¹ /dʒʌdʒ/ noun (countable)
1 someone who decides whether people have done something wrong and how they should be punished
   - The **judge** decided that the man was a thief and sent him to prison for six months.
2 someone who decides who should win a competition
   - The **judge** gave first prize to Alison Shaw for her painting of a tiger.

judge² verb
judging, judged, has judged
choose the winner of a competition, decide who should win
   - It was hard to **judge** who was the best singer.
   judge fairly

juice /dʒuːs/ noun (uncountable)
the liquid in fruit or vegetables
   - Ben likes orange **juice** but not tomato **juice**.
   ↻ fruit juice, vegetable juice

jump /dʒʌmp/ verb
1 move quickly into the air with both feet off the ground
   - How high can you **jump**?
2 go over or cross something by jumping
   - "Can you **jump** (over) this wall?"
     "No, but I can **jump** (across) that stream."
3 move quickly
   - Tom ran away and **jumped** into his car.

jumper /'dʒʌmpə*/ noun (countable)
1 (British English, American English: **sweater**) a piece of clothing which you wear over the top half of your body
   - Wear a **jumper** over your dress: it'll be cold.
2 (American English) a dress without sleeves worn over a blouse
   - She wore a white blouse and blue **jumper**.

jungle /'dʒʌŋgl/ noun (countable, uncountable)
a place in a hot country with tall trees and other plants (all growing closely together)
   - They're lost in the **jungles** of South America.
   - There was **jungle** all round the village.

just /dʒʌst/ (unstressed /dʒəst/) adverb
1 exactly, no more and no less
   - I've got **just** enough money for my bus fare.
   - His new car is **just** like yours.
2 not long before
   - I'm sorry Noora isn't in. She's **just** left.

LANGUAGE NOTE

In British English **just** is used with the Present Perfect tense with the meaning above.
In American English, **just** is usually used with the Past Simple tense with this meaning.
COMPARE I've just done it. (British English)
         I just did it. (American English)

3 now
   - I'm **just** on my way to the bus stop.
4 only
   - Don't believe his story. It was **just** a joke.
5 You can use **just** in many other ways, especially to show that something is not really important or difficult.
   - **Just** go along the street and turn left.
6 **Just a minute/moment/second** = Wait a short time.
   "Are you doing anything next Wednesday?"
   "**Just a second.** I'll get my diary and see."

LANGUAGE NOTE

Note the place of **just** in the following sentences.
He's **just** (= a moment ago) given me what I wanted.
He's given me **just** (= exactly) what I wanted.
We returned home **just** as the clock struck six.

θ	ð	ʃ	dʒ	tʃ	ŋ	ʒ	iː	ɜː	ɪ	æ	ʌ	ɒ
thing	that	shop	jump	chop	sing	measure	been	bird	bit	cat	but	not

Kk

keep /kiːp/ verb

keeping, kept /kept/ , has kept

1. have or hold something and not let it go
   - *You should keep your dog on a chain.*
2. put something somewhere and not move it
   - *Where do you keep sugar and tea?*
3. own (animals)
   - *Do you keep any pets?*
4. keep a diary, a note, etc
   - *I've always kept a diary so that I know what I've done.*
5. continue
   - *Mrs Ervas keeps (on) practising English.*

LANGUAGE NOTE	
NEVER	keep on to do something
ALWAYS	keep on *doing* something

6. stay
   - *Keep calm! Everything will be all right.*
7. not change, not move
   - *Keep still while I take a photograph.*
8. **keep a promise** = do what you said you would do
   - *I must keep my promise and not smoke.*

kept /kept/ verb

past tense and past participle of **keep**
- *Have you ever kept a dog?*

kettle /ˈketl/ noun (countable)

something in which you can boil water
- *I'll put the kettle on and make a cup of tea.*
- put the kettle on (= fill it with water and boil it) ; a kettle boils, a few kettles whistle (when they boil); an electric kettle

key /kiː/ noun (countable)

something which you use to open a door, a gate, a drawer, etc which is locked
- *I lost the key to my flat and couldn't get in.*
- put a key in a lock, turn a key

kick /kɪk/ verb

hit something or someone with your foot

- *Vincent kicked the ball through a window.*

kidnap /ˈkɪdnæp/ verb

kidnapping, kidnapped, has kidnapped

SPELLING NOTE
double *p*: kidna**pp**ing, kidna**pp**ed

take away and hide someone and then ask for money
- *President Aiwa's daughter was kidnapped, but the police found her and caught the kidnappers.*

kill /kɪl/ verb

make someone die
- *Two passengers were killed in the accident.*
- See also **die.**

kind[1] /kaɪnd/ noun (countable)

something in the same group as something else
- *Oranges and apples are different kinds of fruit.*

LANGUAGE NOTE	
COMPARE	What kind of fruit *is* this?
	What kind of oranges *are* these?

θ	ð	ʃ	dʒ	tʃ	ŋ	ʒ	iː	ɜː	ɪ	æ	ʌ	ɒ
thing	that	shop	jump	chop	sing	measure	been	bird	bit	cat	but	not

kind [2] adjective

nice, good
- *Mary is a very **kind** person. She gave me two of her sandwiches.*

> **LANGUAGE NOTE**
>
> kind *to* someone
> kind *of* someone *to do* something

△ See also **sort**; see also **type** [1].

king /kɪŋ/ noun (countable)

a man who is the head of a country
- *The **king** waved to the crowd as he passed.*

kiss /kɪs/ verb

touch someone with your lips
- *Tamara **kissed** her aunt as she left.*

kitchen /ˈkɪtʃɪn/ noun (countable)

a room where you can cook food
- *Teresa is in the **kitchen** cooking dinner.*

kite /kaɪt/ noun (countable)

narrow pieces of wood covered with paper or cloth with a long string at the end of it

- *Tom and Dave are flying their **kites**.*

kneel /niːl/ verb

kneeling, knelt /nelt/, has knelt
bend down on one's knees
- *We **knelt** down and looked under the table.*

knew /njuː/ verb

past tense of **know**
- *I **knew** the answers to most of the questions.*

knickers /ˈnɪkəz/ noun (plural)

underwear worn by girls and women below the waist
- *"Wear a clean pair of **knickers**," Mrs Small told Mary.*

△ See also **underpants**.

knock [1] /nɒk/ noun (countable)

the noise which is made by someone hitting something
- *There was a loud **knock** at the door.*

knock [2] verb

hit a door, a window, etc several times (usually to let people know you are there)
- *Who's **knocking** at the door?*

↻ knock loudly/softly

knock down /ˌnɒk ˈdaʊn/ phrasal verb

hit so that someone or something falls on the ground
- *Mr Hill was away from work for three months after he had been **knocked down** by a car.*

knot /nɒt/ noun (countable)

a place (in a piece of string or cloth) where two parts have been tied together
- *Please tie a **knot** in the string.*

↻ tie/untie/undo/loosen a knot

know /nəʊ/ verb

knowing, knew /njuː/, has known /nəʊn/
1 learn and understand
   - *How much of the story do you **know**?*
2 have something in your mind
   - *Do you **know** where Mary is?*
3 **know about** = have heard about
   - *Did Victoria **know about** the accident?*
4 **know about** = have studied, have learned about
   - *Paul **knows** a lot **about** collecting stamps.*

θ	ð	ʃ	dʒ	tʃ	ŋ	ʒ	iː	ɜː	ɪ	æ	ʌ	ɒ
thing	that	shop	jump	chop	sing	measure	been	bird	bit	cat	but	not

LANGUAGE NOTE
1 NEVER ~~Do you know to play chess?~~ ALWAYS Do you know **how to** play chess?
2 The verb **know** is not used in the continuous tenses. NEVER ~~We are knowing how you feel.~~ ALWAYS We **know** how you feel.
3 Compare **know** and **learn** in the following sentences. How do you **know** about it? When did you **learn** about it? (= get to know)

Ll

knowledge /ˈnɒlɪdʒ/ noun (uncountable, countable)
what you have learned and understood
- Do you have any **knowledge** of Macao?
- He has a good **knowledge** of English history.

↻ have a good knowledge of (= know a lot about), have a poor knowledge of (= not know much about);
(a) deep/wide/fair/excellent/slight knowledge of

known /nəʊn/ verb
past participle of **know**
- We've **known** Stefan for over ten years.

label /ˈleɪbl/ noun (countable)
a small piece of paper, card or plastic with important information on it (usually the name of someone or something, etc)
- "What's this medicine?"
 "Look at the **label** on the bottle and see."

↻ have/put/stick/tie a label on

ladder /ˈlædə*/ noun (countable)
a wooden or metal frame with steps on it

- Can you climb up the **ladder** and rescue the cat?

↻ climb up/down/go up/come down a ladder, put up a ladder; a rope ladder

lady /ˈleɪdɪ/ noun (countable)
plural: ladies
a woman
- There's an old **lady** crossing the road.

laid /leɪd/ verb
past tense and past participle of **lay**
- The bird **laid** two eggs this morning.

lain /leɪn/ verb
past participle of **lie**
- He's **lain** in bed all day without moving.

θ	ð	ʃ	dʒ	tʃ	ŋ	ʒ	iː	ɜː	ɪ	æ	ʌ	ɒ
thing	that	shop	jump	chop	sing	measure	been	bird	bit	cat	but	not

lake /leɪk/ noun (countable)

a lot of water with land all round it
- *There are several large **lakes** in England.*

> **LANGUAGE NOTE**
>
> Don't use **the** in front of the name of a lake.
> ALWAYS Lake Victoria (NEVER the Lake Victoria)

lamb /læm/ noun (countable, uncountable)

a young sheep

> **LANGUAGE NOTE**
>
> When you are talking about a **lamb** as a living animal in a field, use *a*.
>   There's **a** lamb in the field.
> When you are talking about **lamb** as food on a dish, you should not use *a* before it.
>   Is this mutton or lamb?

lame /leɪm/ adjective

Someone is lame if they cannot walk properly (because their legs or feet hurt, etc).
- *Mr Asoko is **lame** and walks with a stick.*

lamp /læmp/ noun (countable)

a light which you can move
- *It was dark so I switched on the **lamp**.*
- light/turn on/off/ switch on/off a lamp; a reading/table lamp

land¹ /lænd/ noun

1 (uncountable) the part of the earth which is not the sea
   - *We were at sea for a week before we saw **land**.*
   - reach/see land
2 (uncountable) ground, earth
   - *Mr Lee has just bought some **land** in Canada so that he can build a house there.*
3 (countable) a country
   - *Canada is a **land** with very few people.*

land² verb

1 come to the ground
   - *The aeroplane **landed** safely.*
2 make (an aeroplane) come to the ground
   - *Do you know how to **land** the plane?*

lane /leɪn/ noun (countable)

1 a small narrow road in the country
   - *The car's too big to get down the **lane**.*
2 part of a wide road
   - *An accident in the middle **lane** of the motorway caused a traffic jam.*

language /ˈlæŋɡwɪdʒ/ noun (countable)

the words people use (and the way they use them) to talk to one another in a country
- *Mr Low can speak three different **languages**: English, French and Chinese.*
- learn/speak (in) /use a language; your first/second language; a foreign language; bad/strong language (= words which are not polite)

large /lɑːdʒ/ adjective

1 big in size
   - *Elephants are very **large** animals.*
2 big in amount
   - *Can I have a **large** ice cream, please?*

> **LANGUAGE NOTE**
>
> NEVER   a big number of people
>   a big amount of water
> ALWAYS **a large number of** people
>   **a large amount of** water

last¹ /lɑːst/ verb

continuing for some time
- *The film **lasted** for over three hours.*

last² adjective

1 at the end, the only one which remains
   - *My birthday is on the **last** day of the year: December 31st.*
2 the time before this one
   - *They went to see their grandfather **last** week.*

> **LANGUAGE NOTE**
>
> 1 COMPARE I met him last week.
>   (NEVER   I met him the last week.)
>   WITH   I met him in the last week of May.
> 2 last night BUT yesterday evening

last³ adverb
1 after all the others
 • Stephen came **last** in the race.
2 before now
 • I **last** heard from Susie over a year ago.
3 **at last** = in the end
 • She came **at last** after we'd waited an hour.

late¹ /leɪt/ adjective
after the right time
 • Several people were **late** for the meeting.

late² adverb
after the right time (opposite = early)
 • I missed the bus and arrived ten minutes **late**.

later (on) /ˌleɪtər ˈɒn/ adverb
afterwards
 • I'll see you **later (on)** - say, in two hours.

laugh /lɑːf/ verb
make a sound when something is funny
 • We couldn't stop **laughing** at the funny sight.

> **LANGUAGE NOTE**
>
> laugh **at** someone/something/a joke
> laugh **about** something which happened

law /lɔː/ noun (countable)
a set of rules which everyone must obey
 • It is against the **law** to steal.
 ☞ break the law (= do something wrong), obey the law

lawyer /ˈlɔɪə*/ noun (countable)
someone who can advise and help you with the law
 • You should see a **lawyer** before you say anything to the police.

lay /leɪ/ verb
laying, laid /leɪd/, has laid
1 put something on top of something else
 • I'm learning how to **lay** bricks.
2 make an egg
 • This hen has **laid** four eggs.

> **LANGUAGE NOTE**
>
> COMPARE   She **laid** her clothes on the bed.
>   She's **laid** her clothes on the bed.
> WITH   She **lay** on the bed.
>   She's **lain** on the bed.

lazy /ˈleɪzɪ/ adjective
lazier, laziest
not wanting to work
 • Bob is very **lazy**. He watches TV all day.

lead /liːd/ verb
leading, led /led/, has led
1 go in front of others (to show them the way), take
 • I'll **lead** you to the hut in the forest.

> **LANGUAGE NOTE**
>
> It is often better to use **take** instead of **lead**.
> Could you **take** me to the headmaster's office. (NOT lead)

2 go towards
 • Where does this road **lead**?
3 be winning
 • At present our team is **leading**: 3 -1.

leader /ˈliːdə*/ noun (countable)
1 the chief person, the person who gives orders
 • The **leader** of the group told us to be quiet.
 ☞ a born leader (= a very good leader), a strong leader
2 the person who is winning in a race or a competition
 • Only two runners stayed with the **leader**.

leaf /liːf/ noun (countable)
plural: leaves /liːvz/
the green flat parts of plants and trees

θ	ð	ʃ	dʒ	tʃ	ŋ	ʒ	iː	ɜː	ɪ	æ	ʌ	ɒ
thing	that	shop	jump	chop	sing	measure	been	bird	bit	cat	but	not

- *Many trees lose their **leaves** in autumn.*

lean /liːn/ verb

leaning, leant /lent/ or leaned, has leant or has leaned

PRONUNCIATION NOTE

leant is pronounced /lent/
leaned is pronounced /leend/

1 bend your body
   - *She **leant** out of the window to see who was in the street.*
2 put something against something else
   - *Shall I **lean** the ladder against this wall?*

learn /lɜːn/ verb

learning, learnt or learned, has learnt or has learned

study and find out
- *We're **learning** how to use computers.*

LANGUAGE NOTE

learn something *from* someone

least /liːst/ adjective

little, less, least
- *I've got the bottle with the **least** water in it.*
- See also **little**.

least, at adverb phrase

1 You can use **at least** to show the smallest number or amount which is likely.
   - *There were **at least** fifty people at the party.*
2 You can use **at least** to show the smallest thing you could have done.
   - *You should see the headmaster or **at least** phone him.*

leather /'leðə*/ noun (uncountable)

the skin of an animal
- *Is this chair made of **leather** or plastic?*

leave /liːv/ verb

leaving, left /left/, has left
1 put or let something stay in the same place
   - *You can **leave** your car in the car park.*
2 go away or go out
   - *We have to **leave** home early every morning.*

LANGUAGE NOTE

leave Hong Kong *for* Taiwan
(NOT USUALLY leave from Hong Kong)

leaves /liːvz/ noun (countable)

plural of **leaf**
- *The weather is cold and the **leaves** have fallen off the trees.*

led /led/ verb

past tense and past participle of **lead**
- *The narrow path **led** nowhere.*

leek /liːk/ noun (countable)

See box on page 238.

left[1] /left/ verb

past tense and past participle of **leave**
- *Esther **left** home early this morning.*

left[2] adjective

the opposite to **right**
- *I had to write with my **left** hand after I'd broken my right arm.*

leg /leg/ noun (countable)

1 part of a chair, table, etc on which it stands
   - *One of the **legs** of this chair is broken.*
2 part of the body which people and animals use to walk
   - *Oh dear! I've fallen and hurt my **leg**.*
- bend/cross/lift/raise your leg(s)
- See box on page 25.

θ	ð	ʃ	dʒ	tʃ	ŋ	ʒ	iː	ɜː	ɪ	æ	ʌ	ɒ
thing	that	shop	jump	chop	sing	measure	been	bird	bit	cat	but	not

lemon /ˈlemən/ noun (countable, uncountable)
⚠ See box on page 89.

lend /lend/ verb
lending, lent /lent/ , has lent
give someone something to use for a time (but not for always)
* Can you **lend** me ten dollars? I'll pay you back.

LANGUAGE NOTE

lend something **to** someone
 = give something for a certain time
borrow something **from** someone
 = take something for a certain time
ALWAYS   Can I **borrow** your ruler?
OR   Will you **lend** me your ruler?
(NEVER   ~~Can I lend your ruler?~~)

---

length /leŋθ/ noun (uncountable, countable)
how long something is
* "What's the **length** of this wall?"
"I think it's over twelve metres in **length**."

lens /lenz/ noun (countable)
plural: lenses
the special glass in a camera or pair of glasses
* This camera is more expensive than the others because it has a better **lens**.

lent /lent/ verb
past tense and past participle of **lend**
* Paul **lent** me his pen for the exam.

leopard /ˈlepəd/ noun (countable)
female: leopardess /ˈlepədes/
⚠ See box on page 10.

less /les/ adjective
little, less, least
not as much as
* Four is **less** than five.

LANGUAGE NOTE

less rice BUT fewer potatoes (NOT less potatoes)

⚠ See also **little**.

lesson /ˈlesn/ noun (countable)
a short period of time when students are taught about a certain subject: eg English, geography.
* My favourite **lesson** is music.
↻ take lessons (in) a certain subject

let /let/ verb
letting, let, has let
1 allow someone to do something
* Will you **let** me take a photograph of you?

LANGUAGE NOTE

NEVER   ~~I let her to do it.~~
ALWAYS   I let her **do** it.

---

2 allow someone to enter or go out
* The guard refused to **let** me in.
3 You can use **let's** or **let us** to suggest doing something. It shows that you want to do something.
* **Let's** go to the cinema on Saturday.

letter /ˈletə*/ noun (countable)
1 There are 26 letters in the English alphabet: A, B, C, D, E, F, G, etc.
* C is the third **letter** of the alphabet.
2 something you write to someone
* I enjoy writing **letters** to all my pen-friends.
↻ drop a letter into a mailbox (American English), post a letter (British English), mail a letter (American English); send/write/get/receive a letter

lettuce /ˈletɪs/ noun (countable, uncountable)
⚠ See box on page 238.

library /ˈlaɪbrərɪ/ noun (countable)
plural: libraries
a room or a building where books are kept so that people can use them or borrow them to read
* I'm reading a very interesting **library** book.

lid /lɪd/ noun (countable)
the top of a box or a jar
* Take the **lid** off and look inside the box.

θ	ð	ʃ	dʒ	tʃ	ŋ	ʒ	iː	ɜː	ɪ	æ	ʌ	ɒ
thing	that	shop	jump	chop	sing	measure	been	bird	bit	cat	but	not

lie¹ /laɪ/ noun (countable)
something which you say which you know is not true
- *Rick is not very honest and often tells **lies**.*

lie² verb
lying, lied, has lied
say something which you know is not true
- *I'm sure Laura was telling the truth: she never **lies**.*

lie (down) /ˌlaɪ ˈdaʊn/ (phrasal) verb
lying (down), lay /leɪ/(down), has lain /leɪn/ (down)
be in a flat position, rest your body in this position (You usually **lie down** when you go to bed.)

- *Don't **lie** on the grass. It's wet.*

LANGUAGE NOTE

ALWAYS   I lay on the grass yesterday.
NEVER   ~~I'm going to lay on the grass.~~
(Only hens and other birds can lay (eggs) on the grass. People **lie** on the grass.)

⚠ See also **lay** (Language Note).

life /laɪf/ noun (countable)
plural: lives /laɪvz/
1 being alive
   - *He saved my **life**.*
2 the time when you are alive
   - *My grandfather was a farmer all his **life**. He often told people how happy a **life** he had.*

✺ end your life (= die, kill yourself), go through life (= live), lay down your life for someone/something (= die for them, especially during a war), lead a (busy, etc) life, lose your life (= die, be killed), put an end to your life (= kill yourself), save someone's life, shorten your life, spend/live your life, start a new life (= begin again); a busy/quiet/difficult/hard/easy/exciting/dull/long/short/happy/lonely/simple/stormy life

lift¹ /lɪft/ noun (countable)
(American English: elevator)
1 a machine like a large box which carries you up and down a building (from one floor to another)
   - *Let's take the **lift** up to the third floor.*
✺ take/go in the lift
2 a journey in someone's car
   - *Mr Small gave us a **lift** to school.*

lift² verb
pick up something or someone
- *When I **lifted** the rock, ants ran everywhere.*

light¹ /laɪt/ noun
1 (countable) something which helps us to see when it is dark
   - *I can't see. Can you switch on the **light**?*
✺ put on/off/turn on/off/out/switch on/off/out/a light, turn the lights down/up; a bright/strong light
2 (uncountable) being bright so you can see
   - *There isn't enough **light** to read.*
✺ moonlight, sunlight

light² verb
lighting, lit /lɪt/ or lighted, has lit or has lighted
1 make something burn
   - *You can **light** the fire with these sticks.*
2 make something bright (and no longer dark)
   - *Anna uses a candle to **light** the hut.*

θ	ð	ʃ	dʒ	tʃ	ŋ	ʒ	iː	ɜː	ɪ	æ	ʌ	ɒ
thing	that	shop	jump	chop	sing	measure	been	bird	bit	cat	but	not

lightning /ˈlaɪtnɪŋ/ noun (uncountable)
the bright light which suddenly comes from the sky when there is thunder
- *That tree was hit by lightning during the storm.*

like ¹ /laɪk/ verb
liking, liked, has liked
1. enjoy
   - *Do you like chocolate?*
2. think someone or something is nice
   - *I like Linda but I don't like her sister.*
🔁 like someone/something a lot; like someone/something very much
3. **would like** = want
   - *I'd like another cup of coffee, please.*

LANGUAGE NOTE

COMPARE	"*Would* you *like to dance* now?"
	"Yes, please?"
WITH	"*Do* you *like dancing*?"
	"Yes, I do."
(NEVER	Do you like to dance now?)

---

like ² preposition
1. (look or behave) nearly the same as
   - *Do you think Catherine is like her mother?*
2. in the same way as
   - *I wish I could speak English like Mabel.*
3. If you ask what something is **like**, you want someone to describe it.
   - *What was Hong Kong like?*

likely /ˈlaɪklɪ/ adjective
likelier, likeliest
If something is **likely**, it seems that it will be true or it will probably happen.
- *Is it likely to rain today?*

LANGUAGE NOTE

NEVER	We'll likely be late.
ALWAYS	It's likely we'll be late.
OR	We'll probably be late.

---

lime /laɪm/ noun (countable, uncountable)
⚠ See box on page 89.

line /laɪn/ noun (countable)
1. a long, straight piece of string, wire etc
   - *She's hanging the clothes on the line to dry.*
2. a long straight mark
   - *Draw a straight line across the page.*
🔁 a broken line (= - - - -),
   a dotted line (= ....),
   a curved/straight/fine/thin/thick line,
   a wavy line (= 〜〜〜)
3. a row of words
   - *There's a mistake on the first line.*
4. people or things which are side by side or one behind the other
   - *The pupils all stood in a long line outside the classroom.*
🔁 form a line, get into (a) line, stand/wait in (a) line

lion /ˈlaɪən/ noun (countable)
female: lioness /ˈlaɪənes/
⚠ See box on page 10.

liquid /ˈlɪkwɪd/ noun (countable, uncountable)
something like water which can be poured (Water, milk, wine, coffee, tea, oil and petrol are all liquids.)
- *Can you pour the liquid into this bottle?*
🔁 a clear liquid (= a liquid which you can see through), a cloudy liquid (= a liquid which you cannot see through)

list /lɪst/ noun (countable)
names and words which you write under one another or next to one another
- *Before you go shopping, it's always useful to make a list of what you want.*
🔁 draw up/make (up) /go down/ read (down) a list

listen /ˈlɪsn/ verb
give your attention to someone who is speaking, hear what someone is saying, hear noises
- *Maria enjoys listening to music on the radio.*

θ	ð	ʃ	dʒ	tʃ	ŋ	ʒ	iː	ɜː	ɪ	æ	ʌ	ɒ
thing	that	shop	jump	chop	sing	measure	been	bird	bit	cat	but	not

> **LANGUAGE NOTE**
>
> hear someone / something
> BUT listen **to** someone / something

See also **hear**¹.

lit /lɪt/ verb
past tense and past participle of **light**
- Have you **lit** a fire yet?

little /ˈlɪtl/ adjective
less, least
1 small in size
   - There's a **little** mouse in the cupboard.
   See also **small**¹.
2 small in amount
   - Peter wasn't hungry and ate only a **little** fish.

> **LANGUAGE NOTE**
>
> COMPARE There was **a little** salt left.
> (= some but not much)
> There was **little** salt left.
> (= hardly any)

See also **few**; see also **least**; see also **less**.
3 young
   - Henry's **little** brother is only three.
   See also **small** 2.

live¹ /lɪv/ verb
living, lived, has lived
1 be alive, not be dead
   - Shakespeare **lived** four hundred years ago.
2 have your home (in a certain place)
   - Does Mr Tawfic **live** in Cairo?

> **LANGUAGE NOTE**
>
> COMPARE **Does** Anna Lee **live** in Hong Kong?
> (= Is her home there?)
> Is Anna Lee **living** in Hong Kong?
> (= Is she staying there at present?)

live² /laɪv/ adjective
1 having life, not dead
   - Be careful: that's a real **live** snake you're holding!
2 happening now, not recorded
   - The match is being shown **live** on TV tonight.

lives /laɪvz/ noun
plural of **life**
- What interesting **lives** those people have!

living room /ˈlɪvɪŋ rʊm/ noun (countable)
usually the main room of a house or flat, the lounge, the sitting room
- Let's go into the **living room** and watch TV.

load /ləʊd/ verb
put things on a lorry, a ship, etc
- Please **load** the vegetables onto this lorry.

loaf /ləʊf/ noun
plural: loaves /ləʊvz/
a large piece of bread
- Could I have a **loaf**, please?

lock¹ /lɒk/ noun (countable)
something on a door, gate, drawer which you open by using a key
- I can't turn the key in the **lock**.

lock² verb
close something with a key so that no one can open it without the key
- I forgot to **lock** the door of the flat when I left.

lonely /ˈləʊnlɪ/ adjective
lonelier, loneliest
1 without friends or people to talk to
   - I felt very **lonely** when I first started working in London.
2 with few people nearby
   - Mr and Mrs Pearson live in a very **lonely** part of the country.

long /lɒŋ/ adjective
1 not short
   - Bob has **long** legs and can walk very fast.

θ	ð	ʃ	dʒ	tʃ	ŋ	ʒ	iː	ɜː	ɪ	æ	ʌ	ɒ
thing	that	shop	jump	chop	sing	measure	been	bird	bit	cat	but	not

2   You can use **long** to ask how much something measures from one end to the other.
    • *"How **long** is this wall?"*
      *"It's twelve metres **long**."*
3   You can use **long** to ask about the time it will take from the beginning to the end.
    • *How **long** was the concert?*
4   You can also use **long** to show a period of time.
    • *Have you been waiting **long**?*
5   **before long** = soon
    • *They'll catch the thieves **before long**.*

look /lʊk/ verb

1   turn your eyes and watch
    • ***Look** at the blackboard and read the words on it.*

LANGUAGE NOTE
COMPARE I **looked** at you in town this morning. (= I turned my eyes towards you and hoped you would see me.) I **saw** you in town this morning. (= I just happened to turn my eyes towards you when I was there.) I **watched** you in town this morning. (= I stopped to see what you were doing and looked for some time.)

⚠ See also **see**; see also **watch** 2.

2   read or examine (a book, etc)
    • *Have you **looked** at the exercise books yet?*

LANGUAGE NOTE
see or read something BUT look **at** something

3   seem to be
    • *Donald **looked** very happy when I met him.*

look after /ˌlʊk ˈɑːftə*/ phrasal verb
care for
• *Does a nurse **look after** old Mrs Li?*

look for /ˈlʊk fɔː*/ phrasal verb
try to find
• *I've **looked** everywhere **for** my glasses but I can't find them.*

LANGUAGE NOTE
NEVER We looked after Tom for an hour before we found him. ALWAYS We looked **for** Tom for an hour before we found him.

look forward to /ˌlʊk ˈfɔːwəd tuː/ phrasal verb
want something to happen
• *I'm **looking forward to** seeing Bill and Mabel.*

look like /ˈlʊk laɪk/ phrasal verb

1   appear similar
    • *Dave and Sam are brothers. That's why they **look like** each other.*
2   seem to be going to
    • *The sky is very dark now: it **looks like** rain.*

look out /ˌlʊk ˈaʊt/ phrasal verb
be careful
• ***Look out**, Anita! There's a car coming.*

look up /ˌlʊk ˈʌp/ phrasal verb
find out information about something
• *If you don't understand this word, **look** it **up** in the dictionary.*

loose /luːs/ adjective

1   too big and not fitting closely to the body
    • *Mary became very thin after her illness, and all her clothes were too **loose**.*
2   not fixed to something
    • *This screw is **loose**. I think it will fall off.*
⟳ come/cut/let/set/turn loose
⚠ See also **loosen**; see also **lose**.

loosen /ˈluːsn/ verb
make less tight
• *Can you **loosen** this screw, please?*

LANGUAGE NOTE
NEVER Don't loose the screw. ALWAYS Don't **lose** the screw. (= put it somewhere and be unable to find it) OR Don't **loosen** the screw. (= make it loose)

⚠ See also **loose**; see also **lose**.

θ	ð	ʃ	dʒ	tʃ	ŋ	ʒ	iː	ɜː	ɪ	æ	ʌ	ɒ
thing	that	shop	jump	chop	sing	measure	been	bird	bit	cat	but	not

lorry /'lɒrɪ/ noun (countable)
plural: lorries
a kind of large car which is used to carry large and heavy things from one place to another

- The men were putting bricks onto the **lorry**.

lose /luːz/ verb
losing, lost /lɒst/, has lost
1. put something down and forget where you have put it
    - I'm always **losing** my glasses.
2. not have something which you had before
    - I have a small hole in my pocket, and so I often **lose** my money.
3. not win
    - Our team **lost** the match 2 - 0.

⚠ See also **loose**; see also **loosen**.

lot /lɒt/ or **lots** ¹ /lɒts/ noun (countable)
1. a large number, many
    - There were **a lot** of people in the cinema.
    - There were **lots** of people in the cinema.
2. a large amount, much
    - Miss Chan gave us **a lot** of rice.
    - Miss Chan gave us **lots** of rice.
3. **the lot** = all, everything
    - There were seven bars of chocolate: one for each of us. But Susie ate **the lot**.

lot or **lots** ² adverb
1. much
    - Your work is **a lot** better now.
2. often
    - Bob phones Linda **a lot**, doesn't he?

loud /laʊd/ adjective
noisy
- Please turn the television down. It's far too **loud**.

loudly /'laʊdlɪ/ adverb
noisily
- He shouted to his friend as **loudly** as he could.

lounge /laʊndʒ/ noun (countable)
1. usually the main room of a house or flat, the living room, the sitting room
    - Let's go into the **lounge** and have a chat.
2. a very large room at an airport where passengers can wait
    - The airport **lounge** was full of passengers.
    ✍ a transit lounge (= a lounge where you wait when you change aircraft)
3. a large room in a hotel, etc where people can rest, meet or talk
    - Shall we have some coffee in the **lounge**?

love /lʌv/ verb
loving, loved, has loved
1. like someone very much
    - I was sad when she died because I **loved** her.
    ✍ love someone blindly (= be unable to see someone's faults, etc), love someone dearly/deeply/very much
2. like (to do/doing) something very much
    - I **love** eating chocolate.

LANGUAGE NOTE

Be careful when you use *love* for things, especially when you use adverbs like *very much* and *a lot*. It is usually better to use *like a lot*.
NEVER   I love my new camera a lot.
ALWAYS   I *like* my new camera a lot.

---

lovely /'lʌvlɪ/ adjective
lovelier, loveliest
very nice (used about someone or something that you like a lot)
- I think this village is **lovely**.

low ¹ /ləʊ/ adjective
1. not high
    - My small dog can only jump over **low** walls.
2. not loud
    - Mr Mawani spoke in a **low** voice.

low ² adverb
lower, lowest
not high
- The plane flew very **low** over the town.

θ	ð	ʃ	dʒ	tʃ	ŋ	ʒ	iː	ɜː	ɪ	æ	ʌ	ɒ
thing	that	shop	jump	chop	sing	measure	been	bird	bit	cat	but	not

luck /lʌk/ noun (uncountable)
something good which happens by chance
- *I need a lot of luck if I'm going to pass this exam.*
- bring someone luck, have (a lot of) luck; bad/good/hard luck; in luck

luckily /ˈlʌkɪli/ adverb
You use **luckily** to show that you are glad that something good has happened by chance.
- *Luckily I caught the last bus home.*

lucky /ˈlʌki/ adjective
luckier, luckiest
1. having good luck
   - *Nicola was very lucky to win the first prize.*
2. bringing good luck
   - *I think that seven is a lucky number.*

luggage /ˈlʌɡɪdʒ/ noun (uncountable)
bags and cases which you can take with you when you are travelling
- *Can I help you to carry your luggage?*

lunch /lʌntʃ/ noun (uncountable, countable)
plural: lunches
the meal people eat in the middle of the day
- *I usually have sandwiches for lunch.*
- lunch-time (= the time when you have lunch) eat/have lunch, have something for lunch, make/prepare lunch

LANGUAGE NOTES

1. ALWAYS have lunch   NEVER have a lunch
2. Some people in Britain call their midday meal **dinner** (NOT lunch). If they do this, they call their evening meal **tea** or **supper**.

See also **dinner**.

lychee /ˈlaɪtʃiː/ noun (countable)
See box on page 89.

lying /ˈlaɪ-ɪŋ/ verb
1. part of **lie, lay, has lain**
   - *Sam has spent all morning lying in bed.*
2. part of **lie, lied, has lied**
   - *Harry said the camera was new but I'm sure he was lying.*

M m

machine /məˈʃiːn/ noun (countable)
something which uses electricity or another kind of power from an engine to do something
- *Sarah has just bought a new sewing machine.*
- an answering machine (= a small machine which records telephone messages), a sewing/washing machine

made /meɪd/ verb
past tense and past participle of **make**
1. *I made only one mistake in my composition.*
2. **made of** = built from, etc
   - *This chair is made of plastic - not wood.*

LANGUAGE NOTE

COMPARE
This shirt is made of cotton.
(i.e. The cotton hasn't changed: it is a cotton shirt. You can still see and feel the cotton.)
This cake is made *from* flour, raisins and lots of dried fruit.
(ie The flour, raisins and dried fruit have now changed into something new: this cake. You can no longer see and feel the flour, raisins and dried fruit.)

magazine /ˌmæɡəˈziːn/ noun (countable)
a book with a paper cover which is usually printed every week, every month etc
- *Dave gets a magazine on photography every week.*
- a popular magazine (= a magazine which is read by a lot of people)

magic /ˈmædʒɪk/ noun (uncountable)
a strange power to do something which is usually impossible or very unusual

θ	ð	ʃ	dʒ	tʃ	ŋ	ʒ	iː	ɜː	ɪ	æ	ʌ	ɒ
thing	that	shop	jump	chop	sing	measure	been	bird	bit	cat	but	not

- *I didn't believe in **magic** until I saw Dandini pull a rabbit out of a hat.*
- black magic (= magic which is used to do bad things)

magician /məˈdʒɪʃn/ noun (countable)
a man who shows people he can do something which is usually impossible or very unusual

- *Charles Hill is a **magician** and does tricks at children's parties.*

mail /meɪl/ noun (uncountable)
(American English)
See **post** [1] 1.

main /meɪn/ adjective
chief, most important
- *What was the **main** point of the talk?*

make /meɪk/ verb
making, made /meɪd/, has made
1 put things together to build or produce something
   - *Tim's uncle **made** him a kite for his birthday, and his aunt **made** him a cake.*
2 cause someone to do something
   - *Helen's father usually **makes** her do her homework before she can watch TV.*
3 cause something to happen
   - *Stop **making** such a lot of noise.*
4 cause someone to feel something or have something
   - *John's success **made** us all happy.*
5 put or add something to make something else
   - *Black and white **make** grey.*
   - *Seventeen and five **make** twenty-two.*
6 **make friends** = become friends
   - *Ann **made friends** with the new girl.*
7 **make money** = get money by working, etc
   - *Mrs Thompson **made** a lot of **money** by selling the pictures she had painted.*

LANGUAGE NOTE

1		**make** someone better (= cure)
	BUT	**do** better (= improve)
2		**make** tea
	BUT	**do** the cooking
3	COMPARE	He made me do it. (without **to**)
		I was made **to** do it.

make sure /ˌmeɪk ˈʃʊə*/ verb phrase
making sure, made sure, has made sure
See **sure** [3].

make up /ˌmeɪk ˈʌp/ phrasal verb
making up, made up, has made up
1 think of (sometimes to make someone believe something which is not really true)
   - *We're half an hour late. We'll have to **make up** a story to explain.*
2 put powder, lipstick, etc on your face
   - *Linda **made** her face **up** before the party.*

male /meɪl/ noun (countable), adjective
a boy, a man, an animal that cannot have babies
- *Was the thief a **male** or a female?*
See also **female**.

man /mæn/ noun (countable)
plural: men /men/
a person who has grown up but not a woman
- *"There's a **man** at the door." "Oh, it's Mr Smith."*

LANGUAGE NOTE

You can use the word **man** (without a or the) to mean *everyone*, *people*, *men and women*, etc.
   Some people think man will destroy the world.
Sometimes **men** can be used with this meaning:
   Men must learn to live in peace.
Note that a lot of people do not like to use the words **man** and **men** instead of people.

θ	ð	ʃ	dʒ	tʃ	ŋ	ʒ	iː	ɜː	ɪ	æ	ʌ	ɒ
thing	that	shop	jump	chop	sing	measure	been	bird	bit	cat	but	not

☞ a fat/thin man/grown/middle-aged/
old/a young/short/tall/wise man;
a family/married/single man
the common man (= ordinary people),
the man in the street (= an
ordinary person)

manage /ˈmænɪdʒ/ verb
managing, managed, has managed
1 be able to do something
 • *I don't think I can manage to walk up the stairs with this heavy case. I'll go in the lift.*
2 control something
 • *Charles Long manages a hotel in Singapore.*

manager /ˈmænɪdʒə*/ noun (countable)
the person who controls a shop, a factory, etc
 • *Who's going to be the new office manager?*

mango /ˈmæŋɡəʊ/ noun (countable, uncountable)
plural: mangoes
⚠ See box on page 89.

many /ˈmenɪ/ adjective
more, most
1 a lot (of), lots (of)
 • *Do many of your friends play tennis?*

LANGUAGE NOTE

1 many friends   BUT   many *of* my friends
                        many *of* the
2 Use *many* in questions and sentences with *not*;
use *a lot of* or *lots* of in ordinary sentences.
   Did many students go to the meeting?
   I didn't see many students there.
   A lot of students said they were going.

---

2 **how many** = what number of
 • *How many students are absent today?*
⚠ See also **much**.

map /mæp/ noun (countable)
a drawing of a town or country as you would see it from high above it
 • *Can you see Tokyo on your map of Japan?*
☞ draw/make/follow/look at/read a map
(= find out where places are from a map);
a road/weather map

march /mɑːtʃ/ verb
walk (quickly) like a soldier
 • *Did you see the soldiers marching in the town?*

mark ¹ /mɑːk/ noun (countable)
1 a piece of dirt on something
 • *Will these marks come out of my shirt?*
2 a spot, a line, etc
 • *Our dog has a white mark over its left eye.*
3 the points a teacher gives pupils for their work
 • *Mabel got high marks for her homework.*
⚠ See also **exclamation mark**; see also **question mark**.

mark ² verb
1 spoil something by putting a mark on it
 • *Tom's pen broke and marked his new shirt.*
2 put a spot, a line, etc on something so that other people see it or read it
 • *Did you mark the new price on the book?*
3 put a tick (√) or a cross (X) near something to show that it is right or wrong
 • *Has the teacher marked our homework yet?*

market /ˈmɑːkɪt/ noun (countable)
a place where things are bought and sold (especially meat, fish, fruit and vegetables)

 • *Mrs Rodriguez buys fish from the market because it is always fresh.*
☞ a fish/fruit/vegetable market,
a supermarket (= a very large shop which sells all kinds of food and things for the house)

marriage /ˈmærɪdʒ/ noun (countable, uncountable)
1 the act of joining a husband and wife together by law
 • *Mr and Mrs Lee's marriage took place in that church over there.*

θ	ð	ʃ	dʒ	tʃ	ŋ	ʒ	iː	ɜː	ɪ	æ	ʌ	ɒ
thing	that	shop	jump	chop	sing	measure	been	bird	bit	cat	but	not

2 the way a husband and wife feel and behave towards each other
- Mr and Mrs Brown's **marriage** was not happy: they were always quarrelling.
☙ make/end/save a marriage; a marriage breaks up/down; a bad/happy/unhappy marriage

married /ˈmærɪd/ verb
past tense and past participle of **marry**
- Ricardo **married** Mary last year.

married adjective
having a husband or wife
- "Are you **married**?" "Yes, this is my wife."

marry /ˈmærɪ/ verb
marrying, married, has married
1 become someone's husband or wife
- Ali's father asked his mother to **marry** him when she was only eighteen years old.

LANGUAGE NOTE
1 NEVER marry with someone ALWAYS marry someone
2 get married **to** someone = marry someone

2 make two people husband and wife
- This priest is going to **marry** Ann and Ken.

marvellous /ˈmɑːvələs/ adjective
American English: marvelous
wonderful, very good
- The weather was **marvellous**: warm and sunny.

master /ˈmɑːstə*/ noun (countable)
1 the owner of an animal
- That dog always obeys its **master**.
2 a teacher who is a man and who works in a secondary school
- Mr Robinson is our new chemistry **master**.

match /mætʃ/ noun (countable)
plural: matches
1 a small, thin stick of wood which catches fire if you hit it on the side of a matchbox or something rough.
- Can I have a **match** to light my cigarette?
☙ matchbox, matchstick; light/strike a match; put a match to something
2 a game between two players or teams
- Mexico has won all its **matches** against France.

LANGUAGE NOTE
BRITISH ENGLISH a football match
AMERICAN ENGLISH a football game
When the game has come from America, you should use the word **game**: eg **a baseball game**, **a basketball game**. In other cases, use the word match: eg **a tennis match, a hockey match**.
You can use the phrase **a game of** with any game: How about **a game of tennis** tonight? (BUT NEVER a tennis game)

⚠ See also **game**; see also **sport**.

material /məˈtɪərɪəl/ noun (uncountable, countable)
cloth, rubber, metal, etc (= something which can be used to make things)
- "What **material** is your shirt made from?" "Nylon."

matter¹ /ˈmætə*/ noun (countable)
1 something important which causes you to think a lot or makes you give it your attention
- Stealing is a very serious **matter**.
2 **What's the matter?** = What's wrong?
- Samia, you look sad. **What's the matter?**

LANGUAGE NOTE
What's the matter **with** you today?

☙ bring up/take up/clear up/settle/deal with/go into a matter; a difficult/important/serious matter, no laughing matter

θ	ð	ʃ	dʒ	tʃ	ŋ	ʒ	iː	ɜː	ɪ	æ	ʌ	ɒ
thing	that	shop	jump	chop	sing	measure	been	bird	bit	cat	but	not

matter² verb (often negative)

1 be important
- The only thing that **matters** is our love.

2 **It doesn't matter** = It isn't important
- *"Oh dear! I forgot your dictionary."*
  "It doesn't matter. I've got another."

> **LANGUAGE NOTE**
>
> matter **to** someone

may /meɪ/ modal verb
may, might /maɪt/

1 You can use **may** to show what can happen.
- *Simon may not come tonight. He's ill.*

> **LANGUAGE NOTE**
>
> 1 I **may** do it tomorrow.
>   = It is possible I shall do it tomorrow.
> 2 Leila **may have** already left.
>   = It is possible Leila has left (but we don't know).

2 You can also use **may** to ask politely if you can do something.
- *"May I go to the cinema tonight?"*
  "Yes, you may, if you finish your homework."

> **LANGUAGE NOTE**
>
> The verb **can** is used far more than **may** in friendly conversations and letters.
> **Can** we go now?

maybe /ˈmeɪbiː/ adverb
perhaps
- *I'll be going to Athens next week, too. Maybe I'll see you there.*

me /miː/ pronoun
Use **me** after a verb or preposition to mean **I** or **myself**
- *An insect has just bitten me on the leg.*

meal /miːl/ noun (countable)
food which you eat at certain times of the day
- *We have our main meal in the evening.*
- cook/prepare/make/order/serve/eat/have/enjoy a meal; a big/heavy meal; the main meal (of the day), a simple meal, a square meal (= a big meal and usually a healthy meal)

mean¹ /miːn/ verb
meaning, meant /ment/, has meant
When you ask what something means, you want someone to explain it to you.
- *What does the word 'measurement' mean?*
- *I had no idea what you meant when you said Harry was lazy.*

mean² adjective

1 Someone who is mean does not want to give anything to anyone.
- *Sammy, don't be mean. Give your brother some of your chocolate.*

2 unkind
- *Don't pull May's hair and be mean to her.*

meaning /ˈmiːnɪŋ/ noun (countable)
The meaning of a word is what the word says or describes - what it makes you understand.
- *This dictionary gives the meanings of over 2,000 common English words.*
- explain/give/guess/understand the meaning; the general/real/true meaning

measure /ˈmeʒə*/ verb
measuring, measured, has measured
find out how long, high or wide someone or something is
- *Anna measured her desk with a ruler.*
- See also box opposite.

measurement /ˈmeʒəmənt/ noun (countable)
how long, how high or how wide someone or something is
- *What are the measurements of this car?*
- take a measurement, take (someone's) measurements

θ	ð	ʃ	dʒ	tʃ	ŋ	ʒ	iː	ɜː	ɪ	æ	ʌ	ɒ
thing	that	shop	jump	chop	sing	measure	been	bird	bit	cat	but	not

Measures

10 mm (millimetres)	= 1 cm (centimetre)
100 cm (centimetres)	= 1 m (metre)
100 m (metres)	= 1 km (kilometre)
10 mg (milligrams)	= 1 cg (centigram)
100 cg (centigrams)	= 1 g (gram)
100 g (grams)	= 1 kg (kilogram)
10 ml (millilitres)	= 1 cl (centilitre)
100 cl (centilitres)	= 1 l (litre)
100 mm^2 (square millimetres)	= 1 cm^2 (square centimetre)
100 cm^2 (square centimetres)	= 1 m^2 (square metre)
100 m^2 (square metres)	= 1 are
100 ares	= 1 hectare
100 ha (hectares)	= 1 km^2 (square kilometre)

meat /miːt/ noun (uncountable)
the part of an animal or bird which you can eat (ie NOT the bones and skin, etc)
- *Is there enough **meat** for everyone?*
- cook/cut/eat meat; fatty/lean/fresh meat, raw meat (= meat which has not been cooked), tender meat (= meat which is soft and easy to eat), tough meat (= meat which is hard to eat)

mechanic /mɪˈkænɪk/ noun (countable)
someone who repairs machines, cars, etc
- *Bob is working as a **mechanic** in a garage.*
- a garage mechanic

medal /ˈmedl/ noun (countable)
a small round piece of metal which is usually given to someone for doing something very good or brave
- *Six soldiers were given **medals** for bravery.*

medical /ˈmedɪkl/ adjective
You can use the word **medical** when you are talking about medicine and looking after sick people.
- *Dr Ito is giving me a **medical** (examination).*
- a medical (examination), a medical student, a (medical) doctor

medicine /ˈmedsɪn/ noun (countable)
something you take (especially drink) when you are ill to make you feel well again
- *Dr Hill told me to take the **medicine**.*
- take some medicine

medium /ˈmiːdiəm/ adjective
in the middle, not large and not small
- *"What size shirt do you want?"*
  *"**Medium**, please."*

meet /miːt/ verb
meeting, met /met/, has met
1 find or see someone because you are in the same place
   - *I **met** our old teacher in the street.*
2 come together
   - *Let's **meet** at my flat before the cinema.*

LANGUAGE NOTE

BRITISH ENGLISH	The principal is meeting the teachers tomorrow.
AMERICAN ENGLISH	The principal is meeting **with** the teachers tomorrow.

3 get to know someone for the first time
   - *I'd like to **meet** your new neighbour.*

θ	ð	ʃ	dʒ	tʃ	ŋ	ʒ	iː	ɜː	ɪ	æ	ʌ	ɒ
thing	that	shop	jump	chop	sing	measure	been	bird	bit	cat	but	not

meeting

4 introduce someone

- "Mary, I'd like you to **meet** Kevin Mawani."
  "Pleased to **meet** you, Kevin."
  "Pleased to **meet** you, Mary."

meeting /ˈmiːtɪŋ/ noun (countable)
1 people coming together to do something (or to talk about something)
   - There will be a **meeting** in the hall at 1 pm to choose a football team.
   ↻ arrange/call/attend/have/hold a meeting; a friendly/long/short/noisy/stormy successful/useful meeting
2 come together by chance
   - Our **meeting** at the station was not planned.

melon /ˈmelən/ noun (countable, uncountable)
⚠ See box on page 89.

melt /melt/ verb
turn into liquid
   - Put the ice cream in the fridge before it **melts**.

member /ˈmembə*/ noun (countable)
a person who belongs to a group
   - Is Rita a **member** of the school choir?

memory /ˈmeməri/ noun (countable)
plural: memories
1 We use our memory to remember things.
   - Do you have a good **memory**?
   ↻ improve/lose your memory; an amazing/excellent/a good/poor/long/short memory
2 something which you remember
   - I have happy **memories** of my school days.
   ↻ bring back memories, have (happy) memories

men /men/ noun (countable)
plural of **man**
   - How many **men** have joined the army?

mend /mend/ verb
repair something, make it right again
   - Why don't you **mend** your torn shirt?

menu /ˈmenjuː/ noun (countable)
plural: menus
a list of the kind of food which is sold in a restaurant or hotel
   - I looked at the **menu** and decided to have fish.

mess /mes/ noun (countable, usually singular)
something which is very untidy
   - Susie, brush your hair. It looks a **mess**!
   ↻ clean away/up a mess, clear up a mess, leave/make a mess; in a mess

message /ˈmesɪdʒ/ noun (countable)
some information you want to give or send to someone
   - Mr Cole phoned and asked me to give my parents a **message**.
   ↻ get/give someone a message, leave a message for someone, pass on/send/take a message

metal /ˈmetl/ noun (countable, uncountable)
something hard such as iron, steel, lead, tin, copper, etc
   - Iron is a very useful **metal**.

microphone /ˈmaɪkrəfəʊn/ noun (countable)
something you use to make things louder or to record your voice or music

   - No one will hear you unless you speak into the **microphone**.
   ↻ sing/speak into a microphone, use a microphone

θ	ð	ʃ	dʒ	tʃ	ŋ	ʒ	iː	ɜː	ɪ	æ	ʌ	ɒ
thing	that	shop	jump	chop	sing	measure	been	bird	bit	cat	but	not

midday /ˌmɪdˈdeɪ/ noun (uncountable)
twelve o'clock during the day, the middle of the day
- *We always eat lunch at midday.*

middle /ˈmɪdl/ noun (uncountable, singular)
1 the centre
   - *Put the flowers in the middle of the table.*
2 halfway between two points, etc
   - *I am the middle child: I have an older brother and a young sister.*

midnight /ˈmɪdnaɪt/ noun (uncountable)
twelve o'clock during the night, the middle of the night
- *The party didn't finish until midnight.*

might /maɪt/ modal verb
part of **may**
1 something which could have happened
   - *We thought it might rain, but it didn't.*
2 something which could happen
   - *Beatrice might come if she feels better.*

> **LANGUAGE NOTE**
>
> She *may* come. (= It is possible she will come.)
> She *might* come. (= It is possible she will come but it is also possible she will not come.)

milk /mɪlk/ noun (uncountable)
a white liquid from cows which you can drink
- *Many children in Britain like to drink milk.*

mind¹ /maɪnd/ noun (countable)
1 You use your mind to think and to remember things.
   - *I don't know what you're thinking. I can't tell what's in your mind.*
   ☞ make up your mind (= decide), bring / call to mind (= remember), keep in mind, take your mind off something; be in two minds about (doing) something
2 what you think about something
   - *I've changed my mind about the picnic. I don't want to go now.*

mind² verb
1 be careful (of), take care (about)
   - *Mind the step.*
2 care about something
   - *"Would you like to sit in the front of the car?" "I don't mind. It doesn't matter at all."*

> **LANGUAGE NOTE**
>
> mind + me/you/her, etc + *ing* form
> I don't mind them *making* a lot of noise.

3 **Do you mind** or **Would you mind**
You can use **Do you mind** or **Would you mind** to ask someone if something you do will annoy them.
   - *"Would you mind if I opened this window?" "Not at all."*

> **LANGUAGE NOTE**
>
> mind + ing form
> Would you mind helping me a minute?
> (NEVER Would you mind to help me a minute?)

4 **Never mind** = It doesn't matter
   - *"I failed my test." "Never mind. You'll pass next time."*

mine /maɪn/ pronoun
belonging to me
- *That case is mine. My name is on it.*

minibus /ˈmɪnɪbʌs/ noun (countable)
plural: minibuses
a small bus (like a van with seats inside it)
- *Ten of us went to the beach in a minibus.*

> **LANGUAGE NOTE**
>
> COMPARE   a friend of mine (= one of my friends)
>   my friend

θ	ð	ʃ	dʒ	tʃ	ŋ	ʒ	iː	ɜː	ɪ	æ	ʌ	ɒ
thing	that	shop	jump	chop	sing	measure	been	bird	bit	cat	but	not

minus /ˈmaɪnəs/ preposition
made less by
- Eight **minus** three equals five: 8 - 3 = 5.

minute /ˈmɪnɪt/ noun (countable)
1 part of an hour (There are sixty minutes in an hour.)
   - Each student spoke for four **minutes** about what was happening in the world.
2 a short time
   - I'll be back in a **minute**.
3 **the minute** = as soon as
   - He began to complain **the minute** he arrived.

✎ See also **moment**.

mirror /ˈmɪrə*/ noun (countable)
a piece of glass which you look at to see yourself
- She looked at her face in the **mirror**.

Miss /mɪs/
Use **Miss** in front of the surname of a lady who is not married.
- "Who's your teacher?" "**Miss** Green."

LANGUAGE NOTE	
NEVER	~~Miss Ann, Miss Mabel~~
ALWAYS	Ann, Mabel
NEVER	~~Green, Wong, etc~~
ALWAYS	Miss Green, Miss Wong, etc

miss verb
1 fail to hit something
   - I kicked the ball at the goal but just **missed**.
2 fail to catch something
   - Dave threw the ball to Emma but she **missed** it, and it hit the teacher.
3 be too late to get a bus, a train, a plane, etc
   - We'll **miss** the bus if we don't hurry.
4 fail to see or meet someone or something
   - We wanted to meet Susie at the station but we **missed** her.
5 be sad because someone is not there
   - I **missed** Ricardo a lot when he left.

mistake[1] /mɪˈsteɪk/ noun (countable)
1 something which is wrong
   - You've made five **mistakes** in the exercise, and so you've got 15 marks out of 20.
   ✍ make/correct a mistake, excuse someone's mistake; a bad/big/serious/careless/common mistake, a costly mistake (= a mistake which takes a lot of money or time to put right), a silly/foolish mistake
2 **by mistake** = If you do something which you did not want to do, you can say that you did it by mistake.
   - Someone has taken my pen **by mistake**.

mistake[2] verb
mistaking, mistook, has mistaken
think wrongly about someone or something
- I **mistook** her for my aunt and spoke to her.

mix /mɪks/ verb
put different things together
- I **mixed** the flour and eggs, and made a cake.

mixture /ˈmɪkstʃə*/ noun (countable)
different things which are put together
- The meal was an unusual **mixture** of Malaysian, Chinese and Portuguese food.

model /ˈmɒdl/ noun (countable)
a small copy of something
- Ben's hobby is making **model** aeroplanes.

modern /ˈmɒdən/ adjective
more modern, most modern
new
- There are a lot of **modern** buildings in Japan.

moment /ˈməʊmənt/ noun (countable)
1 slightly more or less than a minute, a very short period of time
   - Can you wait a **moment** until I've finished?
2 a short time
   - Susie was here a **moment** ago; she can't be far away.

θ	ð	ʃ	dʒ	tʃ	ŋ	ʒ	iː	ɜː	ɪ	æ	ʌ	ɒ
thing	that	shop	jump	chop	sing	measure	been	bird	bit	cat	but	not

3 **at the moment** = now
 • *I'm sorry. Tina isn't in **at the moment**.*
4 **at that moment** = just then
 • *Tom opened his mouth to sing but **at that moment** I started to cough.*
5 **at any moment** = at any time after now, soon
 • *Be quiet! Mr Lee may come in **at any moment**.*
6 **the moment** = as soon as
 • *He began to complain **the moment** he arrived.*
⚠ See also **minute**.

money /ˈmʌnɪ/ noun (uncountable)
1 something you use to buy things
 • *I had to walk home because I hadn't got enough **money** for the bus fare.*
🔗 borrow/lend/earn/make/raise/save/ spend money
2 **pocket money** = money which parents give their children
 • *Anna gets $2 **pocket money** a week.*

monkey /ˈmʌŋkɪ/ noun (countable)
⚠ See box on page 10.

moon /muːn/ noun (singular countable, often with the)
the round object which you can usually see in the sky at night after the sun goes down

 • *Do you think people will ever live on the **moon**?*
🔗 the moon comes out/rises/shines; a big/full/new moon

more ¹ /mɔː*/ determiner, pronoun
much, more, most
many, more, most
1 a larger number or amount (of)
 • *Can I have some **more** milk in my coffee.*

LANGUAGE NOTE

more cars	BUT	more **of** these cars
		more **of** them
more rice	BUT	more **of** this rice
		more **of** it

2 extra, something added to what has already been given, done, said, etc
 • *"I liked the fish which you cooked." "Good. Would you like any **more**?"*
⚠ See also **much**; see also **many**.

more ² adverb
much, more, most
1 You can use **more** in front of longer adjectives when you want to show that something is bigger, smaller, better, worse, etc than something else.
 • *Is Hong Kong **more** beautiful than London?*
2 You can use **more** after verbs when you want to show that you do, like, want something, etc better, a greater number of times or in a greater way than something else.
 • *I like swimming **more** than cycling.*
⚠ See also **much**.

morning /ˈmɔːnɪŋ/ noun (countable)
the time of day between sunrise and lunchtime
 • *I get up early every **morning**.*

LANGUAGE NOTE

in the morning BUT *on* Saturday morning

mosque /mɒsk/ noun (countable)
a building where people pray to Allah
 • *Rahim goes to the **mosque** every Friday.*

most ¹ /məʊst/ determiner, pronoun
much, more, most
many, more most
1 nearly all (of)
 • ***Most** girls of her age would like this dress.*

> **LANGUAGE NOTE**
>
> most cars   BUT   most **of** these cars
>   most **of** them
> most rice   BUT   most **of** this rice
>   most **of** it

  2 nearly all
   • Did **most of** your friends go to the meeting?
   ⚠ See also **much**; see also **many**.

most ² *adverb*
much, more, most
  1 You can use **most** in front of longer adjectives when you want to show that something is the biggest, smallest, best, worst, etc.
   • Hong Kong harbour is the **most** beautiful in the world.
  2 You can use **most** after verbs when you want to show that you do, like, want something, etc best of all, the greatest number of times or in the greatest way.
   • I like swimming more than cycling. In fact, I like it **most** of all.
  3 very
   • I'm **most** interested in what you say.
   ⚠ See also **much**.

mostly /ˈməʊstlɪ/   *adverb*
nearly all
   • There were **mostly** old women at the meeting.

moth /mɒθ/   *noun (countable)*
   ⚠ See box on page 114.

mother /ˈmʌðə*/   *noun (countable)*
a woman who has a child or some children, the woman who is one of someone's parents
   • My father is a doctor and my **mother** is a nurse.

motor /ˈməʊtə*/   *noun (countable)*
the part of a machine which makes the other parts move
   • The **motor**'s broken, and so the machine won't work.
  ↻ start/turn off a motor;
    a motor runs, a motor works

motorbike /ˈməʊtəbaɪk/   *noun (countable)*
a bike which has an engine
   • Mr Law goes to the office on his **motorbike**.
  ↻ ride (on) a motorbike

motorcycle /ˈməʊtəsaɪkl/   *noun (countable)*
  ⚠ See **motorbike**.

motorway /ˈməʊtəweɪ/   *noun (countable)*
a wide road on which cars can travel very fast for a long way
   • Have you been on the new **motorway** yet?

mountain /ˈmaʊntɪn/   *noun (countable)*
a very high hill
   • Mount Everest is the highest **mountain** in the world.
  ↻ climb a mountain; a high mountain

mouse /maʊs/   *noun (countable)*
plural: mice /maɪs/
  ⚠ See box on page 10.

mouth /maʊθ/   *noun (countable)*
plural: mouths /maʊðz/
  1 the space between your lips in which you put food to eat
   • Vincent put a big piece of cake in his **mouth**.
  ↻ close/shut/open your mouth;
    have your mouth full (of something)
  ⚠ See also box on page 25.
  2 the place where a cave, etc opens
   • Let's hide in the **mouth** of this cave.
  3 the end of a river
   • The city is near the **mouth** of the River Ganges.

move /muːv/   *verb*
moving, moved, has moved
  1 take something from one place to another
   • I **moved** my desk in front of the window.
  2 change place, not be still
   • I was so scared that I couldn't **move**.
  3 leave one place to live in another place
   • When are you **moving** to London?

θ	ð	ʃ	dʒ	tʃ	ŋ	ʒ	iː	ɜː	ɪ	æ	ʌ	ɒ
thing	that	shop	jump	chop	sing	measure	been	bird	bit	cat	but	not

movie /ˈmuːvɪ/ noun (countable)
(American English)
1   See **film 2**.
✊ make/see/watch a movie
2   **the movies** = a cinema
   • *We usually go to **the movies** on Fridays.*
⚠ See also **cinema**.

Mr /ˈmɪstə*/
Use **Mr** in front of the surname of a man.
• *Mr Jones is my brother's new teacher.*

LANGUAGE NOTE
1   You should write **Mr** (NEVER Mister): Mr Jones
2   Don't say **Mister** when you speak to someone (if you don't know his name). It is much better to say **Sir**.

Mrs /ˈmɪsɪz/
Use **Mrs** in front of the surname of a woman who is married.
• *Mrs Mawani is talking to Mr Low.*

LANGUAGE NOTE
1   You should write **Mrs** but say **Missus** :- ie. Write **Mrs Hill** but say **Missus Hill**.
2   Don't say **Missus** when you speak to someone (if you don't know her name). It is much better to say **Madam**.
3   NEVER   ~~Mrs Jenny, Mrs Rose~~
    ALWAYS Jenny, Rose
    OR   Mrs Smith, Mrs Alvarez

Ms /mɪz, məz/
Use **Ms** in front of the surname of a woman who does not want to be called **Mrs** or **Miss**.
• *I'm going to talk to **Ms** Low for a moment.*
⚠ See also **Miss** (Language Note); see also **Mrs** (Language Notes).

much¹ /mʌtʃ/ determiner, pronoun
much, more, most
1   a lot (of)
   • *Do you eat **much** fish?*

LANGUAGE NOTE
1   much money   BUT   much *of* my money
                       much *of* it
2   Use much in questions and sentences with **not**; use **a lot of** in ordinary sentences.
    Was **much of the furniture** broken?
    I didn't see **much furniture** in the room.
    There was **a lot of furniture** outside the room.

2   **how much**?
   • *How much bread shall I buy?*
   • *How much does a new car like this cost?*
⚠ See also **many**.

much² adverb
much, more, most
1   a lot
   • *Your chair is **much** more comfortable than mine.*
2   very often
   • *I don't see Jonathan Lee **much** now.*

mud /mʌd/ noun (uncountable)
wet earth
• *The car was stuck in the **mud**; no one could move it.*

muddy /ˈmʌdɪ/ adjective
muddier, muddiest
(covered in) wet earth
• *Please leave your **muddy** shoes outside.*

multiply /ˈmʌltɪplaɪ/ verb
multiplying, multiplied, has multiplied
make a number or an amount increase
• *Twelve **multiplied** by three is thirty-six: 12 x 3 = 36.*

mum /mʌm/ noun (countable)
a name which some people call their mother
• *His **mum** will take us to college this morning.*

mummy /ˈmʌmɪ/ noun (countable)
a name which some people (especially children) usually call their mother
• ***Mummy**, can I go to Helen's flat, please?*

θ	ð	ʃ	dʒ	tʃ	ŋ	ʒ	iː	ɜː	ɪ	æ	ʌ	ɒ
thing	that	shop	jump	chop	sing	measure	been	bird	bit	cat	but	not

museum /mjuːˈziːəm/ noun (countable)
a building where interesting (and old) things are kept for people to see
- *Were there any old toys in the museum?*

mushroom /ˈmʌʃrʊm/ noun (countable)
⚠ See box on page 238.

music /ˈmjuːzɪk/ noun (uncountable)
pleasant sounds you hear from a cassette, radio, TV set, someone singing or people playing
- *Do you like all kinds of music or just pop?*
↻ listen to/play/read/write music; dance/light/modern/pop/rock music

musical /ˈmjuːzɪkl/ adjective
1 playing music, making music, for music
- *Let's have a musical evening. Bill can play the guitar, you can sing and I can play the piano.*
2 good at music, liking music a lot
- *Anna Richardson is very musical and she can play the piano and sing very well.*

musician /mjuːˈzɪʃn/ noun (countable)
someone who plays the piano, the guitar, etc very well indeed or who earns a living by playing
- *Mabel asked the musicians to play for her.*

must /mʌst/ (unstressed /məst/) modal verb
1 something which you have to do
- *You must be very careful when you cross this busy road.*

LANGUAGE NOTE

1 Use **must** for the present and future; use **had to** for the past.

		I **must** go now.
		When **must** we arrive tomorrow?
BUT		How long **had** you **to** stay yesterday?
OR		How long **did you have to** stay yesterday?
2	COMPARE	You **must** stop singing: I can't study.
		You**'ll have to** stop singing: you'll lose your voice if you continue.

---

2 You can use **must** to show that something is possible or certain.
- *It must be twelve o'clock. I'm hungry.*

mustn't /ˈmʌsnt/ modal verb
must not
- *You mustn't be late again.*
⚠ See also **must**.

LANGUAGE NOTE

COMPARE	You **mustn't** eat too many sweets. (= Don't eat too many sweets.)
WITH	You **needn't** stay any longer.
OR	You **don't have to** stay any longer. (= It isn't necessary to stay any longer if you don't want.)

---

my /maɪ/ adjective
belonging to me
- *This isn't your book. It must be my book.*

myself /maɪˈself/ pronoun
1 You can use **myself** as the object of a verb or preposition.
- *I fell and hurt myself.*
2 You can use **myself** to make the subject or object seem more important or to make the pronoun I stronger.
- *I myself don't think that the painting is very good.*
3 without any help
- *I painted this picture (all by) myself.*
4 **by myself** = without any other person
- *I went to the cinema by myself last night.*

mystery /ˈmɪstərɪ/ noun (countable)
plural: mysteries
a strange thing which happens and which you cannot explain
- *I don't know how I lost the book. It's a mystery!*
↻ clear up/solve a mystery

N n

nail /neɪl/ noun (countable)
1. A nail is a small piece of metal which is sharp at one end and flat at the other end. You can hit the flat end to push the nail into something like wood.
   - *The picture hung from a **nail** on the wall.*
2. the hard parts at the top of your fingers and toes
   - *Your **nails** are too long. I'll cut them.*

   ↻ bite/cut your nails; fingernails, toenails

name /neɪm/ noun (countable)
what someone or something is called
- *My first **name** is Mary, and my surname is Law.*

↻ give someone a name, call someone (bad) names; your Christian name(s) (= your first name(s), your family name, your first name(s), a woman's maiden name (= a woman's name before she was married), a woman's married name (= a woman's husband's surname), your surname (= your family name)

⚠ See also **family 3**.

narrow /ˈnærəʊ/
thin, not wide

- *The road was too **narrow** for the big lorry.*

nasty /ˈnɑːstɪ/ adjective
nastier, nastiest
not pleasant
- *There's a **nasty** smell here. Is it gas?*

nationality /ˌnæʃəˈnælɪtɪ/ noun (countable)
plural: nationalities
You can use **nationality** to show the country to which someone belongs.
- *"What **nationality** is Mabel Lee?" "She's Chinese."*

⚠ See also box on page 51.

naughty /ˈnɔːtɪ/ adjective
naughtier, naughtiest
Children are naughty when they behave badly.
- *Peter, you're very **naughty**. As soon as I tidy the room, you make it untidy again.*

near /nɪə*/ preposition, adverb and adjective
not far away (from), close (to)
- *My home isn't **near** my school: it's quite far away. I wish I lived **nearer** (to) my school.*
- *Tom lives twenty kilometres from the **nearest** town.*

nearby /nɪəˈbaɪ/ adverb, adjective
close by, not far away
- *I'll walk home; I live **nearby**.*
- *Shall we wait under a **nearby** tree until it stops raining?*

nearly /ˈnɪəlɪ/ adverb
near to, almost
- *We should go now. It's **nearly** nine o'clock.*

neat /niːt/ adjective
tidy
- *I've tidied my room. It looks very **neat**.*

neatly /ˈniːtlɪ/ adverb
in a tidy way
- *I can't read this. Try to write **neatly**.*

θ	ð	ʃ	dʒ	tʃ	ŋ	ʒ	iː	ɜː	ɪ	æ	ʌ	ɒ
thing	that	shop	jump	chop	sing	measure	been	bird	bit	cat	but	not

necessary /ˈnesəsəri/ adjective
If something is necessary, it must be done.
- "Is it **necessary** for me to lock the door?"
  "Yes, if you don't, a burglar will get in."

See also **have to**; see also **must**.

LANGUAGE NOTE

necessary **for** someone **to do** something
It's necessary for us to arrive early tomorrow.
= We must arrive early tomorrow.
= We('ll) have to arrive early tomorrow.

---

need /niːd/ verb
1 must have, want
- I'm very thirsty. I **need** a drink as soon as possible.
- Your hair **needs** cutting. It's too long.
2 must (do)
- We **need** to book seats if we want to see this film tonight.

See also **have to**; see also **must**.

---

needle /ˈniːdl/ noun (countable)
a very thin piece of steel with a sharp point (used for sewing)

- Put the **needle** back in this box after you've finished sewing.

a knitting needle, a sewing needle

---

needn't /ˈniːdnt/ verb
need not
- We **needn't** go to college tomorrow. It's Sunday.

LANGUAGE NOTE

1 needn't do = it isn't necessary to do
    Must we go now?
    No, you **needn't** go yet. Stay longer.
2 ALWAYS   You need to see a doctor at once.
   BUT   You **needn't see** a doctor yet.
   NEVER   ~~You needn't to see a doctor yet.~~
3 COMPARE We had a holiday yesterday, and Tina **needn't have gone** to school.
            = Tina went to school, but it wasn't necessary.
   WITH   We had a holiday yesterday, and Tina **didn't need to go** to school.
            = Tina didn't go to school because we had a holiday and it wasn't necessary.

See also **must**; see also **mustn't**; see also **need**.

---

neighbour /ˈneɪbə*/ noun (countable)
(American English: neighbor)
a person who lives near you, especially someone who is next door to you
- When we go away on holiday, our **neighbour** looks after our house.

your next-door neighbour

---

neighter¹ /ˈnaɪðə*/ pronoun, determiner
not one nor the other of two things
- I've seen **neither** of the men you asked about.
- **Neither** book is mine.

LANGUAGE NOTE

1 Use a singular countable noun after **neither** in such sentences as:
   Neither **book** will be suitable.
2 Use **of** after **neither** when there are other determiners: eg **the, these, your,** etc. However, remember that you must use a singular verb.
   Neither **of** those pupils **has** done it.

See also **either**.

θ	ð	ʃ	dʒ	tʃ	ŋ	ʒ	iː	ɜː	ɪ	æ	ʌ	ɒ
thing	that	shop	jump	chop	sing	measure	been	bird	bit	cat	but	not

news 147

neither² adverb
also not (Often used in short answers after sentences with **no**, **not** and **never**.)
- "I can't swim." "**Neither** can I."

neither .... nor /ˌnaɪðə*....'nɔː*/ conjunction
(fail to do) one thing or another, not either
- Ali has **neither** written to us **nor** phoned us.

LANGUAGE NOTE

Take care to use **neither .... nor** in the correct place in a sentence.
  Neither a pen **nor** a pencil will be necessary for this exam. It's a test of speaking.
  You'll need **neither** a pen **nor** a pencil for this exam. It's a speaking test.
  You'll need a pen **neither** for the exam **nor** for your homework. All you have to do is to read Chapter 2.
  I could **neither** borrow a pen **nor** buy a pen.

⚠ See also **either .... or**.

nephew /'nefjuː/ noun (countable)
the son of your brother or sister
- My sister has two sons and my brother has three, and so I have five **nephews**.

nervous /'nɜːvəs/ adjective
afraid or worried
- I'm a little **nervous** about singing in the school concert.

nest /nest/ noun (countable)
the place where a bird lays its eggs

- There are three eggs in this **nest**.
- build/make a nest

net /net/ noun (countable)
1 something made with strings, wires, etc to catch fish, butterflies, etc
   - The small boy caught five fish in his **net**.
   - a fishing-net
2 something made with string, wire, etc to use in a game
   - The ball hit the **net**.

never /'nevə*/ adverb
1 not at any time
   - I've **never** been to Australia. Have you?

LANGUAGE NOTE

Note the place of **never** in the following sentences.
  I **never** get a lift to my office.
  I've **never** caught a bus there.
  I am **never** late.

2 **never mind**
⚠ See **mind²** 4.

new /njuː/ adjective
1 not old, recently bought
   - Is that a **new** dress you're wearing?
2 different, not done before
   - I've just got a **new** job and I've now got to learn two **new** languages.

news /njuːz/
1 (uncountable) new information about things which have happened recently
   - I've got some good **news**. I passed my test.

LANGUAGE NOTE

NEVER   ~~a news~~
ALWAYS the news, some news, or news

- break the news (= tell some surprising news), get/pass on/give/tell some news, spread the news; good/welcome/bad/sad/great/happy/important news, interesting news, the latest news

θ	ð	ʃ	dʒ	tʃ	ŋ	ʒ	iː	ɜː	ɪ	æ	ʌ	ɒ
thing	that	shop	jump	chop	sing	measure	been	bird	bit	cat	but	not

148 newspaper

2 the news
a television or radio programme which gives you information about recent events
- *I heard on **the news** that there will soon be a new government in your country.*

↻ hear (something on) the news, listen to/watch/turn on the news

newspaper /ˈnjuːspeɪpə*/ noun (countable)
large sheets of paper which you buy to find out information about recent events
- *Mr Uchida reads his **newspaper** on his way to work every morning.*

↻ a daily/weekly/morning/evening newspaper

next¹ /nekst/ determiner, adjective
1 the following person or thing
   - *The **next** pupil who speaks will be sent out.*
2 the one that comes after
   - *He phoned Linda the **next** day.*

LANGUAGE NOTE

1 If you are talking about the past, you can say EITHER **the next day** OR **next day**.
However, you must say **the next week**, **the next month**, and **the next year** when you are talking about the past.
  I met her again **(the) next day**.
BUT I met her again **the next week/month/year**.
2 If you are talking about the future (from now), you should say **next week, next month** and **next year** (without **the**).
  I'm going to see her again **next week**.
3 If you use the word **time**, you can say EITHER **the next time**, etc OR **next time**, etc.
  I'll ask her **(the) next time** I see her.

3 **next door** = on one side of (a building)
   - *Mr and Mrs Hill live **next door** to me.*

next² adverb
1 just after, immediately following
   - *What do you think will happen **next**?*
2 the first time afterwards
   - *I **next** went to Hong Kong ten years later.*

next to /ˈnekst tuː/ preposition
at the side of, beside
- *Sarah's school is **next to** a cinema.*

nice /naɪs/ adjective
1 pleasant, kind
   - *It was **nice** of you to visit Dave in hospital.*
2 **nice and** = You can use **nice and** in a friendly conversation to make another adjective seem stronger and more pleasant.
   - *This tea is **nice and** hot! I already feel warmer.*

niece /niːs/ noun (countable)
the daughter of your brother or sister
- *Nicola is Susie's **niece**. She's the youngest daughter of Susie's brother.*

night /naɪt/ noun (countable)
the time when it is dark, not day
- *The **night** was very dark. There was no moon.*

LANGUAGE NOTE

1 **in the** morning, **in the** afternoon, **in the** evening
  at night
2 She works hard **during the day** and she goes out **at night**.

↻ spend the night (with friends); a clear/dark/stormy night

no¹ /nəʊ/ negative
Use **no** to show that you don't agree with something or someone.
- *"Are there seven oranges in the bowl?" "**No**, there are only five."*

LANGUAGE NOTE

1 "Are you meeting Tony tonight?"
  "No, I'm not. I'm staying at home."
2 "You aren't meeting Tony tonight, are you?"
  "No, I'm not. I'm staying at home."

⚠ See also **yes**.

θ	ð	ʃ	dʒ	tʃ	ŋ	ʒ	iː	ɜː	ɪ	æ	ʌ	ɒ
thing	that	shop	jump	chop	sing	measure	been	bird	bit	cat	but	not

no [2] determiner

not one, not any
- There's **no** book in this desk.

LANGUAGE NOTE

Use **no** to mean **not any** or **not one**.
This room has got **no** windows.
= This room has **not** got **any** windows.

---

noise /nɔɪz/ noun (countable, uncountable)

a loud or unpleasant sound someone makes
- Stop making so much **noise**!

↻ make a noise; a big/loud/strange/terrible noise

noisy /'nɔɪzɪ/ adjective

noisier, noisiest

making a loud and unpleasant sound
- The children were very **noisy** this morning.

none /nʌn/ pronoun

not any, not a single thing or person
- "Do you have any money?"
  "I'm sorry. I have **none** at all."

LANGUAGE NOTE

1 The words **at all** are often used after **none**.
I'm sorry I couldn't get you a newspaper. There were none left **at all**.
2 Note the singular verb **is** after **none** (meaning **not even one**).
None of these apples **is** bad. (= not even one)
None of these apples **are** bad. (= not any)
Although **are** is often used in sentences like the second sentence above, some people think such sentences are not correct.
3 COMPARE He drank **no milk**.
           (= He didn't drink any milk at all.)
  WITH   He drank **none of the milk**.
           (= He didn't drink any of the milk we gave him but he might have drunk some milk given by someone else.)

---

nonsense /'nɒnsəns/ noun (uncountable)

You use **nonsense** to describe words or ideas which are silly or stupid.
- Rice doesn't grow on trees! That's **nonsense**!

↻ speak/talk nonsense; complete/perfect/total nonsense

noon /nuːn/ noun (uncountable)

twelve o'clock in the middle of the day
- We usually stop work for an hour at **noon**.

normal /'nɔːml/ adjective

usual, what is expected
- Don't worry. It's **normal** for young children to cry when they first leave their mothers.

north [1] /nɔːθ/ noun (singular with the)

1 the part of a country, etc which is on your left if you look at the place where the sun rises, the direction up from the centre of the earth on a map
- Mr and Mrs Lawson live in the **north** of England.

north [2] adjective

the part of a country, a building, a place, etc which is on your left if you look at the place where the sun rises.
- **North** America is **north** of South America.

north [3] adverb

towards your left if you look at the place where the sun rises
- You travel **north** to go from Africa to Europe.

northern, Northern /'nɔːðən/ adjective

in or from the north part of a country
- Beijing is in **northern** China.

nose /nəʊz/ noun (countable)

part of your face which is above your mouth and through which you breathe
- I had a bad cold, and my **nose** was very red.

↻ blow/pick/wipe your nose; a running nose (= when you have a cold and want to blow your nose very often)

⚠ See also box on page 25.

θ	ð	ʃ	dʒ	tʃ	ŋ	ʒ	iː	ɜː	ɪ	æ	ʌ	ɒ
thing	that	shop	jump	chop	sing	measure	been	bird	bit	cat	but	not

not /nɒt/ negative

1 You use **not** to give the opposite meaning to a word.
 • *Mr and Mrs Law are **not** going out tonight.*

LANGUAGE NOTE

1 Note that **not** is often shortened to **n't** with verbs like **be**, **have**, **do**, **can**, etc.
  Mr and Mrs Law **aren't** going out tonight.
  We **haven't** met your brother.
  I **didn't** see Helen Lee.
  They **can't** come with us tonight.
2 Note the use of **not** after verbs like **hope**, **wish**, **think**, etc in such sentences as the following.
  "Will it rain today?" "I hope **not**."
  "Is Ann coming?" "No, I'm afraid **not**."
3 Note the use of **not** in the following sentences.
  Not many people came.
  Not everyone here speaks English.

---

2 **not one** = none
 • *There was **not one** person who wanted to leave.*
 ⚠ See also **no²**.
3 When we want to say **No** very strongly (especially after the verb **mind**), we use **Not at all**.
 • *"Do you mind if I open this window?" "**Not at all**."*
4 **not only**
 ⚠ See **only** 5.

note /nəʊt/ noun (countable)
1 a short letter which you send or give to someone
 • *Let's call and tell Mabel. We can leave her a **note** if she's out.*
 ⟳ drop/send someone a note, leave a note (for someone), write (someone) a note
2 something which you write in order to remember something
 • *I want to make a **note** of your birthday.*
 ⟳ add a note, make a note of something

LANGUAGE NOTE

COMPARE take note of something (= don't forget it)
AND   take notes (= write down the main points of a talk)

---

3 a piece of paper money (American English: bill)
 • *His pocket was full of £20 **notes**.*

notebook /ˈnəʊtbʊk/ noun (countable)
a (small) book for writing notes in
 • *The policeman took out a small **notebook**.*

nothing /ˈnʌθɪŋ/ pronoun
not anything
 • *I told my mother **nothing** about the accident.*

notice¹ /ˈnəʊtɪs/ noun
1 (countable) something (usually a piece of paper or wood) with writing on it to give people information
 • *There's a **notice** about the times when the bridge will be closed.*
 ⟳ put up a notice
2 **take notice (of)** (uncountable) = know about something and change the way you behave
 • ***Take notice of** what I say and do your homework in future. If you don't, you'll fail.*
3 **take no notice (of)** (uncountable) = know about something but not change the way you behave
 • *The little boy **took no notice of** his parents and continued laughing and shouting.*

notice² verb
noticing, noticed, has noticed
see something or someone, look at something or someone (carefully)
 • *Did you **notice** anything strange about him?*

LANGUAGE NOTE

notice something
notice **that** something has happened
notice someone **do** something
notice something happen**ing**

θ	ð	ʃ	dʒ	tʃ	ŋ	ʒ	iː	ɜː	ɪ	æ	ʌ	ɒ
thing	that	shop	jump	chop	sing	measure	been	bird	bit	cat	but	not

Numbers

Write	Say	Write	Say
1	one	1st	first
2	two	2nd	second
3	three	3rd	third
4	four	4th	fourth
5	five	5th	fifth
6	six	6th	sixth
7	seven	7th	seventh
8	eight	8th	eighth
9	nine	9th	ninth
10	ten	10th	tenth
11	eleven	11th	eleventh
12	twelve	12th	twelfth
13	thirteen	13th	thirteenth
14	fourteen	14th	fourteenth
15	fifteen	15th	fifteenth
16	sixteen	16th	sixteenth
17	seventeen	17th	seventeenth
18	eighteen	18th	eighteenth
19	nineteen	19th	nineteenth
20	twenty	20th	twentieth
21	twenty- one	21st	twenty-first
22	twenty- two	22nd	twenty-second
23	twenty- three	23rd	twenty-third
30	thirty	30th	thirtieth
40	forty	40th	fortieth
50	fifty	50th	fiftieth
60	sixty	60th	sixtieth
70	seventy	70th	seventieth
80	eighty	80th	eightieth
90	ninety	90th	ninetieth
100	a /one hundred	100th	hundredth
101	one hundred and one	101st	hundred and first
200	two hundred	200th	two hundredth
1,000	a /one thousand	1,000th	thousandth
1,001	one thousand and one	–	–
1,101	one thousand, one hundred and one	–	–
2,000	two thousand	2,000th	two thousandth
1,00,000	a/one hundred thousand	100,000th	hundred thousandth
1,000,000	a/one million	1,000,000th	millionth

now /naʊ/ adverb
at the present time
- We must leave **now** or we'll miss the train.

nowhere /ˈnəʊweə*/ adverb
not in any place
- The poor man had **nowhere** to live.

number /ˈnʌmbə*/ noun (countable)
1 1,2,3,4,5,6,7,8,9,10 are the first ten numbers.
   - Some people think seven is a lucky **number**.
   ☞ an even number (= 2, 4, 6, etc), an odd number (= 1, 3, 5, etc), a high/low number
   ⚠ See also box on page 151.
2 the numbers which you dial when you phone someone
   - What's your new **number**?
   ☞ call/phone/ring/dial a number
3 **a number of** = some, several
   - There were **a number of** people from Redlow at the match.
   ☞ a large/small/growing/certain number
4 **a large number of** = many, a lot of
   - The police have just said that **a large number of** cars are not safe to drive.

LANGUAGE NOTE

COMPARE	The number of students who passed the test **was** greater than last year. (the number of + singular verb)
WITH	A large number of students **have** passed the test. (a large number of + plural verb)

⚠ See box on page 151.

nurse /nɜːs/ noun (countable)
a person who looks after sick people and helps doctors

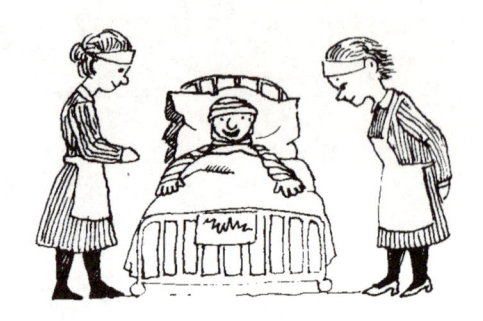

- When I saw Vincent in hospital, two **nurses** were talking to him.

nursery /ˈnɜːsərɪ/ noun (countable)
plural: nurseries
a place where very young children are looked after while their parents are working
☞ Mr and Mrs Law take both their small children to a **nursery** near their home.
a nursery (school), a nursery rhyme

nylon /ˈnaɪlɒn/ noun (uncountable)
a kind of strong cloth which has been made by machines
- Is your shirt made of cotton or **nylon**?

θ	ð	ʃ	dʒ	tʃ	ŋ	ʒ	iː	ɜː	ɪ	æ	ʌ	ɒ
thing	that	shop	jump	chop	sing	measure	been	bird	bit	cat	but	not

O o

obey /əˈbeɪ/ verb
do what you are told to do
- *When the teacher tells you to walk, you shouldn't run. You must always **obey** her.*

object /ˈɒbdʒɪkt/ noun (countable)
a thing
- *"What's that black **object** under your chair?" "It's the top of my pen."*

ocean /ˈəʊʃn/ noun (countable)
a large sea
- *The Atlantic **Ocean** is the **ocean** between Europe and America.*

o'clock /əˈklɒk/ adverb
You use **o'clock** after the numbers from 1 to 12 to show what hour it is.
- *The next lesson starts at starts at three **o'clock**.*

LANGUAGE NOTE		
1	three o'clock BUT ten past three (NEVER ~~ten past three o'clock~~)	
2	BRITISH ENGLISH	five to three / ten past four, etc
	AMERICAN ENGLISH	five before three / ten after four, etc

odd /ɒd/ adjective
1 unusual, strange
- *"There's no one at the college today. It's very **odd**." "Not really. It's Sunday."*
2 one of a pair of things (different from the other)
- *Margaret was wearing **odd** stockings: one was light blue and the other was dark blue.*
3 **an odd number** = a number which will not divide by two
- *1, 3, 5, 7, 9 and 11 are all **odd numbers**.*

of /ɒv/(unstressed /əv/) preposition
1 You can use **of** to show that something belongs to someone.
- *Sammy, is this one **of** your socks?*

LANGUAGE NOTE
's and **s'** are usually used to show that something belongs to someone:
These are Tony**'s** books.
(NOT These are the books of Tony.)
Those are the other pupil**s'** books.
(NOT Those are the books of the other pupils.)

2 You can use **of** to show place or direction.
- *Florence is to the north **of** Rome.*
3 You can use **of** to measure or show an amount or quantity.
- *Can I have a kilo **of** rice, please?*
4 You can use **of** to mean **containing**.
- *Could I have a cup **of** coffee, please?*
5 You can use **of** before pronouns when talking about numbers.
- *Look at those cats. There are six **of** them in that tree.*
6 You can use **of** with **more, most, best, easiest**, etc
- *This is the cheapest and most useful **of** the cameras in the shop.*
7 You can use **of** in phrases like: **a kind of, a sort of, of course**.
- *"A mountain bike is a special kind **of** bicycle." "**Of course**, I know that."*
8 You can use **of** with **think**.
- *What do you think **of** the film?*
9 You can use **of** after **made**.
- *All the houses were made **of** wood.*

off¹ /ɒf/ adverb
1 (come) away or down from
- *The door handle has just fallen **off**.*
2 (go) away to another place
- *The two boys ran **off** as soon as we arrived.*

θ	ð	ʃ	dʒ	tʃ	ŋ	ʒ	iː	ɜː	ɪ	æ	ʌ	ɒ
thing	that	shop	jump	chop	sing	measure	been	bird	bit	cat	but	not

3 (remove) from another place
  • Take **off** your hat and coat and sit down.
4 stop working
  • Switch **off** the TV before you go to bed.

off [2] preposition
1 not on, away or down from
  • Susan fell **off** her bicycle and broke her arm.
2 not in a place, absent
  • John's got toothache and is **off** school today.

LANGUAGE NOTE

COMPARE She was off work. (= absent)
         She was out of work. (= without a job)
---

offer /ˈɒfə*/ verb

SPELLING NOTE

ONLY ONE r: offer, offering, offered
---

1 hold out something to give someone
  • The old lady **offered** us some chocolate.
2 show or say you want to give someone something
  • Bill always **offers** his seat to old people on the bus.

office /ˈɒfɪs/ noun (countable)
1 a room where people work in business
  • Mr Law works in a large **office** in Kowloon.
2 a department of a firm or government
  • Mrs Jones works in the Education **Office**.
୫ a branch/head/main office; a booking office, a box office (= the place in a cinema or theatre where tickets are sold), a ticket office, a lost property office (= the place at a railway station, etc where things which have been left or lost are kept)

officer /ˈɒfɪsə*/ noun (countable)
1 an important person in the army
  • The **officer** led his men towards the enemy.

LANGUAGE NOTE

An **officer** is NOT the same as an **office worker**.
COMPARE an officer
         (= an army officer, a police officer)
         an office worker
         (= someone who works in an office)
---

2 **police officer** = a policeman or policewoman
  • There were two **police officers** at the accident.
⚠ See also **police**.

often /ˈɒfn/ adverb
many times, happening a lot
  • I **often** walk home with Maria.

LANGUAGE NOTE

Note the place of **often** just before the main verb.
I **often** see Anna with Mary.
I have **often** seen Anna with Mary.
---

oil /ɔɪl/ noun (uncountable)
1 a thick liquid which is made from plants and animals and which can often be used for cooking
  • This egg has been cooked in vegetable **oil**.
୫ cooking oil
2 a thick brown liquid which comes from under the ground and which is used in machines
  • This engine needs some more **oil**.

okay/OK /ˌəʊˈkeɪ/ adverb, interjection
(used only in speaking - not writing)
You use **OK** to show that you agree or that you will do something or that you are all right
  • "How are you?" "I'm **okay**."
  • "Shall we go to the cinema tonight?" "**OK!**"
⚠ See **all right**.

old /əʊld/ adjective
1 not young, having lived for many years
  • Mrs Hill is an **old** lady. She's seventy.

2 Use **old** when you give someone's age.
- *"How **old** is your brother?"*
  *"He's seventeen years **old**, and I'm twelve."*
3 not new, not fresh, having been there for a long time
- *Maria, don't wear that **old** dress. It's torn.*

on /ɒn/ preposition

1 You can use **on** to show where something or someone is.
- *Put the cup **on** the table and sit **on** this chair.*
2 You can use **on** with the words paper, page, etc.
- *Can you write your name **on** this envelope?*
3 You can use **on** to show that something is fastened to a wall, a ceiling, etc.
- *There was a picture **on** the wall.*
4 You can use **on** to show that something is working.
- *Could you put the television **on**, please?*
5 You can use **on** to show when something happens.
- *We're going for a picnic **on** Tuesday.*

LANGUAGE NOTE

COMPARE	**on** Thursday (= days of the week)
	on my birthday, on New Year's Day (= special days)
	on 19 May (= dates)
BUT	**at** four o'clock (= clock times)
	at Christmas, at the weekend (= holiday periods)
	in May (= months)
	in winter (= seasons)
	in 1994 (= years)

6 You can use **on** to show what something is about.
- *The talk tonight will be **on** Chinese medicine.*

once /wʌns/ adverb

1 only one time
- *I've only met my uncle **once**.*

2 one time during a period of time
- *Susie goes for singing lessons **once** a week.*
3 a long time ago
- ***Once** people travelled everywhere on horses.*
4 **at once** = this moment, immediately
- *Please come **at once**. I need help.*

one /wʌn/ pronoun
plural: ones

1 a certain person or thing
- *I've got several books by Charles Dickens. Which **ones** would you like to borrow?*
2 you, people in general
- ***One** should be very careful when **one** travels in foreign countries.*

LANGUAGE NOTE

1 **One of** is followed by a plural noun and a singular verb
One of the **men** I saw **was** holding a knife.
2 COMPARE   I need a pencil.
Can I borrow **one**?
I need your pencil.
Can I borrow **it**?
I need your pencils.
Can I borrow **them**?
3 In British English **one** and **he/she** are not usually mixed in the same sentence.
NEVER   ~~One should always try her best.~~
ALWAYS **One** should always try **one's** best.
Note, however, that in American English both sentences are correct.

⚠ See also **another 2**.

onion /ˈʌnjən/ noun (countable, uncountable)
⚠ See box on page 238.

only /ˈəʊnlɪ/ adverb

1 just one of something
- *I am the **only** one in my family who is a doctor.*
2 just, no more than
- *There were **only** five oranges left.*

θ	ð	ʃ	dʒ	tʃ	ŋ	ʒ	iː	ɜː	ɪ	æ	ʌ	ɒ
thing	that	shop	jump	chop	sing	measure	been	bird	bit	cat	but	not

LANGUAGE NOTE

Only should be placed as near as possible to the word it goes with.
1. *Only* Maria lent me ten dollars.
   (= Maria - and no one else lent me ten dollars.)
2. Maria *only* lent me ten dollars.
   (= Maria lent me ten dollars - she didn't give me ten dollars.)
3. Maria lent *only* me ten dollars.
   (= Maria didn't lend anyone else ten dollars.)
4. Maria lent me *only* ten dollars.
   (= It was only ten dollars Maria lent me - no more than that.)

Note that sentence (2) may also be used with the same meaning as sentence (4).

3. You can use **if only** when you want to show a wish.
   - *If only* I could see her now.
     (= I wish I could see her now.)
4. You can use **only just** when you want to show that it was nearly not so.
   - I *only just* passed the exam.
5. **not only .... but also** = and
   - He's brought *not only* some balls *but also* a racquet.

LANGUAGE NOTE

Note the word order (and the place of the subject and verb in the first sentence):
1. *Not only* did Dave give me a pen *but* he *also* bought me some ink.
2. Dave *not only* gave me a pen *but also* bought me some ink.
3. Dave gave me *not only* a pen *but also* some ink.

open¹ /ˈəʊpən/ verb
1. push or lift something so that it is no longer shut
   - *Open* the window and let some fresh air in.
2. move something to look inside it or take something out
   - Mabel *opened* the letter at once.
3. turn the cover of a book
   - *Open* your books at page 31.
4. When a shop or business opens, it begins to work and people can go in and use it.
   - The shops here *open* at 8.30 a.m.

open² adjective
not shut, not closed
- Don't leave the door *open*. Please close it.

LANGUAGE NOTE

Only **open** (NOT opened) is an adjective.
NEVER The shop will be opened tomorrow.
(Unless you mean that someone is going to give a speech, have a party, etc and open the shop.)
ALWAYS The shop will be open tomorrow.

opposite¹ /ˈɒpəzɪt/ noun (countable, usually with the)
completely different
- I'm the *opposite* of my brother. He likes games but I like reading and drawing.

opposite² adjective
1. The opposite side of a street or road is the side which is farther away.

- The hotel is on the *opposite* side of the road to our college.
2. completely different
   - He walked away in the *opposite* direction.

opposite³ preposition, adverb
facing
- We live in a small flat *opposite* the park.

θ	ð	ʃ	dʒ	tʃ	ŋ	ʒ	iː	ɜː	ɪ	æ	ʌ	ɒ
thing	that	shop	jump	chop	sing	measure	been	bird	bit	cat	but	not

or /ɔː*/ conjunction

1 You can use **or** when you want someone to choose between two things or when you want to give a list of things and ideas which are possible.
- "Would you like tea **or** coffee?" "Tea, please."

> **LANGUAGE NOTE**
>
> When **or** joins two singular nouns as subjects, the verb which follows is singular.
> A pen or a pencil **is** necessary for this test.

2 You can use **or** to warn someone that something unpleasant will happen if they (don't) do something.
- Hurry up **or** you'll miss the bus.

orange [1] /ˈɒrɪndʒ/ noun (uncountable, countable), adjective

the colour of an orange, the colour between red and yellow
- The setting sun was like a big **orange** ball.

orange [2] noun (uncountable, countable)
- See box on page 89.

order [1] /ˈɔːdə*/ noun

1 (countable) something which must be done
- Who gave the police the **order** to fire?
- carry out/obey/get/receive/give an order, take orders from (someone)

2 **in order** = the way things are put
- Will you put these books away **in order**?

3 **in good order** = working well
- This video camera's quite old, but it's **in good order**.

4 **out of order** = not working
- The lifts were **out of order**, so we walked up the stairs.

order [2] verb

1 tell people what they must do
- The captain **ordered** the soldiers to fire.

2 ask for food and drink in a restaurant
- "Would you like to **order** now, sir?" the waiter asked.

ordinary /ˈɔːdənrɪ/ adjective

not special or different
- I like Mr Hyde's house although it's just an **ordinary** small house.

organization /ˌɔːgənaɪˈzeɪʃn/ noun (countable)

1 a group of people who meet to do something; a club, a business, etc
- The students are forming an **organization** to send food to poor children in Africa.

2 the way things are planned or arranged
- "Your composition is good but the **organization** is poor," the teacher told me.

organize /ˈɔːgənaɪz/ verb

organizing, organized, has organized

plan things, arrange things
- "Who's **organizing** the concert next month?" "I'm selling the tickets and Mr Lee's getting the singers."

> **SPELLING NOTE**
>
> Also organi**s**ation in British English.
> Also organi**s**e in British English.

other /ˈʌðə*/ pronoun, determiner

1 not the person or people you have just mentioned, not the things you have just talked or written about
- Some pupils were inside while (the) **others** were in the playground.

> **LANGUAGE NOTE**
>
> ALWAYS use **the**, **this**, **that**, **any**, **no**, **my**, etc in front of **other**.
> One arm was broken but **the** other was all right.
> Only Tina and Ann were present: there were **no** other students there.

2 another person or thing, someone or something extra
- She brought two **other** girls with her.

θ	ð	ʃ	dʒ	tʃ	ŋ	ʒ	iː	ɜː	ɪ	æ	ʌ	ɒ
thing	that	shop	jump	chop	sing	measure	been	bird	bit	cat	but	not

3 **the other day** = a few days ago
 • "Isn't it time you visited your uncle again?" "I went to see him **the other day**."
4 **each other**
⚠ See **each** 3.

ought to /'ɔːt tuː/   modal verb
should
 • We all **ought to** try to help the poor.

LANGUAGE NOTE

1 I **must** get up now: I'm very late.
   = I have to get up now or I'll be late.
   I **ought to** get up now or I may be late.
   = I should get up now or I may be late.
2 Note the patterns in sentences with **not** and in questions.
   You **oughtn't to** say that.
   Ought we **to** tell Harry?
3 Use **ought to have** for things you should have done in the past.
   You **ought to have** seen a doctor yesterday.

---

our /'aʊə*/   pronoun
of us, belonging to us
 • **Our** flat is quite near the bus station.

ours /'aʊəz/   pronoun
the one connected with us, something belonging to us
 • Your holiday was different from **ours**.
   You went to the beach and we went climbing.

ourselves /aʊə'selvz/   pronoun
1 You can use **ourselves** as the object of a verb or preposition.
   • We really enjoyed **ourselves** at the party.
2 You can use **ourselves** to make the subject or object seem more important or to make the pronoun **we** stronger.
   • We swept the classroom **ourselves**.
3 without any help from anyone
   • We painted the flat (all by) **ourselves**.
4 **by ourselves** = without anyone else
   • We were left in the cave **by ourselves**.

out /aʊt/   adverb
1 not in, not at home
   • I called to see you but you were **out**.
2 outside, away from
   • Is this the way **out**?
3 no longer burning
   • The fire's **out**. It went **out** an hour ago.
↪ come/go/walk/run/rush/hurry/ get/fall /bring/take/carry /ask/invite/ tear/pull /stay/shut/keep/clean/ empty/wash/cross/ burn/give/hand/ cry/shout/call **out**

out of /'aʊt ɒv/   preposition
1 outside, away from
   • Is this the way **out of** the building?
2 **come out of, go out of** = leave (a room, a building, etc)
   • Ann **went out of** the room when Jim came in.

SPELLING NOTE

go **out of** the room
(NOT go out from the room NOR go out the room)

↪ **out of** town, **out of** date (= too old), **out of** order (= broken), **out of** sight (= too far away, etc to be seen), **out of** the question (= impossible), **out of** doors (= outside)

outdoors /aʊt'dɔːz/   adverb
in the open air, not in a building
 • Mr Saleh likes working **outdoors**.

outside¹ /'aʊtsaɪd/   noun (countable)
the part which is not in a building, etc
 • The **outside** of the building needed painting.

outside²   adjective
out of something, not in a building, a room, etc, in the open air
 • The **outside** walls are made of brick.

outside³ /aʊt'saɪd/   adverb
out of something, not in a building, a room, etc, in the open air
 • I was too hot so I went **outside** to get some fresh air.

θ	ð	ʃ	dʒ	tʃ	ŋ	ʒ	iː	ɜː	ɪ	æ	ʌ	ɒ
thing	that	shop	jump	chop	sing	measure	been	bird	bit	cat	but	not

oven /ˈʌvn/ noun (countable)
something like a box in which you can cook food
- *The meat has been in the **oven** for almost an hour. I think it's ready now.*
- light an oven, turn off/on an oven; an electric/gas oven, a microwave (oven)

over¹ /ˈəʊvə*/ adverb
1 down
   - *The small child's fallen **over** and cut his knee.*
   - fall over, bend/lean over/knock/kick/push over
2 up and out
   - *The water's boiling **over**. Turn the kettle off.*
   - boil/flow/run over
3 onto the other side
   - *Turn the page **over** now and begin the test.*
4 across, towards
   - *Let's go **over** and talk to Stella.*
   - go/walk/run/drive/hurry over
5 finished
   - *The meeting will soon be **over**.*

over² preposition
1 above
   - *There was a small light **over** the table.*
2 covering, on top of
   - *He put a handkerchief **over** his mouth.*
3 to the other side of
   - *Can you jump **over** this wall?*
4 across
   - *Is there a bridge **over** the river near here?*
5 down
   - *I fell **over** that piece of wood.*
6 more than
   - *My pen cost **over** $50.*

owe /əʊ/ verb
owing, owed, has owed
If you owe money to someone, you have borrowed money from them and not paid it back to them.
- *How much do I **owe** you?*

LANGUAGE NOTE
| NEVER | I am owing you twenty dollars. |
| ALWAYS | I owe you twenty dollars. |

own¹ /əʊn/ verb
have something (have bought it or have been given it)
- *Who **owns** that lovely house?*

LANGUAGE NOTE
| NEVER | Mr Small is owning six race horses. |
| ALWAYS | Mr Small owns six race horses. |

own² adjective
something which belongs to someone (and no one else)
- *Mr Manawa has his **own** car now.*

own³
(all) on one's own = alone

- *Ruth sat **on her own** on the bus so that she could read her book.*

owner /ˈəʊnə*/ noun (countable)
the person to which something belongs
- *Will the **owner** of the blue car in the car park please move it at once?*

ox /ɒks/ noun (countable)
plural: oxen /ˈɒksn/
⚠ See box on page 10.

| θ | ð | ʃ | dʒ | tʃ | ŋ | ʒ | iː | ɜː | ɪ | æ | ʌ | ɒ |
| thing | that | shop | jump | chop | sing | measure | been | bird | bit | cat | but | not |

P p

pack /pæk/ verb
1. put away clothes to take with you when you go away
   - It took him two hours to **pack** before he left.
2. put things into boxes, bags, etc
   - Sarah's job is to **pack** food into boxes.

package /'pækɪdʒ/ noun (countable)
(American English)
⚠ See **parcel**.

packet /'pækɪt/ noun (countable)
a bag, box, etc of something
- I was so hungry that I ate a **packet** of biscuits.
↪ a packet of biscuits/cigarettes/envelopes/flour/sugar

page /peɪdʒ/ noun (countable)
a single piece of paper in a book or newspaper
- There are 270 **pages**, and I'm up to **page** 90.
↪ open (a book) at a certain page, turn over a page

paid /peɪd/ verb
past tense and past participle of **pay**
- I **paid** a lot of money for this camera.
↪ highly paid (= earning a lot of money)

pain /peɪn/ noun
1. (uncountable) something which hurts
   - Paul's broken ankle gives him a lot of **pain**.
2. (countable) a sharp unpleasant feeling in part of the body
   - I've got a bad **pain** in the middle of my back.
↪ ease the pain, give someone (a lot of) pain, feel pain, have a pain, kill the pain; be in pain; a pain comes on/goes away/wears off/disappears; a dull/great/slight/sharp pain

painful /'peɪnfl/ adjective
hurting a lot
- My arm was very **painful** for a long time after I'd broken it.

LANGUAGE NOTE
Note that **painful** does NOT mean **full of pain**: it means **causing pain**.
NEVER I was very painful after the accident.
ALWAYS **My legs** were very **painful** after the accident.

paint¹ /peɪnt/ noun (uncountable)
a coloured liquid which you can use to change the colour of things or to make a picture
- I've bought some blue **paint** for Tony's room and yellow **paint** for Mary's.
↪ put paint on, mix paint; a coat of paint (= when you cover something once with paint), put on/need a coat of paint

paint² verb
1. cover something with paint
   - We've **painted** our living room white.
2. make a picture
   - Helen **painted** a picture of some flowers.

painting /'peɪntɪŋ/ noun (countable)
a picture which someone has painted
- I like this **painting** of mountains.
↪ do a painting; an oil/water-colour painting

pair /peə*/ noun (countable)
1. two (parts) of something
   - Jenny wore her new **pair** of shoes today.
2. something which has two parts: eg a pair of pyjamas, a pair of shorts, a pair of trousers, etc
   - Can you lend me a **pair** of scissors, please?

θ	ð	ʃ	dʒ	tʃ	ŋ	ʒ	iː	ɜː	ɪ	æ	ʌ	ɒ
thing	that	shop	jump	chop	sing	measure	been	bird	bit	cat	but	not

LANGUAGE NOTE

1. Note the use of a singular verb after **pair**.
   This new pair of shoes is hurting me.
   (BUT   These shoes are hurting me.)
2. You cannot say *two trousers*, *three scissors*, etc (although you can say *two shoes*.) Say:- **two pairs of trousers**, **three pairs of scissors**, etc.

pale / peɪl/   adjective
1. light in colour
   - *The sky was dark earlier this morning, but now it is **pale** blue and the sun is shining.*
   ↻ pale blue/yellow, etc, a pale colour
2. with little colour in your face (often because you are ill or frightened)
   - *Do you feel all right, Mary? You look very **pale**.*
   ↻ go/turn/look pale

palm / pɑːm/   noun (countable)
1. a kind of tree with long leaves at the top and no branches (usually grown in hot countries)
   - *Sit in the shade under this **palm** (tree).*
2. the part of your hand which is flat
   ⚠ See also box on page 25.

pan / pæn/   noun (countable)
something for cooking food in
- *You can boil the rice in this **pan**.*

pants, / pænts/ **panties** / ˈpæntɪz/ noun (plural)
1. **pants, panties**
   ⚠ See **knickers**.
2. **pants**
   ⚠ See **underpants**.
3. **pants** (American English)
   ⚠ See **trousers**.

papaya / pəˈpaɪə/   noun (countable, uncountable)
⚠ See box on page 114.

paper /ˈpeɪpə*/   noun
1. (uncountable) something on which you can write
   - *Start the exercise on a clean sheet of **paper**.*
   ↻ a piece/sheet of paper; lined/plain paper/typing/writing/ cigarette/tissue/toilet paper
2. (countable) a newspaper
   - *Is there anything interesting in the **paper**?*
   ↻ a daily/Sunday/morning/evening paper
3. (countable) an examination
   - *I thought that the Maths **paper** was very difficult, but the History **paper** was easy.*
   ↻ an exam/test/question paper

paragraph / ˈpærəɡrɑːf/   noun (countable)
part of a piece of writing which always begins on a new line
- *You've written only one **paragraph** but you've described three different people.*

parcel /ˈpɑːsl/   noun (countable)
American English: package
something which is wrapped in paper to send or give to someone
- *I sent a **parcel** to my sister for her birthday.*
↻ address/post/send/get/receive/open a parcel

Pardon? /ˈpɑːdn/   verb
You can say **Pardon?** when you have not heard what someone has just said and you want them to say it again.
- *"I've just seen Anna Melrose." "**Pardon?**" "I said I've just seen Anna Melrose."*

parent / ˈpeərənt/   noun (countable)
Your mother and father are your parents.
- *Paul's **parents** are taking him to London.*

park [1] / pɑːk/   noun (countable)
1. a piece of land with grass, trees, etc, where people can walk, rest and enjoy themselves
   - *Let's take the children to play in the **park**.*
2. ⚠ See **car park**.

θ	ð	ʃ	dʒ	tʃ	ŋ	ʒ	iː	ɜː	ɪ	æ	ʌ	ɒ
thing	that	shop	jump	chop	sing	measure	been	bird	bit	cat	but	not

park² verb
1 leave your car for a (short) time
- You can **park** your car outside the shop.
2 **No parking** = You must not park here.
- You can't stop here: there's a **No Parking** sign.

LANGUAGE NOTE	
COMPARE	Two cars were parking near the school. (= The drivers were parking their cars near the school: ie the cars were moving.)
WITH	Two cars were parked near the school. (= The drivers had already parked their cars near the school: ie the cars were standing still.)

parrot /ˈpærət/ noun (countable)
⚠ See box on page 22.

part /pɑːt/ noun (countable)
1 a piece of something
- This clock doesn't work: a small **part** is missing.
2 some, but not all
- The word "made" is **part** of the verb "make".
3 the words someone says in a play or a film
- I've got a **part** in a film about Columbus.
4 **take part in** = do something with other people
- Are you **taking part in** the school concert?

partly /ˈpɑːtlɪ/ adverb
not completely, in some way only
- "Where is Delhi?" "It's in the middle of India." "That's only **partly** right. Delhi is in India but it's in the north."

party /ˈpɑːtɪ/ noun (countable)
plural: parties
1 a group of people doing something together
- A small **party** of students visited the new factory yesterday.
2 a group of people meeting to enjoy themselves
- I'm going to Mabel's birthday **party** today.

↻ attend/give/throw a party (BUT NOT make a party), have/hold a party; a birthday/Christmas/New Year('s Eve)/cocktail/dinner/tea/farewell/going-away party

pass /pɑːs/ verb
1 go by someone or something (without stopping)
- Tony **passes** Mr Cheng's shop every day.
2 give someone something which they cannot reach
- Could you **pass** the sugar, please?
3 be successful in a test or an examination, not fail
- Leila **passed** her test with the highest mark.

passage /ˈpæsɪdʒ/ noun (countable)
1 a narrow way joining one place to another
- In the flat there is a narrow **passage** from the hall to the living room.
2 a part of a book or piece of music
- Which **passage** from this book should I read?

passenger /ˈpæsɪndʒə*/ noun (countable)
someone who travels on a bus, an aeroplane, a train or a boat
- Most of the **passengers** on the bus started singing.

passport /ˈpɑːspɔːt/ noun (countable)
a small book which has information about yourself and which you usually need to travel to other countries
- Show your **passport** to that man over there.

past¹ /pɑːst/ noun (singular with the)
the time before now
- In the **past** this city was a small fishing village.

↻ belong/forget/remember the past

past² adjective
before now
- I've not been feeling well for the **past** few days.

past³ preposition
1 by, near
- We always walk **past** the post office on our way to school.

θ	ð	ʃ	dʒ	tʃ	ŋ	ʒ	iː	ɜː	ɪ	æ	ʌ	ɒ
thing	that	shop	jump	chop	sing	measure	been	bird	bit	cat	but	not

2 after (used in telling the time)
- "You'll have to hurry. It's half-**past** six." "No, it isn't. It's only twenty-five **past**."

LANGUAGE NOTE	
BRITISH ENGLISH	ten past six
AMERICAN ENGLISH	ten after six

path /pɑːθ/ noun (countable)
plural: paths /pɑːðz/
a narrow piece of ground for people to walk on
- Is there a **path** through the wood?
↻ clear/make a path

patient[1] /ˈpeɪʃnt/ noun (countable)
someone who is ill in hospital or who is being looked after by a doctor or a nurse
- Dr Smith was popular with all his **patients**.
↻ examine/see/look after/nurse/cure/treat a patient

patient[2] adjective
not annoyed easily, always calm
- Anna is very **patient** and never gets angry.

patiently /ˈpeɪʃntlɪ/ adverb
without getting annoyed
- Mike waited **patiently** for or Elsa to arrive.

pattern /ˈpætən/ noun (countable)
the way shapes and colours are put together
- I like the **pattern** on your shirt.
↻ arrange something in a pattern, form/make a pattern; a simple/an unusual pattern

pavement /ˈpeɪvmənt/ noun (countable)
American English: sidewalk
a path for people to walk on at the side of a road
- Walk on the **pavement**, not in the middle of the road.

paw /pɔː/ noun (countable)
an animal's foot (used chiefly for cats, dogs and bears)

- The dog held out its **paw**, and I saw a nail in it.

pay /peɪ/ verb
paying, paid /peɪd/, has paid
1 give money to someone who does some work
- We **paid** $800 to have the car repaired.
2 give money when you buy something
- Have you **paid** the waiter yet?

LANGUAGE NOTE

1 pay someone, pay a bill, etc
  Have you **paid** Ken the money you owe him?
  I've just **paid** the bill. Let's go.

2 pay *for* someone
  How did Ken go to the cinema? He hadn't got any money. *I paid for* him.

3 pay *for* something
  Who **paid for** the meal?

3 **pay a visit** = visit
- It's my uncle's birthday next Tuesday, and so we're going to **pay** him **a visit**.
4 **pay attention** = attend, take notice, listen
- **Pay attention** when I speak to you.

pea /piː/ noun (uncountable)
⚠ See box on page 238.

peace /piːs/ noun (uncountable)
1 a time when there is not a war, when people are not fighting
- There has been **peace** between China and Japan since 1945.
↻ bring about peace, make peace with, work for peace

θ	ð	ʃ	dʒ	tʃ	ŋ	ʒ	iː	ɜː	ɪ	æ	ʌ	ɒ
thing	that	shop	jump	chop	sing	measure	been	bird	bit	cat	but	not

2 being calm, quiet
- *I like walking by myself in the country because I can find **peace** there.*

☞ be at peace with, find peace, leave someone in peace

peach /piːtʃ/ noun (uncountable)
plural: peaches
⚠ See box on page 89.

pear /peə*/ noun (uncountable)
⚠ See box on page 89.

pedestrian /pɪˈdestrɪən/ noun (countable)
someone who is walking (and not travelling by car or bus, etc)
- ***Pedestrians** should walk on the pavement.*

pen /pen/ noun (countable)
something which you write with
- *Shall I write the letter in pencil or in **pen**?*

☞ a ballpoint/felt-tip/fountain pen

⚠ See also **ball-point (pen)**; see also **biro**; see also **felt-tip pen**.

pence /pens/ noun (plural)
singular: penny /ˈpenɪ/, pence or p /piː/
the name of some small coins used in Britain (There are a hundred **pence** in a pound.)
- *Here's your change, sir – eight **pence**.*

LANGUAGE NOTE

Also ***p***: eg 50 p; 1 p.

---

pencil /ˈpensl/ noun (countable)
something which you write or draw with (but without ink in it)
- *My **pencil** is blunt. I'll just sharpen it.*

pen-friend /ˈpen frend/ noun (countable)
someone in another city or country to whom you write letters and who sends you letters
- *I've got an interesting letter from my **pen-friend** in Chile.*

penguin /ˈpeŋgwɪn/ noun (countable)
⚠ See box on page 22.

people /ˈpiːpl/ noun (plural)
singular: person
1 men, women and children
- *How many **people** were at the meeting?*

☞ a crowd/a group/lot/a number of people; common/ordinary/working/city/country/brave/hard-working/proud people

---
LANGUAGE NOTE

COMPARE Only one person **wants** to go.
A lot of people **want** to go.

⚠ See also **person**.
2 everyone
- *I don't care what **people** say: I like him.*
3 **the people** = ordinary men and women
- ***The people** are happy with the government.*

pepper¹ /ˈpepə*/ noun (uncountable)
a powder which you can put on your food (like salt) to make it taste hot
- *Could you pass the salt and **pepper**, please?*

☞ black/white pepper

pepper² noun (uncountable, uncountable)
⚠ See box on page 238.

per /pɜː*/ preposition
1 for each
- *The car can reach a speed of 160 kilometres **per** hour.*

LANGUAGE NOTE

1 160 kilometres per hour = 160 kph
2 Often in conversations ***an*** is used instead of ***per***.
"How fast are we going?"
"About sixty kilometres an hour."

---

2 **per cent** = one part for each hundred
- *"Ten out of fifty students were absent yesterday." "That means that twenty **per cent** of the students didn't come to school."*

θ	ð	ʃ	dʒ	tʃ	ŋ	ʒ	iː	ɜː	ɪ	æ	ʌ	ɒ
thing	that	shop	jump	chop	sing	measure	been	bird	bit	cat	but	not

perfect /ˈpɜːfɪkt/   adjective
1 without any mistakes at all
   - My homework was **perfect**. I didn't make one mistake!
2 just right, as good as possible
   - This dress is **perfect**. It's just the right size and length, and it looks very pretty.

perhaps /pəˈhæps/   adverb
Use **perhaps** when you are not sure whether something is going to happen or whether it is possible, etc.
   - **Perhaps** it will rain tomorrow. I think it may.

period /ˈpɪərɪəd/   noun (countable)
1 a length of time
   - The day will be cloudy with fairly long **periods** of rain.
⟲ a brief /difficult/long/short period
2 a lesson
   - I have three English **periods** a week.
3 the time when blood flows from a woman's body every month
   - Ann isn't feeling too well: I think she's having her **period**.
4 (American English)
⚐ See **full stop**.

person /ˈpɜːsn/   noun (countable)
plural: people or persons
a man, woman or child
   - I'm the only **person** who lives here.

LANGUAGE NOTE

The plural of **person** is usually **people**. The plural **persons** is used only very rarely (in notices, etc).
   Only 12 **persons** allowed standing.
   (From a notice on a bus.)

⚐ See also **people**.

pet /pet/   noun (countable)
an animal, bird or fish which you enjoy keeping in your home or garden
   - We have three **pets**: a bird, a cat and a dog.

petrol /ˈpetrəl/   noun (uncountable)
American English: gas
a liquid which you put into a car to make it go
   - Mr Anderton's car ran out of **petrol** on his way to work yesterday, and he had to walk to the office.
⟲ petrol pump/station, petrol station attendant

pharmacy /ˈfɑːməsɪ/   noun (countable)
American English: drug store
a shop which sells medicines
   - Can you get me some tablets from the **pharmacy**?

phone[1] /fəʊn/   noun (countable)
something you can use to talk to people a long way away: a telephone
   - Have you got a **phone** in your new flat?

LANGUAGE NOTE

1 The word **phone** is a short form of **telephone**.
2 BRITISH ENGLISH   talk to someone **on/over** the phone
   AMERICAN ENGLISH   talk to someone on/over the phone or **by phone**

⟲ answer a/ the phone, make a phone call
   a phone rings
⚐ See also **telephone**[1].

phone[2]   verb
phoning, phoned, has phoned
use a telephone to speak to someone a long way away
   - Shall I **phone** for a taxi?
⚐ See also **telephone**[2].

photocopier /ˈfəʊtəkɒpɪə*/   noun (countable)
a machine which makes a copy of a piece of paper, etc (like a photograph)
   - You can copy the letter on this **photocopier**.

photocopy[1] /ˈfəʊtəkɒpɪ/   noun (countable)
plural: photocopies
a copy of a piece of paper, etc (like a photograph) made by using a photocopier
   - Can you make a **photocopy** of this letter for me.
⟲ make a photocopy

θ	ð	ʃ	dʒ	tʃ	ŋ	ʒ	iː	ɜː	ɪ	æ	ʌ	ɒ
thing	that	shop	jump	chop	sing	measure	been	bird	bit	cat	but	not

photocopy² verb
photocopying, photocopied, has photocopied
make a copy of a piece of paper, etc (like a photograph) with a special machine
• *Photocopy this letter: it's very important.*

photo /ˈfəʊtəʊ/
or **photograph** /ˈfəʊtəɡrɑːf/ noun (countable)
a picture you make when you use a camera
• *Alice showed me her holiday photographs.*

LANGUAGE NOTE
The word **photo** (plural: **photos**) is a short form of **photograph**.

☙ take a photo(graph); a family/group photo(graph)

photographer /fəˈtɒɡrəfə*/ noun (countable)
someone who takes pictures using a camera
• *The photographer took a photo of the class.*

piano /pɪˈænəʊ/ noun (countable)
plural: pianos
something you can play music on by pressing the black and white keys on it

• *Are you learning to play the piano?*

LANGUAGE NOTE
| NEVER | Can you play piano? |
| ALWAYS | Can you play **the** piano? |

pick /pɪk/ verb
1 choose
• *Have they picked the school hockey team?*
2 pull (fruit and flowers from their plants) with your hands
• *We picked some flowers in the country.*

pick up /ˌpɪk ˈʌp/ phrasal verb
1 lift something or someone off the ground, off a table, etc
• *Mr Lee bent down and picked up the child.*
2 give someone a ride in a car, etc
• *The driver stopped to pick up the two old women and took them home.*

picnic /ˈpɪknɪk/ noun (countable)
a meal (usually sandwiches, etc) which you eat outdoors (often in the country or on the beach)
• *Let's go on a picnic to Lake Capilano.*
☙ go on/have a picnic

picture /ˈpɪktʃə*/ noun (countable)
a drawing, painting or photograph
• *Look at the pictures in that book.*
☙ draw/paint/take a picture

piece /piːs/ noun (countable)
a part of something, not all of it
• *Mrs Robinson gave us each a big piece of cake.*
• *Have you got a piece of paper I can use?*

LANGUAGE NOTE
NEVER	an advice (uncountable noun)
ALWAYS	advice, some advice, **a piece of** advice
NEVER	two furnitures (uncountable noun)
ALWAYS	two **pieces of** furniture
BUT	three handkerchiefs (countable noun)
(NEVER	three pieces of handkerchiefs)

pig /pɪɡ/ noun (countable)
⚠ See box on page 10.

piglet /ˈpɪɡlɪt/ noun (countable)
a young pig
⚠ See box on page 10.

pill /pɪl/ noun (countable)
medicine which is small and round and which you swallow
- *The doctor told me to take one of these **pills** four times a day after meals.*
- ↻ swallow a pill, take a pill

pillow /ˈpɪləʊ/ noun (countable)
something soft on which you rest your head when you sleep
- *Anita always likes to sleep with two **pillows**.*

pilot /ˈpaɪlət/ noun (countable)
a person who flies a plane
- *The **pilot** says we'll land at Madrid soon.*

pin¹ /pɪn/ noun (countable)
a very small thin piece of metal with a point at one end
- *I used a **pin** when the button came off my shirt.*
- ↻ drawing pin (American English: thumbtack), safety pin
- ⚠ See also **safety pin**.

pin² verb
pinning, pinned, has pinned
fasten something (to something else) with a pin
- *Can you **pin** this piece of paper on the notice-board?*

pineapple /ˈpaɪnæpl/ noun (uncountable, countable)
⚠ See box on page 89.

pink /pɪŋk/ noun (uncountable, countable), adjective
the colour between white and red
- *Cats have rough **pink** tongues.*

ping pong /ˈpɪŋ pɒŋ/ noun (uncountable)
⚠ See **table tennis**.

pipe /paɪp/ noun (countable)
1 Pipes are used to carry water, oil, gas, etc to buildings.
- *Look at all that water in the street. I think a water **pipe** must have broken.*

2 something which people (usually men) use to smoke
- *Mr Hill likes smoking a **pipe**.*
- ↻ light a pipe, smoke a pipe

pity¹ /ˈpɪtɪ/ noun
1 (uncountable) If you feel **pity** for someone, you feel very sorry for them.
- *I feel great **pity** for that poor man.*
- ↻ feel/show pity for someone, have/take pity on someone
2 (a + singular noun) If it is **a pity** that something has happened, you feel sorry about it.
- *What **a pity** Tom didn't come, either!*

pity² verb
pitying, pitied, has pitied
If you pity someone, you feel sorry for them.
- *I **pity** people who think about money all the time.*

place /pleɪs/ noun (countable)
1 any point, building, village, town, city or country
- *London is the first **place** which most tourists visit when they come to Britain.*
2 any point or position (compared with others)
- *Where's the best **place** to leave our coats?*
- ↻ get/win/keep a place, take your place; an empty/suitable/good/excellent place; your own place (= your home, etc)
3 **place of birth** = where you were born
- *Can you write your name, address, date and **place of birth** on this form, please?*

plain /pleɪn/ adjective
1 clear, easy to understand
- *It was **plain** that Mary didn't like Dave.*
2 simple, without a pattern
- *Jane was wearing a **plain** dress.*

plan¹ /plæn/ noun (countable)
1 an idea about doing something in the future
- *What are your **plans** for this evening?*

θ	ð	ʃ	dʒ	tʃ	ŋ	ʒ	iː	ɜː	ɪ	æ	ʌ	ɒ
thing	that	shop	jump	chop	sing	measure	been	bird	bit	cat	but	not

☞ carry out/draw up/make a plan/plans
keep to a plan; a clever/wise/useful/
secret plan
2 drawings of machines, buildings and towns
• Here's a street **plan** of Hong Kong.

plan² verb
planning, planned, has planned
think or say something about the future
• What do you **plan** to do when you leave school?

plane /pleɪn/ noun (countable)
a machine (with wings and an engine) which flies in the air
• Look at that large **plane**. It's just landing.

LANGUAGE NOTE

1 The word **plane** is a short form of **aeroplane** or **airplane**.
2 go by plane   BUT   take **a** plane

☞ board/fly/get off/land/pilot/take a plane;
a plane takes off, a plane flies/lands/
touches down
⚠ See also **aeroplane**; see also **aircraft**.

planet /ˈplænɪt/ noun (countable)
something large and round in space (like the Earth) but not a star
• Soon men will visit **planets** like Mars and Venus.

LANGUAGE NOTE

the planet Mars   BUT   Mars (without **the**)
the planet Venus   BUT   Venus (without **the**)

---

plant¹ /plɑːnt/ noun (countable)
living things which grow in soil and which have leaves but are smaller than trees
• This **plant** will die if you don't give it any water.
☞ grow/water plants

plant² verb
put flowers, vegetables and trees in soil so that they can grow
• The president is coming tomorrow to **plant** a special tree in the centre of our town.

plaster /ˈplɑːstə*/ noun
1 (countable) a thin piece of cloth to put over a cut, etc

• Wash the blood off your finger and put a **plaster** over the cut.
☞ sticking plaster
2 (uncountable) something you put on walls or ceilings to make them smooth
• Some **plaster** is coming off this wall.
3 **in plaster** = When you break your arm or leg, it will be put in plaster until it is better.
• I saw Leila with her arm **in plaster** yesterday. I didn't know she'd broken it.

plastic¹ /ˈplæstɪk/ noun (uncountable)
a material which is made in factories and which is very useful for making many things used today
• This desk is made of **plastic**.

plastic² adjective
made from plastic
• Let's put the food in a **plastic** bag to keep it fresh.

plate /pleɪt/ noun (countable)
a flat dish from which you eat food
• Shall I put some vegetables on your **plate**?

platform /ˈplætfɔːm/ noun (countable)
1 something flat which people stand on when they talk to a lot of people

---

θ	ð	ʃ	dʒ	tʃ	ŋ	ʒ	iː	ɜː	ɪ	æ	ʌ	ɒ
thing	that	shop	jump	chop	sing	measure	been	bird	bit	cat	but	not

- The principal stood on a small **platform** and talked to all the students in the college.
2   a place in a station where you get on and off a train
- The train for Rome will leave from **Platform** 3.

play [1]   / pleɪ /   noun (countable)

a story which you act
- How many students will act in the school **play**?

↻ act in/put on/produce/write a play; an amusing/funny/good/bad/boring/interesting/serious play

play [2]   verb

1   take part in a game
- Can you **play** tennis?
2   have fun (usually used about small children)
- Look at the children **playing** in the park.
3   make music
- Helen **plays** the piano and I **play** the guitar.

LANGUAGE NOTE

play **the** piano, etc BUT play tennis, etc (without **the**)

---

player   /ˈpleɪə*/   noun (countable)

1   a person who plays a game
- Two of the **players** were hurt in the football match.
2   a person who plays music
- I thought the guitar **player** was very good.

playground   /ˈpleɪɡraʊnd/   noun (countable)

the place outside a school building where children play

- The children are running around in the **playground**.

pleasant   /ˈpleznt/   adjective

When something is pleasant, it makes you happy and you like it.
- The weather is very **pleasant** today, isn't it?

please [1]   / pliːz /   interjection

You often say **please** in English when you are asking someone to do something for you.
- Could you pass the salt and pepper, **please**?

LANGUAGE NOTE

Note the place of **please** in the following sentences.
   Please lend me your pen.
   Could you **please** lend me your pen?
   Lend me your pen, **please**.

---

please [2]   verb

pleasing, pleased, has pleased
make someone feel glad or happy
- Mr Wong tries very hard to **please** his wife.

pleased   / pliːzd/   adjective

glad, happy
- Everyone was **pleased** that Tony had passed his exams because he had worked so hard.

plenty   /ˈplentɪ/   pronoun

a lot of something
- Have some more ice cream. We've got **plenty**.

plough   / plaʊ/   verb

turn over the earth in a field
- The farmer was **ploughing** one of his fields.

plug   / plʌɡ/   noun (countable)

a small plastic object which you use to connect something to the electricity
- Can you put a **plug** on this light, please?

plug in   /ˌplʌɡ ˈɪn/   phrasal verb

plugging in, plugged in, has plugged in
connect a plug to the electricity
- "This light won't work."
   "You haven't **plugged** it **in**."

θ	ð	ʃ	dʒ	tʃ	ŋ	ʒ	iː	ɜː	ɪ	æ	ʌ	ɒ
thing	that	shop	jump	chop	sing	measure	been	bird	bit	cat	but	not

plum /plʌm/ noun (countable)
⚠ See box on page 89.

plus /plʌs/ preposition
made more by
- Eight **plus** three makes eleven: 8 + 3 = 11.

LANGUAGE NOTE
Also: eight **and** three **are** eleven.

pocket /ˈpɒkɪt/ noun (countable)
1 a small bag which is joined to the cloth in a pair of trousers, a skirt, a jacket or a coat
- The key fell though this hole in my **pocket**.

LANGUAGE NOTE	
NEVER	He put his hand in the pocket.
ALWAYS	He put his hand in **his** pocket.
OR	He put his hand in **the** pocket of **his** coat.

☞ pocket book/knife
2 **pocket money**
⚠ See **money** 2.

poem /ˈpəʊɪm/ noun (countable)
A poem is a piece of writing in lines of a certain length. Sometimes the last word of one line sounds like the last word of a line before.
- Have you read any of Wordsworth's **poems**?
☞ write a poem

poetry /ˈpəʊɪtri/ noun (uncountable)
poems
- "Did Shakespeare write any **poetry**?" "Yes, he wrote plays and **poetry**."
☞ read/write poetry

point[1] /pɔɪnt/ noun (countable)
1 a sharp part of something
- The **point** of my pencil is broken.
2 a fact, an idea or an opinion
- This is the most important **point**: think of other people before you do something.

☞ come/get/keep to the point, make a point, miss the point; a difficult/good/important/key/main/strong/weak point
3 a time when something happens
- At this **point** in the talk, Mr Almado began to show some pictures.
☞ arrive at/reach a point
4 a dot, a particular place
- Measure the distance between **point** A and **point** B.
5 a mark in a game or sport
- How many **points** did our team score?

point[2] verb
hold out your finger or a stick to make it easier for someone to see something
- Can anyone **point** to Canada on this map?

LANGUAGE NOTE
point **to** someone or something
point a gun, etc **at** someone or something

point out /ˌpɔɪnt ˈaʊt/ phrasal verb
draw attention to
- The teacher **pointed** several mistakes **out** to me.

police /pəˈliːs/ noun (plural with the)
the people who make sure that everyone obeys the law
- Call the **police**. Someone's stolen my bag!

LANGUAGE NOTE	
1 NEVER	a police
ALWAYS	a policeman
2	The noun **police** is always plural. The police **are** coming!

☞ a police car/station

policeman /pəˈliːsmən/
policewoman /pəˈliːswʊmən/ noun (uncountable)
plural: policemen, policewomen
a man or a woman who is a member of the police
- There was only one **policeman** at the bank.
⚠ See also **officer** 2; see also **police**.

θ	ð	ʃ	dʒ	tʃ	ŋ	ʒ	iː	ɜː	ɪ	æ	ʌ	ɒ
thing	that	shop	jump	chop	sing	measure	been	bird	bit	cat	but	not

polish¹ /'pɒlɪʃ/ noun (uncountable)

You can put polish on something to clean it and make it shine.
- *Why don't you clean your shoes and put some black **polish** on them?*
- furniture/nail/shoe polish

polish² verb

make something shine
- *I **polished** the car yesterday. It looks like new.*

polite /pəˈlaɪt/ adjective

politer or more polite, politest or most polite
behaving or talking in a pleasant way to others, not rude
- *It's **polite** in Britain to say "Excuse me" if you walk in front of someone.*

politely /pəˈlaɪtlɪ/ adverb

(behaving or talking) in a pleasant way to others, not rudely
- *You should ask for things **politely** – not shout.*

pond /pɒnd/ noun (countable)

a small lake
- *Are there any fish in the village **pond**?*

pool /puːl/ noun (countable)

1. part of the ground (usually a very small hole) full of liquid
   - *There was a small **pool** of water where the baby had been sitting!*
2. a place where you can swim

- *We go to the swimming **pool** every Saturday.*
- an indoor/outdoor/swimming pool
- See also **swimming**.

poor /pʊə*/ adjective

1. If you are poor, you have very little money.
   - *The **poor** man had to beg for food.*
2. Sometimes you can use poor about someone to show you feel sorry for them.
   - ***Poor** Tina is ill in hospital.*
3. not good
   - *Vince's letter was **poor** and full of mistakes.*

pop /pɒp/ noun (uncountable)

modern popular music which a lot of people (especially young people) like very much
- *There's a good **pop** concert next Saturday.*

popular /ˈpɒpjʊlə*/ adjective

liked by a lot of people
- *Football is the most **popular** game in Britain.*

population /ˌpɒpjʊˈleɪʃn/ noun (countable)

the number of people who live in a place
- *China has a very large **population**.*
- the population falls/grows/rises/increases; a small/tiny/large population

porch /pɔːtʃ/ noun (countable)

1. an entrance (with a roof on it) to a house or church
   - *Please leave your wet shoes in the **porch**.*
2. (American English)
   See **veranda, verandah.**

pork /pɔːk/ noun (uncountable)

meat from a pig
- *Chinese people like to eat **pork**.*

position /pəˈzɪʃn/ noun (countable)

1. a place where something or someone is
   - *Show me the **position** of our camp on the map.*
2. way of sitting or lying
   - *Sit in a comfortable **position** on the floor.*
- a comfortable/uncomfortable/kneeling/lying/sitting/standing/upright position

θ	ð	ʃ	dʒ	tʃ	ŋ	ʒ	iː	ɜː	ɪ	æ	ʌ	ɒ
thing	that	shop	jump	chop	sing	measure	been	bird	bit	cat	but	not

possible /ˈpɒsɪbl/ adjective

When something is **possible**, it can happen or you can do it.
- It's **possible** to live without food for several weeks but you can't live without water.

post¹ /pəʊst/ noun
1 (American English: mail) (uncountable) letters and parcels which people send
 - Is there any **post** for me this morning?
2 (countable) a piece of wood or metal which stands in the ground
 - Someone has put a notice on the **post** near our house.

post² verb
send a letter or parcel to someone
- I **posted** a letter to Mr Watson on Monday morning, but it didn't arrive until Friday.

postcard /ˈpəʊstkɑːd/ noun (countable)
A postcard is a card with a picture on one side and a space for you to write on the other side. People usually write postcards to their family or friends when they go away on holiday.
- We must send a **postcard** to Rita to tell her how much we enjoyed our holiday.
↻ send someone a **postcard**

postman /ˈpəʊstmən/
postwoman /ˈpəʊstwʊmən/ noun (countable)
plural: postmen, postwomen
someone who takes letters and parcels to people's homes and offices
- Has the **postman** been yet?

post office /ˈpəʊst ˌɒfɪs/ noun (countable)
a place where you can buy stamps and post letters and parcels
- I'll post the parcel when I pass the **post office**.

poster /ˈpəʊstə*/ noun (countable)
a large picture to put on a wall in order to show people or tell them about something
- There was a **poster** about the concert on the wall.
↻ put up/take down a poster

pot /pɒt/ noun (countable)
1 something which you use for cooking food in
 - Put the rice in this **pot** and boil it.
2 something round (like a bowl) which you use to put liquid or food in
 - Is there any tea in the **teapot**?
↻ a coffee pot, a flowerpot, a teapot

potato /pəˈteɪtəʊ/ noun (countable, uncountable)
plural: potatoes
⚠ See box on page 238.

pour /pɔː*/ verb
make liquid come out
- Can you **pour** me some more water, please?

powder /ˈpaʊdə*/ noun (uncountable, countable)
something which is full of tiny pieces almost like dust
- This is very good washing **powder**.
↻ baby/face/soap/washing/baking/curry powder

power /ˈpaʊə*/ noun (uncountable)
1 If you have power, you can make other people do what you want.
 - You don't have the **power** to make us work longer hours. Only our boss can do that.
2 something which makes a machine or an engine work by using electricity, oil, etc
 - This new machine uses wind **power**.

powerful /ˈpaʊəfl/ adjective
very strong
- This car has a very **powerful** engine.

practice /ˈpræktɪs/ noun (uncountable)
doing something often so that you can do it well
- Juanita has had a lot of **practice** speaking English: one of her uncles is an Englishman.

θ	ð	ʃ	dʒ	tʃ	ŋ	ʒ	iː	ɜː	ɪ	æ	ʌ	ɒ
thing	that	shop	jump	chop	sing	measure	been	bird	bit	cat	but	not

SPELLING NOTE

practice = noun   practise = verb

practise /ˈpræktɪs/ verb
practising, practised, has practised
do something often so that you can do it well
- Eddie **practises** the guitar every evening.

praise /preɪz/ verb
praising, praised, has praised
tell someone how good at (doing) something they are
- We all **praised** Maria for doing so well in the test.
- ✜ praise highly

pray /preɪ/ verb
praying, prayed, has prayed
talk to God or ask God for something
- When my sister was very ill, I **prayed** for her.

LANGUAGE NOTE

pray **to** God, pray **to** someone
pray **for** someone, pray **for** something (to happen)

✜ pray silently

prefer /prɪˈfɜː*/ verb
preferring, preferred, has preferred
like one thing, place or person better than another
- "Do you like fish?" "Yes, but I **prefer** meat."

LANGUAGE NOTE

1 prefer something **to** something else (NOT than)
   I prefer rice to potatoes.
2 prefer **doing** something (usually)
   Do you prefer swimming to playing tennis?
3 prefer **to do** something (at one certain time)
   "Would you like to go to the cinema tonight?"
   "No, thanks. I'd prefer to watch TV at home."
   (OR "I'd prefer to watch TV rather than go to the cinema.")

prepare /prɪˈpeə*/ verb
preparing, prepared, has prepared
get ready for something, make something ready
- I'm just **preparing** for the test.
- ✜ prepare a meal, prepare carefully/well

present¹ /ˈpreznt/ noun (countable)
1 (countable) something you give to someone (for their birthday, at Christmas, at the New Year, when you visit them)
   - Did you get a lot of birthday **presents**?
   ✜ a birthday/wedding present, a Christmas/New Year present
2 (singular with the) the time which is now
   - You must stop thinking about the past and live in **the present.**
3 **at present** = now
   - **At present** Connie wants to be a doctor, but a few months ago she wanted to be a teacher.

present² /ˈpreznt/ adjective
1 here, not absent, not away
   - Were you **present** when the fire started?
2 the one now
   - The **present** headmistress is very popular.

press /pres/ verb
1 push something with your finger

- I **pressed** the bell several times but no one answered the door.
✜ press hard
2 use an iron to make cloth smooth
   - Ken **pressed** his trousers very carefully before he went out.

pretend /prɪˈtend/ verb
act in a different way from the true way
- *Tom was very sad when Mary left him but he **pretended** to be happy.*

> **LANGUAGE NOTE**
> pretend to do something
> pretend that something has happened

pretty /ˈprɪtɪ/ adjective
prettier, prettiest
nice to look at, beautiful
- *Jane has a **pretty** face: she's got a lovely smile.*

prevent /prɪˈvent/ verb
stop something happening, stop someone doing something
- *I wish we could **prevent** the river from flooding.*

price /praɪs/ noun (countable)
the amount of money something costs, how much you have to pay for something
- *What's the **price** of this camera, please?*
- bring down/lower/reduce/keep down/put up/push up/increase/raise prices, pay/set/fix a price, put a price on something; prices drop/fall/go down/rise go up/ shoot up; a drop/fall/rise in prices; the bottom/top price, a high/low/fair/right price
- See also **cost** 1.

priest /priːst/ noun (countable)
a person who is the leader of a church or who works in a church
- *We knelt down as the **priest** began to pray.*

primary /ˈpraɪmərɪ/ adjective
the first, the earliest
- *Does Elsa go to **primary** or secondary school?*

prince /prɪns/ noun (countable)
1 the son of a king or queen
- ***Prince** Charles is the son of the Queen.*
2 the ruler of a small country
- *The **prince** sent his soldiers away.*

princess /ˈprɪnses/ noun (countable)
plural: princesses
the daughter of a king or queen, or the wife of a prince
- *The king gave the **princess** everything but she still wasn't happy.*

principal /ˈprɪnsɪpl/ noun (countable)
the head of a school or college
- *The teacher sent six students to the **principal**.*

print /prɪnt/ verb
put words onto paper with a special machine
- *This newspaper was **printed** in London.*

prison /ˈprɪzn/ noun (countable)
the place where people are put if they break the law
- *The thief was sent to **prison** for seven years.*
- be in/ be sent/ break out of/come out of/ escape/go to prison
- See also **jail**.

prisoner /ˈprɪznə*/ noun (countable)
someone who is not free or who is in prison
- *Three **prisoners** have escaped from Norton Jail.*
- take prisoners, take somebody prisoner (in a war)

prize /praɪz/ noun (countable)
something you win, something you receive for doing something well
- *"Leila won the first **prize** for English." "Good. I hear the **prize** was $1000."*
- get/win/give/receive a prize

probable /ˈprɒbəbl/ adjective
If something is probable, you think it is likely to happen or be true.
- *It's **probable** that this is the cause of the disease.*

probably /ˈprɒbəblɪ/ adverb
If something will probably happen, you think it is likely to happen.
- *She'll **probably** arrive late: she usually does.*

θ	ð	ʃ	dʒ	tʃ	ŋ	ʒ	iː	ɜː	ɪ	æ	ʌ	ɒ
thing	that	shop	jump	chop	sing	measure	been	bird	bit	cat	but	not

> **LANGUAGE NOTE**
>
> Note the place of **probably** in the following sentences.
> **Probably** he'll be there.
> He **probably** arrived early.
> She's **probably** switched off the TV.

problem / ˈprɒbləm/ noun (countable)
1 something which causes you difficulty
   • The **problem** with learning English is that I cannot practise it enough.
   ☞ cause/raise/run into/run up against/settle/solve a problem; a difficult/real/serious/big/small problem, the main problem
2 a question which is difficult to answer
   • Our mathematics teacher gave us several **problems** to do for homework.
   ☞ do/give/set/solve a problem; a difficult/easy/a simple problem

produce / prəˈdjuːs/ verb
producing, produced, has produced
1 make something
   • Watches are now **produced** in Hong Kong.
2 take something out to show someone
   • The man **produced** a rabbit out of his hat.
3 grow fruit or vegetables
   • Thailand **produces** very good rice.

programme / ˈprəʊgræm/ noun (countable)
(American English: program)
1 something shown on television or heard on the radio
   • What's your favourite TV **programme**?
   ☞ a radio/television programme
2 a piece of paper or a very thin book which tells you something about a concert or a play you are watching
   • Can we buy a **programme** to find out the songs the choir will be singing tonight?

project / ˈprɒdʒekt/ noun (countable)
a special piece of work which you plan to do
   • Lily is doing a **project** on fishing in the Arctic.
   ☞ carry out /draw up /work on a project

promise¹ / ˈprɒmɪs/ noun (countable)
something which you say you will do
   • I made a **promise** to my father that I wouldn't smoke any more.
   ☞ go back on/break/give/make (someone)/keep a promise

promise² (verb)
promising, promised, has promised
say you will do something
   • Maria **promised** her mother that she would stay at home.

> **LANGUAGE NOTE**
>
> promise someone something
> promise someone **that** you will do something
> promise **to do** something
> promise **not to do** something

pronounce / prəˈnaʊns/ verb
pronouncing, pronounced, has pronounced
say a letter or a word in a certain way
   • Which English words are difficult to **pronounce**?

pronunciation / prəˌnʌnsɪˈeɪʃn/ noun

> **SPELLING NOTE**
>
> ALWAYS pronunciation
> NEVER ~~pronounciation~~

1 (uncountable) the way someone says a letter or a word, the way someone speaks a language
   • Mr Yamaguchi's **pronunciation** of English is perfect: he sounds just like an Englishman.
2 (countable) the way in which a letter or word is pronounced
   • Which of these two **pronunciations** of the adjective P-R-E-S-E-N-T is correct?

properly / ˈprɒpəlɪ/ adverb
the right way, correctly
   • You're not holding your chopsticks **properly**.

θ	ð	ʃ	dʒ	tʃ	ŋ	ʒ	iː	ɜː	ɪ	æ	ʌ	ɒ
thing	that	shop	jump	chop	sing	measure	been	bird	bit	cat	but	not

protect /prəˈtekt/ verb
make or keep something or someone safe
- These dark glasses will **protect** your eyes from the sun.

proud /praʊd/ adjective
feeling happy or pleased with what you have done or with what someone else has done
- We're all very **proud** that Ann passed her exam.

proudly /ˈpraʊdli/ adverb
in a proud way
- Martin **proudly** walked up to collect his prize.

prove /pruːv/ verb
proving, proved, has proved
(American English: also has proven)
show something is true
- Everyone thought Simon had stolen the watch but no one could **prove** it.

public¹ /ˈpʌblɪk/ noun (singular with the)
all people in general
- Is the building open to the **public**?
- the general public

public² adjective
belonging to all people in general
- Is there a **public** telephone in this building?

pull /pʊl/ verb
move something towards yourself

- It took two horses to **pull** the heavy cart
- pull hard

pull up /ˌpʊl ˈʌp/ phrasal verb
stop
- A big car **pulled up**, and two men got out.

pump¹ /pʌmp/ noun (countable)
a machine which moves air or liquids into or out of something
- Use my **pump** to put some air into this tyre.
- bicycle/petrol/water pump

pump² verb
move air or liquid into or out of something
- Can I help **pump** the water out of the boat?

punctuation /ˌpʌŋktʃuˈeɪʃn/ noun (uncountable)
marks like full stops, commas, question marks, etc which are put into a piece of writing
- Can you do the following **punctuation** exercise? did you see victor in georgetown yesterday

punish /ˈpʌnɪʃ/ verb
hurt someone in some way because they have done something wrong
- The teacher **punished** all the students who didn't do their homework.

punishment /ˈpʌnɪʃmənt/ noun (uncountable)
something you do to hurt someone when they have done something wrong
- Peter didn't do his homework last night and will be given more as a **punishment**.
- escape/ be given/hand out/take (a lot of) punishment; cruel/harsh/severe/light punishment

pupil /ˈpjuːpl/ noun (countable)
a student
- Sue was a lazy **pupil** and never did her homework.

LANGUAGE NOTE	
ALWAYS	a pupil at a primary school
	a pupil/student at a secondary school
BUT	a student at a college or university

puppy /ˈpʌpi/ noun (countable)
a young dog
See box on page 10.

| θ | ð | ʃ | dʒ | tʃ | ŋ | ʒ | iː | ɜː | ɪ | æ | ʌ | ɒ |
| thing | that | shop | jump | chop | sing | measure | been | bird | bit | cat | but | not |

purple /ˈpɜːpl/ noun (uncountable, countable)
the colour between red and blue, like violet
- *The grapes were **purple** in colour.*

purpose /ˈpɜːpəs/ noun (countable)
1 the reason for doing something
   - *Isn't the chief **purpose** of going to work to earn money?*
   ↻ answer/serve a purpose; put something to a good purpose; the chief/main/the real/true purpose, a useful purpose
2 **on purpose** = not by accident
   - *I wasn't late for the meeting **on purpose**: I missed the bus because it left early.*

purse /pɜːs/ noun (countable)
(American English: change purse)
1 a small bag in which people (especially women) keep their money
   - *She opened her **purse** and took out ten cents.*
2 (American English)
⚠ See **handbag**.

push /pʊʃ/ verb
1 press against something to move it
   - *The door won't open. Can you **push** hard?*
2 move forward by pressing against someone or something
   - *We had to **push** our way past a lot of people.*

put /pʊt/ verb
putting, put, has put
1 move or place something somewhere
   - *I **put** my books on the table.*
2 **put away** = keep in a cupboard, desk, drawer, etc
   - ***Put** your books **away** when you've finished your homework.*
3 **put on** = wear
   - ***Put** your coat **on** before you go out. It's very cold.*
4 **put on** = turn on, press, make work
   - *Can you **put** the light **on**, please?*
5 **put out** = turn out, stop working
   - *The room was very dark when we **put** the light **out**.*

puzzle /ˈpʌzl/ noun (countable)
a question or a game which we have to think a lot about to get the correct answer
- *Tim likes to do crossword **puzzles**.*
↻ solve a puzzle; a crossword/jigsaw puzzle

pyjamas /pəˈdʒɑːməz/ noun (plural)
a thin shirt and pair of trousers which you can wear when you go to bed
- *Mr Sillito bought himself a new pair of **pyjamas**.*

LANGUAGE NOTE	
ALWAYS	a pair of pyjamas or some pyjamas
NEVER	~~a pyjamas, two pyjamas~~

pyramid /ˈpɪrəmɪd/ noun (countable)
a shape with three triangular sides.
- *There are lots of huge **pyramids** in Egypt, where kings and queens were buried.*

θ	ð	ʃ	dʒ	tʃ	ŋ	ʒ	iː	ɜː	ɪ	æ	ʌ	ɒ
thing	that	shop	jump	chop	sing	measure	been	bird	bit	cat	but	not

Q q

quality /ˈkwɒlɪtɪ/ noun (uncountable)
You can use the word **quality** when you want to say how good or bad something is.
- *These shirts are very good **quality**.*
- bad/excellent/first-rate/good/high/perfect/poor/top quality

quantity /ˈkwɒntɪtɪ/ noun
plural: quantities
1 (countable) an amount you can count or measure
- *The **quantity** of food was all right: it was the quality which I didn't like.*
- a large/small/tiny quantity, an unknown quantity
2 (uncountable) amount, number (especially large)
- *Tom's happy when there is plenty of food; he prefers **quantity** to quality.*
3 **in quantity** = in large amounts, a lot of
- *Rubber is produced **in quantity** in Malaysia.*

quarrel[1] /ˈkwɒrəl/ noun (countable)
any angry conversation when two or more people do not agree about something
- *My brothers had a big **quarrel** last week.*

LANGUAGE NOTE
a quarrel **between** two or more people
a quarrel **with** someone over something

- cause/have/lead to/pick/start/settle a quarrel; a quarrel breaks out/starts

quarrel[2] verb
quarrelling, quarrelled, has quarrelled

SPELLING NOTE
double *r* and double *l* : quarrelling, quarrelled

not agree with someone and talk to them in an angry way
- *Maria and Alfredo began to **quarrel** in the library: they both wanted the same book.*

quarter /ˈkwɔːtə*/ noun (countable)
1 a fourth part
- *There was only one apple but there were four of us, and so Tina gave us each a **quarter**.*
2 fifteen minutes
- *It's (a) **quarter** to three. (= fifteen minutes before three o'clock)*

queen /kwiːn/ noun (countable)
1 the woman ruler of a country
- ***Queen** Elizabeth is the **Queen** of England.*
2 the wife of a king
- *King George married Mary and made her his **queen**.*

question /ˈkwestʃən/ noun (countable)
1 You can ask a question when you want to find out an answer or learn something.
- *Can anyone answer this **question**? What is sixty-two and thirty-five?*

LANGUAGE NOTE
1 Ask me another question.
2 What was the first question in the exam about?
3 The question is what to do next.
4 The question whether to leave or stay was the cause of great argument.

- reply to/answer/ask/raise/put a question (to someone)
2 **question mark**
the mark you must use at the end of a question when you write / ? /
- *How old are you?*

queue[1] /kjuː/ noun (countable)
a line of people who are waiting to buy something or do something

θ	ð	ʃ	dʒ	tʃ	ŋ	ʒ	iː	ɜː	ɪ	æ	ʌ	ɒ
thing	that	shop	jump	chop	sing	measure	been	bird	bit	cat	but	not

- There's a long **queue** at the bus stop. We won't get on the bus.

↻ form/join/ jump/stand in a queue; a long/short queue

queue² (up) /ˌkjuː ˈʌp/ (phrasal) verb
queuing, queued, has queued
stand in a line to wait for something

- We **queued (up)** for an hour to get tickets for the concert.

LANGUAGE NOTE

queue up **for** something = queue up to get something

quick /kwɪk/ adjective
fast, not slow
- Be **quick** or we'll be late for school.

quickly /ˈkwɪklɪ/ adverb
fast, not slowly
- It's very cold. Let's walk **quickly** to keep warm.

quiet /ˈkwaɪət/ adjective
with very little noise or sound
- Be **quiet** or you won't hear me call out the names of the winners.

quietly /ˈkwaɪətlɪ/ adverb
making very little noise
- Anna returned home late and entered the house very **quietly**.

quite /kwaɪt/ adverb
1 in some way (but not completely)
  - My car is **quite** new, only two years old.
2 completely
  - That's **quite** right. I **quite** agree.

LANGUAGE NOTE

The problem here is the meaning of **quite**.
1 When you can put **very** before an adjective, **quite** means **in some way (but not completely)** in British English:
   very good   **quite** good
   very exciting   **quite** exciting
   very comfortable   **quite** comfortable
   (Note, however, that in American English **quite** usually means **very** in such phrases as those above.)
2 When you cannot usually put **very** in front of an adjective or make it stronger in any way, **quite** can be used to mean **completely** in British English:
   perfect   **quite** perfect
   impossible   **quite** impossible
   right   **quite** right
3 In a few cases **quite** may have either of the two meanings given above. Only the sentence or paragraph in which it is used will give you the correct meaning of **quite**.
   She was **quite** beautiful. (quite = very or rather)
4 When **quite** is used with adverbs, it usually means **fairly** in British English:
   quite well   **quite** hard   **quite** fast

quiz /kwɪz/ noun (countable)
plural: quizzes
A quiz is a competition in which you are asked questions to find out how much you know about certain things.
- I enjoy watching **quiz** programmes on television.

↻ quiz programme/show

quotation marks /kwəʊˈteɪʃn ˌmɑːks/
noun (usually plural)
These are quotation marks " " . You should use quotation marks to show that you are saying or writing the words which someone else has used.
- In the following sentence Linda's words are in **quotation marks**. "Go away," Linda said.

θ	ð	ʃ	dʒ	tʃ	ŋ	ʒ	iː	ɜː	ɪ	æ	ʌ	ɒ
thing	that	shop	jump	chop	sing	measure	been	bird	bit	cat	but	not

R r

rabbit /ˈræbɪt/ noun (countable, uncountable)

> **LANGUAGE NOTE**
>
> When you are talking about *a rabbit* as a living animal, use *a*.
>   The farmer's caught *a* rabbit.
> When you are talking about *rabbit* as a food on a dish, you should not use *a* before it
>   Mrs Lee's cooking rabbit for dinner.

See box on page 10.

race¹ /reɪs/ noun (countable)

a competition to run, walk, ride or drive the fastest or to finish something first
- *Mary ran much faster than anyone else and easily won the race.*
- lose/win/run a race; a close race (= a race with only a very small difference between the first and second runners, etc), an exciting race

race² verb

racing, raced, has raced

try to run, walk, ride, or drive the fastest; do something quickly to see who is the first to finish
- *Let's race one another to the beach.*

racket /ˈrækɪt/ noun (countable)

> **SPELLING NOTE**
>
> Sometimes spelt *racquet*.

something you play tennis or badminton with
- *I can't play tennis: I've broken a string in my racket.*
- a badminton/tennis racket

radar /ˈreɪdɑː*/ noun (uncountable)

a machine which shows the position of things which you cannot see
- *The police are using radar to find out which cars are travelling too fast.*

radio /ˈreɪdɪəʊ/ noun

1 (uncountable) music, news and other programmes which are sent out over the air
   - *I like listening to foreign radio.*
2 (countable) something you use (like a small box) for listening to music, news and other programmes
   - *I'm going to buy a new radio today.*
- hear something on the radio, listen to the radio, put/switch/turn the radio off/on, turn down/up the radio

rail /reɪl/ noun (countable)

1 a long piece of wood or metal
   - *Hang your wet towel on the towel rail.*
2 a piece of wood or metal which a train runs on
   - *The train was late because there was snow on the rails.*
3 **by rail** = by train
   - *"Are you going to London on a bus?" "No, I'm going by rail. It's much faster."*

railway /ˈreɪlweɪ/ noun (countable)
(American English: railroad)

1 the lines on which trains run
   - *Is there a bridge over the railway?*
2 trains, rails, etc
   - *Have you ever travelled on the Bombay – Calcutta railway?*

θ	ð	ʃ	dʒ	tʃ	ŋ	ʒ	iː	ɜː	ɪ	æ	ʌ	ɒ
thing	that	shop	jump	chop	sing	measure	been	bird	bit	cat	but	not

railway station / ˈreɪlweɪ ˌsteɪʃn/ noun (countable)
⚐ See **station 1**.

rain[1] / reɪn/ noun (uncountable)
drops of water which fall from clouds in the sky
- We get a lot of **rain** in this part of Africa.
↻ rain falls/pours down/starts/stops; heavy/light/ steady rain; be caught in the rain

rain[2] verb
fall from clouds in the sky as drops of water
- We couldn't play tennis last night because it was **raining** too heavily.
↻ start/stop raining

raincoat / ˈreɪnkəʊt/ noun (countable)
a light coat which you can wear to keep dry when it is raining
- I brought my umbrella but forgot my **raincoat**.

rainy / ˈreɪnɪ/ adjective
rainier, rainiest
wet, when it is raining
- I like to stay in on **rainy** days.

raise /reɪz/ verb
raising, raised, has raised
1 lift up
   - Don't shout out. **Raise** your hand if you want to ask a question.
2 make (prices or wages) higher
   - Mr Skelton's wage has just been **raised** from $1200 a week to $1500 a week.

LANGUAGE NOTE	
raise + object	She **raised** her hand.
rise (without an object)	She **rose** when Ann came in.

⚐ See also **rise**.

raisin /ˈreɪzn/ noun (countable)
⚐ See box on page 89.

ran / ræn/ verb
past tense of **run**
- I **ran** all the way to the station to catch the bus.

rang / ræŋ/ verb
past tense of **ring**
- Who **rang** the fire bell?

rare / reə*/ adjective
very unusual
- It's **rare** for Tim to be late for school.

raspberry /ˈrɑːzbərɪ/ noun (countable)
plural: raspberries
⚐ See box on page 89.

rat /ræt/ noun (countable)
⚐ See box on page 10.

rather[1] / ˈrɑːðə*/ verb phrase
would rather = want to do something more than something else
- Joe **would rather** swim than play football.

rather[2] adverb
a little, quite
- I'm feeling **rather** tired today, and so I'm going to stay at home and have a rest.

reach / riːtʃ/ verb
1 put out your hand to try to touch or hold something
   - I had to stand on a chair to **reach** the light.
2 arrive at (a place)
   - It took two hours to **reach** the top.

LANGUAGE NOTE
ALWAYS reach a place   NEVER ~~reach to a place~~

θ	ð	ʃ	dʒ	tʃ	ŋ	ʒ	iː	ɜː	ɪ	æ	ʌ	ɒ
thing	that	shop	jump	chop	sing	measure	been	bird	bit	cat	but	not

read /riːd/ verb
reading, read /red/, has read /red/

PRONUNCIATION NOTE
The past forms of **read** are pronounced like **red**.

look at written words and understand them
- I **read** an interesting book on China last week.

↻ **read** aloud/silently; **read** a book/letter/(news)paper/story; **read** about someone/something in a book, etc

reader /ˈriːdə*/ noun (countable)
1 a person who reads
   - This newspaper has over 800,000 **readers**.
2 a book for teaching or practising reading
   - Dave's class **reader** is "Oliver Twist".

ready /ˈredɪ/ adjective
1 in a position to start doing something, waiting to do it
   - "Are you **ready** to leave yet?"
   "Almost. I've just got to put my shoes on."
2 willing, happy (to do something)
   - Ann is always **ready** to help anyone.

real /rɪəl/ adjective
1 not false, not a copy
   - Are those flowers **real**? They look like plastic.
2 You can sometimes use **real** to make the meaning of a word much stronger.
   - He's a **real** fool!

really /ˈrɪəlɪ/ adverb
1 truly, certainly
   - "Have you **really** been to Canada?"
   "Yes, I have. We visited my aunt there last year."
2 You can use **really** as a reply to show surprise.
   - "It's Joe's birthday today."
   "**Really!**"

reason /ˈriːzn/ noun (countable)
the cause of something, why something has happened
- "What was the **reason** for Jenny's absence?"
"She had to go to the dentist's."

LANGUAGE NOTE		
1	NEVER	The reason for my absence was because I felt ill.
	ALWAYS	The reason for my absence was **that** I felt ill.
2		Do you know the reason **why** they did it?
		Do you know the reason **that** they did it?
		Do you know the reason they did it?
		Do you know the reason **for** them doing it?

↻ find out/ask the reason, give/have a reason

receive /rɪˈsiːv/ verb
receiving, received, has received

SPELLING NOTE
e before **i**: receive

be given something, get something
- Have you **received** my letter yet?

recent /ˈriːsnt/ adjective
happening a short time ago
- Did you enjoy your **recent** holiday in Canada?

recently /ˈriːsntlɪ/ adverb
not long ago
- "John, have you seen Sammy **recently**?"
"No. I last saw him two weeks ago."

recess /rɪˈses/ noun (countable, uncountable)
a short break from lessons when pupils can play, talk or have a rest
- Let's have a game of table tennis during **recess**.

⚠ See also **break** [1].

θ	ð	ʃ	dʒ	tʃ	ŋ	ʒ	iː	ɜː	ɪ	æ	ʌ	ɒ
thing	that	shop	jump	chop	sing	measure	been	bird	bit	cat	but	not

recognize /ˈrekəgnaɪz/ verb
recognizing, recognized, recognized

> **SPELLING NOTE**
>
> Also recogni**s**e in British English

If you recognize someone or something, you know them because you have seen, heard about or read about them before.
- *It'll be easy to **recognize** me. I'll be wearing a red hat and a yellow suit.*

record[1] /ˈrekɔːd/ noun (countable)
a round, flat piece of plastic on which music and sounds are kept to be played back
- *Ken's got a lot of pop **records**.*
↻ play/put on/listen to/make a record; a record player

record[2] /rɪˈkɔːd/ verb
put sounds on a CD, record or tape
- *Let's **record** a short message for Mr Law.*

rectangle /ˈrektæŋgl/ noun (countable)
a shape with two longer sides (of equal length) and two shorter sides (of equal length)
- *This isn't a square: it's a **rectangle**.*

red /red/ noun (countable, uncountable), adjective
the colour of blood
- *He gave her a **red** rose.*

refrigerator /rɪˈfrɪdʒəreɪtə*/ noun (countable)
a cupboard or box for keeping food cold
- *Put the fish in the **refrigerator** to keep it cool.*
⚠ See also **fridge**.

refuse /rɪˈfjuːz/ verb
refusing, refused, has refused
say no to someone, not agree (to do something)
- *Tina's boss **refused** to let her take a holiday.*

relative /ˈrelətɪv/ noun (countable)
member of your family
- *"Is Harry a **relative** of yours?" "He's my cousin."*
↻ a close/distant relative

remain /rɪˈmeɪn/ verb
1 stay
- *Ten students left but the others **remained**.*
2 be left
- *After we had all eaten some cake, only a small piece **remained**.*

remember /rɪˈmembə*/ verb
1 not forget, keep in your mind
- *I must **remember** Mary's birthday card.*
2 forget something and then bring it back into your mind
- *Peter said he'd met me before but I couldn't **remember** where.*

> **LANGUAGE NOTE**
>
> COMPARE   I didn't remember **doing** it.
>   (= Perhaps I did it but I don't remember whether I did it or not.)
> WITH   I didn't remember **to do** it.
>   (= I didn't do it and I can remember that I didn't do it.)

remind /rɪˈmaɪnd/ verb
help or make someone remember something
- ***Remind** me to give you this book when I go.*

> **LANGUAGE NOTE**
>
> remind someone **of** something
>   He reminded me of your brother.
> remind someone **to do** something
>   Can you remind me to give Ann her book.
> remind someone **that** something is happening, etc.
>   She reminded me that I still had Ann's book.

rent[1] /rent/ noun (countable)
money which you pay someone to use a flat, a house, an office, etc
- *How much **rent** do you pay for your flat?*

θ	ð	ʃ	dʒ	tʃ	ŋ	ʒ	iː	ɜː	ɪ	æ	ʌ	ɒ
thing	that	shop	jump	chop	sing	measure	been	bird	bit	cat	but	not

rent [2] verb

pay money to use a house, an office, a car, etc
- Mr Saleh **rents** a large office in the city centre.

> **LANGUAGE NOTE**
>
> COMPARE We decided to rent a flat in London.
> We decided to hire a car in London.
> You usually **rent** something when you pay money several times over a long period. You usually **hire** something when you pay only once.
> (Note that there is not this difference in meaning between **rent** and **hire** in American English.)

repair /rɪ'peə*/ verb

mend something which is damaged or broken
- Has anyone been to **repair** the TV set yet?

repeat /rɪ'piːt/ verb

say or write something again, say something which has already been said
- Will you **repeat** what you have just said?

reply [1] /rɪ'plaɪ/ noun (countable)

plural: replies

something you say or write as an answer
- Did you send me a **reply** to my letter?
- get/have/receive/give/make/send a reply; a blunt reply (= a very honest reply, often impolite), a brief/early/immediate reply (to a letter), a prompt reply (= a quick reply)

reply [2] verb

replying, replied, has replied

give an answer
- Sarah, why didn't you **reply** to my letter?

> **LANGUAGE NOTE**
>
> reply **to** = answer
> **reply** to a letter, **reply** to a question
> NEVER **reply** to the door NOR **reply** to the phone
> ALWAYS **answer** the door and **answer** the phone

report [1] /rɪ'pɔːt/ noun (countable)

a piece of writing (or sometimes something spoken) which tells you about something
- There was a short **report** in the Daily News about our school competition.
- give/make/write a report; a newspaper/school/traffic/weather report

report [2] verb

tell about something which has happened
- Shall I **report** the accident to the police?

reporter /rɪ'pɔːtə*/ noun (countable)

someone who writes for the newspaper about what has happened or someone who talks on the radio or TV about what has happened
- A lot of **reporters** came to see the film star.

rescue /'reskjuː/ verb

rescuing, rescued, has rescued

save

- Mr Low **rescued** a child who fell into the lake.

reservoir /'rezəvwɑː*/ noun (countable)

a place (like a lake) where water is kept for use by people
- There's very little water in the **reservoir**.

respect [1] /rɪ'spekt/ noun (uncountable)

If you have respect for someone, you think well of them.
- I've got a lot of **respect** for Mr Carvalho: he's worked hard and always been very honest.
- earn someone's respect, have/show respect for someone/something, win/lose someone's respect; a deep/great respect

θ	ð	ʃ	dʒ	tʃ	ŋ	ʒ	iː	ɜː	ɪ	æ	ʌ	ɒ
thing	that	shop	jump	chop	sing	measure	been	bird	bit	cat	but	not

respect [2] verb
think well of someone
- Everyone **respects** an honest man.

rest [1] /rest/ noun
1 (singular with the) what is left, what remains
   - I'll have a quarter of the apple, and you can have **the rest**.

LANGUAGE NOTE

The rest of the rice **has** now been eaten.
The rest of the potatoes **have** now been eaten.

---

2 (countable, uncountable) a short time sitting or lying down and not doing anything
   - Rosa was so tired that she had to have a **rest**.
↻ have/take a rest; bed rest (= resting in bed), complete rest, a short/long rest

rest [2] verb
sit and not do anything
- After a day's work, I like to **rest** and watch TV.

restaurant /ˈrestərɒnt/ noun (countable)
a place where you can have a meal
- Let's go to a good **restaurant** for dinner.

result [1] /rɪˈzʌlt/ noun (countable)
what happens when someone does something or when something else happens
- "What was the **result** of the recent change in the exam?" "More students passed."
↻ an excellent/good/poor/satisfactory/pleasing/surprising result

result [2] verb
happen because of something
- All the hard work which Dave did **resulted** in him going to university.

return [1] /rɪˈtɜːn/ noun (countable)
a ticket for a bus, a train, etc which allows you to travel somewhere and back again
- Two **returns** from Leeds to London, please.
⚠ See also **single** [1].

return [2] verb
1 go back, come back
   - Rita left early for college, but she **returned** later because she'd forgotten her books.
2 send or give something back
   - Have you **returned** your library book yet?

LANGUAGE NOTE

return **to** school, etc   BUT   return home

---

revise /rɪˈvaɪz/ verb
revising, revised, has revised
study again or learn something again (usually for an examination)
- I must **revise** some dates for our History test.

revision /rɪˈvɪʒn/ noun (uncountable)
what you study again for an examination
- Have you done any **revision** for the exams yet?
↻ do (some) revision

reward [1] /rɪˈwɔːd/ noun (countable)
something which you receive for working well, being brave, finding something, etc
- I hope I get a **reward** for finding the watch.

reward [2] verb
give something to someone for working well, being brave, finding something, etc
- Peter was **rewarded** for finding the watch.

rhyme /raɪm/ verb
rhyming, rhymed, has rhymed
When two words rhyme, they have a similar sound.
- The word "two" **rhymes** with "blue" and "three" **rhymes** with "sea".

rice /raɪs/ noun (uncountable)
very small brown or white pieces of food
- Would you like some more fish with your **rice**?

rich /rɪtʃ/ adjective
having a lot of money
- I'll buy a big car and a big house when I'm **rich**.

θ	ð	ʃ	dʒ	tʃ	ŋ	ʒ	iː	ɜː	ɪ	æ	ʌ	ɒ
thing	that	shop	jump	chop	sing	measure	been	bird	bit	cat	but	not

ride ¹ /raɪd/ noun (countable)

a journey on a horse, on a bicycle, on a bus or in a car, etc
- *Would you like to come for a **ride** in my new car?*
↻ come/go for/have/take a ride

ride ² verb

riding, rode /rəʊd/, has ridden /ˈrɪdn/
make a journey on a horse, on a bicycle, on a bus or in a car, etc
- *Mr Law likes to **ride** his bicycle for ten kilometres every day after work.*

LANGUAGE NOTE

ride **in** a car, **in** a bus, **in** a train
BUT ride **on** a horse, **on** a bicycle

---

right /raɪt/ adjective
1 correct
   - *How many answers did you get **right**?*
2 fair, just
   - *You were **right** to ask for your money back.*
3 satisfactory
   - *Things are not **right** between Mr and Mrs Samson.*
4 suitable
   - *This coat is just **right** for me. Thanks.*
5 not left
   - *Most people write with their **right** hand.*
6 **right now** = immediately, this minute
   - *Do it **right** now. Don't leave it until later.*
7 all right
   ⚠ See **all right**.

ring ¹ /rɪŋ/ noun (countable)
1 a small circle of metal which you can wear on your finger
   - *Mrs Uchida always wears her wedding **ring**.*
↻ a diamond/gold/wedding/key ring, an engagement ring (= a ring given when two people agree to marry each other)

2 a circle
   - *The small children sat in a **ring** round their teacher.*

ring ² verb

ringing, rang /ræŋ/, has rung /rʌŋ/
1 call someone on the telephone
   - *I'll **ring** you (up) tonight to discuss this.*
2 make a noise like a bell
   - *The phone's **ringing**. Can you answer it?*

ripe /raɪp/ adjective
fully grown and ready to be eaten
- *These bananas are still green: they aren't **ripe**.*

rise /raɪz/ verb
rising, rose /rəʊz/, has risen /ˈrɪzn/
1 stand up, get up
   - *The class **rose** when the headmaster entered.*
2 become higher
   - *Bread **rises** when you bake it.*
⚠ See also **raise**.

risk /rɪsk/ verb
take a chance even when something bad or unpleasant could happen
- *Mr Robinson **risked** his life when he jumped into the sea to save the small girl.*

river /ˈrɪvə*/ noun (countable)
a large stream of fresh water which flows between banks to the sea or a lake
- *Several people were fishing on the **river**.*
↻ cross/sail up/sail down a river; a river flows/overflows (its banks) / dries up/winds (its way); a big/small/wide/narrow river

road /rəʊd/ noun (countable)
hard ground for cars, lorries, buses, etc to drive on
- *Don't run across the **road**: it's dangerous.*

a busy/fast/good/main/major/minor/ straight/winding/wide/narrow road; a road goes/runs/leads somewhere, a road winds

See also **street**.

roar /rɔː*/ verb

make a very loud noise (like a lion)
- The crowd **roared** when Dave Travis scored.

rob /rɒb/ verb

robbing, robbed, has robbed

SPELLING NOTE

double **b** : ro**bb**ing, ro**bb**ed BUT ro**b**s

---

steal something from someone, take things which are not yours
- The police caught the men who **robbed** the bank.

LANGUAGE NOTE

rob a person, a bank, etc
BUT steal something *from* a person, a bank, etc

See also **steal**.

robber /'rɒbə*/ noun (countable)

someone who steals or takes things which do not belong to them (often by using force or frightening people)
- The police caught the **robbers** who had stolen Mrs Smith's watch and handbag.

See also **burglar**; see also **thief**.

robbery /'rɒbərɪ/ noun (countable)

plural: robberies

the crime of taking money, etc from a bank, a house, a shop, etc
- There was a **robbery** at Mr Lee's new shop, and a lot of cameras were stolen.

carry out/ plan a robbery; armed robbery (= using guns to rob people)

robot /'rəʊbɒt/ noun (countable)

a machine which can work and do things which people do
- Many factories now use **robots** to make cars.

rock /rɒk/ noun

1 (uncountable) stone
   - Machines are now used to break **rock**.
2 (countable) a piece of stone
   - There's a big **rock** on top of that hill.

rocket /'rɒkɪt/ noun (countable)

1 a machine which can travel to the moon and further
   - The Americans have sent a **rocket** to Mars.
2 the engine of a machine which can travel into space
   - A **rocket** lifted the spacecraft into space.
3 a bomb
   - The planes fired several **rockets** at the enemy ship.

rode /rəʊd/ verb

past tense of **ride**
- Ann **rode** home from school on her new bicycle.

roll [1] /rəʊl/ noun (countable)

1 something which has been turned round itself
   - I bought a **roll** of paper and some paints.
2 a small round piece of bread
   - Would you like a **roll** with your soup?

roll [2] verb

1 move by turning over and over many times
   - The football **rolled** under the lorry.
2 make something round
   - **Roll** the painting up and put it away.

roof /ruːf/ noun (countable)

plural: roofs

the cover on top of a building

- The winds were so strong that they blew the **roof** off the hut.

θ	ð	ʃ	dʒ	tʃ	ŋ	ʒ	iː	ɜː	ɪ	æ	ʌ	ɒ
thing	that	shop	jump	chop	sing	measure	been	bird	bit	cat	but	not

room /ruːm/ noun
1 (countable) part of a flat or house (with four walls)
- *Peter came out of the bed**room** and turned on the TV in the sitting **room**.*
❀ book/let/rent a room; a bathroom, a bedroom, a common room (= a room in a school or college where people can sit and talk), a dining room, a double room, a drawing room (= a living room in a house (British English), a living room, a sitting room (the main room of a house where you can sit, rest, talk or watch TV), a guest room, a showroom, a single room, a spare room (= a room in a house or flat which is empty or not usually used), a waiting room (= a room in a station, in a hospital, at the doctor's or dentist's where people can sit and wait)
2 (uncountable) space
- *As there were ten in the family, they had very little **room** in their flat.*

root /ruːt/ noun (countable)
part of a plant which grows under the ground
- *Don't cut the **roots** of the tree: you'll kill it.*

rope /rəʊp/ noun (uncountable, countable)
strong, thick string (made by twisting threads round one another)
- *Tie the horse to a tree with a strong **rope**.*
❀ a bit/length/piece of rope; loosen/tighten a rope

rose ¹ /rəʊz/ noun (countable)
a beautiful flower with a sweet smell
- *Mr Dawson gave his wife twelve red **roses**.*

rose ² verb
past tense of **rise**
- *The class **rose** when Mrs Chan came in.*

rough /rʌf/ adjective
1 not calm
- *It's very windy and the sea is very **rough**.*
2 not smooth
- *I cut my hand on the **rough** edge of the desk.*
3 not gentle
- *The policeman was very **rough** with the thief.*
4 not properly finished
- *I did a **rough** drawing of the scene before I started to paint it.*

round ¹ /raʊnd/ adjective
like a ball in shape
- *The earth isn't flat, is it? It's **round** like a ball.*

round ² adverb
1 When something moves round, it moves in the shape of a circle.
- *The police are walking **round** the building to make sure no one is there.*
2 When you **turn round** or **look round**, you face the opposite direction.
- *I **turned round** when as I heard her behind me.*

roundabout /ˈraʊndəbaʊt/ noun (countable)
1 a circle at a place where roads meet (and the traffic goes round it)
- *Take the first turning off at the **roundabout**.*
2 a large machine (usually in a fair or a playground) which turns round
- *Let's go for a ride on the **roundabout**.*

row ¹ /rəʊ/ noun (countable)

> **PRONUNCIATION NOTE**
>
> The word **row** rhymes with **go**.

several of the same things in a line or next to one another
- *I've booked seats on **Row** J at the theatre.*

row ² verb
use pieces of wood in the water to make a boat move through the water
- *A man was **rowing** a boat across the lake.*

rub /rʌb/ verb
rubbing, rubbed, has rubbed

> **SPELLING NOTE**
>
> double **b** : ru**bb**ing, ru**bb**ed BUT ru**b**s

θ	ð	ʃ	dʒ	tʃ	ŋ	ʒ	iː	ɜː	ɪ	æ	ʌ	ɒ
thing	that	shop	jump	chop	sing	measure	been	bird	bit	cat	but	not

1 move your hand up and down or backwards and forwards over something
   - *He was **rubbing** his hands to keep warm.*
2 **rub out** = make disappear
   - *Sarah **rubbed** the mistake **out**.*

rubber /ˈrʌbə*/ noun
1 (uncountable) the soft material from a special tree, out of which tyres are made
   - *Malaysia produces a lot of **rubber**.*
2 (countable) something which you can use to make pencil marks disappear (American English: eraser)
   - *I've made a mistake. Can you lend me a **rubber**?*

rubbish /ˈrʌbɪʃ/ noun (uncountable)
(American English: garbage)
something which you do not need and which you want to throw away
   - *You shouldn't throw **rubbish** in the street.*
   - a **rubbish** bin (= something for putting rubbish in)

rude /ruːd/ adjective
not polite
   - *Mary, don't be **rude**. You haven't said "Hello".*

LANGUAGE NOTE

rude *to* someone

---

rudely /ˈruːdlɪ/ adverb
do something in a way which is not polite
   - *Mr Lee felt sorry for speaking **rudely** to us.*

rugby /ˈrʌgbɪ/ noun (uncountable)
(also: rugger /ˈrʌgə*/)
a kind of football where players can throw and kick the ball to one another
   - *Australia beat England at **rugby** last week.*

rule ¹ /ruːl/ noun (countable)
something you must obey (a kind of law)
   - *One of the college **rules** is that students should not eat and drink in the classroom.*
   - keep to/follow/break/ make a rule

rule ² verb
ruling, ruled, has ruled
1 be the king, queen or most important person in a country
   - *Queen Victoria **ruled** England for more than sixty years.*
2 draw a straight line using a piece of wood, metal or plastic with a straight edge
   - ***Rule** a line under the picture.*

ruler /ˈruːlə*/ noun (countable)
1 a piece of wood, metal or plastic which you use to measure things
   - *Measure the length of your desk with your **ruler**.*
2 a king, a queen or the most important person in a country
   - *No one liked the new **ruler** of the country.*

run /rʌn/ verb
running, ran /ræn/ , has run
1 move more quickly than when you walk

   - *You'll catch the bus if you **run**.*
2 go
   - *"Are the buses still **running**?" "No, the last bus left an hour ago."*
   - run early/late/on time
3 flow
   - *The River Seine **runs** through Paris.*
4 arrange
   - *Mrs Jones is **running** a competition.*

rung /rʌŋ/ verb
past participle of **ring**
   - *Has anyone **rung** the fire bell yet?*

runner /ˈrʌnə*/ noun (countable)
a person who runs in a race
   - *Several **runners** didn't finish the race.*

rush /rʌʃ/ verb
go quickly
   - *I'm **rushing** home to watch a TV programme.*

θ	ð	ʃ	dʒ	tʃ	ŋ	ʒ	iː	ɜː	ɪ	æ	ʌ	ɒ
thing	that	shop	jump	chop	sing	measure	been	bird	bit	cat	but	not

Ss

sad /sæd/ adjective
sadder, saddest
1 not happy
 • *I was very **sad** to hear of your uncle's death.*
2 A **sad** story or film makes you feel very unhappy.
 • *Maria always cries when she sees a **sad** film.*

sadly /ˈsædlɪ/ adverb
not happily
 • *The old man walked **sadly** away from his home.*

safe [1] /seɪf/ noun (countable)
plural: safes
a heavy metal box or cupboard in which you put money, jewels, etc so that it will be difficult for thieves to steal them
 • *Tim keeps his money in a **safe** in his bedroom.*

safe [2] adjective
1 not dangerous
 • *Is it **safe** for the children to play here?*
2 in no danger, free from danger
 • *I won't feel **safe** until I reach home.*

safely /ˈseɪflɪ/ adverb
without danger, without hurting yourself
 • *"Goodnight. Drive home **safely**."*

safety /ˈseɪftɪ/ noun (uncountable)
a place where you can be out of danger
 • *We ran to the nearest building for **safety** when we heard the sound of guns.*

safety pin /ˈseɪftɪ pɪn/ noun (countable)
a special kind of pin
 • *I need a **safety pin** to fasten up my skirt.*
⚠ See also **pin** [1].

said /sed/ verb
past tense and past participle of **say**
 • *Who **said** I was absent?*

sail /seɪl/ verb
sailing, sailed, has sailed
travel by boat on the sea
 • *We **sailed** from Italy to India.*

sailor /ˈseɪlə*/ noun (countable)
someone who works on a boat at sea
 • *I want to be a **sailor** and travel round the world.*

salad /ˈsæləd/ noun (countable)
cold vegetables
 • *"Would you like a salad with your cold meat?" "Yes, please, I'll have some lettuce and tomatoes."*

sale /seɪl/ noun
1 (uncountable, countable) the act of selling
 • *He got enough money from the **sale** of his small flat to send his son to university.*
2 (countable and often used in the plural) the time when a shop sells goods at a lower price than normally
 • *I bought a new carpet in the **sale(s)** today.*
3 **for sale** = offered to be sold by someone
 • *"Is this flat **for sale**?" "Yes, it is."*
4 **on sale** = offered to be sold in a shop
 • *The new cameras are **on sale** in this shop.*

salesman /ˈseɪlzmən/
saleswoman /ˈseɪlzwʊmən/ noun (countable)
plural: salesmen, salewomen
someone who works in a shop and sells things to you
 • *I couldn't decide which dress to buy, but the **saleswoman** was very helpful.*

salt /sɔːlt/ noun (countable)
white powder you put on food to make it taste better
 • *Put some more **salt** on your meat.*

salty /ˈsɔːltɪ/ adjective
saltier, saltiest
with salt in it
 • *Sea water is **salty**. You can't drink it.*

θ	ð	ʃ	dʒ	tʃ	ŋ	ʒ	iː	ɜː	ɪ	æ	ʌ	ɒ
thing	that	shop	jump	chop	sing	measure	been	bird	bit	cat	but	not

same [1] /seɪm/ pronoun
not different, like something else
- *Three plus one is the **same** as two plus two.*

same [2] adjective
not different, not changed, not another
- *Is that the **same** shirt which you wore yesterday?*
- almost/nearly the same, exactly the same

LANGUAGE NOTE

1 ALWAYS *the* same
   NEVER   ~~same~~ OR ~~a same~~

2 the same as / the same that
   Helen was reading *the **same*** book *as* I was.
   Helen was reading *the **same*** book *that* she had read a month ago.

---

same [3] adverb
not differently
- *He does everything the **same** as his brother.*

sand /sænd/ noun (uncountable)
tiny pieces of broken rock (like powder) which you see on the beach or in a desert
- *I've been on the beach and got **sand** in my hair.*

sandal /'sændl/ noun (countable)
light shoe suitable for warm weather
- *I'll take my **sandals** with me on holiday.*

LANGUAGE NOTE

EITHER Whose are *these* new ***sandals***?
OR   Whose is *this* new ***pair of sandals***?

---

sandwich /'sænwɪdʒ/ noun (countable)
plural: sandwiches
A sandwich is two pieces of bread with some meat, tomatoes, cheese, etc between them.
- *I take **sandwiches** to work for lunch.*
- a cheese sandwich, a tomato sandwich, etc

sang /sæŋ/ verb
past tense of **sing**
- *Ted **sang** several songs at the party.*

sank /sæŋk/ verb
past tense of **sink**
- *The ship hit some rocks and soon **sank**.*

sat /sæt/ verb
past tense and past participle of **sit**
- *Jenny **sat** down in an armchair and fell asleep.*

satisfactory /ˌsætɪsˈfæktəri/ adjective
good enough
- *The teacher says my homework isn't **satisfactory**, and so I have to do it again.*
- highly satisfactory (= very satisfactory)

sauce /sɔːs/ noun (countable, uncountable)
a thick liquid which you can put on food to make it taste better
- *The meat was covered with a lovely **sauce**.*
- apple/ soy/tomato sauce, etc

saucer /ˈsɔːsə*/ noun (countable)
a small plate on which you put your cup
- *Could we have another cup and **saucer**, please?*

save /seɪv/ verb
saving, saved, has saved
1 stop something unpleasant or dangerous happening to someone
   - *Peter caught hold of Pat's dress and **saved** her when she began to fall off the balcony.*
2 not spend money
   - *Anita has **saved** $1200 for a holiday.*
3 keep for later
   - *Let's take a taxi. It'll **save** us a lot of time.*
- save money/ time; save someone a place/seat

saw [1] /sɔː/ noun (countable)
something for cutting wood
- *Lend me your **saw** to cut a branch off this tree.*

saw [2] verb
sawing, sawed, has sawn /sɔːn/
(American English: has sawed)
1 cut with a saw
   - *Tony's **sawn** several branches off the tree.*
2 past tense of **see**
   - *I **saw** Ben getting into a car yesterday.*

θ	ð	ʃ	dʒ	tʃ	ŋ	ʒ	iː	ɜː	ɪ	æ	ʌ	ɒ
thing	that	shop	jump	chop	sing	measure	been	bird	bit	cat	but	not

say /seɪ/ verb
saying, said /sed/, has said
speak
- I couldn't hear what Leila was **saying** because the radio was very loud.

LANGUAGE NOTE

1. Note the pattern:
   say something **to** someone

2. You often use **say** without a direct object BUT you must always use **tell** with a direct object.
   Ann **said** that she would come soon.
   She **told me** that she would come soon.

3. You can often use **say** for reported speech.
   "I'm very sorry."
   I **said** I was very sorry.
   (NOT I told I was very sorry.)

4. Use **tell** (NOT **say**) for reporting orders.
   "Come early," I said to her.
   I **told** her to come early.
   (NOT I said to her to come early.)

5. Note the following phrases:
   tell the truth, **tell** lies, **tell** a story
   speak the truth, **speak** French, etc
   say what you think

See also **speak**; see also **talk**[2]; see also **tell**.

scarf /skɑːf/ noun (countable)
plural: scarves
a thick piece of cloth which you wear round your neck
- Wear a **scarf** if you feel cold.

school /skuːl/ noun (countable)
the place where you go to learn things
- How old were you when you left **school**?

LANGUAGE NOTE

go to school BUT go to **a** good school

attend /go to/start/finish/leave school; nursery/infant/primary/junior/middle/high/secondary/grammar/comprehensive/public/boarding/prep(aratory)/day/evening/night school

See box below.

science /ˈsaɪəns/ noun (uncountable, countable)
the study of things in the world, how they are made and how they behave
- The government is spending a lot of money on the teaching of **science** in our schools.

School and College Subjects

	Monday	Tuesday	Wednesday	Thursday	Friday
9–10	Art	Biology	Chemistry	English	Spanish
10–12	Domestic Science / Home Economics	Crafts	Civics	Environmental Studies	Russian
11–12	General Science	Social Studies	Technical Drawing	Wood work	Chinese
12–1	Lunch	Lunch	Lunch	Lunch	Lunch
1–2	Games	Metalwork	Physics $E = Mc^2$	French	Geography
2–3	Gymnastics	History	Arabic	Mathematics $2 + 2 = 4$	Physical/Sports Education

θ	ð	ʃ	dʒ	tʃ	ŋ	ʒ	iː	ɜː	ɪ	æ	ʌ	ɒ
thing	that	shop	jump	chop	sing	measure	been	bird	bit	cat	but	not

scientist /ˈsaɪəntɪst/ noun (countable)
someone who studies things in the world, how they are made and how they behave
- *Scientists study changes in the world's climate.*

scissors /ˈsɪzəz/ noun (plural)
two pieces of sharp metal which are joined at the middle and used for cutting paper, cloth, etc
- *Use this pair of scissors to cut the cardboard.*

LANGUAGE NOTE	
ALWAYS	a pair of scissors OR some scissors
NEVER	a scissor

scold /skəʊld/ verb
speak angrily to someone because they have done something wrong
- *The teacher scolded us for laughing.*

score [1] /skɔː*/ noun (countable)
the result of a game or the number of points which a person or team has won
- *The score at the end of the match was 2-3.*

score [2] verb
scoring, scored, has scored
1 get points
   - *Ali's parents were very proud when their son scored most points in the test.*
2 write down points
   - *Mary, will you score for our competition?*

scratch [1] /skrætʃ/ noun (countable)
plural: scratches
1 a mark which you make when you rub something sharp against something else
   - *The cat made a long scratch on the table with its claws.*
2 a small cut
   - *I had a few scratches when I fell off my bike.*

scratch [2] verb
move something sharp across something and mark it
- *The cat scratched my hand when I picked it up.*

scream [1] /skriːm/ noun (countable)
a loud cry
- *There was a loud scream when I fired the gun.*

scream [2] verb
make a loud cry
- *Mary screamed when the dog ran towards her.*

screen /skriːn/ noun (countable)
the part of a cinema or television set where pictures appear

- *Don't sit near the screen. You'll hurt your eyes.*

screw [1] /skruː/ noun (countable)
a sharp piece of metal which you can turn and which is often used to hold pieces of wood together
- *Use these screws to make the cupboard.*

screw [2] verb
1 turn round and round
   - *Can you screw the top on this bottle?*
2 fasten with screws
   - *Jonathan screwed the picture to the wall.*

sea /siː/ noun (countable with *the*, uncountable)
the large amount of salt water which covers most of the earth
- *Swimming in the sea is better than in a pool.*

LANGUAGE NOTE
go **by** sea   BUT   sail on **the** sea, swim in **the sea**

✍ a calm/choppy sea (= with small waves)/ smooth/rough/stormy sea, rough/stormy seas

θ	ð	ʃ	dʒ	tʃ	ŋ	ʒ	iː	ɜː	ɪ	æ	ʌ	ɒ
thing	that	shop	jump	chop	sing	measure	been	bird	bit	cat	but	not

season /'siːzn/ noun (countable)
1 The year in some countries is divided into four seasons: spring, summer, autumn and winter.
 • *Autumn is my favourite **season**.*
2 a part of the year when something happens
 • *We go to the beach in the holiday **season**.*
↪ the dry/wet/rainy season
⚠ See also box on page 57.

seat /siːt/ noun (countable)
something on which you can sit, a chair, etc
 • *Are there any empty **seats** on the bus?*
↪ book a seat (in a theatre, etc), give up a seat to someone (on a bus, etc) (= stand so that someone can sit down), have a seat (= sit down), take your seat (= sit down, usually at a concert, etc); an empty seat

seat belt /'siːt belt/ noun (countable)
something to fasten across your body in a car or on an aeroplane

 • *Can you put on your **seat belt**, please?*
↪ do up/fasten/unfasten your seat belt, wear a seat belt

second /'sekənd/
1 (noun) There are sixty seconds in one minute.
 • *The train should leave in twenty **seconds**!*
2 (adverb) something which follows or is behind
 • *Mabel was beaten by Anne and came **second**.*
⚠ See also box on page 151.

secret [1] /'siːkrɪt/ noun (countable)
something which you don't tell anyone else
 • *Don't tell Dave I'm here. It's a **secret**.*
↪ give away/tell (someone)/keep a secret; a big secret, a close secret (= a secret which only one or two people know), an open secret (= a secret which everyone knows!)

secret [2] adjective
If something is secret, other people don't know about it.
 • *The old man keeps his money in a **secret** drawer.*

secretary /'sekrətrɪ/ noun (countable)
plural: secretaries
someone who types, answers the phone and does office work
 • *Rita works as a **secretary** in the college office.*

secretly /'siːkrɪtlɪ/ adverb
in a way which no one will know about
 • *Tim **secretly** hoped to be chosen for the team.*

see /siː/ verb
seeing, saw /sɔː/, has seen /siːn/
1 use your eyes
 • *Harry can't **see**. He's been blind since he was ten.*
2 notice
 • *I didn't **see** Sue because she was standing behind me.*
3 visit
 • *Ted wasn't in. He'd gone to **see** Tony.*
4 meet
 • *Wait here until I'm ready to **see** you.*
5 understand
 • *I don't **see** why you must leave. Stay a while.*

LANGUAGE NOTE

1 Do not use **see** in the continuous tense when **see** means **use your eyes** (1), **notice** (2) or **understand** (5).
NEVER What are you seeing?
ALWAYS What **do** you **see**?

2 You can often use **can** and **could** with **see** in place of the continuous tense.
  What are you doing?
  I'm standing on top of the hill and I can see lots of things.

3 When **see** is used to mean **visit** (3) or **meet** (4), you can use the present continuous forms.
  Are you **seeing** Joe tonight?

⚠ See also **look** [1]; see also **watch** [2].

θ	ð	ʃ	dʒ	tʃ	ŋ	ʒ	iː	ɜː	ɪ	æ	ʌ	ɒ
thing	that	shop	jump	chop	sing	measure	been	bird	bit	cat	but	not

seed /siːd/ noun (countable)
a small hard part of a plant which can grow into a plant or tree
- Look at the farmer sowing **seeds** in his field.
↻ plant/sow seeds

seem /siːm/ verb
appear, make someone think it is
- "Mary **seems** to be a nice girl."
  "Perhaps, but you don't know her, do you?"

LANGUAGE NOTE

1. Use an adjective after the verb **seem** (not an adverb).
   The music seems **loud**. (NOT loudly)
   You seem **happy**. (NOT happily)
2. Use **to be** after **seem** when there is a noun by itself (without an adjective).
   He seemed **to be** the manager.
3. Note the following patterns.
   You always seem **to** be late.
   The taxi driver seems **to** have got lost.
   There seems to be something wrong.
   It seems **like** a good time to finish now.
   It seems **as if** he doesn't want to come.

seen /siːn/ verb
past participle of **see**
- Have you **seen** Susan anywhere?

selfish /ˈselfɪʃ/ adjective
thinking only about yourself
- Don't be so **selfish**. Think how I feel.

sell /sel/ verb
selling, sold /səʊld/, has sold
give something to someone who pays you money
- We're **selling** our flat so we can buy a house.

semi-colon /ˌsemi ˈkəʊlən/ noun (countable)
This is a semi-colon ;
- You can use a **semi-colon** to separate two parts of a long sentence.

send /send/ verb
sending, sent /sent/, has sent
1. arrange for something to be taken from one place to another
   - Did you **send** Teresa a birthday card?
2. make someone go somewhere
   - Mrs Lee **sent** Linda to buy some bread.

LANGUAGE NOTE

send someone something
OR send something **to** someone

sent /sent/ verb
past tense and past participle of **send**
- Who **sent** the parcel?

sentence /ˈsentəns/ noun (countable)
a group of words which begins with a capital letter and ends with a full stop
- A **sentence** usually has a verb and either tells us something or asks a question.

separate [1] /ˈsepəreɪt/ verb
separating, separated, has separated
1. move one thing or person away from another
   - Mrs Dawson **separated** Mary and Helen because they always talked in class.
2. divide
   - A small wall **separated** Mr Swindon's garden from his neighbour's.
3. go different ways
   - We walked together to the bank before **separating**.

separate [2] /ˈseprət/ adjective
not joined, not together
- My sister and I have **separate** bedrooms: this is my bedroom and that is hers.

separately /ˈseprətli/ adverb
not together with someone or something, alone
- Although Sarah and I live next door to each other, we go to school **separately**.

θ	ð	ʃ	dʒ	tʃ	ŋ	ʒ	iː	ɜː	ɪ	æ	ʌ	ɒ
thing	that	shop	jump	chop	sing	measure	been	bird	bit	cat	but	not

serious /ˈsɪərɪəs/ adjective
1 something which is bad or which makes you worried
   • *I saw a serious accident on my way to the college today: two people were killed.*
2 not funny, not joking
   • *Was Shirley serious when she said she was going to work in Tokyo for a year?*

seriously /ˈsɪərɪəslɪ/ adverb
in a way which shows that you think something is important or that you mean what you say
   • *Pam talked very seriously about her new job.*

servant /ˈsɜːvənt/ noun (countable)
a person who works in someone's house (usually to clean, cook, etc)
   • *Mr Cheung is so rich he has two servants.*

serve /sɜːv/ verb
serving, served, has served
1 sell things to people in a shop
   • *Which shop assistant served you?*
2 bring or take food
   • *Serve yourselves and take what you want.*
↪ serve food/a meal, serve someone

service /ˈsɜːvɪs/ noun
1 (uncountable) selling in a shop or taking food to people in a restaurant
   • *The service in that restaurant is very slow.*
↪ excellent/good/poor/polite/quick/slow service
2 (countable) something which is done for the public (and which is necessary or important)
   • *Bus services to Bristol are much better now.*
3 (countable, plural only) some work which is done for people
   • *We need the services of a doctor.*

set¹ /set/ noun (countable)
a group of things which belong together
   • *Harry's just got a new chess set.*
↪ a chess/coffee/tea/dinner set, a radio/television/TV set

set² verb
setting, set, has set
1 **set an example** = do something good so that other people will follow and do it
   • *Be quiet and set an example to others.*
2 **set free** = make free
   • *All the prisoners have now been set free.*
3 **set off/out** = go somewhere, start out
   • *We set off for the beach at half-past six.*
4 **set on fire** = make something burn
   • *The police think that someone set the building on fire by accident.*

several /ˈsevərəl/ adjective, pronoun
more than a few (but not a large number)
   • *I went to see Maria several times but she was never in.*

sew /səʊ/ verb
sewing, sewed, has sewn /səʊn/
(American English: also has sewed)
join pieces of cloth together with thread

   • *Could you sew this button on my shirt, please?*

shade /ʃeɪd/ noun (uncountable, usually with the)
a dark area not in the sunlight
   • *The sun is very strong. Let's sit in the shade.*

shadow /ˈʃædəʊ/ noun (countable)
a dark shape
   • *The sun is very bright this morning. Can you see the shadows of those trees?*

shake /ʃeɪk/ verb
shaking, shook /ʃʊk/, has shaken /ˈʃeɪkən/
move quickly from side to side or up and down
   • *We felt the building shake during the storm.*
↪ shake a bottle, shake hands, shake your head

θ	ð	ʃ	dʒ	tʃ	ŋ	ʒ	iː	ɜː	ɪ	æ	ʌ	ɒ
thing	that	shop	jump	chop	sing	measure	been	bird	bit	cat	but	not

shall /ʃæl/ (unstressed /ʃəl/)   modal verb
1 You can use **shall** to show the future (= **will**).
   • I must go now or I **shall** be late.
2 You can use **shall** to ask certain questions.
   • **Shall** I make a cup of tea?

LANGUAGE NOTE

1 The short form of both **shall** and **will** is '**ll**.
   I'**ll** see you tomorrow.
   They'**ll** stay in Japan for over a month.
2 Don't use **to** after **shall**.
   NEVER   ~~We shall to do it tomorrow.~~
   ALWAYS   We **shall do** it tomorrow.
3 You can use **will** instead of **shall** in most cases. In the past **will** was used after **I** and **we** to show a promise or an order. Now you can use EITHER **shall** OR **will** after **I** and **we**.
   I **shall/will** help you.
4 Also in the past **shall** was used after **you, he, she** and **they** to show a promise or an order. Now it is better to use **will** after **you, he, she** and **they** in all cases.
   They **will** help you.
5 Use **shall** after **I** and **we** when you want to make an offer or a suggestion.
   Shall I tell you the answer now?
   Shall we meet at seven tonight?

⚠ See also **will**.

shallow   /'ʃæləʊ/   adjective
only a short way from the top to the bottom, not deep
• If you aren't a good swimmer, you should stay where the water is **shallow**.

shan't   /ʃɑːnt/   modal verb
shall not
• I **shan't** tell anyone your secret.
⚠ See also **shall**.

shape   /ʃeɪp/   noun (countable)
The shape of a person or an object is how it looks from its outside edges (eg whether it is round, square, fat, thin, etc)
• A ring is the **shape** of a circle.

share   /ʃeə*/   verb
sharing, shared, has shared
1 have or use something while someone else has it or uses it
   • Can I **share** your book? I've lost mine.
2 **share (out)** = divide something
   • We had to **share** the cake **(out)** between the four of us, and so we got a quarter each.

shark   /ʃɑːk/   noun (countable, uncountable)
a large fish which swims in the sea and is often very dangerous

• Come out at once! There's a **shark** in the water!

LANGUAGE NOTE

When you are talking about **a shark** as a fish swimming in the sea, use **a**.
   Be careful. Someone saw a shark near here yesterday.
When you are talking about **shark** as a food on a dish, you should not use **a** before it.
   A lot of people like eating **shark**.

---

sharp   /ʃɑːp/   adjective
1 having a very thin edge which will cut things easily
   • Don't play with the knives: they're very **sharp**.
2 sudden, quick
   • Drive carefully. There's a **sharp** bend in the road.

sharpen   /'ʃɑːpən/   verb
make something sharp (ie come to a thin edge or a point)
• My pencil was broken so I had to **sharpen** it.
↻ sharpen a knife/a pencil/some scissors

θ	ð	ʃ	dʒ	tʃ	ŋ	ʒ	iː	ɜː	ɪ	æ	ʌ	ɒ
thing	that	shop	jump	chop	sing	measure	been	bird	bit	cat	but	not

sharpener /ˈʃɑːpnə*/ noun (countable)
something you use to sharpen things
- *May I borrow your pencil **sharpener**, please?*

shave /ʃeɪv/ verb
shaving, shaved, has shaved
cut hair from your face, your arms or legs
- *Are you growing a beard? You haven't **shaved**.*

she /ʃiː/ pronoun
You can use **she** to talk about a woman or a girl.
- *"What's Anna doing?" "**She's** watching TV."*
⚠ See also **he** (Language Note).

she'd /ʃiːd/
1 she would
  - *I'm sure **she'd** come if you invited her.*
2 she had
  - *I never found out what **she'd** done to her husband.*

sheep /ʃiːp/ noun (countable)
plural: sheep

LANGUAGE NOTE

The meat from a young **sheep** is called **lamb**..

⚠ See box on page 10.

sheet /ʃiːt/ noun (countable)
1 a large thin piece of cloth (usually like a rectangle in shape)
  - *Are there clean **sheets** on the bed?*
2 a piece of paper (like a square or rectangle in shape)
  - *Begin your exercise on a new **sheet** of paper.*

shelf /ʃelf/ noun (countable)
plural: shelves /ʃelvz/
a flat piece of wood, metal, glass, etc which is fixed to a wall or inside a cupboard
- *The book I'd like to borrow is on the top **shelf**.*

she'll /ʃiːl/
she will
- *"Where's Teresa?" "**She'll** be here soon."*

shell /ʃel/ noun (countable)
1 the hard cover of some kinds of small fish
  - *There were lots of **shells** on the beach.*
2 the thin, hard cover of an egg
  - *Use your knife to break the **shell** of the egg.*

shelter /ˈʃeltə*/ verb
1 stay in a place where you are safe
  - *During the storm several people **sheltered** under the big tree.*
2 keep someone safe
  - *The high wall **sheltered** us from the wind.*

shelves /ʃelvz/ noun (countable)
⚠ See **shelf**.

she's /ʃiːz/
1 she is
  - ***She's** living in Hong Kong now.*
2 she has
  - *Helen says **she's** already met Ann.*

shine /ʃaɪn/ verb
shining, shone /ʃɒn/, has shone
1 give out bright light
  - *There aren't any clouds and the sun is **shining**.*
  ↻ shine brightly
2 look bright
  - *If you polish your shoes, they'll **shine**.*

ship /ʃɪp/ noun (countable)
a large boat which can travel across the sea
- *There are a lot of **ships** in the harbour today.*
↻ build/sail a ship; a ship sails/ sinks

shirt /ʃɜːt/ noun (countable)
a piece of clothing which you wear on the top half of your body
- *They won't let you go in the restaurant unless you wear a **shirt** and tie.*
↻ put a shirt on, take your shirt off, wear a shirt

θ	ð	ʃ	dʒ	tʃ	ŋ	ʒ	iː	ɜː	ɪ	æ	ʌ	ɒ
thing	that	shop	jump	chop	sing	measure	been	bird	bit	cat	but	not

shoe /ʃuː/ noun (countable)
something which you wear on your feet
- *My new **shoes** are hurting my feet.*
- put on/wear some shoes, take off your shoes; a pair of shoes; gym/running/sports/tennis shoes
- See also **trainers**.

shone /ʃɒn/ verb
past tense and past participle of **shine**
- *A light **shone** from the small house.*

shook /ʃʊk/ verb
past tense of **shake**
- *He **shook** the bottle before he opened it.*

shoot /ʃuːt/ verb
shooting, shot /ʃɒt/ , has shot
1 fire a gun (at)
   - *The thieves **shot** (at) a policeman.*
2 move very quickly
   - *A mouse suddenly **shot** out of the hole.*

shop /ʃɒp/ noun (countable)
a place (in a building) where you can go to buy things
- *I must go to the **shop** to get some bread.*
- a baker's (shop), a bookshop, a butcher's (shop), a chemist's (shop), a gift shop, a (green)grocer's (shop), a toy shop

LANGUAGE NOTE

1 The word **shop** is used in British English for smaller places which sell things while **store** and **department store** are used for larger places which sell things. The word **store** is used more in American English than in British English. It can be used in American English for small shops.

2 the baker's = the baker's shop
   the butcher's = the butcher's shop

shop assistant /'ʃɒp əˌsɪstənt/ noun (countable)
a person who works in a shop
- *One of the **shop assistants** has gone to look for the shoes I asked to see.*

shopkeeper /'ʃɒpkiːpə*/ noun (countable)
a person who owns a small shop
- *Do you know the **shopkeeper** in the new shop?*

shopping /'ʃɒpɪŋ/ noun (uncountable)
1 what you do when you go to shops to buy things
   - *Have you done all your **shopping** yet?*
- do the shopping, go shopping
2 the things which you have bought in a shop
   - *Can I carry your **shopping** for you?*

LANGUAGE NOTE

ALWAYS shopping   NEVER ~~shoppings~~

shore /ʃɔː*/ noun (countable)
the land at the edge of the sea or by the side of a lake

- *It's nice to walk along the sea **shore**.*

short /ʃɔːt/ adjective
1 not long (in time)
   - *The students in Form Four have a **short** break between the third and fourth lessons.*
2 not tall
   - *Mr Meredith is quite **short**: he is only one metre and twenty centimetres tall.*
3 not long (in length)
   - *Do you think this skirt is too **short**?*
4 not far
   - *She goes for a **short** walk every evening.*

shorts /ʃɔːts/ noun (plural)
trousers with very short legs which do not cover your knees
- *I wear **shorts** when I play football.*

θ	ð	ʃ	dʒ	tʃ	ŋ	ʒ	iː	ɜː	ɪ	æ	ʌ	ɒ
thing	that	shop	jump	chop	sing	measure	been	bird	bit	cat	but	not

200　shot

LANGUAGE NOTE	
ALWAYS	a pair of shorts, some shorts, shorts
NEVER	~~a shorts~~

shot /ʃɒt/　verb
past tense and past participle of **shoot**
- *He shot the tiger but didn't kill it.*

should /ʃʊd/ (unstressed /ʃəd/)　modal verb
1 You can use **should** when you think something will happen.
- *I should be able to go to the cinema tonight.*
2 You can use **should** when you think it is a good idea if something happens.
- *You should eat a lot of apples.*
3 You can use **should** to ask for advice, information, etc.
- *Where should we go tonight?*
4 You can use **should** before **like** when you are polite and want to do something.
- *I should like to come with you if I can.*

⚠ See also **would**.

shouldn't /'ʃʊdnt/　modal verb
should not
- *You shouldn't go out every night.*

⚠ See also **should**.

shout /ʃaʊt/　verb
cry or call loudly
- *There's no need to shout. I'm not deaf!*

show /ʃəʊ/　verb
showing, showed, has shown /ʃəʊn/
or (rarely) has showed
1 let someone look at something
- *Peter wanted to show Dave his new camera.*
2 take someone to a certain place
- *Will you show Joe where the library is?*
3 teach by acting or doing
- *Can you show me how to use this machine?*

shower /'ʃaʊə*/　noun (countable)
1 You stand under a **shower** to wash yourself. It is a pipe fitted with several small holes through which water pours.
- *I'm hot. I think I'll have a cold shower.*
↻ have/take a shower
2 a fall of rain or snow which lasts only a short time
- *It'll be sunny tomorrow morning but there'll be some showers in the afternoon.*

shut [1] /ʃʌt/　verb
shutting, shut, has shut
close something
- *Please shut the door when you go out.*

shut [2]　adjective
not open (ie you cannot go in)
- *We didn't buy any bread because the shop was shut.*

shut up /ˌʃʌt 'ʌp/　phrasal verb
shutting up, shut up, has shut up
stop talking, be quiet
- *Shut up and listen to me for a minute.*

LANGUAGE NOTE
Be quiet is more polite than **Shut up**.

shy /ʃaɪ/　adjective
shyer, shyest
1 not happy to meet people because you are afraid or because you don't know what to say to them
- *Peter was very shy and never spoke to me.*
2 easily frightened
- *Rabbits are shy and run away if you touch them.*

sick /sɪk/　adjective
ill, not well
- *I wasn't at college yesterday because I was sick.*
⚠ See also **ill**.

side /saɪd/　noun (countable)
1 to the right or to the left of something
- *On which side of the room is the door?*
the left/right/east/west/north/south side
2 the flat outside part of something
- *A box has six sides.*

θ	ð	ʃ	dʒ	tʃ	ŋ	ʒ	iː	ɜː	ɪ	æ	ʌ	ɒ
thing	that	shop	jump	chop	sing	measure	been	bird	bit	cat	but	not

3 **side by side** = next to one another, not in front and not behind
- Stand **side by side** and hold hands.

sidewalk /'saɪdwɔːk/ noun (countable)
(American English)
⚠ See **pavement**.

sight /saɪt/ noun
1 (uncountable) being able to see
- Didn't you know Mrs Ralston was blind? She lost her **sight** in a car accident.
↻ lose your sight
2 (countable) something which is seen
- The fire was a frightening **sight**.
↻ a beautiful/lovely/pleasant/wonderful/ welcome/funny/rare/sad/sorry/terrible sight; in /out of sight
3 **catch sight of** = see (someone or something) suddenly or for a moment
- I **caught sight of** John Robertson at the football match but I don't think he saw me.
↻ lose sight of someone/something

sign[1] /saɪn/ noun (countable)
a word, a mark or picture which tells you something
- You mustn't talk in the library. Can't you see the **signs** with the word "Silence" on them?

sign[2] verb
write your name
- **Sign** (your name) at the bottom of the page.

signal /'sɪgnəl/ noun (countable)
a kind of sign which gives a certain message to someone

- The train has just stopped at a **signal**.
↻ a railway signal

silence /'saɪləns/ noun (uncountable)
When there is silence, everything is quiet and there is no noise at all.
- The new teacher waited until there was **silence** before she began to talk.
↻ complete/perfect/ total silence

silent /'saɪlənt/ adjective
quiet, without making any noise or sound
- The pupils had to be **silent** in the library.
↻ be/keep/stay silent

silently /'saɪləntlɪ/ adverb
quietly, without making any noise
- When I arrived, everyone was working **silently**.

silk /sɪlk/ noun (uncountable)
very smooth cloth which is made with soft, thin threads
- All these shirts are made of **silk**. Have you ever worn a **silk** shirt?

silly /'sɪlɪ/ adjective
sillier, silliest
foolish
- Stop being **silly**. You know the earth is round.

silver[1] /'sɪlvə*/ noun (uncountable)
Silver is a grey metal which shines and is very valuable. People use **silver** to make jewelry.
- Coins used to be made of **silver**.

silver[2] adjective
1 made of a shining grey metal
- Do you like this **silver** plate?
2 grey and white (and shining)
- The moon made the lake **silver** in colour.

similar /'sɪmɪlə*/ adjective
almost (but not completely) the same
- This dark blue colour looks **similar** to black.

LANGUAGE NOTE

similar **to** someone/something (NEVER as)

simple /'sɪmpl/ adjective
1 easy, not difficult
  • *Do you think that learning English is **simple**?*
2 plain, without extra things
  • *I like **simple** food, especially chicken and rice.*
3 not clever, stupid
  • *Don't be so **simple**. How can nought times five be five?*

since /sɪns/ preposition, conjunction, adverb
1 from a time in the past until now
  • *I've been waiting for you **since** seven.*
2 because, as
  • *It's very noisy in Susie's flat **since** she lives near the bus station.*

LANGUAGE NOTE

1 You should usually use tenses formed with **has/have** or **had** with **since**.
   We **have been** here since 1992.
   Tim **has been waiting** since two o'clock.
   I **haven't seen** Ruth since I last met you.
2 NEVER Ann has been sleeping from six o'clock.
   ALWAYS Ann has been sleeping **since** six o'clock.
3 NEVER I have lived here since three years ago.
   ALWAYS I have lived here **for** three years.

---

sincerely /sɪnˈsɪəlɪ/ adverb
1 honestly (You use **sincerely** when you really feel or mean something.)
  • *I'll be sad to leave my old school, and I mean that very **sincerely**.*
2 **Yours sincerely** = Write **Yours sincerely** at the end of a letter to someone you don't know (well).
  • *I look forward to hearing from you.*
                    Yours sincerely,
                    John Grey

sing /sɪŋ/ verb
singing, sang /sæŋ/, has sung /sʌŋ/
make music with your voice
  • *I like to hear Tina **sing**: she's got a sweet voice.*

singer /'sɪŋə*/ noun (countable)
someone who makes music with their voice
  • *David's sister is a well-known **singer** on TV.*

single ¹ /'sɪŋgl/ noun (countable)
a bus, train, plane ticket to a certain place
  • *A **single** to Queenstown, please.*
  ⚠ See also **return** ¹.

single ² adjective
1 only one
  • *There wasn't a **single** apple left on the tree.*
2 not married
  • *Are you married or **single**?*
3 for one person
  • *Would you like a **single** room or a double?*

sink ¹ /sɪŋk/ noun (countable)
a basin with water taps

  • *Put the dishes in the **sink** and I'll wash them.*
  ↻ the bathroom sink, the kitchen sink

sink ² verb
sinking, sank or (rarely) sunk, has sunk
move slowly downwards or beneath the water
  • *The boat hit a rock and **sank**.*

sir /sɜː*/
You can use the word **sir** when you want to be polite to a man.
  • *"Good morning. I'm your new teacher." "Good morning, **sir**."*

sister /'sɪstə*/ noun (countable)
a girl or woman with the same parents as someone else
  • *I've got three **sisters** but only one brother.*

θ	ð	ʃ	dʒ	tʃ	ŋ	ʒ	iː	ɜː	ɪ	æ	ʌ	ɒ
thing	that	shop	jump	chop	sing	measure	been	bird	bit	cat	but	not

sit /sɪt/ verb

sitting, sat /sæt/, has sat

1. bend at the waist and rest the lower part of your body on the ground or a chair, etc
   - Please come in and **sit** down.
2. **sit (for) an exam** = take an examination
   - Are you going to **sit (for)** the English exam?

size /saɪz/ noun (countable)

how large or small something is
- "What's the **size** of your bed?" "It's a single bed."
- "What **size** does Anna take in shoes?" "**Size** six."

� take/wear size 4, 5, etc; the right/wrong size; a size too big/too small

skate¹ /skeɪt/ noun (countable)

piece of metal you wear under your feet when you move over ice
- Let's take our **skates** and go to the frozen lake.

skate² verb

skating, skate, has skated
move smoothly over the ice on pieces of metal or move on the ground on small wheels
- Have you ever been **skating**?

☞ ice skating, roller skating (= skating on skates with small wheels)

skeleton /'skelɪtən/ noun (countable)

all the bones in someone's body
- I was very frightened when I saw the **skeleton**.

ski¹ /skiː/ noun (countable)

plural: skis
long flat pieces of wood, metal or plastic which you can put under your feet to move quickly and easily on snow
- Let's take our **skis** with us to Switzerland.

ski² verb

skiing, skied, has skied
move quickly and easily on snow wearing long, flat pieces of wood, metal or plastic under your feet
- I'm going **skiing** tomorrow.

skin /skɪn/ noun

1. (uncountable) what all animals and people are covered with
   - Her **skin** is very white, isn't it?

☞ dark/light/fair/dry/oily/rough/smooth/soft skin

2. (countable) the outside part of a vegetable or fruit
   - Leila slipped on the banana **skin** and fell.

☞ a thick/thin skin

skip /skɪp/ verb

skipping, skipped, has skipped

1. jump while running
   - Tina was so happy that she **skipped** all the way home.
2. jump up and down over a rope
   - The children were **skipping** in the playground.

skirt /skɜːt/ noun (countable)

a piece of clothing which is worn by women and girls, and which hangs from their waist (like the bottom half of a dress)
- Ann's **skirt** was made of cotton.

☞ a long/short skirt; lengthen/shorten a skirt

sky /skaɪ/ noun (countable, usually singular with the)

plural: skies
the space above the earth where the clouds, sun, moon and stars are
- Look at that aeroplane high in the **sky**.

☞ a blue/bright/clear/cloudless sky, blue/bright/clear/cloudless skies, a cloudy/dull/stormy/starry sky, cloudy/dull/stormy/starry skies

sleep¹ /sliːp/ noun

1. (uncountable) not being awake
   - Children need more **sleep** than adults.

☞ go to sleep

2. (singular with a) the time when you are asleep
   - You'll feel better after you've had a **sleep**.

☞ a long/short/deep sleep/a light sleep (= almost awake), a sound sleep (= a good sleep)

LANGUAGE NOTE

go to sleep   BUT   have **a** short sleep

θ	ð	ʃ	dʒ	tʃ	ŋ	ʒ	iː	ɜː	ɪ	æ	ʌ	ɒ
thing	that	shop	jump	chop	sing	measure	been	bird	bit	cat	but	not

sleep [2] verb
sleeping, slept /slept/ , has slept
rest and close your eyes, stop being awake
- *Cats **sleep** during the day and go out at night.*

sleepy /ˈsliːpɪ/ adjective
tired and ready to go to sleep
- *I must get some exercise. I feel very **sleepy**.*

sleeve /sliːv/ noun (countable)
the piece of clothing which covers your arms
- *The **sleeves** of her dress are far too long.*

slept /slept/ verb
past tense and past participle of **sleep**
- *I was so tired that I **slept** for over twelve hours.*

slide [1] /slaɪd/ noun (countable)
something which children can play on
- *Henry likes going down the **slide**.*

slide [2] verb
sliding, slid /slɪd/ , has slid
move smoothly without stopping or sticking
- *The soap **slid** out of my hands onto the floor.*

slight /slaɪt/ adjective
very small
- *There's been a **slight** increase in the number of people without work.*

slightly /ˈslaɪtlɪ/ adverb
a bit, a little, rather
- *This is **slightly** heavier than the other one.*

slip /slɪp/ verb
slipping, slipped, has slipped
You slip when your foot moves forward by accident and you fall down (or almost fall down).
- *I **slipped** on the banana skin and broke my leg.*

slipper /ˈslɪpə*/ noun (countable)
loose, soft shoes which people often wear inside their home
- *I was in such a hurry I went out in my **slippers**.*
- put your slippers on, take your slippers off, wear (some) slippers

slope [1] /sləʊp/ noun (countable)
something flat which is higher at one end than at the other

- *We ran down the **slope** to the bottom of the hill.*
- a gentle/steep slope

slope [2] /sləʊp/ verb
sloping, sloped, has sloped
When something slopes, it is higher at one end than at the other end.
- *The road **slopes** down the hill to the river.*
- slope steeply

slow /sləʊ/ adjective
1 not fast, taking a long time
- *Don't be so **slow**. Hurry up!*
2 showing the time earlier than it is
- *My watch is very **slow**. The time is now twenty past eight but by my watch it is only ten to eight.*

slow down /ˌsləʊ ˈdaʊn/ phrasal verb
move or go more slowly
- *Don't walk so fast. **Slow down** a little.*

slowly /ˈsləʊlɪ/ adverb
without much speed
- *The old man walks very **slowly**. We'll wait.*

small /smɔːl/ adjective
1 little, not big in size, amount, weight, etc
- *Mrs Hill was too **small** to reach the shelf.*
- *I'm not hungry. I want only a **small** piece of cake.*
- See also **little**.

θ	ð	ʃ	dʒ	tʃ	ŋ	ʒ	iː	ɜː	ɪ	æ	ʌ	ɒ
thing	that	shop	jump	chop	sing	measure	been	bird	bit	cat	but	not

snow 205

2 young
- A **small** child began to cry.

LANGUAGE NOTE

Use little (NOT small) if you want to show that you like or don't like someone/something.
ALWAYS   What a nice little girl!
NEVER   What a nice small girl!

---

smart /smɑːt/   adjective
1 clean and neat
- Vincent looks very **smart** in his new suit.
2 clever
- Mr Hill is very **smart** - he's a businessman.

smell¹ /smel/   noun (countable)
something which you can tell with your nose
- There's a bad **smell** here. Is this meat fresh?
- ಜಿ a bad/terrible/faint/strong/sweet smell

smell² verb
smelling, smelled or smelt /smelt/, has smelled or has smelt
1 become aware of something with your nose
- I could **smell** gas, so I opened the windows.
2 have a smell
- These flowers **smell** very sweet.

LANGUAGE NOTE

smell + adjective	They smell **sweet**.
smell + noun	I can smell **petrol**.
smell + -ing form	Do you smell **burning**?
smell **of**	It smells **of** roses.

---

smile¹ /smaɪl/   noun (countable)
if someone has a smile on their face it usually means they are happy
- It's nice to see Mary; she always has a big **smile**.
- ಜಿ a big/broad/cheerful/happy/nice/faint smile

smile² verb
smiling, smiled, has smiled
move your mouth to show you are happy
- Elsa looked at her husband and **smiled**.

LANGUAGE NOTE

smile **at** someone/something

---

smoke¹ /sməʊk/   noun (uncountable)
gas (often white or grey) which you see when something is burning
- There was a lot of **smoke** in the kitchen because Harry had burnt the food!
- ಜಿ thick smoke, give off (thick) smoke, clouds of smoke

smoke² verb
smoking, smoked, has smoked
1 have a cigarette, etc in your mouth
- Don't **smoke** if you want to stay healthy.
2 give off a white or grey gas (ie smoke)
- Even when the fire was put out, the wood continued **smoking**.

smooth /smuːð/   adjective
1 not rough, even, without any holes in it
- The steps were very **smooth** as people had walked up and down them for many years.
2 moving comfortably in the same way without any sudden changes
- The flight to England was quite **smooth**.

snack /snæk/   noun (countable)
a small meal or something small which you can eat between meals
- I have a **snack** for lunch - usually a sandwich.

snake /sneɪk/   noun (countable)
⚠ See box on page 10.

snow¹ /snəʊ/   noun (countable)
soft white frozen rain
- The **snow** made everything look clean.
- ಜಿ snow falls/melts; heavy/light snow

θ	ð	ʃ	dʒ	tʃ	ŋ	ʒ	iː	ɜː	ɪ	æ	ʌ	ɒ
thing	that	shop	jump	chop	sing	measure	been	bird	bit	cat	but	not

snow [2]   verb

fall from the sky as soft white frozen rain
- *It began to **snow** as we crossed the mountains.*

� snow heavily/lightly

so [1]   /səʊ/   adverb

1. You can often use **so** when you talk about how much, how big, how thin, etc something is.
   - *My bag was **so** heavy that I couldn't carry it.*

LANGUAGE NOTE

1. You can often miss out **that**.
   My bag was so heavy I couldn't carry it.
2. NEVER   It was a so bad meal that I didn't eat it.
   ALWAYS   It was **so** bad a meal that I didn't eat it.
   OR   It was **such** a bad meal that I didn't eat it.
   OR   The meal was **so** bad that I didn't eat it.

---

2. also, too
   - *Sammy wanted to go home, and **so** did I.*
3. You can use **so** to show something that you or someone has already spoken about.
   - *"I hope our team wins tonight." "I hope **so**, too."*
4. You can use **so** in polite sentences to mean **very**.
   - *It was **so** kind of you to invite me.*
5. You can use **so** before **much** and **many**.
   - *I saw **so much** snow I wanted to play in it.*

so [2]   conjunction

1. as a result
   - *It was still very early in the morning, and **so** I decided to stay in bed.*
2. with the purpose that
   - *I got up early **so** (that) I would be the first to arrive.*

soap   /səʊp/   noun (uncountable)

something which is used with water for washing and cleaning
- *Here's a bar of **soap** to wash yourself with.*

� a bar/cake/piece of soap; soap flakes/powder

sock   /sɒk/   noun (countable)

a piece of clothing which you can wear over your feet (inside your shoes)
- *The strange man was wearing a black **sock** on one foot and a white one on the other.*

� a pair of socks

sofa   /ˈsəʊfə/   noun (countable)

a long comfortable seat which two or more people can sit on
- *Mr and Mrs Perry sat together on the **sofa**.*

soft   /sɒft/   adjective

1. bending gently when you push against it, not hard
   - *Henry likes a **soft** pillow when he sleeps but Ken prefers a hard one.*
2. pleasant to listen to
   - *Helen spoke in a very **soft** voice.*
3. smooth, not rough, gentle
   - *Your hands are very **soft**.*
4. **a soft drink** = a cold drink such as fruit juice (BUT NOT beer, wine, etc)
   - *Would you like a **soft drink** or a cup of coffee?*

soil   /sɔɪl/   noun (uncountable)

something which covers part of the earth and in which plants can grow
- *Plants will do well here: the **soil** is very good.*

soldier   /ˈsəʊldʒə*/   noun (countable)

a person who is in the army
- *We watched the **soldiers** marching.*

solve   /sɒlv/   verb

solving, solved, has solved
find an answer or an explanation
- *Have the police **solved** the crime yet?*

� solve a crime/a (crossword) puzzle/a problem

some   /sʌm/ unstressed /səm/   determiner, pronoun

1. an amount of (but not much)
   - *Would you like **some** tea or **some** coffee?*
2. a number of (but not many)
   - ***Some** of the pupils started to laugh.*

θ	ð	ʃ	dʒ	tʃ	ŋ	ʒ	iː	ɜː	ɪ	æ	ʌ	ɒ
thing	that	shop	jump	chop	sing	measure	been	bird	bit	cat	but	not

sort — 207

LANGUAGE NOTE

1. You should usually use **any** instead of **some** in questions and sentences with **not**.
   Is there **any** bread left?
   There weren't **any** cars in the car park.
   However, you can also use **some** in questions, especially when you offer something to someone.
   Would you like **any** more coffee?
   Would you like **some** more coffee?

2. **Some students** were at the meeting.
   Some of the students you met were at the meeting.
   Some of those students were at the meeting.

See also **any** [1]; see also **any** [2].

somebody /ˈsʌmbədɪ/
(someone) /ˈsʌmwʌn/ pronoun
a person (but no special person)
- **Somebody** has taken my book. Who was it?

something /ˈsʌmθɪŋ/ pronoun
a thing (but no special thing)
- We looked up and suddenly saw **something**. Later we found it was a small aeroplane!

LANGUAGE NOTE

You should put an adjective AFTER **somebody**, **something**, and **somewhere**.
I'm sure he'll marry somebody **very rich**.
I've got something **nice** for you.
Are we going somewhere **nice** on the picnic?

sometimes /ˈsʌmtaɪmz/ adverb
at different times, now and then
- **Sometimes** I go to my uncle's on Sundays and **sometimes** I go to the beach with my friends.

somewhere /ˈsʌmweə*/ adverb
(in, at, or to) some place (but no special place)
- I suppose we'll be going **somewhere** for our holidays, but we don't know where yet.

son /sʌn/ noun (countable)
someone's child who is a boy
- Mrs Manson was very proud of her **son** when he went to university.

song /sɒŋ/ noun (countable)
words and music which you sing
- What's your favourite **song**?
- play/sing/write a song; a love/folk song

soon /suːn/ adverb
sooner, soonest
in a short time
- We ought to go **soon** or we'll be late.

LANGUAGE NOTE

Soon we shall leave.
We shall **soon** leave.
We shall leave **soon**.

sore /sɔː*/ adjective
hurting, giving pain
- I've fallen off my bike. My leg's very **sore**.

sorry /ˈsɒrɪ/ adjective

1. You can say **sorry** when you wish you hadn't done something.
   - "Could you be quiet? I'm trying to study." "I'm very **sorry**."

2. Sometimes you say **sorry** when you cannot do (or don't want to do) what someone wants.
   - "Let's go to the cinema tomorrow evening." "I'm **sorry**. I'm meeting Nadia tomorrow."

3. sad (for someone)
   - I feel very **sorry** for Ted. He's failed again.

LANGUAGE NOTE

be sorry **to do** something
be sorry **for doing** something
be sorry **that** you have done something
feel/be sorry **for** someone

sort /sɔːt/ noun (countable)
kind of person or thing, belonging to a certain group
- What **sort** of music do you enjoy?

See also **kind** [1]; see also **type** [1].

θ	ð	ʃ	dʒ	tʃ	ŋ	ʒ	iː	ɜː	ɪ	æ	ʌ	ɒ
thing	that	shop	jump	chop	sing	measure	been	bird	bit	cat	but	not

sound¹ /saʊnd/ noun (countable)
something which you can hear
- *The **sound** of a child crying woke me.*
- make/hear a sound; a beautiful/sweet/sad/sharp/tiny/welcome sound

sound² verb
1 seem when you hear something
- *Your cough **sounds** just as bad as it **sounded** yesterday.*
2 make a sound
- *The bell's **sounded** for the end of the lesson.*
3 **sound as if/though** = seem
- *From what you say, it **sounds as if** you enjoyed yourself very much.*
4 **sound like** = seem
- *That **sounds like** a very good thing to do.*

soup /suːp/ noun (uncountable)
a liquid food which is made from boiling vegetables, meat or fish in water
- *Could I have some more **soup**, please?*
- eat/make soup; chicken/tomato/vegetable soup, etc

sour /ˈsaʊə*/ adjective
a kind of sharp taste like a lemon, not sweet
- *Put sugar on the fruit: it's very **sour**.*

south¹ /saʊθ/ noun (singular with the)
1 the part of a country, etc which is on your right if you look at the place where the sun rises, the direction down from the centre of the earth on a map
- *Mr and Mrs Law live in the **south** of England.*

LANGUAGE NOTE
You can also use a capital **S**.
He comes from **the South**.

south² adjective
the part of a country, a building, a place, etc which is on your right if you look at the place where the sun rises
- *The **south** side of the flat is hot in summer.*

south³ adverb
towards your right if you look at the place where the sun rises
- *You travel **south** to go from Norway to Egypt.*

southern, Southern /ˈsʌðən/ adjective
in or from the south part of a country
- *Seville is in **southern** Spain.*

souvenir /ˌsuːvəˈnɪə*/ noun (countable)
something which you buy to remember a holiday or visit somewhere
- *This shop sells very nice **souvenirs** of Rome.*

sow /səʊ/ verb
sowing, sowed, has sown /səʊn/ or has sowed
throw seeds on the ground, plant seeds
- *The farmer has just **sown** some seeds in the field.*

space /speɪs/ noun
1 (countable) an empty place

- *I kept two **spaces** in the theatre for my friends.*
- a big/large/small/ blank/empty/wide/narrow/open space
2 (uncountable) an empty area in a place
- *Is there enough **space** for me to park my car?*
3 (uncountable) the area around all the stars
- *The first rocket was sent into **space** over thirty years ago.*
- space-age (= very modern), spacecraft, spaceship, space station

spade /speɪd/ noun (countable)
something which you use for digging in the ground
- *Use this **spade** to dig a hole.*

spat /spæt/ verb
past tense and past participle of **spit**
- *He looked at his old enemy and **spat** at him.*

θ	ð	ʃ	dʒ	tʃ	ŋ	ʒ	iː	ɜː	ɪ	æ	ʌ	ɒ
thing	that	shop	jump	chop	sing	measure	been	bird	bit	cat	but	not

speak /spiːk/ verb

speaking, spoke /spəʊk/, has spoken /ˈspəʊkən/

1 talk, say words
- *Anne was so frightened that she couldn't **speak**.*
- speak quickly/slowly/loudly/softly/quietly/clearly/correctly/speak freely (= say whatever you want to say), speak openly (= not keep any secrets, etc)

LANGUAGE NOTE

speak *about* someone/something
speak *of* someone/something (less common)
speak *to* someone
speak *with* someone (less common in British English but common in American English)

---

2 use a language
- *Can you **speak** Arabic?*

See also **say**; see also **talk** 2; see also **tell**.

special /ˈspeʃl/ adjective

different, not ordinary, not usual, important
- *Tomorrow is a **special** day. It's your birthday!*

speech /spiːtʃ/ noun (countable)

plural: speeches

a talk to a group of people
- *The headmaster gave a long **speech** at the opening of the new library.*
- give/make a speech; a boring/interesting/good/excellent/important/long/short/simple speech, a moving speech (= a speech which makes you feel very sad, very angry, etc), a simple speech

speed /spiːd/ noun (countable)

how fast or how slowly something or someone moves
- *"At what **speed** is the train travelling now?" "I think it's doing over 150 kph."*
- drive/go/travel at a certain speed, keep to a certain speed; at great/high speed

spell /spel/ verb

spelling, spelt /spelt/ or spelled, has spelt or has spelled

put the correct letters together to form words
- *"How do you **spell** the word we use to talk about the floors in a block of flats?" "S-T-O-R-E-Y-S: storeys, of course."*

spelling /ˈspelɪŋ/ noun

1 (uncountable) putting the correct letters together to form words, the ability to put correct letters together to form words
- *Henry isn't much good at **spelling**.*
2 (countable) the way letters are put together to form a word
- *Is the British **spelling** of "colour" different from the American **spelling**?*

spend /spend/ verb

spending, spent /spent/, has spent

1 use money, pay money
- *Have you **spent** all the money I gave you?*
2 use time, pass time
- *"How did you **spend** the weekend?" "I **spent** all weekend at the beach."*

LANGUAGE NOTE

1 spend money *on* (doing) something
  spend time doing something
2 ***spend*** time doing something = enjoy or use the time
  pass time doing something = do something to make the time go by (ie better than doing nothing)

---

spider /ˈspaɪdə*/ noun (countable)

See box on page 114.

spill /spɪl/ verb

spilling, spilt /spɪlt/ or spilled, has spilt or has spilled

let liquid fall by accident
- *"I'm afraid I've **spilt** some tea on the carpet."*

spinach /ˈspɪnɪdʒ/ noun (countable)

See box on page 238.

θ	ð	ʃ	dʒ	tʃ	ŋ	ʒ	iː	ɜː	ɪ	æ	ʌ	ɒ
thing	that	shop	jump	chop	sing	measure	been	bird	bit	cat	but	not

spit /spɪt/ verb
spitting, spat /spæt/, has spat
(American English: also spit, has spit)
throw water or food out of your mouth
- *The woman was so angry she **spat** at me.*

splash¹ /splæʃ/ noun (countable)
plural: splashes
the noise which is made when something hits some water or when some water falls somewhere
- *There was a loud **splash** as he fell into the sea.*

splash² verb
throw water or (any liquid), move or hit water
- *The sea **splashed** against the rocks.*

spoil /spɔɪl/ verb
spoiling, spoilt /spɔɪlt/ or spoiled, has spoilt or has spoiled
make something useless or unsatisfactory
- *I used red paint on my painting and **spoilt** it.*

spoke /spəʊk/ verb
past tense of **speak**
- *The old man **spoke** about his youth.*

spoken /ˈspəʊkən/ verb
past participle of **speak**
- *Has anyone **spoken** to Joe about the party?*

spoon /spuːn/ noun (countable)
something we use for eating food and drinking liquid as well as for moving food and putting it on plates
- *Here's a **spoon** for your medicine.*
- a dessert/soup spoon, a tablespoon, a teaspoon

spoonful /ˈspuːnfʊl/ noun (countable)
the amount which a spoon can hold
- *Take two **spoonfuls** of medicine twice a day.*

sport /spɔːt/ noun (countable, uncountable)
the games you play and the things you do for exercise
- *Swimming is a very healthy **sport**.*
- an exciting sport

LANGUAGE NOTE

sports = (1) kinds of sports: eg tennis, football, etc
Our favourite sports are running and basketball.
(2) a meeting where people run, jump, etc
When is your school sports day?

See also **game**; see also **match** ².

spot /spɒt/ noun (countable)
1 a small round mark on something
- *Vincent had some **spots** on his face and went to the doctor's.*
2 a place
- *We had our picnic at a **spot** near the river.*

spread /spred/ verb
spreading, spread, has spread
1 cover thinly
- *He used a knife to **spread** butter on the bread.*
2 go out or move over a wide area
- *Maria soon **spread** the news that her sister was going to university.*

spring¹ /sprɪŋ/ noun (countable)
1 a piece of metal which is turned round and round, and which will jump back into place after you pull or push it
- *The watch won't work because the **spring** inside it has broken.*
2 a season
See box on page 57.

spring² verb
springing, sprang /spræŋ/, has sprung /sprʌŋ/
(American English: also sprung)
suddenly move or jump
- *The tiger **sprang** on the small animal.*

square¹ /skweə*/ noun (countable)
1 a shape with four sides of equal length
- *Write YES or NO in the small **square**.*
See also **shape**.
2 an open place in a town or city (often in the shape of a square)
- *There is a market today in the city **square**.*

θ	ð	ʃ	dʒ	tʃ	ŋ	ʒ	iː	ɜː	ɪ	æ	ʌ	ɒ
thing	that	shop	jump	chop	sing	measure	been	bird	bit	cat	but	not

square [2]   *adjective*
1 in the shape of a square
   • *The post office is a* **square** *building next to the railway station.*
2 the measurement of an area which is square in shape
   • *The forest is fifty kilometres* **square**.

squeeze   /skwiːz/   *verb*
squeezing, squeezed, has squeezed
hold or press tightly
   • *Don't* **squeeze** *my arm. It hurts!*

staff   /stɑːf/   *noun (uncountable)*
the people who work for a school, a hospital, a business, a factory, etc
   • *All the* **staff** *were at the meeting with the pupils' parents.*
   ⟳ hospital/office/teaching staff

LANGUAGE NOTE	
the staff of a school	NEVER the staffs of a school
a member of staff	NEVER a staff

stair   /steə*/   *noun (countable, usually plural)*
a set of steps from one floor to another in a building
   • *He soon gets tired if he has to climb up the* **stairs** *to his flat on the third floor.*
   ⟳ come/go up/down the stairs, climb (up/down) the stairs

stall   /stɔːl/   *noun (countable)*
a small, open shop in a street or market
   • *Old Mr Lee has a fruit* **stall** *in the market.*

stamp [1]   /stæmp/   *noun (countable)*
a small piece of paper which we stick on an envelope before we post it
   • *Put an 80-cent* **stamp** *on this envelope if you want to send it by air to Britain.*
   ⟳ put/stick a stamp on (an envelope, a letter, a parcel)

stamp [2]   *verb*
When you stamp your foot, you put it down very hard.
   • *Simon was very angry and* **stamped** *up the stairs.*

---

starve   211

stand   /stænd/   *verb*
standing, stood /stʊd/, has stood
1 have your legs and body straight and both feet on the ground

   • *All the seats on the bus were taken, and so I had to* **stand**.
2 **stand (up)** = get up on your feet after sitting or lying down
   • *Everyone* **stood (up)** *when Linda came in.*

star   /stɑː*/   *noun (countable)*
1 a bright light which you can see in the sky when it is dark
   • *Look at all those* **stars** *in the sky.*
   ⟳ a bright star
2 a shape
   • *The teacher gave Lina a* **star** *for her maths.*
3 **(film) star** = a famous actor or actress in a film
   • *She wants to be a* **(film) star**.

starfruit   /'stɑː fruːt/   *noun (countable)*
   ⚠ See box on page 89.

start   /stɑːt/   *verb*
begin, do something which you were not doing before
   • *We* **started** *to play football when Tim came.*
   ⚠ See also **begin**.

starve   /stɑːv/   *verb*
starving, starved, has starved
not have enough food (and sometimes die)
   • *Thousands of people in Africa will* **starve** *to death unless they receive food very quickly.*

θ	ð	ʃ	dʒ	tʃ	ŋ	ʒ	iː	ɜː	ɪ	æ	ʌ	ɒ
thing	that	shop	jump	chop	sing	measure	been	bird	bit	cat	but	not

station /ˈsteɪʃn/ noun (countable)
1 the place where you catch a bus or train
 • *Let's meet at the railway **station** at 1.10 pm.*
☞ bus station, railway station
2 a building where policemen or firemen work
 • *I had to go to the police **station** to tell them that my bag had been stolen.*
☞ fire station, police station

stay /steɪ/ verb
staying, stayed, has stayed
1 continue to be in a place, not go away
 • *We **stayed** at home because it was raining.*
2 live for a short time (with someone)
 • *I **stayed** with my uncle and aunt when I visited Singapore.*

steak /steɪk/ noun (countable)
a thick piece of meat or fish
 • *I'd like a large **steak**, please.*

steal /stiːl/ verb
stealing, stole /stəʊl/, has stolen /ˈstəʊlən/
take something which is not yours
 • *A man was jailed for **stealing** a watch from this shop.*
⚠ See also **rob**.

steam /stiːm/ noun (uncountable)
hot gas which rises from boiling water
 • *The **steam** from the kettle has made the wall wet.*

steep /stiːp/ adjective
with a big slope (which may be difficult to go up or down)
 • *I can't cycle up such a **steep** hill.*

step¹ /step/ noun (countable)
1 a single stair
 • *There were several **steps** into the garden.*
2 If you take a step, you move backwards or forwards when you walk.
 • *Susan took a short **step** back when she saw us.*

step² verb
stepping, stepped, has stepped
If you step on something, you put your foot on it. If you step forwards or backwards, you put one foot in front of or behind the other
 • *Be careful! You've just **stepped** on my foot.*

stick¹ /stɪk/ noun (countable)
1 a thin piece of wood
 • *Paul picked up some **sticks** and lit a fire.*
2 a thin, round piece of wood to help you walk.
 • *Old Ned can't walk without his (walking) **stick**.*
☞ a hockey/walking stick

stick² verb
sticking, stuck /stʌk/, has stuck
1 join together using glue, etc
 • *Can you **stick** the handle back on the cup?*
2 push (in)
 • *The nurse **stuck** a needle in my arm.*
3 be unable to move
 • *The car was **stuck** in the mud, and so we had to walk home.*
4 not know what to do, be unable to do something
 • *I couldn't do my maths homework. I was **stuck**.*

still /stɪl/ adverb
1 up till now, up to that time

LANGUAGE NOTE	
NEVER	~~The students still are writing.~~
ALWAYS	The students are still writing.

 • *Leila isn't ready yet. She's **still** in bed.*
2 **be still, keep still, stay still** = not move
 • *Please **keep still** while your hair is being cut.*

stir /stɜː*/ verb
stirring, stirred, has stirred
move round and round with a spoon, stick, etc
 • *Put some sugar in your tea and **stir** it.*

stocking /ˈstɒkɪŋ/ noun (countable)
a piece of clothing which you can wear over your feet and legs
 • *There was a small hole in Emma's **stockings**.*
☞ a pair of stockings

θ	ð	ʃ	dʒ	tʃ	ŋ	ʒ	iː	ɜː	ɪ	æ	ʌ	ɒ
thing	that	shop	jump	chop	sing	measure	been	bird	bit	cat	but	not

stole /stəʊl/ verb
past tense of **steal**
- *The thieves stole a TV set from the shop.*

stolen /ˈstəʊlən/ verb
past participle of **steal**
- *My television set's just been stolen.*

stomach /ˈstʌmək/ noun (countable)
the part of your body where food goes after you swallow it
- *Dave must have a very big stomach: he can eat enough food for ten people!*

See also box on page 26.

stomachache /ˈstʌmək eɪk/
noun (uncountable, countable)
(American English: a stomachache)
a pain in your stomach
- *Oh dear. I've got (a) bad stomachache after eating those apples. I don't think they were ripe.*

See also **ache** [1].

stone /stəʊn/ noun
1 (uncountable) something hard which is found in the ground and used for building houses, walls, bridges, etc
- *A lot of houses in Britain are built of stone – in Canada they are built of wood.*
2 (countable) a small piece of rock
- *There were a few small stones in the garden.*

stood /stʊd/ verb
past tense and past participle of **stand**
- *He stood (up) as we came in.*

stop [1] /stɒp/ noun (countable)
1 a place where you can get on or off a bus
- *We should get off the bus at the next stop.*
2 the moment when something no longer moves
- *The train came to a sudden stop.*

a brief/smooth/sudden stop

stop [2] verb
stopping, stopped, has stopped
1 finish
- *Stop being so noisy. I'm trying to sleep.*

2 not move
- *She suddenly stopped as if she'd seen something.*

LANGUAGE NOTE

COMPARE stop **to do** something
= stop moving or finish doing something in order to do something else
I stopped (writing) **to talk** to Anna.

WITH stop **doing** something
= finish doing something
I stopped **talking** to Anna and began to write a letter.

---

store [1] /stɔː*/ noun (countable)
a shop
- *The village has a very big store.*

See also **department store**; see also **shop**.

store [2] verb
storing, stored, has stored
keep (usually to use later)
- *When we moved into a smaller flat, we had to store some of our furniture at Mr Lee's house.*

storeroom

stories /ˈstɔːrɪz/ noun (countable)
plural of **story**
- *Do you like love stories or adventure stories?*

storm /stɔːm/ noun (countable)
very bad weather with strong winds and a lot of rain
- *Several small boats sank during the storm.*

story /ˈstɔːrɪ/ noun (countable)
plural: stories
a description of things which have happened or which you imagine have happened
- *Have you read the story about Oliver Twist?*

make up/read/tell (someone)/write a story; a children's/detective/fairy/funny/ghost/long/love/short/true story

straight /streɪt/ adjective, adverb
1 neither bent nor round in any way
- *Rule a straight line from A to B.*
2 by the shortest way
- *Come straight home after school.*

θ	ð	ʃ	dʒ	tʃ	ŋ	ʒ	iː	ɜː	ɪ	æ	ʌ	ɒ
thing	that	shop	jump	chop	sing	measure	been	bird	bit	cat	but	not

strange /streɪndʒ/ adjective
1 something or someone you have not seen before
  • There was a **strange** man at the door.
2 odd, unusual
  • You say that Alice didn't speak to you. That was very **strange**, wasn't it?

stranger /ˈstreɪndʒə*/ noun (countable)
1 someone you have not seen before
  • A **stranger** stopped me in the street.
  a complete/perfect stranger
2 You are a stranger when you are in a place to which you haven't been before.
  • "Can you tell me where the city hall is?" "I'm sorry. I'm also a **stranger** here."

strawberry /ˈstrɔːbərɪ/ noun (countable)
plural: strawberries
⚠ See box on page 89.

stream /striːm/ noun (countable)
a small, narrow river
  • Can you jump across the **stream**?

street /striːt/ noun (countable)
a road in a village, town, or city (usually with shops or houses along it)
  • There are a lot of good shops in this **street**.

LANGUAGE NOTE

A street is usually in a city, town or village. There are often houses and shops on each side. A road can also be in a city, town or village. However, a road (NOT a street) often goes from one city, town or village to another.
NEVER   This street goes from Milan to Rome.
ALWAYS   This **road** goes from Milan to Rome.
Note that the names of some streets in Britain use the word **road**: eg 21, Dover Road.

✥ cross the street; a back street; a busy/crowded street, a high street (British English), a main street (American English), a narrow/wide/quiet street; street names/numbers
⚠ See also **road**.

streetcar /ˈstriːtkɑ*/ noun (countable)
(American English)
⚠ See **tram**.

string /strɪŋ/ noun (uncountable, countable)
very thin rope (made by twisting threads round one another)

  • The man was holding some balloons on **strings**.
✥ a piece of string

strong /strɒŋ/ adjective
1 able to move heavy things
  • I'm not **strong** enough to lift this sofa all by myself.
2 not easily broken
  • You won't break the chair. It's very **strong**.

student /ˈstjuːdnt/ noun (countable)
someone who learns things in a school, college or university
  • My brother is a **student** at Leeds University.
✥ a good/excellent/poor/bad/weak student; a full-time/part-time student

---
LANGUAGE NOTE

student = anyone studying in a college or university
pupil = anyone studying in a school

Note that in British English the word **student** can also be used for younger people in schools.
In American English **student** is USUALLY used for younger people in schools. However, you should use **pupil** in British English for anyone studying in a primary school.

θ	ð	ʃ	dʒ	tʃ	ŋ	ʒ	iː	ɜː	ɪ	æ	ʌ	ɒ
thing	that	shop	jump	chop	sing	measure	been	bird	bit	cat	but	not

study /ˈstʌdɪ/ verb
studying, studied, has studied
learn about things by reading
- *I want to **study** Geography at university.*
↻ **study** hard

stupid /ˈstjuːpɪd/ adjective
not clever, foolish
- *Don't be **stupid**. You can't go out in your pyjamas.*

subject /ˈsʌbdʒɪkt/ noun (countable)
something which you study at school: eg History, Geography, English, Science, Maths
- *Physics is my favourite **subject**.*
⚠ See also box on page 192.

subtract /səbˈtrækt/ verb
take away one number from another
- *If you **subtract** 5 from 22, you get 17.*

subway /ˈsʌbweɪ/ noun (countable)
(American English)
⚠ See **underground**.

succeed /səkˈsiːd/ verb
manage to do
- *I hope you'll **succeed** in climbing to the top.*

LANGUAGE NOTE	
NEVER	succeed *to* do something
ALWAYS	succeed *in* doing something
OR	succeed *at* something

success /səkˈses/ noun
1 (uncountable) a good result, doing well
   - *I wish you **success** at university.*
2 (countable) someone who has done well
   - *Helen Garton is a great **success** as an actress.*
3 (countable) something which has done well
   - *Mr Shaw's new business was a big **success**.*

successful /səkˈsesfl/ adjective
having done well, having managed to do what you tried to do
- *Barbara was very **successful** in her career.*
↻ highly / very / quite successful

successfully /səkˈsesfəlɪ/ adverb
well and with good results
- *Pat is running her business very **successfully**.*

such /sʌtʃ/ determiner, predeterminer; pronoun
1 of this kind (You can use **such** to show the person or thing which you have just talked about.)
   - *I like gold rings and beautiful dresses but my husband says **such** things cost too much.*
2 You can use **such** and **that** when you want to talk or write about the result of something.
   - *She's **such** a nice girl **that** everyone likes her.*

LANGUAGE NOTE	
NEVER	a such good man
ALWAYS	such *a* good man

⚠ See also **that**³ 2.

3 You can use **such** to show how big, how fat, how nice, how good, etc someone or something is.
   - *You ate **such** a big meal? You'll be ill.*
⚠ See also **so**¹ 1. (Language Notes)

4 **such as** = for example
   - *There were lots of different animals in the zoo, **such as** kangaroos, giraffes and tigers.*

suck /sʌk/ verb
hold something in or with your mouth and try to get liquid from it
- *The baby was **sucking** milk from a bottle.*

sudden /ˈsʌdn/ adjective
something which happens quickly and which you don't expect
- *We were walking home when there was a **sudden** cry for help.*

suddenly /ˈsʌdnlɪ/ adverb
happening quickly and not expected
- *A dog **suddenly** ran in front of our car.*

sugar /ˈʃʊgə*/ noun (uncountable)
something sweet which you can put on food or in tea and coffee
- *Do you have **sugar** in your tea?*

θ	ð	ʃ	dʒ	tʃ	ŋ	ʒ	iː	ɜː	ɪ	æ	ʌ	ɒ
thing	that	shop	jump	chop	sing	measure	been	bird	bit	cat	but	not

suggest /sə'dʒest/ verb
say what you think it is good to do, talk about an idea or a plan for someone to think about
- I **suggest** we take an umbrella. It may rain.

LANGUAGE NOTE

1. Where do you suggest *going* tonight?
   NEVER ~~suggest to do something~~
   ALWAYS suggest *doing* something
2. Where do you suggest (that) *we go* tonight?
3. Where do you suggest (that) *we should go* tonight?

---

suggestion /sə'dʒestʃən/ noun (countable)
an idea or plan for someone to think about
- What should we do now? Have you got any **suggestions**?
- ask for suggestions, make/offer a suggestion; a good/bad/foolish/wise/helpful/useful/kind suggestion

suit /suːt/ noun (countable)
a jacket and trousers
- Peter wore a new **suit** for the interview.
- put a suit on, take your suit off, wear a suit

suitable /'suːtəbl/ adjective
right for a certain purpose
- Is this film **suitable** for young children?

sum /sʌm/ noun (countable)
1. something we do when we add, multiply, subtract and divide numbers
   - Could you do all the **sums** for homework?
2. an amount of money
   - A hundred dollars is a large **sum** to spend on a pen!
- a large/small sum

summer /'sʌmə*/ noun (countable, uncountable)
See box on page 57.

sun /sʌn/ noun (singular with the)
the ball of fire in the sky during the day. The Earth goes round the sun.
- The **sun** is shining and the sky is blue.
- the sun comes out/goes in/shines/comes up/rises/goes down/sets; a/the bright sun, a/the hot/strong/warm sun, a/the red sun; sunlight, sunrise, sunset, sunshine

sung /sʌŋ/ verb
past participle of **sing**
- Have you ever **sung** these songs before?

sunk /sʌŋk/ verb
past participle of **sink**
- The old car has **sunk** to the bottom of the lake.

sunny /'sʌnɪ/ adjective
sunnier, sunniest
with a lot of sun, when the sun is shining brightly
- It was cloudy earlier, but now it's very **sunny**.

supermarket /'suːpəˌmɑːkɪt/ noun (countable)
a large shop where you can buy all kinds of food
- Mary does all her shopping in the **supermarket**.

supper /'sʌpə*/ noun (countable)
the last meal or snack of the day
- What would you like for **supper** tonight?
- eat/have supper, make supper

sure /ʃʊə*/ adjective
1. certain, without any doubt
   - Are you **sure** that Ann was at the meeting?
2. **Sure!** = OK, Yes
   - "Can I borrow your pen, please?" "**Sure!**"
3. **make sure** = do something to be certain
   - I'll phone Alice to **make sure** she's alright.

surprise¹ /sə'praɪz/ noun
1. (uncountable) the way you feel about something which you didn't expect
   - Imagine my **surprise** when I found out I had passed the exam.
- show surprise
2. (countable) something which you didn't expect
   - We're going to have a party for Sarah. Don't tell her because it's a **surprise**.
- a big/great/complete/total/pleasant/unpleasant/nice surprise

surprise [2] verb

surprising, surprised, has surprised

do something which someone doesn't know about or doesn't expect
- *Lesley **surprised** everyone by winning the competition.*

☞ very / greatly surprised

surprising /səˈpraɪzɪŋ/ adjective

not expected, giving someone a surprise
- *My exam result was very **surprising**: I never thought I would pass.*

swallow /ˈswɒləʊ/ verb

make food or liquid go down your throat
- *Andrew **swallowed** his food too quickly and began to cough.*

swam /swæm/ verb

past tense of **swim**
- *I **swam** for an hour in the sea yesterday.*

sweat [1] /swet/ noun (uncountable)

drops of water which come from your skin when you are hot or frightened
- *I wiped the **sweat** off my face before I entered.*

sweat [2] verb

give off drops of water on your skin when you are hot or frightened
- *He **sweated** a lot while he was digging.*

sweater /ˈswetə*/ noun (countable)

something warm which you can wear over the top part of your body
- *I like your new **sweater**. Who made it for you?*

sweep /swiːp/ verb

sweeping, swept /swept/, has swept

push dirt with a brush
- *Use this brush to **sweep** the carpet.*

sweet [1] /swiːt/ noun (countable)

1 a small piece of food (eg chocolate) which is made out of sugar and other things (American English: candy)
- *Too many **sweets** are bad for your teeth.*

2 food with sugar in it which you can eat at the end of a meal
- *I think I'll have a **sweet**. Do you have any ice cream?*

sweet [2] adjective

1 with the taste of sugar
- *This cup of tea is too **sweet**. You've put too much sugar in it.*

2 nice, pleasant
- *What a **sweet** smell these roses have!*

sweetcorn /ˈswiːtkɔːn/ noun (countable)

⚠ See box on page 238.

swept /swept/ verb

past tense and past participle of **sweep**
- *I **swept** the floor this morning.*

swim [1] /swɪm/ noun (countable)

the activity or the time when you move through water by using your arms and legs
- *Would you like to go for a **swim** this afternoon?*

☞ go / have / take a swim

swim [2] verb

swimming, swam /swæm/, has swum /swʌm/

move through water by using your arms and legs
- *"Can you **swim**?" "Yes, I **swam** 500 metres yesterday."*

swimmer /ˈswɪmə*/ noun (countable)

someone who moves through water by using their arms and legs
- *Are you a good **swimmer**?*

swimming /ˈswɪmɪŋ/ noun (uncountable)

moving through water by using your arms and legs
- *My favourite sport is **swimming**.*

☞ swimming bath(s) / costume / pool / trunks

swimming pool /ˈswɪmɪŋ ˌpuːl/
noun (countable)

⚠ See **pool** 2.

θ	ð	ʃ	dʒ	tʃ	ŋ	ʒ	iː	ɜː	ɪ	æ	ʌ	ɒ
thing	that	shop	jump	chop	sing	measure	been	bird	bit	cat	but	not

swing /swɪŋ/ verb
swinging, swung /swʌŋ/, has swung
move forwards and/or backwards or from side to side
- *The door **swung** slowly open.*

switch /swɪtʃ/ noun (countable)
plural: switches
something which you press to make a machine, a radio, etc stop or start
- *We can't turn the light on: the **switch** is broken.*
↻ press a switch, turn off/on a switch

switch off /ˌswɪtʃ ˈɒf/ phrasal verb
make a machine, an engine, a TV, etc stop by pressing a switch
- *Stop the car and **switch off** the engine.*

switch on /ˌswɪtʃ ˈɒn/ phrasal verb
make a machine, an engine, a TV, etc start by pressing a switch
- *Will you **switch** the radio **on**, please?*

sword /sɔːd/ noun (countable)
something sharp which is like a very long knife
- *The soldiers were fighting with **swords**.*

swum /swʌm/ verb
past participle of **swim**
- *Lesley's already **swum** across this river!*

swung /swʌŋ/ verb
past tense and past participle of **swing**
- *I sat on the wall and **swung** my legs.*

syllable /ˈsɪləbl/ noun (countable)
a group of letters with a vowel sound in a word
- *The word today has two **syllables**: to is one **syllable** and day is the other **syllable**.*

Tt

table /ˈteɪbl/ noun (countable)
1 a piece of furniture with a flat top on which you can put things
- *The meal is ready: I'm putting it on the **table**.*
↻ lay/set the table
2 a group of words or numbers in rows
- *The book has interesting **tables** showing the number of people without homes.*

tablespoon /ˈteɪblspuːn/ noun (countable)
⚠ See **spoon**.

table tennis /ˈteɪbl ˌtenɪs/ noun (uncountable)
a game you can play by hitting a small, light ball over a low net on a table (also called ping pong)

- *Betty and I often play **table tennis** after school.*

tablet /ˈtæblɪt/ noun (countable)
a small, hard piece of medicine
- *Dr Short gave me these **tablets** for my sore throat.*
↻ swallow/take a tablet

tail /teɪl/ noun (countable)
the long thin part at the back of an animal's body or a bird's body
- *The small dog wagged its **tail** happily.*

θ	ð	ʃ	dʒ	tʃ	ŋ	ʒ	iː	ɜː	ɪ	æ	ʌ	ɒ
thing	that	shop	jump	chop	sing	measure	been	bird	bit	cat	but	not

tailor /ˈteɪlə*/ noun (countable)
a person who makes clothes
• *I went to the **tailor's** to have a new suit made.*

take /teɪk/ verb
taking, took /tʊk/, has taken /ˈteɪkən/
1 carry, hold
   • *Can you **take** this bread to your aunt?*
   ⚠ See also **bring**.
2 have
   • ***Take** your medicine before you go to bed.*
   ↻ take a bath/chair/seat, take a dislike to someone/something, take a meal, take some medicine, take notes, take a rest
3 pick, choose
   • ***Take** what you want.*
4 need (time)
   • *She **took** a long time to find my book.*

LANGUAGE NOTE
You can often use **it** with **take**.
***It** takes a long time to write a book.*
***It** took us more than an hour to finish.*

5 get on or in
   • *Let's **take** a taxi home.*
   ↻ take a bus/plane/train/tram/taxi
6 show someone the way, lead
   • *Mr Lee promised to **take** me out.*
7 carry something away without telling anyone, steal
   • *Who has **taken** my book?*
8 **take away** = subtract
   • ***Take** 3 **away** from 10.*
9 **take care** = be careful
   • ***Take care** when you cross the road.*
10 **take down** = write down
   • *Will you **take down** a message for Linda?*
11 **take off** = leave the ground
   • *Look! There's a plane **taking off**!*
12 **take part (in)** = work or play with other people (in something)
   • *Are you **taking part** in the school play?*

talk¹ /tɔːk/ noun (countable)
1 a conversation what you say to people, words which you speak
   • *Tina and I had a long **talk** about Harry.*
   ↻ have a talk (with someone)
2 a kind of speech
   • *I went to an interesting **talk** about Australia last night.*
   ↻ give a talk (to a lot of people)

talk² verb
say something (to someone)
• *My brother can't **talk**. He's only one.*

LANGUAGE NOTES
1 The verb **talk** often means **have a conversation**.
   We **talked** about our old school.
2 talk to someone **about** someone/something
   He talked **to** us **about** the accident.
3 talk **to** or **with** someone (American English only)

↻ talk freely (= say whatever you want to say), talk loudly/softly/quietly/quickly/slowly, talk openly (= not keep any secrets, etc)
⚠ See also **say**; see also **speak**; see also **tell**.

tall /tɔːl/ adjective
high, not short
• *Mr Kenning's so **tall** that he has to bend down to get through the door.*
⚠ See also **high** ¹ 1.

tame /teɪm/ adjective
tamer, tamest
not wild, not afraid of people and not wanting to hurt them (used about animals)
• *Don't worry. This lion is very **tame**.*

tap /tæp/ noun (countable)
1 the noise which you make when you hit something gently
   • *I heard a **tap** at the door. It was Alex.*
2 something to let water out of a pipe (into a sink or bath)

• *Harry forgot he'd left the **tap** on, and there was water everywhere.*

θ	ð	ʃ	dʒ	tʃ	ŋ	ʒ	iː	ɜː	ɪ	æ	ʌ	ɒ
thing	that	shop	jump	chop	sing	measure	been	bird	bit	cat	but	not

tape /teɪp/ noun (countable)
1. a narrow piece of cloth, paper, etc
   - *Would you tie this **tape** round the parcel?*
2. something for recording sounds
   - *Play this **tape** on my new cassette player.*
   - play/wind/rewind a tape; a tape recorder

tape measure /'teɪp ˌmeʒə*/ noun (countable)
a narrow piece of cloth or plastic which you can use for measuring things
- *Use a **tape measure** to find out the width of the table.*

tape recorder /'teɪp rɪˌkɔːdə*/ noun (countable)
a machine for recording sounds and playing tapes
- *Let me record you singing on my **tape recorder**.*

taste[1] /teɪst/ noun (countable)
what food is like when you touch it with your tongue
- *This meat has a very salty **taste**.*
- a bad/good/sweet/sour taste; have no taste

taste[2] verb
tasting, tasted, has tasted
1. put a small amount of food in your mouth to see if it is nice
   - *Good cooks always **taste** their dishes first.*
2. give a certain feeling in your mouth
   - *My tea **tastes** very sweet.*

taught /tɔːt/ verb
past tense and past participle of **teach**
- *Ms Jones **taught** us French.*

taxi /'tæksɪ/ noun (countable)
plural: taxis
a car which you pay to ride in and which will take you where you want to go
- *I missed the bus to work, and so I got a **taxi**.*
- go by taxi, get/take a taxi (BUT NOT catch a taxi)

tea /tiː/ noun (uncountable)
1. a drink made from hot water and leaves, roots, flowers etc
   - *Would you like a cup of **tea**?*
   - drink/have/make tea; cold/hot/strong/weak tea; a cup of tea, a glass of tea
2. a small meal which people sometimes eat in the afternoon
   - *I'm going to my aunt's flat for **tea** today.*

teach /tiːtʃ/ verb
teaching, taught /tɔːt/, has taught
tell people things and help them to learn
- *Who is **teaching** Spiros to read?*

LANGUAGE NOTES

teach someone **to** drive
teach someone **how to** drive
teach someone a school subject (eg History)
teach someone **about** electricity

teacher /'tiːtʃə*/ noun (countable)
someone who teaches pupils, especially at a school or college
- *I want to be a **teacher** when I leave college.*

team /tiːm/ noun (countable)
a group of people who play on the same side in a game
- *Suleiman is the best player in our **team**.*
- a baseball/basketball/cricket/football/hockey/volleyball team

LANGUAGE NOTE

COMPARE Our team **is** winning.
AND   Our team **are** quarrelling among themselves.

When you are thinking of the team as ONE group, use **is**, **has**, etc after **team**. When you are thinking of the team as different people, use **are**, **have**, etc after **team**.

teapot /'tiːpɒt/ noun (countable)
something for making tea in and serving it
- *Put tea in the **teapot** and add boiling water.*

θ	ð	ʃ	dʒ	tʃ	ŋ	ʒ	iː	ɜː	ɪ	æ	ʌ	ɒ
thing	that	shop	jump	chop	sing	measure	been	bird	bit	cat	but	not

tear[1] /tɪə*/ noun (countable)
a drop of water which comes from your eye
- *She had **tears** in her eyes when she told me the sad news.*
↻ break/burst into tears, (your) eyes fill with tears; tears flow, tears roll down your cheeks

tear[2] /teə*/ verb
tearing, tore /tɔː*/, has torn /tɔːn/
When you **tear** paper or cloth, you pull it into two or more pieces.
- *Let me sew your jacket: you've **torn** it.*

tease /tiːz/ verb
teasing, teased, has teased
make fun of someone or something
- *Stop **teasing** your sister.*

teaspoon /ˈtiːspuːn/ noun (countable)
a small spoon
- *Stir your coffee with this **teaspoon**.*
△ See also **spoon**.

teaspoonful /ˈtiːspuːnfʊl/ noun (countable)
the amount of a liquid a teaspoon can hold
- *Take two **teaspoonfuls** of this medicine.*
△ See also **spoonful**.

teeth /tiːθ/ noun (countable)
plural of **tooth**
- *Janet's **teeth** are shining white.*

telephone[1] /ˈtelɪfəʊn/ noun (countable)
something you can use to talk to people a long way away: a phone
- *Tony's speaking to Marcel on the **telephone**.*
↻ answer a/the telephone, make a telephone call (to someone); a telephone rings
△ See also **phone**[1].

telephone[2] verb
telephoning, telephoned, has telephoned
use a telephone to speak to someone a long way away
- *Who **telephoned** you a moment ago?*
△ See also **phone**[2].

television /ˈtelɪˌvɪʒn/ noun
(short form: TV)
1 (countable) a box with a screen on which you can see pictures (= a television set)
- *Have you got a **television** in your flat?*
↻ put (the) television on, switch/turn (the) television off/on
2 (uncountable) the things which are shown on television
- *Do you enjoy watching **television**?*
↻ watch television

tell /tel/ verb
telling, told /təʊld/, has told
1 give (someone) information about something
- ***Tell** me what happened this morning.*
↻ tell a story, tell the truth
2 order or ask (someone) to do something
- *Who **told** you to switch on the television?*

LANGUAGE NOTE

Always use an object after ***tell***.
Leila told **us** that she was late for school.
"I'm late for school," Leila told **us**.

△ See also **say**; see also **speak**; see also **talk**[2].

temperature /ˈtemprətʃə*/ noun (countable)
1 The **temperature** of something is how hot or cold it is.
- *The **temperature** has fallen to freezing point.*
↻ the temperature drops/rises/goes down/up; (water boils/ice melts, etc at a certain temperature)
2 how hot or cold your body is
- *The nurse will take your **temperature** now.*
↻ take someone's temperature;
3 **have (got) a temperature** = have (got) a fever
- *You should stay in bed. You've **got a temperature**.*

temple /ˈtempl/ noun (countable)
a building where people pray to a god
- *Mrs Banerjee goes to the **temple** every day.*

tennis /ˈtenɪs/ noun (uncountable)
a game which two or four players can play by hitting a ball across a net
- *Fatima and I played **tennis** for an hour.*
- a tennis match, a game of tennis; a (tennis) court

tent /tent/ noun (countable)
something made of cloth or nylon which you can sleep in when you are camping

- *Can you help me take the **tent** down?*
- put up/take down/pitch a tent

term /tɜːm/ noun (countable)
part of a school year
- *There'll be an exam in the summer **term**.*
- the first/second/third/fourth term, etc, the autumn/spring/summer/winter term

terrible /ˈterəbl/ adjective
1 very serious and unpleasant
   - *I saw a **terrible** accident on my way to school.*
2 very bad, awful
   - *The food at our school was **terrible**.*

LANGUAGE NOTE
NEVER ~~very terrible~~

test¹ /test/ noun (countable)
1 a short examination
   - *We're going to have a Maths **test** on Friday.*
   - fail (in)/pass/get through/give/sit (for)/take a test; a difficult/easy/hard test
2 an experiment
   - *They've carried out some **tests** on the new car.*
   - carry out/fail/pass a test, put something through a test

test² verb
1 give a short examination
   - *The teacher is going to **test** the class now.*
2 use something to see that it is all right
   - *I **tested** several different kinds of bicycles.*
3 look at something carefully
   - *I had my eyes **tested** to see if I needed glasses.*

than /ðæn/ (unstressed /ðən/) preposition, conjunction
You can use **than** to compare two things.
- *This chair is more comfortable **than** the sofa.*

thank /θæŋk/ verb
You thank someone when you want to show how pleased you are for what they have done.
- *Please **thank** your father for helping me.*

thank you, /ˈθæŋk juː/ thanks /θæŋks/
what you say when you tell someone how pleased you are for what they have done
- ***Thank you** for inviting me to your party.*
- *"Here's the book you wanted." "**Thanks** a lot."*

that¹ /ðæt/ determiner, pronoun
1 (plural: those) the one over there
   - *"Is **that** your pen?" "No, this is my pen."*
2 You can use **that** for someone or something which you have already talked about or which you know about.
   - *"Paris is the capital of France, isn't it?" "**That's** right."*

that² /ðət/ relative pronoun
who, which
- *I enjoyed all the stories **that** he wrote.*

that³ /ðət/ conjunction
1 You can use **that** after verbs like say, know, show, etc.
   - *Who said **that** I was afraid of him?*
2 You can use **that** after **so** and **such** to show the result of something.
   - *The cupboard is so big **that** it won't go through the door.*
   - See also **so** ² 1; see also **such** ².

θ	ð	ʃ	dʒ	tʃ	ŋ	ʒ	iː	ɜː	ɪ	æ	ʌ	ɒ
thing	that	shop	jump	chop	sing	measure	been	bird	bit	cat	but	not

the /ðiː/ (unstressed /ðə, ðɪ/) definite article, determiner
1. After you have used **a** in front of a word, you use **the** when you say or write the word again.
   - *Suddenly I caught sight of a gun. **The** gun was pointing at me!*
2. Use **the** when you describe someone or something or say more about them.
   - *That's **the** person I told you about.*
3. You can use **the** when there is only one object (eg there is only one sun).
   - ***The** sun was shining brightly in **the** sky.*
4. Use **the** in front of words like biggest, best, most, etc.
   - *Tony is **the** oldest boy in the class.*
5. Use **the** in front of certain adjectives to show a group of people: **the** poor, **the** rich, **the** old, **the** young, **the** blind, **the** sick, etc.
   - *She's got a job helping **the** blind.*

LANGUAGE NOTES

1. Don't use **the** with a countable noun in the plural when it is used in a general sense.
   NEVER I like to read books about the stamps.
   ALWAYS I like to read books about stamps.
2. Don't use **the** with an uncountable noun when it is used in a general sense.
   NEVER Those shirts are made of the cotton.
   ALWAYS Those shirts are made of cotton.

⚠ See also **a**.

theatre /ˈθɪətə*/ noun (countable)
(American English: theater)
a place where you can go to see a play or a film
- *Let's go to the **theatre** to see the new play there.*
💲 a movie theatre (American English) (= a cinema)

their /ðeə*/ determiner
belonging to certain people, of them
- *Is that **their** new flat?*

theirs /ðeəz/ pronoun
belonging to certain people, belonging to them
- *Look at Tom and Jane. Is that car **theirs**?*

them /ðem/ (unstressed /ðəm/) pronoun
You can use **them** to show two or more people or things.
- *"I met Mr and Mrs Jameson last night." "What did you say to **them**?"*

themselves /ðəmˈselvz/ preposition, conjunction
1. You can use **themselves** as the object of a verb or preposition.
   - *Tom and Henry dried **themselves** as soon as they came out of the sea.*
2. You can use **themselves** to make the subject or object seem more important or to make the pronoun **they** stronger.
   - *The doctors drove the two ambulances **themselves**.*
3. without any help
   - *Did they paint the flat all by **themselves**?*
4. **by themselves** = without anyone else
   - *Ali and Rahim were in the house by **themselves**.*

then /ðen/ adverb
1. at a time in the past
   - *Mr and Mrs Wang were living in England **then**, but now they've returned to Taipei.*
2. at a time which you have just spoken about
   - *I can't play tennis this evening. I'll be at my uncle's **then**.*
3. next, after that
   - *Do your homework first and **then** watch TV.*

LANGUAGE NOTE

Use **and** before **then** to join two parts of sentences.
Have breakfast **and then** clean your teeth.

---

there[1] /ðeə*/ pronoun
You can use **there** before **is**, **are**, etc at the beginning of a group of words.
- ***There's** a cinema near my flat.*

there[2] adverb
in that place
- *"Where's Maria?" "She's (over) **there**."*

θ	ð	ʃ	dʒ	tʃ	ŋ	ʒ	iː	ɜː	ɪ	æ	ʌ	ɒ
thing	that	shop	jump	chop	sing	measure	been	bird	bit	cat	but	not

LANGUAGE NOTE

NEVER go to there   ALWAYS go there

therefore /ˈðeəfɔː*/   adverb

as a result, for this reason
- Mr Lee earns a lot of money and **therefore** he should help the poor.

thermometer /θəˈmɒmɪtə*/   noun (countable)

something which measures how hot or cold a place is or a person is

- Let me put this **thermometer** in your mouth to take your temperature.

these /ðiːz/   determiner, pronoun

singular: this

the ones here
- **These** apples are better than those.

they /ðeɪ/   pronoun

You can use **they** to talk about two or more people, animals, places, or things.
- "I saw Mr and Mrs Long yesterday."
  "Where were **they**?"

LANGUAGE NOTE

1 NEVER   They are a lot of cars in the street.
    ALWAYS   There are a lot of cars in the street.

2 You can also use **they** to mean **people in general**.
       They used to say the world was flat.
       They grow rubber trees in Malaysia.

See also **he** (Language Note); see also **there**[1].

they'd /ðeɪd/
1 they would
   - **They'd** help you if you asked them.
2 they had
   - They told me **they'd** lived in Mexico for five years.

they'll /ðeɪl/

they will
- **They'll** help us if we want them to.

they're /ðeə*/

they are
- "What are Mabel and Susan doing?"
  "**They're** playing table tennis."

they've /ðeɪv/

they have
- "Aren't Mr and Mrs Rosario at home?"
  "No, **they've** gone to London for a fortnight."

thick /θɪk/   adjective

1 not thin
   - These windows are made of **thick** glass which won't break.

LANGUAGE NOTE

Use **thin** for both people and things BUT usually use **fat** for people and **thick** for things.

Tom isn't **thin**: he's very **fat**.
This book isn't **thin**: it's very **thick**.

See also **fat**; see also **thin 2**.
2 We can use **thick** to talk about how wide or deep something is.
   - The walls of the castle are a metre **thick**.
   See also **thin 1**.
3 If a forest, hair, etc is **thick**, the trees, hairs, etc are very close together.
   - There's a **thick** forest near the village: you can easily get lost in it.
4 If fog or smoke is **thick**, it is difficult to see through it.
   - **Thick** smoke was coming out of the building.

θ	ð	ʃ	dʒ	tʃ	ŋ	ʒ	iː	ɜː	ɪ	æ	ʌ	ɒ
thing	that	shop	jump	chop	sing	measure	been	bird	bit	cat	but	not

thief /θiːf/ noun (countable)
plural: thieves /θiːvz/
someone who takes things which do not belong to them
- The **thief** who stole your watch has been caught.

See also **burglar**; see also **robber**.

thin /θɪn/ adjective
thinner, thinnest
1. only a small way between each of its two sides, not thick
   - This suit is made out of very **thin** cloth: it won't keep you warm in winter.

See also **thick 1** and **2**.

2. only a small way between each of a person's two sides, not fat
   - Sammy is very **thin**. He looks as if he hardly eats anything.

See also **fat**.

thing /θɪ/ noun (countable)
1. an object (not a plant nor a person nor an animal)
   - A watch, a ring, a pen and two or three other **things** were stolen.
2. You can use **thing** instead of another word or group of words when you have talked about it or when you are going to talk about it.
   - A terrible **thing** happened while I was on my way to college.

a bad/good/difficult/easy/nice/silly/strange/terrible thing; the right/wrong thing

---

LANGUAGE NOTE

Note the sentences:
It was **a** bad/silly/foolish thing to do.
I was **the** right/wrong/best thing to do.

---

3. **things** = what belongs to you
   - I've put your **things** in the spare room.

think /θɪŋk/ verb
thinking, thought /θɔːt/, has thought
1. use your mind to get ideas
   - I **thought** for a long time but couldn't decide what to buy Maria for her birthday.

think clearly, think hard

2. believe something is true (but not be sure)
   - I **think** Harry will come tonight.
3. **(can/can't) think of** = remember
   - I can't **think of** her name now, but I'll remember it later.

thirsty /ˈθɜːstɪ/ adjective
thirstier, thirstiest
You feel thirsty when you want a drink very much or when you haven't had a drink for a long time.
- Tina was so **thirsty** that she drank four cups of tea!

this /ðɪs/ determiner, pronoun
plural: these
the one here
- "Is **this** your book?" "No, that's my book over there." "Whose is **this** then?"

those /ðəʊz/ determiner, pronoun
singular: that
the ones over there
- These shoes are not mine but **those** are.

though /ðəʊ/ conjunction
yet, even so
- I was late for school (even) **though** I caught the early bus. It broke down on the way there.

See also **although**.

thread /θred/ noun (uncountable, countable)
a thin piece of cotton which you can use to sew things together
- Have you any black **thread** to mend my trousers?

threw /θruː/ verb
past tense of **throw**
- She **threw** the ball to me and ran away.

θ	ð	ʃ	dʒ	tʃ	ŋ	ʒ	iː	ɜː	ɪ	æ	ʌ	ɒ
thing	that	shop	jump	chop	sing	measure	been	bird	bit	cat	but	not

through /θruː/ preposition
1 from one end to the other, from one side to the other
- We have to go **through** this room to reach the bedrooms.
2 while, during a whole period of time
- I was so tired that I slept **through** the film.
3 by way of
- The burglar got in **through** an open window.

throw /θrəʊ/ verb
throwing, threw /θruː/, has thrown /θrəʊn/
make something move quickly through the air

- Don't **throw** stones: someone might get hurt.

thunder /ˈθʌndə*/ noun (uncountable)
the loud noise which you can hear in the sky during a storm
- The **thunder** was so loud that I thought the wall had fallen down.

thus /ðʌs/ adverb
for this reason, therefore, so
- It hasn't rained much this year. **Thus** the farmers are short of water for their fields.

tick[1] /tɪk/ noun (countable)
a mark (√) which a teacher puts against a right answer
- How many **ticks** have you got for this exercise?

tick[2] verb
make a mark against a right answer
- Will you **tick** all the sums which I've got right?

ticket /ˈtɪkɪt/ noun (countable)
a piece of paper which shows you have paid to travel somewhere or go to the cinema, a sports ground, etc
- Don't forget to bring the **tickets** for the concert.
↻ buy/get a ticket; a return ticket (= a ticket for a journey to a certain place and back), a single ticket (= a ticket for a journey to a certain place), a season ticket (= a ticket to travel every day to a certain place for a period of time: eg three months); airline/bus/train/tram/library ticket

tide /taɪd/ noun (countable)
the rising and falling of the sea twice a day
- You can't play on the beach yet: the **tide** is still in.
↻ full/high/low tide; the tide is in/out

tidy[1] /ˈtaɪdɪ/ verb
tidying, tidied, has tidied
put things away and in the right place
- Sam's mother made him **tidy** (up) his room.

tidy[2] adjective
tidier, tidiest
with things in the right place, neat
- Mrs Uchida told Yoko to put her toys away so that the room would look **tidy**.

tie[1] /taɪ/ noun (countable)
a narrow piece of cloth which men and boys sometimes wear round their necks
- What colour is your school **tie**?

tie[2] verb
tying, tied, has tied
fasten something with string, rope, a narrow piece of cloth, leather, etc
- Can you help me **tie** up this parcel?

tiger /ˈtaɪgə*/ noun (countable)
female: tigress /ˈtaɪgrɪs/
⚠ See box on page 10.

tight[1] /taɪt/ adjective
not loose, safely fastened, fitting closely,
- This string is very **tigh**t. I can't take it off.
- Tony is so fat that his trousers are too **tight**.

tight[2] adverb
tight/tightly = not loosely, closely
- Tie the string round the parcel as **tight** / **tightly** as you can.

θ	ð	ʃ	dʒ	tʃ	ŋ	ʒ	iː	ɜː	ɪ	æ	ʌ	ɒ
thing	that	shop	jump	chop	sing	measure	been	bird	bit	cat	but	not

tighten /ˈtaɪtn/ verb
become or make tight(er), make something fit closely, fasten something safely
- *Could you **tighten** these screws, please?*

tights /taɪts/ noun (plural)
Tights are like women's stockings but they cover the lower part of the body as well as the legs.
- *"Are you wearing **tights**?" "No, I'm wearing stockings."*

till /tɪl/ preposition, conjunction
⚠ See **until**.

time /taɪm/ noun
1 (uncountable) a certain point in the day
- *"What **time** is it?" "It's seven thirty." "Is that really the **time**? I must go."*
2 (uncountable, countable) a certain period
- *It's dinner **time**.*
- *A long **time** ago people lived in caves.*

LANGUAGE NOTE	
CORRECT	I'll see you in a month's time.
BUT	It'll take a month to do.
NOT	It'll take a month's time to do.

↻ have/lose/pass (your)/save/spend (your)/waste (your)/take your time (= don't hurry); time flies, time passes; a bad/good/difficult/easy/happy/sad/busy/exciting/pleasant time
3 (countable) when something happens or happened
- *The last **time** I was on a boat, I was sick.*
4 **How many times** = How often
- *"**How many times** have I told you not to shout?" "Only five times."*

times /taɪmz/ preposition
multiplied by
- *Six **times** three is eighteen: 6 x 3 = 18.*

LANGUAGE NOTE
Also: six times three **equals** eighteen

timetable /ˈtaɪmteɪbl/ noun (countable)
a list with different times written on it to show when something will happen
- *"What's the next lesson?" "Look at the **timetable** and find out."*
↻ draw up/follow/keep to a timetable

tin /tɪn/ noun
1 (uncountable) a soft silver metal
- *Malaysia produces a lot of **tin**.*
2 (countable) something often round in which food is stored
- *Let's buy two **tins** of soup.*

tinned /tɪnd/ adjective
anything which has been put in a tin to keep it a long time
- *I prefer fresh fruit to **tinned** fruit. Don't you?*

tiny /ˈtaɪnɪ/ adjective
tinier, tiniest
very small
- *The bird was so **tiny** we could hardly see it.*

tip /tɪp/ noun (countable)
1 the top of something
- *I've cut the **tip** of my finger.*
2 some money which you give to someone who has done something for you
- *Did you give the waiter a **tip**?*
↻ give (someone)/leave (someone) a tip; a big/small tip

tired /ˈtaɪəd/ adjective
1 feeling sleepy or needing a rest
- *I was so **tired** that I sat down and fell asleep.*
2 bored, not wanting to continue doing the same thing
- *I'm **tired** of homework. I'm going to see Ann.*

tire /ˈtaɪə*/ noun (countable)
(American English)
⚠ See **tyre**.

| θ | ð | ʃ | dʒ | tʃ | ŋ | ʒ | iː | ɜː | ɪ | æ | ʌ | ɒ |
| thing | that | shop | jump | chop | sing | measure | been | bird | bit | cat | but | not |

to[1] /tuː/ (unstressed /tə, tʊ/) preposition
1 You can use **to** to show that someone or something is moving towards a place.
   • *We're going **to** Singapore for a holiday.*
2 You can use **to** to mean **before** when you are telling the time.
   • *It's already five **to** one.*
3 You can use **to** before the names of people, etc who receive things.
   • *Give this letter **to** your mother.*
4 You can use **to** to show something which is joined to something else.
   • *The small boy tied his uncle **to** the chair.*

to[2] (followed by infinitive)
Use **to** with verbs to form the infinitive.
• *I want **to** go shopping to buy some bread.*
• *I'd like **to** meet Patricia.*
• *I've forgotten **to** tell Henry about the meeting.*
• *She's learning **to** play the piano.*

today /tə'deɪ/ noun (uncountable), adverb
the day on which you are speaking or writing
• ***Today** is Tuesday.*
• *What are you doing **today**?*

LANGUAGE NOTE	
EITHER	Have you read ***today's*** newspaper?
OR	Have you read the newspaper ***today***?

⚠ See also **tonight**.

together /tə'geðə*/ adverb
1 with each other
   • *Linda and Alison always work **together**.*
2 next to each other
   • *Put these pencils **together**. Now can you see which is longer?*
3 at the same time
   • *Everyone began to talk **together**, and so I couldn't understand a word that was said.*

toilet /'tɔɪlɪt/ noun (countable)
1 a lavatory (= a large bowl with a seat)
   • *This **toilet** is broken.*
🔗 toilet paper, a toilet roll
2 a room with a lavatory, sink, etc in it
   • *Can you tell me where the **toilets** are?*

told /təʊld/ verb
past tense and past participle of **tell**
• *I **told** you that Pauline would come.*

tomato /tə'mɑːtəʊ/ noun (countable)
plural: tomatoes
⚠ See box on page 238.

tomorrow /tə'mɒrəʊ/ noun (uncountable), adverb
the day after the day on which you are speaking or writing
• *Today is Monday; **tomorrow** will be Tuesday.*

tonight /tə'naɪt/ noun (uncountable), adverb
the evening or night of the day on which you are speaking or writing
• ***Tonight** is the only evening I'm not going out.*
⚠ See also **today**.

too /tuː/ adverb
1 also, as well
   • *We're going to a football match tonight. Would you like to come, **too**?*

LANGUAGE NOTE	
1	Never use **too** at the beginning of a sentence.
NEVER	~~Too, I'd like to borrow this book.~~
ALWAYS	I'd like to borrow this book, too.
OR	I'd also like to borrow this book.
2	Use too only in sentences without **not**. Use **either** in sentences with **not**.
NEVER	~~I don't like English food and Ann doesn't, too.~~
ALWAYS	I don't like English food and Ann doesn't **either**.
OR	I like English food and Ann does, too.

⚠ See also **either**[2].
2 more than enough, more than what is needed
   • *I feel ill because I've eaten **too** much.*

LANGUAGE NOTE

Remember that **too** means **more than enough**.
NEVER ~~I am too happy that you'll come.~~
ALWAYS I am **very** happy that you'll come.

See also **very** ¹.

took /tʊk/ verb
past tense of **take**
- It **took** me a long time to do my homework.

tool /tuːl/ noun (countable)
something which can help you to make something
- Pedro brought us a saw, a knife, and a lot of other **tools**.

tooth /tuːθ/ noun (countable)
plural: teeth /tiːθ/
something hard and white in your mouth which helps you to eat food
- How often do you brush your **teeth**?
- brush/clean your teeth, fill a tooth (= put something in the hole of a tooth to stop it from going bad), pull (out)/take out a tooth; back/front/lower/upper teeth, wisdom teeth (= the four teeth at the back of your mouth); toothbrush, toothpaste

See also box on page 25.

toothache /ˈtuːθeɪk/ noun (uncountable)
(American English: a toothache)
You have toothache when one of your teeth is bad and gives you a lot of pain.
- Pam has to go to the dentist's because she's got bad **toothache**.
- get (a) toothache, have (a) toothache

See also **ache** ¹·

top /tɒp/ noun (countable)
1 highest point
   - Can you walk to the **top** of the hill?
2 highest part
   - Cover the **top** of the table with this cloth.

torch /tɔːtʃ/ noun (countable)
plural: torches
a light or a lamp which you can carry

- Take a **torch** with you if you're going camping.
- shine a torch, turn off/on a torch

tore /tɔː*/ verb
past tense of **tear**
- I **tore** my dress on a nail this morning.

torn /tɔːn/ verb
past participle of **tear**
- Who's **torn** this page out of my exercise book?

total ¹ /ˈtəʊtl/ noun (countable)
the amount when you add everything together
- Can you add up the bill and tell me the **total**?

total ² adjective
complete (after everything has been added together)
- What was the **total** number of people at the concert?

totally /ˈtəʊtl-ɪ/ adverb
completely
- Poor Bob was **totally** deaf and couldn't hear anything at all.

touch /tʌtʃ/ verb
1 When something or someone touches something else, there is no space between them.
   - One of the branches is **touching** the wall.
2 put your hand on something
   - She **touched** my arm and smiled.

θ	ð	ʃ	dʒ	tʃ	ŋ	ʒ	iː	ɜː	ɪ	æ	ʌ	ɒ
thing	that	shop	jump	chop	sing	measure	been	bird	bit	cat	but	not

230 tourist

tourist /ˈtʊərɪst/ noun (countable)
someone who visits a place on holiday
- I saw a lot of Japanese **tourists** in London.

towards /təˈwɔːdz/ preposition
1 in the direction of, to
- The dog suddenly ran **towards** us.
2 near (in time)
- It became much cooler **towards** evening.

> **LANGUAGE NOTE**
>
> Use **towards** when you are more interested in showing the direction. Use **to** when you want to show the place.
> USUALLY Who's that walking **towards** us?
> NOT Who's that walking to us?

towel /ˈtaʊəl/ noun (countable)
a piece of cloth which you can use to dry yourself or to dry dishes, etc
- I can't use this **towel**: it's too wet.
↻ a bath/face/hand towel, a tea-towel, a paper towel, a dish towel (= American English)

tower /ˈtaʊə*/ noun (countable)
a tall, narrow building or a tall, narrow part of a building
- The prince was kept a prisoner in the **tower**.

toy /tɔɪ/ noun (countable)
something which a child plays with
- "Ali's got a **toy** from his uncle." "What kind of **toy**?" "It's a **toy** car."

tractor /ˈtræktə*/ noun (countable)
a machine which has large wheels at the back and which is used on a farm
- That's the farmer's new **tractor** in the field.

trade /treɪd/ noun (uncountable)
buying and selling things
- **Trade** with Japan last year was very good.

traffic /ˈtræfɪk/ noun (uncountable)
cars, buses, lorries, etc
- There was so much **traffic** on the road that it took Rosa half an hour to drive one kilometre.
↻ direct traffic (= control the way cars, lorries, etc move), hold up traffic (= stop cars, lorries, etc moving); fast traffic, heavy traffic (= a lot of cars, buses, lorries, etc), light traffic (= only a few cars, buses, lorries, etc)

> **LANGUAGE NOTE**
>
> NEVER a lot of traffics ALWAYS a lot of traffic

train /treɪn/ noun (countable)
some carriages which are pulled by an engine along a railway line
- Has the **train** for Berlin come into the station?
↻ drive/catch/take/ miss a train, change trains, get off/on a train; a train arrives/ pulls in/leaves/pulls out/stops; a fast/ slow/express/local /freight/goods/ passenger train

trainers /ˈtreɪnəz/ noun (plural)
something you wear on your feet (like a very soft shoe)
- Put on your **trainers** and come for a walk.
△ See also **shoe**.

tram /træm/ noun (countable)
(American English: streetcar)
a kind of electric bus which travels on rails in towns and takes people from one place to another
- Do you take a bus or a **tram** to work?
↻ drive/ride/take a tram

translate /trɑːnsˈleɪt/ verb
translating, translated, has translated
say or write something in another language
- Who **translated** this poem into English?

> **LANGUAGE NOTE**
>
> translate something **into** (NEVER to) another language

θ	ð	ʃ	dʒ	tʃ	ŋ	ʒ	iː	ɜː	ɪ	æ	ʌ	ɒ
thing	that	shop	jump	chop	sing	measure	been	bird	bit	cat	but	not

travel /'trævl/ verb
travelling, travelled, has travelled

SPELLING NOTE

British English:
Double *l*: **travelling**, **travelled** BUT **travels**
American English:
Single *l*: **traveling**, **traveled**

---

go from one place to another on a journey
- *I enjoy **travelling** by bus as I can see a lot.*
↻ travel far/widely; travel first-class/second-class

treasure /'treʒə*/ noun
1 (uncountable) a lot of gold, silver, and other valuable things
   - *The thieves hid the box of **treasure** in a hole.*
   ↻ buried treasure
2 (countable) an object which is very valuable
   - *The museum has a lot of rare **treasures**.*

tree /triː/ noun (countable)
a very large, tall plant from which we get wood
- *He climbed to the top of the **tree** to see the way.*
↻ cut a tree down, grow/plant trees

triangle /'traɪæŋgl/ noun (countable)
a shape with three straight sides
- *The strange building was the shape of a **triangle**.*

trick [1] /trɪk/ noun (countable)
a clever joke which you play on someone
- *We played a **trick** on James. We hid his shoes in the kitchen.*

trick [2] verb
play a joke on someone, make someone do something so that you can get what you want or laugh at them
- *Sue **tricked** her younger brother. "What's that in the sky?" she asked him. When her brother looked up, Sue ate one of his sweets.*

trip [1] /trɪp/ noun (countable)
a journey somewhere (for a short time)
- *Mr Law went on a **trip** to Spain last week.*
↻ go on/make/take/plan a trip; a business/long/short/a round-the-world trip

trip [2] verb
tripping, tripped, has tripped
hit your foot against something as you are walking or running
- *I **tripped** on the stairs as I ran down them.*

trouble [1] /'trʌbl/ noun (uncountable, countable)
something which causes difficulty, problems, or worry
- *Are you having **trouble** with your computer?*

trouble [2] verb
troubling, troubled, has troubled
1 When you give someone problems, pain, etc, you are troubling them.
   - *"I hope I'm not troubling you." "It's no trouble at all."*
2 worry
   - *You don't seem very happy. What's **troubling** you?*

trousers /'traʊzəz/ noun (plural)
(American English: pants)
clothes which cover the lower part of your body and each leg

- *He was wearing his new **trousers** at the party.*
↻ button/zip up your trousers, put on (some) trousers, take off your trousers, wear (some) trousers; long/short trousers

---
LANGUAGE NOTE

1 a pair of trousers, some trousers
   NEVER a trousers
2 **trouser** + noun (trouser pocket)

θ	ð	ʃ	dʒ	tʃ	ŋ	ʒ	iː	ɜː	ɪ	æ	ʌ	ɒ
thing	that	shop	jump	chop	sing	measure	been	bird	bit	cat	but	not

truck /trʌk/ noun (countable)
a lorry, a van
- *Several **trucks** carried sand to the village.*

true /truː/ adjective
truer, truest
not wrong, correct
- *"Is it **true** that you're getting married soon?" "Yes, it's **true**. I'm marrying Oliver."*

trust¹ /trʌst/ noun (uncountable)
believing that someone or something is good
- *He put his **trust** in God and stopped worrying.*
- ↻ have trust in someone/something, place/put your trust in God/someone

trust² verb
believe that someone or something is good or honest
- *You can **trust** me. I'll help you.*

LANGUAGE NOTE

trust someone
trust someone **to do** something
trust someone **with** something
trust **in** God
(= believe there is God, believe that God will help you)

---

truth /truːθ/ noun (uncountable)
what is true and correct
- *Tell me the **truth**. Did you borrow my book?*
- ↻ arrive at/find out/discover/hear/speak stick to the truth; the plain/real/whole truth

truthful /ˈtruːθfl/ adjective
honest, saying what is true
- *Bill is very **truthful**. He never tells lies.*

try /traɪ/ verb
trying, tried, has tried
1 do something again and again until you can do it properly
   - *Dave **tried** to reach the branch but he couldn't.*
   - ↻ try your best, try hard
2 use something for the first time, test something, taste something
   - *Let's **try** the fish. It smells good.*

LANGUAGE NOTE

COMPARE   try **to do** something (See 1 above)
          I tried to **climb up** the wall but I couldn't.
WITH   try **doing** something (See 2 above)
          Let's try **adding** some water to see what will happen.

---

3 **try on** = When you **try** clothes **on**, you see if they will fit you.
   - *Why don't you **try on** the new dress?*

tube /tjuːb/ noun (countable)
something long and round in which there is toothpaste, glue, etc
- *Can I use your **tube** of toothpaste, please?*

tunnel /ˈtʌnl/ noun (countable)
a long passage through a hill or under the ground, through which trains or cars travel

- *We drove through the new **tunnel** in the mountain.*
- ↻ build/dig a tunnel

turn /tɜːn/ verb
1 move (something) round
   - *The wheels of the big lorry began to **turn**.*
2 move your body or your head to face the opposite direction
   - *You'll never guess who's standing behind you! Why don't you **turn** (round) and see?*
3 change direction
   - ***Turn** left at the end of the street.*
- ↻ turn back/left/right, turn sharply

θ	ð	ʃ	dʒ	tʃ	ŋ	ʒ	iː	ɜː	ɪ	æ	ʌ	ɒ
thing	that	shop	jump	chop	sing	measure	been	bird	bit	cat	but	not

4 **turn into** (something) = become
   - When water boils, it **turns into** steam.
5 **turn off** = stop, switch off
   - The car stopped, and the driver **turned off** the engine.
6 **turn on** = start, switch on
   - Will you **turn** the radio **on**, please?
7 **turn to** (a page) = find (a page)
   - **Turn to** Page 97 in your readers.

turnip /ˈtɜːnɪp/   noun (countable, uncountable)
  ⚠ See box on page 238.

TV /ˌtiː ˈviː/   noun (uncountable)
  ⚠ See **television**.

twice /twaɪs/   adverb, predeterminer
  two times
  - I've already seen this film **twice**.

twist /twɪst/   verb
  1 hold one end of something while turning the other end
     - **Twist** the string: it'll be much stronger.
  2 turn round and round
     - You have to **twist** the top to open the jar.
  3 bend in many directions
     - The road **twisted** up the side of the hill.

tying /ˈtaɪ-ɪŋ/   verb
  part of **tie**
  - "What are you doing?" "I'm **tying** my horse to the fence."

type ¹ /taɪp/   noun (countable)
  kind, a group of people or things
  - "What **type** of car have you got?" "A sports car."
  ↻ belong to/choose/want/keep to a certain type; a good/bad/well known/ common/rare/new/old/strange/ unusual type
  ⚠ See also **kind** ¹; see also **sort**.

type ²   verb
  typing, typed, has typed
  use a machine (eg a typewriter or a word processor) to write words on a page
  - Ann is learning to **type** because she wants to get a job as a secretary.

typewriter /ˈtaɪpˌraɪtəʳ/   noun (countable)
  a machine which you can use to print words by pressing keys
  - Lesley uses a **typewriter** to type all her letters.

typist /ˈtaɪpɪst/   noun (countable)
  someone whose job is typing
  - Ann's sister works as a **typist** in a big office.

tyre /ˈtaɪəʳ/   noun (countable)
  (American English: tire)
  a piece of thick rubber (usually filled with air) round a wheel
  - We have a flat **tyre**. Can you put some air in it?
  ↻ a flat/worn tyre;
     blow up/change a tyre

θ	ð	ʃ	dʒ	tʃ	ŋ	ʒ	iː	ɜː	ɪ	æ	ʌ	ɒ
thing	that	shop	jump	chop	sing	measure	been	bird	bit	cat	but	not

Uu

ugly /ˈʌglɪ/ adjective
uglier, ugliest
not beautiful, unpleasant to look at
• The rubbish in the street was an **ugly** sight.

umbrella /ʌmˈbrelə/ noun (countable)
something used to keep you dry from the rain

• Why don't you use your **umbrella**? It's raining.
↻ close an umbrella, open an umbrella

uncle /ˈʌŋkl/ noun (countable)
the brother of your mother or father, or your aunt's husband
• Paul often visits his **uncle** at weekends.

under /ˈʌndə*/ preposition
1 below, not on
• Your shoes are **under** your bed.
2 less than
• You can travel half-price if you're **under** 16.

underclothes /ˈʌndəkləʊðz/ noun (plural)
underclothing /ˈʌndəkləʊðɪŋ/ noun (uncountable)
◊ See **underwear**.

underground /ˈʌndəɡraʊnd/ noun (singular with the)
(American English: subway)
a railway under the ground in a town or city
• The **underground** in Hong Kong is one of the best in the world.

underneath /ˌʌndəˈniːθ/ preposition
below, beneath
• Write today's date **underneath** your address.

underpants /ˈʌndəpænts/ noun (plural)
underwear worn by boys and men below the waist
• Is this pair of **underpants** your size?
◊ See also **knickers**.

undershirt /ˈʌndəʃɜːt/ noun (countable)
(American English)
◊ See **vest 1**.

understand /ˌʌndəˈstænd/ verb
understanding, understood, has understood
know what someone or something means
• "Do you **understand** English?" "I think so."
↻ understand clearly/perfectly

underwear /ˈʌndəweə*/ noun (uncountable)
clothes which you wear next to your body (under your shirt, trousers, dress, skirt, etc)
• I wear clean **underwear** every day.

undo /ʌnˈduː/ verb
undoing, undid /ʌnˈdɪd/, undone /ʌnˈdʌn/
When you undo a parcel, you untie or unfasten it (ie take the string off).
• Let's **undo** the parcel and see what's inside.

undress /ʌnˈdres/ verb
take your clothes off
• I turned the light off, **undressed** and got into bed.

unfortunate /ʌnˈfɔːtʃənət/ adjective
unlucky
• It was **unfortunate** there was no empty seat.

unfortunately /ʌnˈfɔːtʃənətlɪ/ adverb
unluckily
• **Unfortunately** the tickets had all been sold.

θ	ð	ʃ	dʒ	tʃ	ŋ	ʒ	iː	ɜː	ɪ	æ	ʌ	ɒ
thing	that	shop	jump	chop	sing	measure	been	bird	bit	cat	but	not

uniform /ˈjuːnɪfɔːm/ noun (countable)
clothes people wear in the army, for school, or for a special job
- Mike looks very smart in his new police **uniform**.
- ✤ put a uniform on, take your uniform off, wear a uniform; a fireman's/nurse's/policeman's/soldier's uniform, etc

university /ˌjuːnɪˈvɜːsətɪ/ noun (countable)
plural: universities
a place where students study for degrees
- Vincent Chan is at **university** in Australia.

> **LANGUAGE NOTE**
>
> 1 go to university BUT go to **a** good university
>   American English: go to a university
> 2 Hong Kong University, Oxford University
>   (place name + university)
>   BUT
>   **the** Chinese University, **the** National University of Singapore
>   (**the** + adjective + university)

unless /ənˈles/ conjunction
You can use **unless** to show what will happen if something else does not happen.
- We're having a picnic tomorrow **unless** it rains.

unlike /ˌʌnˈlaɪk/ preposition
different from, not like
- Sonny is **unlike** Dave: he's good at sports: Dave doesn't like sports at all.

unpleasant /ʌnˈplezənt/ adjective
making you feel bad, frightened, etc
- The smell outside the cinema was very **unpleasant**.

untidy /ʌnˈtaɪdɪ/ adjective
untidier, untidiest
not neat, with nothing in the right place
- Anna's room is very **untidy**: there are clothes, books and records everywhere!

until /ənˈtɪl/ preposition, conjunction

> **SPELLING NOTE**
>
> till BUT until (only one *l*)

up to a certain time
- I'll wait for you **until** quarter past eight.

> **LANGUAGE NOTE**
>
> The present tense (NOT the future tense) is used in the part of the sentence after **until**.
>
> NEVER   I'll stay until you will come.
> ALWAYS   I'll stay until **you come**.
> OR   I'll stay until **you've come**.

up¹ /ʌp/ adverb
1 not down, towards a higher place
   - Susie looked **up** and smiled when I passed.
2 become straight
   - I felt so tired that it was hard to get **up**.
3 **grow up** = become an adult
   - Tim wants to be a doctor when he **grows up**.
4 You can also use **up** to make the meaning of certain verbs much stronger.
   - Eat all your dinner **up**.

up² preposition
1 not down, towards a higher place
   - Tim climbed **up** the ladder to the roof.
2 along
   - Walk **up** the street for a hundred metres.

upon /əˈpɒn/ preposition
on top of
- The small child climbed **upon** her mother's knee.

upside down /ˌʌpsaɪd ˈdaʊn/ adjective, adverb
turned so that the lowest part is above the highest part
- Someone's hung this picture **upside down**.

θ	ð	ʃ	dʒ	tʃ	ŋ	ʒ	iː	ɜː	ɪ	æ	ʌ	ɒ
thing	that	shop	jump	chop	sing	measure	been	bird	bit	cat	but	not

upstairs /ʌpˈsteəz/ adverb
to or on a higher floor
- *She went **upstairs** to her bedroom.*

upwards /ˈʌpwədz/ adverb
towards a higher place
- *The plane flew slowly **upwards**.*

us /ʌs/ (unstressed /əs/) pronoun
Use **us** after a verb to mean **we** or **ourselves**.
- *Please show **us** how to do this exercise.*

use¹ /juːs/ noun
the purpose of something
- *What's the **use** of learning History?*
🔑 find a use for something (= find out what something can be used for), lose the use of (your arm, etc) (= be unable to use your arm, etc), make use of something/someone, put something to (good) use; bad/good/general/common/ordinary/daily/everyday/immediate use, wide use

use² /juːz/ verb
using, used, has used
make something work, do something for a certain purpose
- *How do you **use** this cassette recorder?*

LANGUAGE NOTE	
EITHER	I use it **to** clean my typewriter.
OR	I use it **for** cleaning my typewriter.

used to /ˈjuːst tuː/ verb phrase
1 If you used to do something, you often did it in the past (but you no longer do it now).
- *I **used to** walk five kilometres every day.*
2 If you are used to (doing) something, you have done it often and you know all about it.
- *I've lived in Taiwan for five years so I'm **used to** (eating) Chinese food now.*

LANGUAGE NOTES	
COMPARE WITH	I **used to** eat Chinese food a lot but I don't eat much Chinese food now.
	I'm **used to** eating Chinese food and I enjoy it a lot.
NEVER	I used to eating Chinese food.

useful /ˈjuːsfl/ adjective
with many purposes or uses, helpful
- *How **useful** is a bag with a hole in it?*

useless /ˈjuːslɪs/ adjective
of no use, with no purpose
- *A broken pencil is **useless**.*

usually /ˈjuːʒʊəli/ adverb
often
- *We **usually** go to the cinema on Thursday.*

LANGUAGE NOTE	
EITHER	**Usually** we meet Ruth at four o'clock.
OR	We **usually** meet Ruth at four o'clock.
OR	We meet Ruth **usually** at four o'clock.
OR	We meet Ruth at four o'clock **usually**.

θ	ð	ʃ	dʒ	tʃ	ŋ	ʒ	iː	ɜː	ɪ	æ	ʌ	ɒ
thing	that	shop	jump	chop	sing	measure	been	bird	bit	cat	but	not

Vv

vague /veɪg/ adjective
not clear
- The police have only got a **vague** description of the thief.

valley /ˈvælɪ/ noun (countable)
low land between hills and mountains
- Let's camp for the night in this **valley**.

valuable /ˈvæljʊəbl/ adjective
something which is important or costs a lot
- Gold is the most **valuable** metal in the world.
- quite/very/highly valuable

value /ˈvæljuː/ noun (uncountable, countable)
the amount of money something is worth
- What is the **value** of your flat?
- agree on the value of something; place/put/set a (high) value on something; have (great) value, hold its value, keep/lose its value; great/high/little/low/real/true value, full value

van /væn/ noun (countable)
a vehicle like a large car or a small lorry
- A **van** stopped, and two men took some fruit out.

vase /vɑːz/ noun (countable)
something which you can put flowers in
- Please put these flowers into the **vase**.

vegetable /ˈvedʒtəbl/ noun (countable)
plants (eg potatoes, lettuces, carrots) which you can eat
- Would you like any **vegetables** with your meat?
- grow vegetables; cooked/green/raw vegetables
- See box on page 238.

vehicle /ˈviːɪkl/ noun (countable)
a machine which takes people from one place to another (eg a car, a bus, a lorry, a truck and a van are all vehicles)
- Several **vehicles** are still in the tunnel.

veranda, verandah /vəˈrændə/ noun (countable)
plural: verandas, verandahs
(American English: porch)
an open place at the side of a flat or a house (with a floor and a roof)
- Let's have some fresh air and sit on the **verandah**.

verb /vɜːb/ noun (countable)
a word which tells us what someone or something does or what happens
- "Look", "happen", and "run" are all **verbs**.

very /ˈverɪ/ adverb
1 a lot (You can use **very** to make an adjective stronger.)
   - "Ted's clever, isn't he?" "Yes, he's **very** clever."

LANGUAGE NOTE

1 Use **very** only when a participle (ie the word ending in **-ed**) is an adjective which shows how you feel. Use **very much** in front of all other participles ending in **ed**.

   very bored, very excited, very interested, very pleased, very tired, very worried
   BUT very much liked

2 NEVER very better, very faster, very more
   ALWAYS **much** better, **much** faster, **much** more

2 **very much** = a lot
   - I like chocolate **very much**.

LANGUAGE NOTE

NEVER	Ken likes very much football.
ALWAYS	Ken **very much** likes football.
OR	Ken likes football **very much**.

θ	ð	ʃ	dʒ	tʃ	ŋ	ʒ	iː	ɜː	ɪ	æ	ʌ	ɒ
thing	that	shop	jump	chop	sing	measure	been	bird	bit	cat	but	not

238 vest

Vegetables

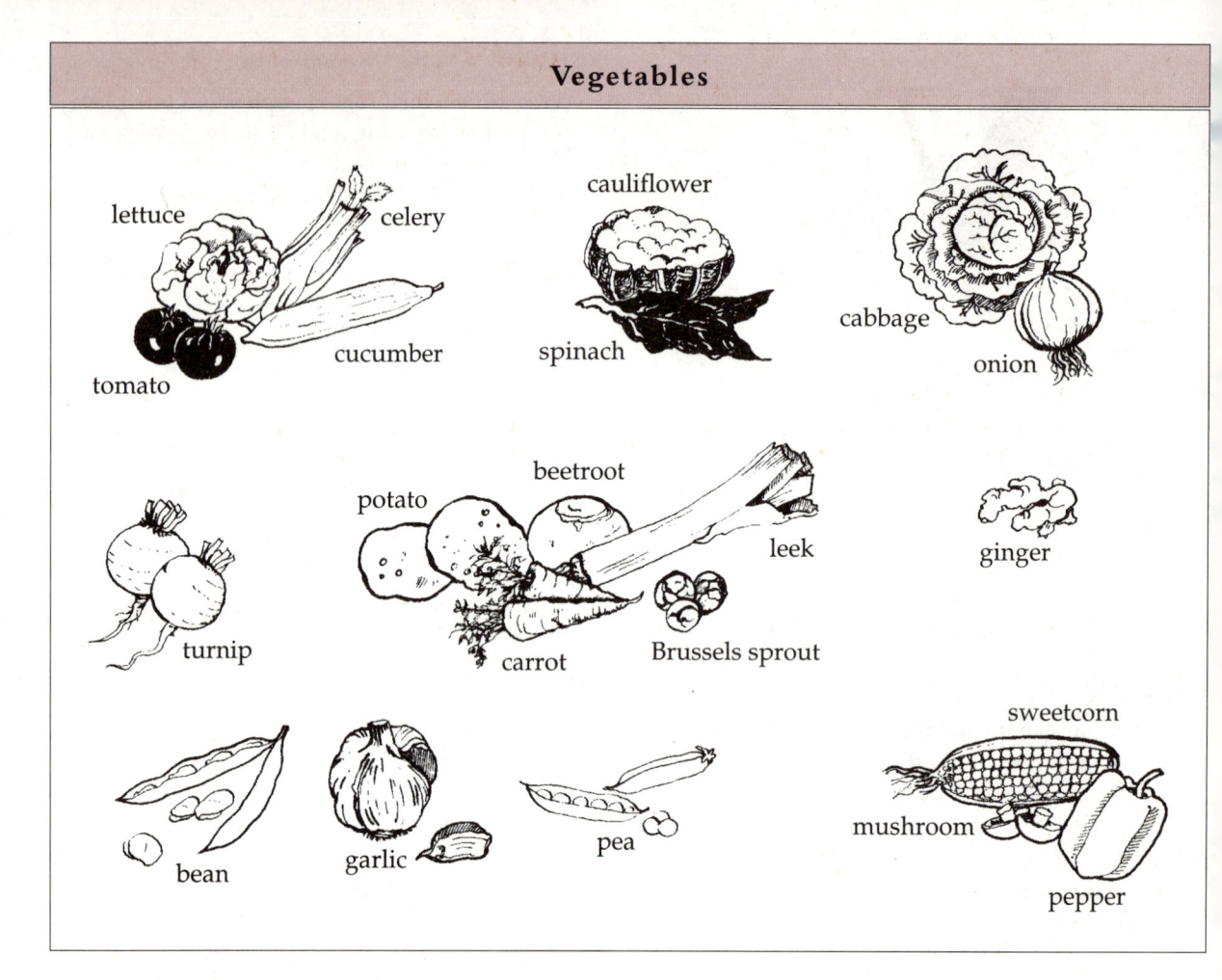

lettuce, celery, cauliflower, cabbage, tomato, cucumber, spinach, onion, turnip, potato, beetroot, leek, ginger, carrot, Brussels sprout, sweetcorn, bean, garlic, pea, mushroom, pepper

vest /vest/ noun (countable)
1 (American English: undershirt) something which people wear over the top part of their body under a dress, a shirt, etc
 • I've forgotten to put my **vest** on today.
2 (American English)
⚠ See **waistcoat**.

video /ˈvɪdɪəʊ/ noun (countable)
1 a film which has been recorded on a tape
 • Let's stay at home and watch a **video**.
2 a machine for making and playing video tapes (also called a **VCR**)
 • Have you just bought a new **video** (recorder)?
↻ a video cassette (= a tape for recording and playing videos); a video recorder (= a video machine); a video tape

view /vjuː/ noun (countable)
1 what you can see from a certain place
 • The **view** from the bedroom window is excellent: you can see a lot of mountains.
2 what you think about something
 • "What are your **views** on smoking?" "It shouldn't be allowed."
↻ agree with someone's views, change your views (on/about something), have/hold a view (on/about something); modern/opposite/strong views, sound views (= good views)

village /ˈvɪlɪdʒ/ noun (countable)
a very small town in the country
 • Mr and Mrs Wright live in a very pretty **village**.

θ	ð	ʃ	dʒ	tʃ	ŋ	ʒ	iː	ɜː	ɪ	æ	ʌ	ɒ
thing	that	shop	jump	chop	sing	measure	been	bird	bit	cat	but	not

violin /ˌvaɪəˈlɪn/ noun (countable)
something which you can play by moving a bow over its four strings (A bow is a long piece of wood with thin hairs fastened along it.)
- *Tina's learning to play the **violin**.*

LANGUAGE NOTE	
NEVER	~~Can you play violin?~~
ALWAYS	Can you play **the** violin?

visa /ˈviːzə/ noun (countable)
a mark in your passport to allow you to visit a certain country
- *Do I need a **visa** to visit Nigeria?*

visit [1] /ˈvɪzɪt/ noun (countable)
When you go to see someone or something, you pay them a visit.
- *We had a **visit** from Mr and Mrs Saleh last night.*
↻ make/pay a visit

visit [2] verb
1 go to see someone
   - *The nurse **visited** my mother yesterday.*
2 go to see a place
   - *We **visited** North Point last week.*

visitor /ˈvɪzɪtə*/ noun (countable)
someone who goes to see someone or something
- *There are always a lot of **visitors** to Stratford-on-Avon, the place where Shakespeare was born.*

voice /vɔɪs/ noun (countable)
When someone speaks or sings, you hear their **voice**.
- *Mr Obasuyi has lost his **voice**, and couldn't teach us.*
↻ drop/lose/lower/raise your voice; an angry/calm/loud/quiet/soft/high/low/rough/gentle/clear/deep/rich voice

LANGUAGE NOTE
speak in a loud voice (NOT with)

volleyball /ˈvɒlɪbɔːl/ noun (uncountable)
a game in which you hit a large ball over a high net with your hand
- *Our team won the **volleyball** competition.*

vowel /ˈvaʊəl/ noun (countable)
a letter of the alphabet the sound of which you make with your mouth open: eg a, e, i, o, u
- *The word "umbrella" begins with a **vowel**.*

voyage /ˈvɔɪ-ɪdʒ/ noun (countable)
a long journey in a ship or on a spacecraft
- *The spacecraft's **voyage** to Mars took several weeks.*
↻ go on a voyage; a long/round-the-world voyage

θ	ð	ʃ	dʒ	tʃ	ŋ	ʒ	iː	ɜː	ɪ	æ	ʌ	ɒ
thing	that	shop	jump	chop	sing	measure	been	bird	bit	cat	but	not

Ww

wage /weɪdʒ/ noun (countable)

the money you are paid for your work
- *Some of the workers have asked for an increase in their **wages**.*
- get/earn/have a (good) wage; a good/high/poor/low wage, good/high/poor/low wages

waistcoat /ˈweɪskəʊt/ noun (countable)

(American English: vest)
a garment which men can wear over their shirts and under their jackets
- *All the men were wearing suits, but only a few were wearing **waistcoats**.*

wait /weɪt/ verb

stay in a place until someone comes or something happens
- *We **waited** for a bus for half an hour.*

LANGUAGE NOTE
wait **for** someone (to do something)

waiter /ˈweɪtə*/ noun (countable)

a man who brings food to you in a restaurant
- *We gave the **waiter** a large tip because he was very polite and quick.*

waitress /ˈweɪtrɪs/ noun (countable)

a woman who brings food to you in a restaurant
- *The **waitress** wrote down what we wanted.*

wake (up) /ˌweɪk ˈʌp/ (phrasal) verb

waking (up), woken (up), has woken (up)
(American English: also waked, has waked)

1 stop sleeping
   - *I **wake (up)** every morning at seven o'clock.*
2 stop someone from sleeping
   - *Will you **wake** me **(up)** at six tomorrow? I want to get up early.*

walk¹ /wɔːk/ noun (countable)

a journey on foot
- *Let's go for a short **walk** this morning.*
- go for/on/have/take a walk; an easy/long/short walk

walk² verb

move by putting one foot in front of the other on the ground (but not run)
- *I **walk** to college every morning.*
- walk fast/quickly/slowly

walkman, Walkman /ˈwɔːkmən/
noun (countable)

plural: walkmans, Walkmans
a small cassette player which you can carry with you and which has wires which you put in your ears to listen to music
- *I always take my **walkman** on the bus.*

wall /wɔːl/ noun (countable)

1 a side of a building or room
   - *We painted the **walls** of the living room white.*
2 something like a fence but made out of bricks or stones (round a garden, a field or a town)
   - *Peter jumped over the **wall** into his neighbour's garden.*
- put up/build/climb/paint a wall; an inside/outside wall, a brick/stone wall

wallet /ˈwɒlɪt/ noun (countable)

something which we put paper money, credit cards, etc in and carry in our pocket
- *My **wallet** has been stolen. I had $250 in it!*

want /wɒnt/ verb

1 wish for something
   - *I **want** to go to Japan some time.*

LANGUAGE NOTE
want someone to do something
Do you want me to bring you a glass of water?

- want badly, want very much

θ	ð	ʃ	dʒ	tʃ	ŋ	ʒ	iː	ɜː	ɪ	æ	ʌ	ɒ
thing	that	shop	jump	chop	sing	measure	been	bird	bit	cat	but	not

2 need
- Tony's hair **wants** cutting. It's too long.

war /wɔː*/ noun (countable)
fighting between two countries
- The **war** between China and Japan came to an end fifty years ago.
- fight (in) a war, go to war (over something), win/lose a war, make war (on another country); a civil war (= a war between different groups of people in the same country), a cold war (= a period when two or more countries are very unfriendly but do not fight against one another), a world war

ward /wɔːd/ noun (countable)
a room with several beds in a hospital
- When Soraya was in hospital, she was put in a **ward** with other girls who had the same illness.

warm /wɔːm/ adjective
neither very hot nor cold
- Put this coat on. It'll keep you **warm**.

warn /wɔːn/ verb
tell someone that something bad or dangerous may happen
- Mrs Banerjee **warned** us about the storm.

was /wɒz/(unstressed /wəz/) verb
part of **be**
- It **was** very sunny earlier today.

wash /wɒʃ/ verb
clean something with water and soap
- Ken **washed** his shirt twice before it was clean.

wash up /ˌwɒʃ ˈʌp/ phrasal verb
clean dirty dishes with water and soap

- Let me help you to **wash up**.

washing-machine
/ˈwɒʃɪŋ məˌʃiːn/ noun (countable)
a machine which washes clothes
- Sarah's just bought a new **washing-machine**.

wasn't /ˈwɒznt/
was not
- It **wasn't** a very nice day yesterday.
- See **be**.

waste¹ /weɪst/ noun (uncountable)
1 rubbish
- Put all your **waste** paper in this bag.
2 not using or doing something that is useful
- Watching TV a lot is a **waste** of time.
- a great/terrible waste (of time and money)

waste² verb
wasting, wasted, has wasted
not use something which is useful
- Kate **wastes** money on sweets.

watch¹ /wɒtʃ/ noun (countable)
plural: watches
something which you wear on your wrist and which tells you the time
- "What time is it by your **watch**?"
  "Sorry. I haven't got it on today."
- set (= put it to the correct time) /wind up your watch; a watch goes/keeps (good) time/runs down/stops; a watch can be fast or slow (fast = in front of the correct time; slow = behind the correct time), a watch can be correct or right

watch² verb
look at something, see

LANGUAGE NOTE
COMPARE watch someone **do** something
(= see them do all of something)
AND watch someone **doing** something
(= see them do all or only part of something)

- Did you **watch** the film on TV last night?
- See also **look** 1; see also **see**.

θ	ð	ʃ	dʒ	tʃ	ŋ	ʒ	iː	ɜː	ɪ	æ	ʌ	ɒ
thing	that	shop	jump	chop	sing	measure	been	bird	bit	cat	but	not

water¹ /ˈwɔːtə*/ noun (uncountable)
a clear liquid which falls from clouds as rain, which is in rivers and lakes and which we drink
- *Could I have another glass of **water**, please?*
↻ boil/drink/pour/run/spill water; cold/warm/hot/boiling/drinking/ice(d)/fresh/clear/rain/salt/sea water

water² verb
put water on plants or over the ground
- *I must **water** these plants before they die.*

wave¹ /weɪv/ noun (countable)
1 a raised area of water on top of the sea
   - *The sea was very rough and big **waves** hit the the sides of the boat.*
↻ a big/small/high/tall wave
2 moving (your hand) from side to side
   - *Elsa gave me a big **wave** when I left.*

wave² verb
waving, waved, has waved
move your hand and arm in the air to say hello or goodbye to someone
- *I **waved** to Ahmed but he didn't see me.*

way /weɪ/ noun (countable)
1 direction (usually singular with the)
   - *Can you tell me the **way** to the bank, please?*
↻ lead/point/show/tell someone the way; on the way to (= going towards)
2 how to do something
   - *That's the wrong **way** to do it. You should do it this **way**.*

LANGUAGE NOTE
EITHER a way *to do* something
OR   a way *of doing* something

↻ choose a way, explain/show someone the way
3 **on my way** = as I am going, as I was going
   - *I'll post the letters **on my way** to work.*

we /wiː/ pronoun
You can use **we** to talk about yourselves.
- *Maria and I arrived early, and **we** were the only people there.*

weak /wiːk/ adjective
1 not strong
   - *Mrs Small is still **weak** after her illness, and so I do her shopping.*
2 poor, not very good
   - *My English is **weak**. I need much more practice.*

wear /weə*/ verb
wearing, wore /wɔː*/, has worn /wɔːn/
1 have (or put) clothes on your body
   - *Are you **wearing** that dress to the party?*
2 become thinner or weaker after being worn or used
   - *These tyres soon **wear**. They're already **worn** (out), and we now need new ones.*
↻ wear out (= wear completely)

weather /ˈweðə*/ noun (uncountable)
how cold, warm, sunny, cloudy, wet, etc it is
- *What's the **weather** like today?*
↻ bad/good/beautiful/clear/cloudy/cold/cool/warm/hot/mild/fair/fine/rainy/wet/nice/pleasant/windy weather; weather forecast (= telling in a newspaper, on TV or on the radio what the weather is going to be like), weather report

wedding /ˈwedɪŋ/ noun (countable)
the time when people get married (and the party which often follows)

- *Maria and Stefan got married on Saturday. It was a lovely **wedding**.*
↻ wedding cake, wedding day

θ	ð	ʃ	dʒ	tʃ	ŋ	ʒ	iː	ɜː	ɪ	æ	ʌ	ɒ
thing	that	shop	jump	chop	sing	measure	been	bird	bit	cat	but	not

we'd /wi:d/
1 we would
- *We'd do it if she asked us.*
2 we had
- *Dave talked to us after we'd finished working.*

week /wi:k/ noun (countable)
a period of seven days from Sunday to Saturday
- *We're going to have a holiday next week.*

LANGUAGE NOTE

1 NEVER ~~a two week's holiday~~
ALWAYS a two-**week** holiday
2 a week **on** Friday (British English)
on Friday week (British English)
a week *from* Friday (American English)
(= a week after next Friday)

☙ last/next/this week

weekday /'wi:kdeɪ/ noun (countable)
any day except Saturday and Sunday
- *We're busy on weekdays, but we can see you on Sunday.*

weekend /wi:k'end/ noun (countable)
Saturday and Sunday
- *What are you doing next weekend?*

LANGUAGE NOTE

on a weekday BUT **at** the weekend

---

weigh /weɪ/ verb
1 measure how heavy something is

- *The shop assistant weighed the potatoes and put them in a bag.*
2 how heavy something is
- *My bag was heavy: it weighed five kilos.*

weight /weɪt/ noun (uncountable, countable)
how heavy something is
- *"What's the weight of the parcel?" "It's eight kilos."*
☙ take off/lose weight (= weigh less), put on weight (= weigh more)

welcome¹ /'welkəm/ noun (countable)
being glad or pleased that someone has arrived or has visited you
- *We got a warm welcome from Tom.*
☙ find/get/receive a (warm, etc) welcome, give someone a (warm, etc) welcome; a cool welcome (= a poor or unfriendly welcome), a warm welcome (= a very friendly welcome), a great/real welcome

welcome² verb
welcoming, welcomed, has welcomed
show someone that you are pleased they have arrived or have visited you
- *We all went to the airport to welcome Uncle Ben back from Canada.*

LANGUAGE NOTE

welcome someone **to** a place

☙ welcome someone warmly

we'll /wi:l/
we will
- *What time do you think we'll arrive?*

well¹ /wel/ noun (countable)
a hole in the ground where you can get water
- *Our well dried up so we had no water.*
☙ dig/sink a well; a well dries up; a deep well

well² adjective
1 healthy, not ill
- *I was ill last week, but I'm well again now.*
2 **well-known** = known by a lot of people, famous
- *Pavarotti is a well-known singer.*

well³ adverb
1 in a good way
- *Susie can play the piano very well.*
2 **as well (as)** = also, and
- *Can you play the piano – and sing as well?*

θ	ð	ʃ	dʒ	tʃ	ŋ	ʒ	iː	ɜː	ɪ	æ	ʌ	ɒ
thing	that	shop	jump	chop	sing	measure	been	bird	bit	cat	but	not

west ¹ /west/ noun (singular with the)
where the sun goes down in the sky
- *It's late in the evening and the sun is going down in **the west**.*

> **LANGUAGE NOTE**
>
> You can use **the West** (with a capital **W**) to mean Europe and/or the United States.

west ² adjective
the part of a country, a building, a place, etc facing where the sun goes down, in the west
- *Nigeria is in **West** Africa, isn't it?*

west ³ adverb
towards where the sun goes down
- *Turkey is to the **west** of India.*

western, Western /ˈwestən/ adjective
in or from the west part of a country
- *He's just bought a house in **Western** France.*

wet /wet/ adjective
wetter, wettest
1 covered with water, rain, etc, not dry
   - *Dry your hands. They're **wet**.*
2 rainy
   - *It was **wet** yesterday but the sun is shining now.*

we've /wiːv/
we have
- ***We've** already seen that film.*

whale /weɪl/ noun (countable)
a very large animal which lives in the sea and looks like a fish

- *We saw a large **whale** from the boat.*

what /wɒt/ determiner, predeterminer; pronoun
1 You can use **what** to ask questions about something you don't know.
   - ***What's** that over there?*

> **LANGUAGE NOTE**
>
> Note the word order in questions with **What**:
> ALWAYS   What does that word mean?
> NEVER   ~~What means that word?~~

2 You can use **what** to mean **which**.
   - ***What** books would you like to borrow?*
3 You can use **what** to show surprise and other things you feel strongly.
   - ***What** a lot you did on your holiday!*
4 You can use **what** in sentences like these:
   - *Tell us **what** you'd like us to do, please.*
   - *I don't know **what** to say.*

wheat /wiːt/ noun (uncountable)
a crop which is used to make bread
- *Look at that field full of **wheat**.*

wheel /wiːl/ noun (countable)
something round which turns
- *He took one of the **wheels** off the car and put another one on.*
- ℘ a wheel turns; be at the wheel (= drive a car)

when /wen/ adverb, conjunction, pronoun
1 at what time
   - ***When** are you going away on holiday?*
2 at a certain time
   - *Come to visit me **when** you are in town.*

where /weə*/ adverb, conjunction, pronoun
1 in what place
   - ***Where** did you put the book?*
2 in a certain place
   - *Is that **where** Mr Tang lives?*

whether /ˈweðə*/ conjunction
1 if (used after verbs like **know, ask, find out**, etc)
   - *Do you know **whether** Leila will be there?*

θ	ð	ʃ	dʒ	tʃ	ŋ	ʒ	iː	ɜː	ɪ	æ	ʌ	ɒ
thing	that	shop	jump	chop	sing	measure	been	bird	bit	cat	but	not

whose 245

2 You can use also use **whether** to decide between two things.
- He doesn't know **whether** to laugh or cry.

which /wɪtʃ/ determiner, pronoun
1 what person or thing
- "**Which** boy spoke to you?" "That one."
2 that
- Is that the book **which** you read last night?

LANGUAGE NOTE	
NEVER	Ali picked up the ball which he had tried to kick it.
ALWAYS	Ali picked up the ball which he had tried to kick.

while[1] /waɪl/ noun (singular)
a period of time
- Can you wait for a **while**? I'll be ready soon.

while[2] conjunction
during the time that
- We saw an accident **while** we were walking to school.

whisper /ˈwɪspə*/ verb
speak very quietly
- Fatima **whispered** a secret to Jonathan.

whistle[1] /ˈwɪsl/ noun (countable)
something you blow through to make a high noise
- The teacher blew her **whistle** to let everyone know the game had finished.
↻ blow (on) a whistle, give a whistle

whistle[2] verb
whistling, whistled, has whistled
make a high noise by blowing air between your lips
- Can you **whistle** this song?

white /waɪt/ noun (uncountable)
the colour of salt, snow, milk
- All the men wore **white** shirts.
- Snow is **white** in colour.

who /huː/ determiner, pronoun
1 which person or persons
- "**Who** phoned you?" "Ted Hill."
2 that (of a person)
- It was Mr Smart **who** helped me.

LANGUAGE NOTE	
NEVER	I smiled at the woman who she was helping Tina.
ALWAYS	I smiled at the woman who was helping Tina.

whole /həʊl/ noun (singular)
all of something
- I missed school on Monday morning because I spent the **whole** morning at the doctor's.

whom /huːm/ determiner, pronoun
1 which person or persons
- "**Whom** did she meet?" "Ted Hall."
2 that
- Is that the man **whom** you phoned?

LANGUAGE NOTE
1 **Whom** does the principal wish to see? (Correct but not often used in speaking) **Who** does the principal want to see? (More usual in speaking)
2 The woman **to whom** we spoke waved. (Correct and usual in writing) Did the woman **who** you spoke **to** wave? (More usual in speaking)

who's /huːz/
1 who is
- **Who's** coming with me?
2 who has
- I wonder **who's** agreed to do it.

whose /huːz/ determiner, pronoun
1 belonging to which person or persons
- **Whose** is that bike?
2 of whom
- That's the woman **whose** dog bit me.

θ	ð	ʃ	dʒ	tʃ	ŋ	ʒ	iː	ɜː	ɪ	æ	ʌ	ɒ
thing	that	shop	jump	chop	sing	measure	been	bird	bit	cat	but	not

why /waɪ/ adverb, conjunction
for what reason
- *Why* did you do that?

wide /waɪd/ adjective
1 large or far from one side to the other
   - "What a *wide* chair! Two people can sit on it." "It isn't a chair. It's a sofa!"
2 from one side to the other
   - How *wide* is the river?
3 fully
   - Please open the window as *wide* as you can.

width /wɪdθ/ noun (uncountable, countable)
how far it is from one side to the other
- The *width* of the classroom is 4.5 metres.

wife /waɪf/ noun (countable)
plural: wives /waɪvz/
the woman a man is married to
- Have you met the headmaster's *wife* yet?

wild /waɪld/ adjective
1 without being controlled, behaving in a free way

- It's wrong to put *wild* animals in cages.
2 living and growing in the country
   - Susie was picked *wild* flowers in the wood.
3 angry, excited
   - Robert had a *wild* look in his eyes.
4 stormy
   - It was a *wild* night when the ship sank.

will /wɪl/ modal verb
part of **be**
- There *will* be a lot of people at the party.
⚠ See also **shall**.

win /wɪn/ verb
winning, won /wʌn/, has won
1 be first in a game or sport
   - Our team *won* the match.
↻ win easily, just win
⚠ See also **beat**.
2 be given something for doing well
   - Rohana *won* a prize for English.

wind¹ /wɪnd/ noun (uncountable, countable)
air which moves
- The strong *wind* blew our hats off.
↻ the wind blows/changes/dies down, the wind gets/picks up (= blows harder); a biting wind (= a very cold wind), a cold/gentle/light/slight/strong wind

wind² /waɪnd/ verb
winding, wound /waʊnd/, has wound
1 turn something (eg a key) to make something else go round
   - My watch has stopped because I forgot to *wind* it (up).
2 turn something round something else
   - *Wind* this piece of cloth round the handle.
3 bend
   - The road *wound* round the side of the hill.

window /ˈwɪndəʊ/ noun (countable)
a space in a wall filled with glass so that light can enter
- Several pupils were looking out of the *window* when the teacher came in the classroom.
↻ open/close/shut a window, look out of/clean/wash a window

windy /ˈwɪndɪ/ adjective
windier, windiest
If it is a windy day, the wind is blowing a lot.
- It's too *windy* to cycle to school today. You'll be blown over.

wing /wɪŋ/ noun (countable)
1 the part of a bird which moves up and down so that it can fly

θ	ð	ʃ	dʒ	tʃ	ŋ	ʒ	iː	ɜː	ɪ	æ	ʌ	ɒ
thing	that	shop	jump	chop	sing	measure	been	bird	bit	cat	but	not

- The little bird couldn't fly because one of its *wings* was broken.
2 the long flat part which sticks out on each side of an aeroplane
    - This plane has two engines on each *wing*.

winner /ˈwɪnə*/ noun (countable)
someone who comes first in a race or competition
- Mary was the *winner*, and Alan was second.

winter /ˈwɪntə*/ noun (countable, uncountable)
⚑ See box on page 57.

wipe /waɪp/ verb
wiping, wiped, has wiped
make clean or dry by rubbing
- Stop crying and *wipe* your eyes with this handkerchief.
↻ wipe something dry

wire /ˈwaɪə*/ noun
1 (uncountable) thin metal thread
    - The fence was made of strong *wire*.
2 (countable) a piece of metal thread
    - The kite hit one of the telephone *wires*.

wise /waɪz/ adjective
able to use your knowledge well, not foolish
- Mr Hill is very *wise* and will know what to do.

wisely /ˈwaɪzlɪ/ adverb
in a wise way
- Catherine *wisely* kept silent and let her sister argue.

wish¹ /wɪʃ/ noun (countable)
1 something good you want or hope for
    - It was my mother's last *wish* that I should go to university.
↻ get your wish(es), have/make a wish; a wish comes true
2 hope that someone will be happy or successful
    - Please give your father my best *wishes*.
↻ your best/good wishes, your warm/warmest wishes

wish² verb
1 hope for something good to happen
    - I *wish* I could go to Switzerland.
⚑ See also **hope**².
2 hope that someone will get something
    - Sue *wished* us success in our examination.
3 want
    - The headmistress *wishes* to see you.

with /wɪð/ preposition
1 If you are **with** someone or something, you are together.
    - I usually walk to school *with* Harry Lee.
2 If you do something **with** an object, you use it to do something.
    - I need a pencil or a pen to write *with*.
3 You can use **with** when you talk about how someone feels when they do something.
    - I was shaking *with* fear when the dog jumped on me.
4 You can use **with** when you talk about something a person or an object has.
    - A man *with* a white beard suddenly spoke.
5 You can use **with** after verbs like **fight**, **argue**, **agree**, etc.
    - I agree *with* Lesley.

without /wɪðˈaʊt/ preposition
1 not with
    - I take my tea *without* sugar.
2 not do something
    - She left home *without* saying goodbye to us.

wives /waɪvz/ noun (countable)
singular: wife
- The village chief had three *wives*.

θ	ð	ʃ	dʒ	tʃ	ŋ	ʒ	iː	ɜː	ɪ	æ	ʌ	ɒ
thing	that	shop	jump	chop	sing	measure	been	bird	bit	cat	but	not

woke (up) /ˌwəʊk ˈʌp/ (phrasal) verb
past tense of **wake (up)**
• I *woke (up)* at four o'clock this morning!

woken (up) /ˌwəʊkən ˈʌp/ phrasal verb
past participle of **wake (up)**
• I hadn't *woken (up)* when Rita left.

wolf /wʊlf/ noun (countable)
plural: wolves /wʊlvz/
⚠ See box on page 10.

woman /ˈwʊmən/ noun (countable)
plural: women /ˈwɪmɪn/
a person who has grown up but not a man
• Dr Kempf isn't a man. She's a *woman*.
🕮 a beautiful/fat/thin/young/middle-aged/ an old/pretty/tall/short/married woman, a single woman (= a woman who is not married)

won /wʌn/ verb
past tense and past participle of **win**
• Who *won* the first prize?
• I've *won* a prize for English.

wonder /ˈwʌndə*/ verb
not know about something but think about it, ask yourself about something
• I *wonder* what she was doing in the garden?

LANGUAGE NOTE

I wonder **what** will happen.
I wonder **whether** they'll come (**or** not).
I wonder **if** they'll come.
(NEVER ~~I wonder that they'll come.~~)

---

wonderful /ˈwʌndəfl/ adjective
very good, making you feel very happy
• "I've passed!" "What *wonderful* news!"

won't /wəʊnt/ modal verb
will not
• I *won't* tell anyone your secret.
⚠ See also **will**.

wood /wʊd/ noun
1 (uncountable) something which you get from trees
• Is that desk made of *wood* or plastic?
2 (countable) a lot of trees in one place

• We went for a walk in the *woods* and got lost.

wool /wʊl/ noun (uncountable)
the soft, thick hair of a sheep or the thread which is made from it
• Is your dress made of *wool* or cotton?

word /wɜːd/ noun (countable)
a group of letters which means something
• "What *word* means the same as 'stormy'?" "It's 'wild': we can talk about 'a wild night'."
🕮 pronounce/say/write a word; angry/sharp/empty words (= words which mean nothing or which are not sincere), kind/ (in) simple/ (in) suitable words

word processor /ˈwɜːd ˌprəʊsesə*/ noun (countable)
a machine like a typewriter with a screen, a kind of computer
• I can soon write these letters on my *word processor*.

wore /wɔː*/ verb
past tense of **wear**
• I *wore* my best suit for the party.

work¹ /wɜːk/ noun (uncountable)
1 a job
• What time do you finish *work* each day?

θ	ð	ʃ	dʒ	tʃ	ŋ	ʒ	iː	ɜː	ɪ	æ	ʌ	ɒ
thing	that	shop	jump	chop	sing	measure	been	bird	bit	cat	but	not

would   249

↻ begin/start/finish/stop/find/get/go to work; boring/interesting/easy/hard/part-time/full-time/important/light/tiring work

2 something you do
- *Mrs Papadimos always checks our **work** to see if we're doing everything right.*

↻ excellent/good/poor work

work²   verb

1 do something to earn money
- *Elena **works** as a secretary in a big office.*

↻ work hard/fast/quickly/slowly

2 go
- *This computer isn't **working**. There's something wrong with it.*

↻ work badly/well

workbook   /ˈwɜːkbʊk/   noun (countable)

a kind of exercise book in which you can write and do exercises
- *Have you done the exercises in your **workbook**?*

worker   /ˈwɜːkə*/   noun (countable)

someone who earns money by working (but who is not a manager)
- *The **workers** asked their boss for a holiday.*

↻ factory/office/full-time/part-time/highly-paid/low-paid workers

workman   /ˈwɜːkmən/   noun (countable)

plural: workmen
a man who earns money by doing things with his hands (eg building roads, etc)
- *Two **workmen** mended the sink.*

world   /wɜːld/   noun (singular with the)

the earth on which everyone lives
- *Who was the first man to sail round the **world**?*

LANGUAGE NOTE

Rio de Janeiro is the most beautiful city **in the world**. (NOT of the world)

---

worn   /wɔːn/   verb

past participle of **wear**
- *This tyre is **worn**. We'll have to get a new one.*

worried   /ˈwʌrɪd/   adjective

sad or frightened because you think something unpleasant may happen or may have happened
- *We were all very **worried** because you were so late. We thought you'd had an accident.*

worry   /ˈwʌrɪ/   verb

worrying, worried, has worried
think about something unpleasant many times and feel sad or afraid
- *I can't stop **worrying** about Hiroshi. He looks so tired and ill.*

worse   /wɜːs/   adjective

bad, worse, worst
more bad
- *Being ill a lot is much **worse** than being poor.*

⚠ See also **bad**.

worst   /wɜːst/   adjective

bad, worse, worst
most bad
- *Poor health is the **worst** thing that can happen.*

⚠ See also **bad**.

worth   /wɜːθ/   preposition

having a value of
- *This old car must be **worth** a few dollars.*

would   /wʊd/   modal verb

1 You can use **would** as a polite way of asking someone to do something.
- ***Would** you pass me the sugar, please?*

LANGUAGE NOTE

It is more polite to use **would** than **will**.
Will you open the window, please?
Would you open the window, please?

θ	ð	ʃ	dʒ	tʃ	ŋ	ʒ	iː	ɜː	ɪ	æ	ʌ	ɒ
thing	that	shop	jump	chop	sing	measure	been	bird	bit	cat	but	not

2. You can use **would** for **will** when you are talking about what someone has said or done.
- *Mary said she **would** come with us.*

LANGUAGE NOTE

DIRECT SPEECH	"I'll come," Mary said.
REPORTED SPEECH	Mary said (that) she *would* come.

See also **should**.

wouldn't /ˈwʊdnt/ modal verb
would not
- *Harry **wouldn't** come to the cinema with us because he had some letters to write.*

would rather /wʊd ˈrɑːðə*/ verb phrase
See **rather**¹.

wrap /ræp/ verb
wrapping, wrapped, has wrapped

SPELLING NOTE

double **p**: wra**pp**ing, wra**pp**ed

cover something all round
- *Alan **wrapped** Samia's birthday present in brown paper to surprise her.*

wrestle /ˈresl/ verb
wrestling, wrestled, has wrestled
fight someone by holding them, twisting their arms and legs, etc or throwing them to the ground

- *I really enjoy watching **wrestling** matches on television.*

write /raɪt/ verb
writing, wrote /wrəʊt/, has written /ˈrɪtn/
put words or numbers on paper
- *Please **write** your name on this line.*
- write your name/address/a letter/report/book

writing /ˈraɪtɪŋ/ noun (uncountable)
1. something which is written on paper
   - *What's that **writing** at the top of the paper?*
2. way of writing
   - *Susan's **writing** is very neat, but Alice's **writing** is hard to read.*

written /ˈrɪtn/ verb
past participle of **write**
- *How many postcards have you **written**?*

wrong /rɒŋ/ adjective
1. not right, not correct
   - *This exercise is **wrong**. Do it again?*
2. bad
   - *It is **wrong** to borrow things without asking.*
3. not satisfactory, not suitable, not right
   - *That's the **wrong** way to hold chopsticks.*

wrote /rəʊt/ verb
past tense of **write**
- *Who **wrote** this sentence on the blackboard?*

θ	ð	ʃ	dʒ	tʃ	ŋ	ʒ	iː	ɜː	ɪ	æ	ʌ	ɒ
thing	that	shop	jump	chop	sing	measure	been	bird	bit	cat	but	not

Xx

X-ray /ˈeks reɪ/ noun (countable)
a picture of the inside of your body using a special machine

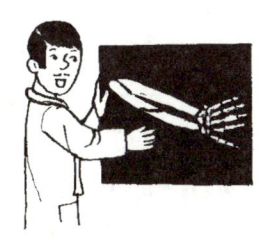

- *Dr Jones looked at an **X-ray** of the broken bone.*
- go for/have/make/take an X-ray

X-ray verb
X-raying, X-rayed, has X-rayed
take a picture of the inside of your body using a special machine
- *The doctor **X-rayed** Ken's broken arm.*

Yy

yard /jɑːd/ noun (countable)
the area of concrete next to a building (often at the back of it)
- *The children played in the **yard** behind the house.*

LANGUAGE NOTE
In American English the word **yard** can be used to mean either a concrete area or a garden with grass and flowers.

- backyard, coalyard, farmyard, dockyard, shipyard, churchyard, graveyard

yawn /jɔːn/ verb
open your mouth wide when you are tired or bored

- *All the pupils **yawned** when Mr Long began to speak.*

year /jɪə*/ noun (countable)
365 days or 12 months or 52 weeks
- *I've been working in Singapore for three **years**.*

LANGUAGE NOTE
COMPARE   a girl who is fifteen years old
a fifteen year old girl
a girl of fifteen

θ	ð	ʃ	dʒ	tʃ	ŋ	ʒ	iː	ɜː	ɪ	æ	ʌ	ɒ
thing	that	shop	jump	chop	sing	measure	been	bird	bit	cat	but	not

↻ begin/have/lose/miss/pass/spend a year; a poor/a bad/a good/excellent/busy/difficult/exciting/happy/important/successful/whole year,
a calendar year (= 365 or 366 days from 1 January to 31 December), a college/school/university year (= the period from the beginning of the first term to the end of the last term); last year, next year, this year, the present year

yellow /ˈjeləʊ/ noun (uncountable, countable), adjective
the colour of the sun or the colour of gold, butter or a lemon
- *Lemons are usually **yellow**.*

yes /jes/
You can use **yes** to show that you agree with someone, etc.
- *"Would you like to play basketball?"*
  *"**Yes**, I would. Thanks."*

⚠ See also **no** ¹.

LANGUAGE NOTE

Read the answers to the questions below.
"Are you going out tonight?"
"Yes, I am."   OR   "No, I'm not."
"Aren't you going out tonight?"
"Yes, I am."   OR   "No, I'm not."
(=Yes, I am going out.)   (=No, I'm not going out.)

---

yesterday /ˈjestədɪ/ noun (uncountable), adverb
the day before today
- ***Yesterday** was Monday; today is Tuesday.*

yet /jet/ adverb
1 up until now
   - *Have you finished your homework **yet**?*
2 but
   - *The exam was very hard **yet** no one failed.*

you /juː/ pronoun
the person or people to whom you are talking
- *Bruno, **you** must be more careful in future.*

you'd /juːd/
1 you would
   - *I knew **you'd** come soon.*
2 you had
   - *Esther arrived soon after **you'd** left.*

you'll /juːl/
you will
- *I hope **you'll** come to the meeting.*

young /jʌŋ/ adjective
not old, not having lived a long time
- *You're too **young** to drive a car.*

your /jɔː*/ determiner
belonging to you
- *Is this **your** book or Dave's?*

you're /jɔː*/
you are
- ***You're** coming to my party, aren't you?*

yours /jɔːz/ pronoun
something which belongs to you
- *That pen over there is **yours**: this one is mine.*

yourself /jɔːˈself/ pronoun
plural: yourselves
1 You can use **yourself** as the object of a verb or preposition.
   - *Dry **yourself** as soon as you come out of the water.*
2 You can use **yourself** to make the subject or object seem more important or to make the pronoun **you** stronger.
   - *Did you see the strange man **yourself**?*
3 without any help
   - *Did you paint this picture all by **yourself**?*
4 **by yourself** = without anyone else
   - *You will be left in the room (all) **by yourself**.*

you've /juːv/
you have
- *Tell me as soon as **you've** finished.*

θ	ð	ʃ	dʒ	tʃ	ŋ	ʒ	iː	ɜː	ɪ	æ	ʌ	ɒ
thing	that	shop	jump	chop	sing	measure	been	bird	bit	cat	but	not

Zz

zebra /ˈzebrə/   noun (countable)
  🔊 See box on page 10.

zebra crossing /ˌzebrə ˈkrɒsɪŋ/ noun (countable)
part of a road with black and white lines (in Britain) where people can cross safely

- *Don't cross the road here. Let's use the **zebra crossing** over there.*

zip /zɪp/   noun (countable)
two rows of metal or plastic which are joined together if you pull something
- *The **zip** on Tina's dress was broken.*
↻ do up/undo a zip

zoo /zuː/   noun (countable)
plural: zoos
a park or cages where wild animals are kept
- *We saw a monkey in the **zoo** yesterday and my aunt said it looked just like me!*

θ	ð	ʃ	dʒ	tʃ	ŋ	ʒ	iː	ɜː	ɪ	æ	ʌ	ɒ
thing	that	shop	jump	chop	sing	measure	been	bird	bit	cat	but	not

Exercises

Finding Words

Exercise 1

Put these groups of words in alphabetical order.

1. garden   meat   careful   very   repeat   exam   produce   bus   sure   add
2. accident   alone   along   ache   ask   allow   already   almost
3. break down   breakfast   break up   break   break out

Now check your order with the words in the dictionary.

Pronunciation

Exercise 2

The pronunciation of each headword is given in the dictionary. Use this information to write out two words in each group on the right containing the same sound as that underlined in the word in capital letters.

1. L<u>A</u>KE   same   famous   am   father
2. C<u>O</u>ME   up   gone   another   together
3. S<u>OU</u>R   shower   colour   flower   now
4. L<u>OO</u>K   wool   but   cushion   pool
5. C<u>Y</u>CLE   like   aisle   lady   yacht
6. TH<u>ERE</u>   here   wear   fair   are
7. <u>O</u>F   even   if   fine   live
8. PR<u>I</u>CE   ice   prize   sight   wise
9. <u>TH</u>IS   that   thin   there   thief
10. <u>A</u>BOUT   woman   hut   enjoy   husband

Exercise 3

Rewrite the following words, using capital letters for the syllable which is stressed.

newspaper   grandfather   bicycle
engineer   business   uniform
travel   holiday   accident
electricity nationality   cinema
neighbour   education   successful
university

Example: *NEWSpaper*

Exercise 4

Use the pronunciation information in the dictionary to find out whether the two words in each pair are pronounced in the same way or in a different way.
Write S (= same) or D (= different) after each number.

1. live (verb)   2. result (noun)
   live (adjective)   result (verb)
3. present (noun)   4. address (noun)
   present (adjective)   address (verb)
5. opposite (noun)   6. record (noun)
   opposite (adjective)   record (verb)

Parts of Speech

Exercise 5

Look at each of the following words and write out what part of speech the word is:

blackboard   clever
it   point out
department store   climb
just   too
easily   colourful
must   upon
chest   hello
per   you

Example: **blackboard - noun**

Exercise 6

You want to find out more about the following underlined words. Write out each underlined word and the part of speech you think it is. Then look up each word in this dictionary and add the correct number of each word entry.
Example: *The small boy began to <u>cry</u> when his parents left him.*   **verb   cry 2**

1. How many students were <u>late</u> for school this morning?
2. The tourists were advised to keep their money in the hotel <u>safe.</u>
3. Bristol is over a hundred miles <u>west</u> of London, isn't it?

4 "How do you feel today?" "<u>Fine</u>, thanks."
5 Why have you left Leila <u>behind</u>?
6 Don't forget to put a <u>stamp</u> on the envelope before you post it.
7 Everyone likes being on holiday <u>better</u> than working.
8 Mr Lee likes to <u>iron</u> his own shirts.
9 I <u>wish</u> you were coming with us.
10 How <u>high</u> did he jump?
11 Who won the <u>race</u>?
12 Have a <u>guess</u> if you don't know the answer.

Exercise 7

Write out what part of speech each of the underlined words is. Then rewrite each sentence, using the same word but this time as the part of speech given in brackets. You can change the words in the sentence as much as you wish but try not to change the meaning of the sentence.
Example: Draw a <u>circle</u> round the word 'left'. (verb)
circle = noun in the sentence above
Circle the word 'left'.

1 There's a slight <u>bend</u> in the road here. (verb)
2 Don't <u>lie</u>. I want to know the truth. (noun)
3 Why don't you <u>rest</u> for a short time if you feel very tired? (noun)
4 Edna and Susan are sitting at the <u>back</u> of the bus. (adjective)
5 Put a <u>chain</u> round your bicycle wheel and the gate if you don't want anyone to steal it. (verb)
6 I think I'll <u>walk</u> for an hour in the park. (noun)
7 An enemy plane dropped a <u>bomb</u> on the building. (verb)
8 Bill is the <u>fastest</u> runner. (adverb)

British and American English

Exercise 8

Here is part of a letter between two pen-friends: an English boy and an American boy.
Can you guess whether it was written by the American boy or by the English boy?
How do you know?

Dear Ken,

I was very happy to receive your letter in the mail this morning. I am glad you want to be my pen-friend. You ask me to tell you about myself. My hair is black and the color of my eyes is blue. I am getting quite fat: my mom says I am fat because I am always eating cookies and candies. She says that is why I often have a stomachache.

We live in a small apartment but the apartment house itself is very big. I watch TV a lot and my favorite program is "Muz". Have you heard of it? It is about ....

Exercise 9

Who stole the missing ring?

Inspector Strange, the famous detective, is interviewing three people who he thinks may have stolen a valuable ring from a shop called Jason's in the centre of Oxford. He asks them what they were doing near Jason's. Here are their replies.

Person 1 "I live in Oxford and I went to Jason's to look at some rings. I wanted to buy a ring for my wife but all the rings were too expensive and so I didn't get one. Later, I went to another shop and got a similar ring, but it isn't the same as the one I saw in Jason's."

Person 2 "I am tourist from Japan. I come to England since last week and I liked to visit Oxford. I want to buy ring for taking back to my country. I not like any rings I saw in the Jason's window and so I not go inside the shop. Please excuse my English. It is very bad."

Person 3 "I am an Englishman and I've lived in London all my life. I was on my way to the drug store next to Jason's. I was standing on the sidewalk outside the shop but I didn't go in. In any case, I have already gotten a lot of rings and I don't want any more."

Which person do you think is not telling the truth? How do you know?

Exercise 10

The following sentences have been written in British English. Use this dictionary to rewrite each sentence in American English.

1. Yesterday I found a handbag on the seat next to me in a restaurant.
2. There was a cinema programme on top of it.
3. Inside the handbag there was a ten-dollar note.
4. There was also a small bag of sweets.
5. I asked for the bill and decided to take the handbag I had found to the nearest police station.
6. Later that night I heard the doorbell ring and I put on my dressing gown to go to see who was there.
7. A man wearing a black suit and a red waistcoat was standing there.
8. He would have looked very smart if he hadn't been wearing an old jumper.

Grammar

Verbs: patterns

Exercise 11

Several of the following sentences contain incorrect verb forms. Write out each sentence, correcting only those sentences containing mistakes. Your dictionary will help you to do this.

1. Did the men succeed to reach the lost village?
2. I enjoy to read books about travel.
3. Someone started to sing in a very low voice.
4. Ken went to swim every day during his holiday.
5. Mr Price decided to leave work early yesterday.
6. Can you imagine to live in a place like that? It must be terrible!
7. I suggested to go to the cinema but no one wanted to go.
8. Do you really want to go out this evening?
9. Would you mind to open the window, please?
10. Several people advised Jonathan to stay at school.

Verbs: forms and meanings

Exercise 12

Read the following pairs of sentences. Then rewrite the incorrect sentence in each pair. Note that all the mistakes result from the incorrect use of verb forms and tenses. Use the dictionary to check your answers.

1. a) I was feeling very cold when the police at last arrived.
   b) The water was feeling very cold when I put my foot in.
2. a) Ken is holding a small child in his arms.
   b) This small case is holding a lot of things.

Verbs: past tenses and participles

Exercise 13

Rewrite the following sentences, putting the verbs in brackets into the correct tense form. Check your answers with the verb forms given in the dictionary.

1. Something strange (happen) last night.
2. Tom and Maria (quarrel) after we left them.
3. I said I (prefer) football to tennis when I was his age.
4. "Why don't you want to see this film?" "I've (see) it."
5. He (become) very famous before he was twenty.
6. Someone's (hide) my book.
7. I was so thirsty that I (drink) six glasses of water.
8. The meeting lasted so long that I (leave) half way through.
9. I (creep) out of the room as someone was beginning to speak.
10. Someone had (stick) a notice on the wall.
11. Tina (drive) her daughter to school this morning.
12. She (light) a cigarette and took a deep breath.
13. Have you (forget) what I told you?
14. I (cut) my hand a moment ago.
15. Who's (sew) your button on?
16. The water in the pond has already (freeze).
17. I was (wake) by a loud noise.
18. The hot iron has (burn) a hole in this shirt.
19. I was so tired that I (lie) down for half an hour.
20. Our team was (beat) by the visitors.

Verbs with and without prepositions

Exercise 14

Rewrite each newspaper headline, completing each blank with the correct word ONLY WHERE NECESSARY. (Note that no word is necessary in 3 headlines.)

New car made .... plastic

Many prefer travelling by rail .... driving a long way

Malaysian reaches .... South Pole on foot

Shops full .... cheap computer games

SOLDIERS ENTER .... KUWAIT

200 firemen fight .... fire at Harold's Supermarket

POLICE LOOK .... THIEF WITH ONLY ONE HAND

President returns .... Singapore

Nouns: countable and uncountable

Exercise 15

Each sentence in the following paragraph contains one mistake in the use of countable and uncountable nouns. Write the paragraph out, correcting all the mistakes.

(1) Mr Robinson has grey hair and white beard. (2) He often wears an old clothing but he is always smiling. (3) He seems happy and in a good health. (4) He enjoys painting picture and he often plays the piano. (5) Every morning I see him buying a bread in the shop near the school. (6) He carries a small radio with him so he can listen to a news. (7) I caught a sight of him yesterday afternoon on his way to the bus station. (8) He was carrying a heavy luggage. (9) "I'm going to spend week with my daughter," he said. (10) "Have good time," I answered.

Exercise 16

Add 's' to each word in bold type wherever possible.

1 The room was full of old **furniture**.
2 A lot of people use **gas** to cook with.
3 Listen carefully to the **instruction** I'm going to give you.
4 Several pupils had **headache**.
5 We've got lots of **homework** to do tonight.
6 When will the **lesson** finish?
7 Is there any interesting news in the **paper** today?
8 We are now having a lot of **practice** for the examinations.
9 The waiters were very rude and the **service** very poor.
10 Look at the lovely tea **set** in the shop window.
11 He was having **supper** when I phoned.
12 I enjoy watching **television** a lot.

Exercise 17

Use the dictionary to help you to write the plural forms of the following nouns.

valley	department store	torch
gentleman	tie	gas
cinema	box	story
person	safe	child
leaf	thief	roof
radio		

Word Meanings

Finding and understanding word meanings

Exercise 18

Try to guess the meaning of each underlined word or phrase from the sentence in which it appears. Then check your answers with the definitions given in the dictionary.

1 Can you phone the college to <u>check</u> what time the concert starts tonight?
2 I don't think you're ill: your temperature is <u>normal</u>.
3 Ben was always smiling: he was <u>hardly ever</u> unhappy.
4 I don't know what's <u>going on</u>? Why hasn't the lesson already started and where is the teacher?

5   There was a <u>cloudy liquid</u> in the bottle.
6   The rich man's son has been <u>kidnapped</u>.
7   I <u>totally</u> agree with everything you have just said.
8   The animal <u>spat</u> at the little boy when he tried to touch it with a stick.
9   There are several large <u>department stores</u> near the new college.
10 Is there a <u>call box</u> nearby?
11 Do Mr and Mrs Jones live in a <u>detached house</u>?
12 I <u>couldn't care less about</u> what you're going to do.

Exercise 19

Choose the letter of the best word to complete each of the following sentences. Then check your answers in the dictionary.

1   The film was very .... I couldn't stop laughing.
    A boring   B interesting
    C amusing   D surprising
2   Tony has a good............ of Chinese history.
    A knowledge   B study
    C examination   D care
3   The name of the medicine will be on the .... on the side of the bottle.
    A notice   B letter
    C stamp   D label
4   "Did you have a pleasant .... to Beijing?"
    "Yes, it was an enjoyable flight."
    A aircraft   B journey
    C voyage   D holiday
5   The damage caused by the storm was a terrible ...., and I had to close my eyes.
    A happening   B sight
    C notice   D event
6   Poor Sheila's been taken to hospital with a rare ....
    A cure   B damage
    C ambulance   D disease
7   I can't tell you what Ann told me. It's a .... !
    A message   B conversation
    C secret   D code
8   Be careful or you'll .... some milk on the carpet.
    A run   B fall
    C flow   D spill

Exercise 20

Try to guess the meaning of each underlined word or phrase in the following sentences. Choose the letter of the correct meaning of the underlined word and then check your answers in the dictionary.

1   Thousands of people will <u>starve</u> if the harvest is poor.
    A not have enough food and sometimes die
    B be hurt or punished
    C leave the country to live in cities
    D have no water at all
2   The river is <u>shallow</u> here.
    A not dirty   B not calm
    C not healthy   D not deep
3   Mr Lee is going to use <u>robots</u> in his new factory.
    A workers who will not ask for high wages
    B new ways of making things
    C machines which can work like people
    D children who are very clever
4   Shall we pay to go in the big house? There are a lot of <u>treasures</u> which we can look at.
    A small paintings
    B pieces of old furniture
    C rooms with beautiful views from their windows
    D things which are very valuable
5   There were several pieces of wood <u>floating</u> near the rocks.
    A sinking to the bottom of the water
    B falling into the water
    C staying on top of the water
    D going round and round in the water
6   Please be quiet and stop <u>annoying</u> everyone.
    A making people angry
    B trying to hurt people
    C amusing people
    D playing tricks on people
7   Attention, please. I have an <u>announcement</u>.
    A something very useful to do
    B something important to tell people
    C something very valuable to present to someone
    D something unusual to sell
8   Don't worry. <u>I'll take care of</u> you while your mother is ill.
    A teach   B give money to
    C look after   D cure

Exercise 21

Read the definitions of the following words in the dictionary. Then write the correct word in each blank.

advise   brief   difficulty
information   surname   sign

First write your............. on the top line and then your other names on the next line. Give .... answers to all the questions. If you have any ...., ask your teachers for help. They will be able to .... you and show you what to do. When you have finished, ... the form and put today's date on it. The .... you have given will not be passed to anyone else.

Words which are similar

Exercise 22

Words which look or sound similar.
Write out each sentence, putting in each blank the correct word in brackets.

1. Big Bill has been in .... for six months for stealing some money. (gaol, goal)
2. Who won the .... for the best composition? (price, prize)
3. Katie and Anna are .... in several ways. (alike, like)
4. Have a short rest and............. down for a few minutes if you're tired. (lay, lie)
5. I'd like to give you a piece of .... (advice, advise)
6. When I didn't see Linda, I wrote a short .... to her to ask her to meet me the next evening. (note, notice)
7. Jonathan wants to become a .... nurse. (mail, male)
8. I'd like a .... of biscuits, please. (package, packet)
9. Mr Wong wore a clean white .... and tie for the meeting. (shirt, skirt)
10. You'll miss the news unless you're .... (quiet, quite)
11. Maria doesn't often .... her glasses: I'm surprised she can't find them now. (loose, lose)
12. If you agree with the speaker, please .... your hand. (raise, rise)

Exercise 23

Read the following pairs of sentences. Then choose the correct word for each sentence. Check your answers in the dictionary.

1. homework / housework
   (a) We have to write a composition for .... tonight.
   (b) My aunt often helps my mother and me with the ....
2. game / sport
   (a) Boxing is still a very popular .... in many countries.
   (b) My favourite .... is chess.
3. floor / ground
   (a) I put my books on the edge of the desk but they fell on the ....
   (b) Don't put the tent so near the river: the .... is too soft and wet.
4. been / gone
   (a) Have you ever .... to London?
   (b) Mr and Mrs Saito are abroad at present: they've .... to Switzerland.
5. hard / hardly
   (a) Why don't you read more? I .... ever see you with a book.
   (b) I'm sure you'll go to university if you continue to work ....
6. high / tall
   (a) There were several .... trees in the big garden.
   (b) The mountain over there isn't as .... as the one near my house.
7. hire / rent
   (a) Mr Low is going to .... a small boat to go fishing today.
   (b) Are you going to buy a flat or .... one?
8. cost / price
   (a) The .... of having the car repaired was very high.
   (b) The .... of a new car has not risen in the last year.

Finding the most suitable meaning

Exercise 24

Each underlined word below can have more than one meaning. Using this dictionary, find out which meaning it has in the sentence below and then write the number of the meaning.
Example: Where I went is my business. I'm not going to tell you. **business 3**

1. I found it hard to describe what actually happened.
2. I think he went in that direction.
3. Mr Baker stopped to put some gas in his car.
4. Where are you going on holiday this year?
5. The engine is pulling twelve carriages.
6. Who was the first man in space?
7. These shoes are just right. They're perfect.
8. The river twisted in the valley below.
9. The visitors began to argue among themselves.
10. The pupils wrote the letters B-A-K-E.
11. Poor Dave is hopeless at games.
12. We live near the fire station.

Exercise 25

The word **take** has more than one meaning. Write after each of the following sentences the number of the meaning given in this dictionary.

1. Take this book to Mr Primrose, please.
2. Don't forget to take this medicine three times a day.
3. Take as much fruit as you want.
4. Is Mrs Long taking a bus to Bristol or is she going by train?
5. Someone's been in the house and taken our TV set.
6. I'm taking Tina to the cinema this evening.
7. The last exercise took me a long time to do.
8. Take 17 away from 40.
9. Listen carefully and take down everything he says.
10. Take care when you go on the picnic.
11. What time does your plane take off?
12. Are you taking part in the school concert tonight?

Phrasal verbs

Exercise 26

Remember that the meaning of a phrasal verb is often different from the meaning of the verb itself (without the addition of the adverb or preposition). Here are the meanings of the verbs underlined in the following sentences, but they are given in the wrong order. Can you match each underlined verb with the correct meaning? Check your answers in the dictionary.

think of   stop   write   happen   be quiet
continue   try harder   escaped from

1. Could you speak a little slower? I can't get down everything you are saying.
2. Ken and Susie carried on talking when the teacher entered the classroom.
3. Shut up and let me speak for a moment.
4. Please pull up here so that I can get out of the car.
5. Peter made up a good excuse to explain why he was late for work.
6. Come on. I know you can win.
7. Three of the men who broke out of gaol have already been caught.
8. The teacher had no idea what was going on when she entered the classroom.

Collocations

Exercise 27

Which of the following words can be put with the word in capital letters?

1.
                                 clearly
                                   truly
     UNDERSTAND something fairly
                                   well
                                 perfectly

2.   near
     close
 a good   RELATIVE
     far
     distant

3   carry on
    have
    hold   a CONVERSATION with someone
    keep
    bring in

4   poor
        strong
    have large   DIFFICULTY with something
        great
        serious

5   ruin
    bring down   a GOVERNMENT
    make
    form
    set up

6   big
    bad
    a terrible   SMELL
    faint
    good

7   ask
    demand
    raise   a QUESTION
    lower
    answer

8   song
            rhyme
    a NURSERY school
            place
            story

Exercise 28

One of the words in each of the underlined collocations is wrong. Rewrite the sentences, correcting all the collocations. Use your dictionary to check each collocation.
1 My father sends you his <u>hot</u> <u>wishes</u>.
2 The <u>thick traffic</u> made me late for the meeting.
3 This <u>motor is flowing</u> very smoothly.
4 There has been a <u>blunt drop</u> in the price of oil.
5 He <u>signed out a cheque</u> for a hundred dollars.
6 The new teacher found it difficult to <u>carry</u> the pupils' <u>attention</u>.
7 The doctor asked me to take <u>a long breath</u>.
8 Mr and Mrs Simpson are <u>catching a party</u> tomorrow.
9 It was a very <u>windy meeting</u>: everyone argued.
10 Ken's got very <u>keen eyes</u>.

11 Two years in prison for such a small crime seems <u>a very serious punishment</u>.
12 Don't <u>give away hope</u>: you may still be successful.

Exercise 29

Complete each of the following sentences with the most suitable collocation taken from this dictionary. Your sentence should have almost the same meaning as the first sentence in each pair.
1 Prices have increased very much indeed in the last month.
   There has been a ....
2 Can you fry an egg for me?
   Can you make me a ....?
3 The trees in the forest we entered were planted very close together.
   We entered a ....
4 Thank you for replying so quickly to my letter.
   Thank you for your.............................. .
5 The old man died from his illness.
   The old man had a ....
6 Can you answer Questions 2, 4, 6, 8, 10 and 12 while I answer 1, 3, 5, 7, 9 and 11?
   Can you answer the ....
   while I answer the ....?
7 Poor Anna wanted to blow her nose all the time because of her bad cold.
   Poor Anna had a ....
8 Mr Law earns a lot of money in his job.
   Mr Law has a ....

Exercise 30

Choose the correct word in each phrase and use the phrase in a sentence of your own. Then check your answers with the dictionary.

rub out/clean **the blackboard**
bring/take **a break**
a light/lamp **bulb**
take big/great **care**
complete/whole **nonsense**
save/earn **time**
good/excellent **luck**
cheap/low **wages**
a bad/poor **cold**
big/thick **smoke**
draw/paint **the curtains**
pleasant/pleasing **journey**

a train/railway **carriage**
weak/pale **tea**
a slight/narrow **difference**
make/give **a small charge**
a desk/table **job**
popular/common **mistake**
knock strongly/loudly
a watch is fast/quick

Exercise 31

Find out the meaning of the following words which are formed from two nouns. Each is given in the list of collocations under one of the words in each pair.
Example: a packing case = the box in which something new is sold

an answering machine	a heavy fine
white coffee	a light sleep
sound advice	a return ticket
a handy guide	a close race
a broken line	a biting wind

Exercise 32

The following are the meanings of certain phrases (ie collocations) which are given in the dictionary. However, the meanings given here do not contain the headwords under which they are listed in the dictionary. Try to guess the headword where you would look for each collocation and then write out the correct collocation.
 Example: a crash in which someone is killed
   ACCIDENT   *a fatal accident*

1   a very honest reply, often not polite
2   a way across a street or road marked with black and white lines
3   during the day
4   far enough away from someone or something so as not to be dangerous
5   a very poor reason (which is difficult to believe)
6   something which someone has done wrong and which takes a lot of time or money to put right
7   words which are not polite

If you have not been able to guess all the headwords, look at the following list. Note, however, that the headwords are not given in order here.

DISTANCE   ANSWER   MISTAKE
EXCUSE   CROSSING DAYLIGHT
LANGUAGE

Exercise 33

What is the difference between each word in the following pairs? Write sentences to show the difference.

out of order	out of the question
health food	healthy food
a light sleep	a sound sleep
a detached house	a terraced house

Exercise 34

The meaning of each of the underlined phrases (collocations) is idiomatic and cannot always be guessed from a knowledge of the individual words in the collocation. Look up each collocation in the dictionary and then use the collocation in a sentence of your own.

1   He <u>lay down his life</u> for his country.
2   <u>My heart sank</u> when I heard the disappointing news.
3   "<u>Take a seat</u>, please, and tell me what's wrong with you."
4   <u>Make up your mind</u> and either stay or leave.
5   You can <u>talk freely</u>. No one can hear us now.